Judaisms and Their Messiahs at the Turn of the Christian Era

Edited by

JACOB NEUSNER
Brown University

WILLIAM SCOTT GREEN
University of Rochester

ERNEST S. FRERICHS
Brown University

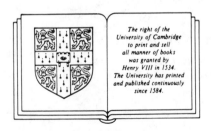

The right of the
University of Cambridge
to print and sell
all manner of books
was granted by
Henry VIII in 1534.
The University has printed
and published continuously
since 1584.

CAMBRIDGE UNIVERSITY PRESS

Cambridge
New York   Port Chester   Melbourne   Sydney

Published by the Press Syndicate of the University of Cambridge
The Pitt Building, Trumpington Street, Cambridge CB2 1RP
40 West 20th Street, New York, NY 10011, USA
10 Stamford Road, Oakleigh, Melbourne 3166, Australia

First published 1987
Reprinted 1990

Printed in the United States of America

Library of Congress Cataloging-in-Publication Data
Judaisms andTheir Messiahs at the Turn of the Christian
    Era.
    Includes index.
    1. Messiah – History of doctrines.   2. Judaism – History
– Post-exilic period, 586 B.C.–210 A.D.   3. Jesus Christ
– History of doctrines – Early church, ca. 30–600.
I. Neusner, Jacob, 1932–   .   II. Green, William Scott.
III. Frerichs, Ernest S.
BM615.J84   1987   296.3'3   87–10374

British Library Cataloguing in Publication Data
Judaisms and Their Messiahs at the Turn of the Christian
    Era.
    I. Messiah   2. Judaism
1. Neusner, Jacob   II. Green, William Scott
III. Frerichs, Ernest S.
296.3'1 BM615

ISBN 0 521 34146 9 hard covers
ISBN 0 521 34940 0 paperback

**Judaisms and Their Messiahs
at the Turn of the Christian Era**

To the memory of
GEORGE MACRAE, S. J.
teacher of us all
in the science of religion
especially Gnosticism
and
in the art of collegiality.
We miss him every day.

Contents

Preface

A Judaism comprises a world view and a way of life that together come to expression in the social world of a group of Jews. The "Judaisms" of the title therefore constitute several such ways of life and world views addressed to groups of Jews. A Messiah in a Judaism is a man who at the end of history, at the eschaton, will bring salvation to the Israel conceived by the social group addressed by the way of life and world view of that Judaism. Judaisms and their Messiahs at the age of the beginning of Christianity therefore encompass a group of religious systems that form a distinct family, all characterized by two traits: (1) address to "Israel" and (2) reference to diverse passages of the single common holy writing ("Old Testament," "written Torah").

In this book we propose to describe how several Judaisms treat the Messiah-theme. These diverse systems may define teleology by invoking that theme or may do so by referring to some other, nonmessianic explanation altogether. What we want to know is where the Messiah-theme matters when it does, and, when that theme proves uninteresting, why, as in the Mishnah's system and in the thought of Philo, the Messiah-theme makes no contribution to the definition and symbolization of a Judaism's teleology. Ultimately, of course, we should like to propose a rule to predict and to explain when and why a system's teleology will reach expression in an eschatological form (hence, in the world at hand, using the Messiah-theme) and when and why it will not. So we hope to contribute toward the formation of a rule, a generalization, in that generalizing science known as the study of religion. In all inquiry into the study of religion, what we learn about a given religion should at some point tell us something beyond it. A religion in particular may exemplify a trait of religion in general, presenting us with a "what else?" Our goal here is to clarify, for religion, the rule on when teleology will, and will not, reach definition in an eschatological, hence a messianic, doctrine.

The Judaisms under discussion here do not wholly conform to a single pattern, and the evidence at hand also proves diverse. So we stand a long way from our goal of systematic description, then analysis through comparison and contrast, and finally interpretation through the framing of a useful hypothesis subject to testing among a number of systems. Some of the systems at hand reach us only in fragmentary form, such as the rather broad category of systems we call, all together, the apocalyptic, treated by George W. E. Nickelsburg in the case of Enoch, Michael Stone in the case of Fourth Ezra, and the like. In other cases we have writings produced by not a social group but a political institution, discussed in the case of the Maccabees' writings by Jonathan A. Goldstein and John J. Collins. In one instance we have not a social group but a solitary philosopher, Philo, dealt with by Richard Hecht. In yet another, we deal with a book composed by a social group of a rather special character, the philosophers who stand behind the Mishnah, whom I describe. Two Judaisms come to representation in sources that address a community of a distinctive character, the Essene writings of Qumran, dealt with by Shemaryahu Talmon, and the Christian community represented by Mark's Gospel, treated by the late George MacRae, of blessed memory, and by Howard Clark Kee. Among this evidence, all of a literary character, one chapter treats not a single book or a small library, as in the case of Enoch, Ezra, Maccabees, Mark, Philo, and the Mishnah, but an ongoing literary genre. Burton L. Mack on the Wisdom writings describes a set of sources not wholly congruent in type with the cogent books of Mark and the Mishnah, on the one side, and the coherent writings of Qumran and of the apocryphal writings of Fourth Ezra and Enoch, on the other. Finally, reflecting in more conventional terms on the two subdivisions of ancient Israel in the first century, James H. Charlesworth attempts some broader generalizations. The contribution of William Scott Green, setting the stage for the sustained studies to follow, requires no introduction.

Since, as we see, what we treat here are books and no religion ever was born in a book or lived in a book or even died by a book, we had best return to the notion of a Judaism, a system. For a book is not a system, and what we hope, in time to come, is to learn how to describe a system, not merely to paraphrase and to analyze what is in a book. But a book does form a detail of a system, and, in the study of a religion, God lives in the details. So, as in everything we undertake to study, we have to teach ourselves to move from the detail to the whole, to generalize on the basis of only a part, but then to test our generalization. The reader may well wonder why, if at all, the conception of a Judaism proves helpful and suggestive, as we believe it does. For are we not merely working our way through fairly standard, and well-known, received sources? Indeed so, but we take a road of our own. So let us revert to this notion of a Judaism, which is our map.

If we insist that we speak not of Judaism but of Judaisms, does that mean we have also to speak not of Christianity but of Christianities? Indeed it does – and that proves our point. People familiar with the rich diversity of Christianity today and throughout the history of the Christian faith will find routine the allegation that, just as history has yielded its diverse Christianities – in some ways autonomous, in some connected, in some continuous – so history testifies to more than one Judaism. Why does everyone understand that there is not now, and never was, a single Christianity (except, I hope, from God's perspective)? Because people consider the alternative: a construct of total confusion, of a harmony of opposites. Imagine the Christianity we should define and describe, were we to treat all evidence as uniform in the manner in which we treat the evidence about "Judaism." That would be a Christianity to which Orthodox and heterodox, Arian and Athanasian, Greek and Russian, Armenian and Latin, Catholic and Gnostic, not to mention Protestant and Roman Catholic today, equally testify – and all totally out of context. Such a single Christianity unites around the cross, but divides on all else.

Then how about the Christianity of the first century? Do we not here, at least, deal with a single Christ? Few who have studied the problem would say so. The Gospels speak for diverse records of a single person. Each represents matters in a way distinctive to its authorship. All address points of disharmony in the nascent and tiny churches of the day. From the explanation of repeated stories and sayings settled by the theory of a Sermon on the Mount and a Sermon on the Plain (parallel to the harmonization of the two versions of the Ten Commandments, the one in Exodus, the other in Deuteronomy, by the theory that "remember" and "keep" were said at one and the same time), nearly all scholarship has taken a fond farewell. The last persuasive harmony of the Gospels found its original audience in the third century. For Christians it is routine therefore to read Matthew's Gospel as the statement of his school and its version of matters, not as part of "the Gospels'" single testimony to the one and uniform "life of Jesus." To speak of Mark's viewpoint, the particular perspective of the author of Hebrews, not to mention the Christian systems of Aphrahat on east, Chrysostom in the center, or Augustine in the far West – that is routine. No one proposes to force all evidence to testify to one *Christianity*.

So too with *Judaism*. In ancient times, as in every age of the history of the Jewish people, diverse groups of Jews have defined for themselves distinctive ways of life and world views. A Judaism therefore constitutes the world view and the way of life that characterize the distinctive system by which a social group of Jews works out its affairs. True, these several systems produced by different groups of Jews assuredly do exhibit traits in common. For example, they universally appeal to the same Hebrew Scriptures. But in fact points in common underline the systems' essential diversity. For if we ask a group to specify those verses of Scripture it finds critical and to explain their meaning, we rarely hear from one a repertoire of verses found equally central in the system of some other distinct group. Still less do the interpretations of those verses of Scripture shared among the several groups coincide. It follows that, in the history of Judaism, we can identify numbers of different Judaisms. Whether we deal with a long period of time, such as a millennium, or a brief period of just a few centuries, the picture is the same. Like Christianities, these Judaisms relate to one another in diverse ways. Some stand essentially autonomous, as the Christian Judaisms of the first century came to do. Some proved connected to one another, yielding shared holy books, for example. All together, of course, we observe continuities, but these prove hardly definitive of the distinctive traits of any one system. So, in all, Judaisms flourished side by side. Or they took place in succession to one another. Or they came into being out of all relationship with one another. Thus, some Judaisms took shape all by themselves, remaining autonomous; other Judaisms related to one another through connections whereby shared doctrine or practice joined one Judaism to the next; and still other Judaisms turn out, upon inspection, to have formed a continuity and stood in sequence with one another, so that the frontier between one and the next proves difficult to delineate.

So far I have written as though people in general used such words as "a Judaism" and understood that the Messiah-theme in diverse Judaisms either may take an important systemic position or may contribute little to the system at hand. But this very mode of thought is fresh to the study of Judaism. People have written books on the messianic doctrine in Judaism, but this is the first book on the Messiah-theme in Judaisms. So let me back up and deal with the terms and categories people do know. How do people ordinarily define categories in sorting out Judaic data? What modes of thought dictate the questions they ask and methods of answering them and why do we reject the received modes of description? There is one category, "Judaism," and a single mode of thought, collecting and arranging Judaic data to testify to doctrines and practices of that Judaism, which people call Orthodox. Accordingly, people invoke the term "Judaism," meaning, "the Jewish religion." They further employ the category of "messianism," or "the messianic doctrine in Judaism." Hence, as I just said, we have books constructed upon the foundation of the species, "Judaism," within the genus, religion, "messianic." What follows? Books on "the messianic idea in Judaism." Here we turn matters on their head. How so? We ask about the classification, or genus, Judaisms, and we invoke the Messiah-theme to help us differentiate one species of the genus, Judaisms, from another, thus, Judaisms and their messiahs. We accordingly move from one set of categories and modes of analysis to another.

What is wrong with the established view is simple. People join together books that do not speak the same language of thought, that refer to distinctive conceptions and doctrines of their own. If books so close together in topic and sentiment as the four Gospels no longer yield harmonization, books so utterly remote from one another as the Mishnah and Philo and Fourth Ezra and Enoch should not contribute doctrines to a common pot: Judaism. But if we do not harmonize, then what we have to do is quite the opposite: analyze. In fact all we propose is to describe things item by item, and to postpone the work of searching for connections and even continuities until all the components have had their say, one by one. For, as we see throughout this book, each of the components – the distinct books – makes its own distinctive statement.

I cannot imagine a more self-evidently right approach to any problem of learning. We take each relevant item of information as it comes, working inductively from item to item, building a larger picture out of smaller components. That work of sifting and sorting of evidence characterizes all fields of Western learning. The analytical method has defined all learning from the beginning, in Greek science and philosophy, to our own day: observation, reflection. Curiosity reaches expression then in the questions, why? what if? and why not? and, above all, so what? But that mode of thought, based on observation and testing through experiment, scarcely characterizes the deductive system commonplace in the received and established methods of Judaic learning, a system that shamelessly invokes *a priori* facts of history, and that knows things before proof or without proof. So the present approach – so self-evidently right to us – contradicts the established conviction, which is that all pieces of evidence deriving from Jews, whoever they were, wherever and whenever they lived without regard to context and circumstance, testify to one and the same Judaism. That proposition remains to be demonstrated. What we cannot show we do not know, and here we propose to begin to find out. We propose in the setting of the public (hence, not theological) inquiry into the nature of religion to describe, analyze, and interpret. The "we" in this book is made up of learning people – atheists, Christians, and Jews alike – who respect the religions that have emerged from late antiquity to define the civilization of the West and of the world – the Christianities, the Judaisms. But we come to this study because we are children of the tradition of Western philosophy, that is, because we want to know how things came to be the way they are: What if? and why? and why not?

The book speaks for us all and is the work of us all. The three editors consulted throughout, both in organizing the papers, as some were originally read orally, and in planning the project, beginning to end. We consulted also with Professor Jonathan Z. Smith. The book emerges from sessions of the American Academy of Religion, which, from 1982 on, provided the meeting place and the occasion for our continuing conversation, over a period of years, on a common topic. Our tribute to the Academy finds a place on every page of this book. We pay tribute also to our editor at Cambridge University Press, David Emblidge, who knew just what he wanted, and who always was right.

A principal partner in the organization of these studies, George MacRae, died in September 1985. We grieve at his death and our loss and offer this book as a tribute to him. He had a mind of remarkable clarity; he could lead us through confused and difficult data; he not only enlightened our learning, but, to those of us fortunate enough to enjoy his friendship, he also illuminated our lives. We dedicate our work to his memory.

Jacob Neusner

Contributors

J. H. Charlesworth is the George L. Collord Professor of New Testament Language and Literature at Princeton Theological Seminary. His critical books include *The Odes of Solomon* and *The Pseudepigrapha and Modern Research with a Supplement*. He edited the two-volume work, *The Old Testament Pseudepigrapha*.

John J. Collins is Professor of Theology at the University of Notre Dame. His publications include *Between Athens and Jerusalem: Jewish Identity in the Hellenistic Diaspora*, *The Apocalyptic Imagination*, and *Daniel, with an Introduction to Apocalyptic Literature*. He was a contributor to J. H. Charlesworth's *The Old Testament Pseudepigrapha*.

Jonathan A. Goldstein is Professor of Ancient History and Classics at the University of Iowa. He has written *The Letters of Demosthenes* and, for the Anchor Bible, *I Maccabees* and *II Maccabees*.

William Scott Green is Professor of Religious Studies at the University of Rochester. He is the author of *The Traditions of Joshua ben Hananiah* and other studies of ancient Judaism. He has edited five volumes of *Approaches to Ancient Judaism* and is editor of the *Journal of the American Academy of Religion*.

Richard D. Hecht is Associate Professor of Religious Studies at the University of California at Santa Barbara. He is coauthor, with Ninian Smart, of *Sacred Texts of the World: A Universal Anthology*, an editor of *Studia Philonica*, and is completing a book with Roger Friedland entitled *To Rule Jerusalem*.

Howard Clark Kee is the William Goodwin Aurelio Professor of Biblical Studies at Boston University and the author of *Jesus in History, Miracle in the Early Christian World,* and *Medicine, Miracle and Magic.*

Burton L. Mack is Professor of New Testament Studies at the School of Theology at Claremont. He is the author of *Wisdom and the Hebrew Epic: Ben Sira's Hymn in Praise of the Fathers* and *A Myth of Innocence: Mark and the Christian Origins,* and an editor of *Studia Philonica.*

George MacRae, S.J., was the Stillman Professor of Roman Catholic Theology at Harvard Divinity School, and became the Acting Dean in 1985. His publications include *Faith in the Word: The Fourth Gospel* and *Invitation to John: A Commentary on the Gospel of John with Complete Text from the Jerusalem Bible.*

Jacob Neusner is University Professor and Ungerleider Distinguished Scholar of Judaic Studies at Brown University. He is the author and editor of more than 150 works, including *The Mishnah: A New Translation, Judaism and Christianity in the Age of Constantine,* and *Vanquished Nation, Broken Spirit.*

George W. E. Nickelsburg is Professor of New Testament and Early Judaism at the University of Iowa in Iowa City. He is the author of *Jewish Literature Between the Bible and the Mishnah,* and, with Michael E. Stone, coauthor of *Faith and Piety in Early Judaism: Texts and Documents.*

Michael Stone teaches at the Hebrew University of Jerusalem. He is the author of *Scriptures, Sects and Visions: A Profile of Judaism from Ezra to the Jewish Revolts* and *Signs of the Judgment: Onomastica Sacra and The Generations from Adam,* and, with George W. Nickelsburg, coauthored *Faith and Piety in Early Judaism.*

Shemaryahu Talmon is the Judah Leib Magnes Professor of Bible Studies at the Hebrew University of Jerusalem. He is the author of *King, Cult and Calendar in Ancient Israel* and an editor of the Hebrew University Bible Project. Together with F. M. Cross, he edited a volume of essays entitled *Qumran and the History of the Biblical Text.*

1

Introduction: Messiah in Judaism: Rethinking the Question

WILLIAM SCOTT GREEN

What is found at the historical beginning of things is not the inviolable identity of their origin; it is the dissension of other things. It is disparity.

Michel Foucault[1]

Probably no religious category appears more endemic to Judaism than the messiah. That the messiah is a Jewish idea is a Western religious cliché. A broad academic and popular consensus holds that the messiah, a term conventionally taken to designate Israel's eschatological redeemer,[2] is a fundamental Judaic conception and that conflicting opinions about the messiah's appearance, identity, activity, and implications caused the historical and religious division between Judaism and Christianity. It is standard practice to classify Jewish messianism as national, ethnic, political, and material, and to mark Christian messianism as universal, cosmopolitan, ethical, and spiritual. That Jewish anticipation of the messiah's arrival was unusually keen in first century Palestine and constituted the *mise en scène* for the emergence of Christianity is a virtual axiom of western history. The study of the figure of the messiah thus is inextricable from the quest for "Christian origins" and persists as a major scholarly strategy for discerning early Christianity's filiation and divergence from the Jewish religion of its day.

At the outset of his influential essay on the messianic idea in Judaism, Gershom Scholem observed: "Any discussion of the problems relating to Messianism is a delicate matter, for it is here that the *essential conflict* between Judaism and Christianity has developed and continues to exist."[3] Scholem's claim embodies three suppositions that have guided most research on the question and figure of the messiah. First, it assumes the constant centrality of the messiah in the morphology and history of Judaism and in the Jewish–Christian argument. Second, it makes the object of

1

inquiry "messianism" – an ideology or theology – rather than "the messiah" – a concrete textual term or category. Third, by proposing an "essential conflict" between Judaism and Christianity, it construes both religions as invariable monoliths that share a single fixed point of mutual exclusivity.

In harmony with these suppositions, most scholarship on the messiah has postulated for both Judaism and its Israelite precursor(s) a single, uniform religious pattern in which messianic belief was both decisive and generative. Consequently, scholarly work on the topic has tended to be neither analytical nor interpretive, but crudely historical. The major studies have sought to trace the development and transformations of putative messianic belief through an incredible and nearly comprehensive array of ancient literary sources – from its alleged genesis in the Hebrew Bible through the New Testament, rabbinic literature, and beyond – as if all these writings were segments of a linear continuum and were properly comparable. Such work evidently aims to shape a chronological string of supposed messianic references into a plot for a story whose ending is already known; it is a kind of sophisticated proof-texting. This diegetical approach to the question embeds the sources in the context of a hypothetical religion that is fully represented in none of them. It thus privileges what the texts do not say over what they do say.

Any notion of a messianic belief or idea in ancient Judiasm necessarily presupposes that "messiah" was a focal and evocative native category for ancient Jews. But a review of Israelite and early Judaic literature, the textual record produced and initially preserved by Jews, makes such a conclusion dubious at best. The noun *mashiaḥ* ("anointed" or "anointed one") occurs 38 times in the Hebrew Bible, where it applies twice to the patriarchs, six times to the high priest, once to Cyrus, and 29 times to the Israelite king, primarily Saul and secondarily David or an unnamed Davidic monarch.[4] In these contexts the term denotes one invested, usually by God, with power and leadership, but never an eschatological figure. Ironically, in the apocalyptic book of Daniel (9:25f), where an eschatological messiah would be appropriate, the term refers to a murdered high priest.[5]

The term "messiah" has scant and inconsistent use in early Jewish texts.[6] Most of the Dead Sea Scrolls and the Pseudepigrapha, and the entire Apocrypha, contain no reference to "the messiah."[7] Moreover, a messiah is neither essential to the apocalyptic genre nor a prominent feature of ancient apocalyptic writings.[8] A rapid survey of the most pertinent materials helps to justify these generalizations.

The Maccabean documents, which disdain the revival of the Davidic dynasty, ignore the term. There is no messiah in Jubilees, nor in Enoch 1–36 and 91–104, nor in the Assumption of Moses, nor in 2 Enoch, nor in the Sibylline Oracles, though, as Morton Smith observes, "all of these contain prophetic passages in which some messiah might reasonably have been expected to make an appearance." [9] The messiah is absent from Josephus' description of Judaism in both *Antiquities* and *Against Apion,* and also from the writings of Philo.

In Ben Sira, which has no interest in a future redeemer, the "anointed one" or "messiah" is the Israelite king. The Qumran scrolls report at least two messiahs, one Davidic and one priestly, who are not necessarily eschatological figures. [10] The scrolls also apply the term to the prophets. In Psalms of Solomon 17, which is neither apocalyptic nor eschatological, the messiah is an idealized, future Davidic king who also exhibits traits of sage and teacher. The term appears only twice in the Similitudes of Enoch (1 Enoch 37–71), where it denotes not a king but a transcendent, heavenly figure. In any case, its use in Enoch is dwarfed by other titles, such as "the Chosen One" and "the Son of Man." The half-dozen references in the first century text 4 Ezra offer conflicting pictures of the messiah. In 7:28ff. the messiah dies an unredeeming death before the eschaton, but later chapters portray him as announcing and executing the final judgment. In 2 Baruch, which contains five references, the term applies primarily to a warrior, the slayer of Israel's enemies. In the Mishnah's legal contexts, messiah refers to an anointed priest, and the messiah as redeemer is negligible.

Nearly a quarter century ago, Morton Smith assessed these data as follows:

> Now all this variety in the matter of messianic expectations is merely one detail – though a particularly striking one – of the even greater variety of eschatological expectations current in the two centuries before and after the time of Jesus. To say nothing of mere differences in personnel and program, these expectations run the whole gamut of concepts, from ordinary kingdoms in this world, through forms of this world variously made over and improved, through worlds entirely new and different, to spiritual bliss without any world at all. But the point to be noted is that these contradictory theories evidently flourished side by side in the early rabbinic and Christian and Qumran communities which copied the texts and repeated the sayings. What is more, quite contradictory theories are often preserved side by side in the same document. [11]

The disparate uses surveyed above conform to Smith's judgment. They offer little evidence of sustained thought or evolving Judaic reflection about the messiah. In early Jewish literature, "messiah" is all signifier with no signified; the term is notable primarily for its indeterminacy.

In view of these facts, one may legitimately wonder about the reasons for conceiving "the messiah" as a fundamental and generative component of both Israelite religion and early Judaism. One may wonder about the justification for the assertion that "from the first century B.C.E., the Messiah was the central figure in the Jewish myth of the future,"[12] or for the claim that "belief in the Messiah" is one of the four "good gifts which the people of Israel have left as an inheritance to the entire world,"[13] or for the widespread assumption that "In the time of Jesus the Jews were awaiting a Messiah."[14] One may wonder, in other words, how so much has come to be written about an allegedly Jewish conception in which so many ancient Jewish texts manifest such little interest.

The primacy of "the messiah" as a subject of academic study derives not from ancient Jewish preoccupation, but from early Christian word-choice, theology, and apologetics. Early Christians, and particularly the earliest Christian writers, had to establish a discourse that made Jesus' career reasonable, his unexpected death believable, and their audacious commitment and new collective life plausible.[15] The New Testament's gingerly application of multiple titles to Jesus[16] suggests a crisis of classification, the dilemma of a signified without a signifier. The New Testament records various solutions to this problem. Two of them were determinative for the study of the messiah.

First, early Christian writers gave Jesus a surname. From all the titles and adjectives that are applied to him in the New Testament, they elected *christos,* the Greek for *masshiah,* to attach to Jesus' name. That *christos* was perceived as a name rather than a title seems likely from its use in the Pauline epistles and from the addition to it of the designation "son of God" in the superscription of the Gospel of Mark. Despite such initial indeterminacy, the usage valorizes *christos* and thereby makes "messiah" seem a revealing and important category, and thus a subject to be studied.[17] To be persuaded that the word *christos* itself was pivotal in shaping later understanding, one need simply imagine the consequences for western history, religion, and theology had, for example, "lord," "son of man," or "rabbi" prevailed instead.

Second, in addition to tagging Jesus with the name "messiah," New Testament authors, particularly of the gospels of Matthew and Luke, made the Hebrew scriptures into a harbinger of his career, suffering, and death. The "promise-fulfillment" motif, which casts Jesus as a foreseen figure, is perhaps the major achievement of New Testament apologetics. Apparently a later development of early Christian writing, the motif is a major focus of neither Paul's letters, nor the Q source, nor the Gospel of Mark.[18]

It is richly articulated and elaborated in the Gospel of Matthew, particularly in Matthew's distinctive use of fulfillment formulas ("All this happened in order to fulfill what the Lord declared through the prophet ... ") to make various prophetic statements into predictions of Jesus' birth and career. That nearly half of those statements are not predictions, but the prophets' comments about Israel's past or their own present,[19] suggests that the fulfillment formulas and their attached verses are strategic devices, the results of *post facto* choice, rather than remnants of an exegetical heritage. The ideology for the motif is explicit at Luke 24:13–27. On the road to Emmaus, two disciples unknowingly encounter the risen Jesus and express their disbelief at his death, which seems to disconfirm their early supposition about him ("But we had been hoping that he was the man to liberate Israel"). Jesus rebukes their lack of perception and claims that his death was predicted in the Hebrew scriptures ("Then he began with Moses and all the prophets, and explained to them the passages which referred to himself in every part of the scriptures"). The Hebrew scriptures are thus classified as anterior literature, to be read only as the messiah's textual antecedent, as a story that moves in a single direction and points beyond itself.

The "promise-fulfillment" motif, along with the geneologies devised by Matthew and Luke, embed Jesus in the Hebrew scriptures and forge an indelible continuity between him (and thus the early Christians) and Israel. The strategy solved the crisis of classification in three ways. First, it legitimated Jesus by giving him an Israelite pedigree. Second, it rendered his death intelligible by making it predetermined. Third, it made early Christian community plausible by providing an instant and urgently needed tradition. As Jaroslav Pelikan remarks, the "struggle over the authority of the Old Testament and over the nature of the continuity between Judaism and Christianity was the earliest form of a quest for a tradition that has, in other forms, recurred throughout Christian history."[20] The success and implications of this tactic should not be underestimated.

By naming Jesus *christos* and depicting him as foretold and expected – "not something brand-new, but something newly restored and fulfilled"[21] – early Christian writers gave the figure of the messiah a diachronic dimension. They situated the messiah's origin not in the present but in Israelite antiquity and thus established the Hebrew scriptures as a sequence of auguries. Reading scripture became, and to a large extent has remained, an exercise in deciphering and tracing a linear progression of portents. In Gerhard Von Rad's words, "The Old Testament can only be read as a book of ever increasing anticipation."[22] Or, as Joachim Becker puts it, "the Old Testament itself and even the history that lies behind it possess a unique messianic luminosity."[23] It was not simply, as Paul claimed, that the messiah exhibited a typological similarity to important biblical characters such as Adam.[24] Rather, the messiah was rooted in Israel's past, and his appearance could be tracked and plotted, perhaps even calculated, through time. On the model provided by Matthew and Luke, the messiah emerges not as an abrupt response to a contemporary crisis, but as the ultimate fulfillment of centuries of accumulated hope and intensifying expectation. He is a constant desideratum, an inevitability, an evolutionary rather than a revolutionary figure. In a word, the messiah is the culmination and completion of an ancient Israelite tradition.

This strategy of representation established on enduring convention of western discourse about the messiah. The model limned by an apologetic use of scripture was accepted by later scholarship as a literary fact and a historical reality, not only of scripture itself, but also of Israelite and Jewish religion. To preserve the model against the challenge of a textual record incongruent to it, scholars have been forced to resort to evasive argument.

We have seen that in Jewish writings before or during the emergence of Christianity, "messiah" appears neither as an evocative religious symbol nor as a centralizing native cultural category. Rather, it is a term of disparity, used in few texts and in diverse ways. Not surprisingly, therefore, studies of the messiah in ancient Judaism that employ the inherited model tend to assign little importance to the function or meaning of the term in discrete documents. For example, Franz Hesse's widely used article asserts that " . . . none of the Messianic passages in the OT can be exegeted Messianically. Nevertheless, the so-called Messianic understanding is implied in many of the passages, although this is more evident in texts in which the term *mashiah* is not used."[25] Nearly a quarter of his study of the use of *mashiah* in the Hebrew Bible deals with passages in which the term does not appear. Likewise, Geza Vermes acknowledges that the meaning of "messiah" will appear variable " . . . if each single usage of the term in the Pseudepigrapha, Dead Sea Scrolls and early rabbinic sources is taken into account and accorded equal importance." But Vermes doubts the value of such a procedure: "It would seem more appropriate to bear in mind the difference between the general Messianic *expectation* of Palestinian Jewry, and the peculiar Messianic *speculations* characteristic of certain learned and/or esoterical minorities."[26]

These arguments, which are representative of a type, appear to suggest that the best way to learn about the messiah in ancient Judaism is to study texts in which there is none. Indeed, the devaluation of empirical textual references and the concomitant emphasis on such terms as "understanding" and "expectation" show that the real object of research is not a figure entitled "messiah" but the religious ideology that purportedly made one possible. Thus, the standard works on the topic typically devote less attention to concrete textual references than to discussion of a religious attitude allegedly at the core of Israelite and Jewish experience: the so-called "future hope." In Mowinckel's words, "An eschatology without a Messiah is conceivable, but not a Messiah apart from a future hope."[27] The revised version of Emil Schürer's monumental history depicts that hope as the driving force of ancient Judaism:

> ... it was ... expected that Israel's faithfulness would be suitably rewarded in the life both of the nation and of the individual. Yet it was obvious that in actual experience the reward came neither to the people as a whole, nor to individuals, in the proportion anticipated. Accordingly, the more deeply this awareness penetrated into the mind of the nation and the individual, the more they were forced to turn their eyes to the future; and of course, the worse their present state, the more lively their hope. It may therefore be said that in later eras religious consciousness was concentrated upon hope for the future. A perfect age to come was the goal to which all other religious ideas were teleologically related. As the conduct of the Israelite was essentially observance of the Torah, so his faith was centered on awaiting God's kingdom.[28]

The establishment of future hope as the subject of study has three important consequences. First, it makes it possible to collect an extraordinary number and range of biblical and postbiblical texts under a single "messianic" category and to treat their contents as species of a genus. Almost any textual reference to the future, or to eternity, or to an idealized figure – to say nothing of verses with unclear temporal limits – is an immediate candidate for inclusion. The absence of eschatology or of the title "messiah" is no barrier. With this rubric, Joseph Klausner could begin his history of the messiah idea in Israel not even with David, but with Moses!

Second, the use of future hope as the primary taxon of messianism also permits those varied texts to be arranged chronologically and cast as components of a continuous and unitary tradition. Indeed, the notion that messianic belief or expectation originated in Israel's experience and then developed in Judaism is the cornerstone of nearly every major scholarly treatment of the subject. This supposition has been relentlessly applied to the study of the messiah even when the evidence admittedly fails to support it or even contradicts it. For instance, Hesse concluded his survey of messianic references in biblical and postbiblical writings with the following claim:

It is very difficult, if not impossible, to reconstruct a history of the Messianic movement in Israel and post-exilic Judaism from these scanty passages, many of which cannot be dated with any certainty. There undoubtedly must have been such a movement. This is shown by the examples given and it may also be concluded from the fact that Messianism emerges into the clear light of history in later centuries, not merely as a trend that has just arisen in Judaism, but as a movement with hundreds of years of history behind it.[29]

If, by Hesse's own admission, the evidence is minimal and inconclusive, it is difficult to understand how to know that there "must have been" a messianic movement in Israelite religion and Judaism, much less that later versions of it were the product of "hundreds of years of history."

To violate ordinary scholarly principles of evidence and inference with such forced arguments requires powerful external motivations. It would be disingenuous and unhelpful to pretend that a question as significant and sensitive as the messiah has escaped the vagaries of theological interests, both Christian and Jewish. Joachim Becker makes some of these explicit:

We have seen that the messianic prophecies cannot be considered visionary predication of a New Testament fulfillment. In fact, there was not even such a thing as a messianic expectation until the last two centuries B.C. Does this eliminate the traditional picture of messianic expectation? Such a conclusion would contradict one of the most central concerns of the New Testament, which insists with unprecedented frequency, intensity, and unanimity that Christ was proclaimed in advance in the Old Testament. Historical-critical scholarship can never set aside this assertion of the New Testament. We must therefore find an explanation that does justice to both this historical approach and the witness of the New Testament. A synthesis must be sought in which both are preserved. To appeal to the light of faith for this synthesis is not a schizophrenic act of intellectual violence, for revelation and faith go hand in hand with a manifestation of their rationality. . . . The christological actualization of the Old Testament in the New is so commanding that it confronts exegesis with the question of conscience whether the historical-critical methods . . . is in fact a way at all of carrying out the exegesis of the Old Testament *as such.*[30]

If, in a Christian context, scholars have used the model of an Israelite–Judiac messianic tradition to claim the Israelite legacy and thus demonstrate Christianity's authenticity, scholars in a Judaic context have employed the same model for the opposite purpose. Mowinckel, for example, concluded his classic work with the claim that Jesus definitively refashioned the Israelite–Judaic messianic tradition. In Jesus, he asserted,

> The Jewish Messianic concept is . . . transformed and lifted up to a wholly other plane. If fact, the Jewish Messiah, as originally conceived, and as most of Jesus' contemporaries thought of him, was pushed aside and replaced by a new redeemer and mediator of salvation. . . . For Jesus, the Jewish Messianic idea was the temptation of Satan, which he had to reject. The new conception of a saviour, which Jesus created, unites in itself the loftiest elements in both the Jewish and Aryan spirit, and fuses them in a true unity, which is realized in Jesus himself.[31]

Likewise, Klausner's judgment that " . . . in the belief in the Messiah of the people of Israel, *the political part goes hand in hand with the ethical part, and the nationalistic with the universalistic*"[32] surely makes the ethical-universal messianism he attributes to Christianity seem a mere shadow of the real thing. In both instances, the scholarly results leave something to be desired.

Third, the postulate of a proto-messianic or messianic hope as coextensive with, and the generative force of, Israelite and Jewish religions presupposes that the practitioners of both understood themselves to have lost on the temporal plane. Schürer's assertion that a "perfect age to come was the goal to which all other religious ideas were teleologically related" entails a prior claim of explicit Jewish awareness of religious failure and defeat. The demarcation of "future hope" as a primary category of Israelite and Judaic experience suggests that those who had it regarded their present existence as both provisional and ultimately unredeeming. Scholem developed the idea more abstractly and applied it to the entire history of Judaism:

> There is something grand about living in hope, but at the same time there is something profoundly unreal about it. It diminishes the singular worth of the individual, and he can never fulfill himself, because the incompleteness of his endeavors eliminates precisely what constitutes its highest value. Thus in Judaism the Messianic idea has compelled *a life lived in deferment,* in which nothing can be done definitively, nothing can be irrevocably accomplished. . . . Precisely understood, there is nothing concrete which can be accomplished by the unredeemed. This makes for

the greatness of Messianism, but also for its constitutional weakness.[33]

If, as the established consensus holds, the messiah really is indigenous to Judaism, then, on the arguments of Schürer and Scholem, it must follow that Judaism was and is constitutionally incapable of success.

The model of an Israelite–Judaic tradition driven by a "future hope" is finally unpersuasive because it uses so little to account for so much. It makes disappointment and defeat the sole cause of both the origination and development, the genesis and crystallization, of messianism. It also requires the postulation of a chronic and endemic religious problem in Judaism, to which the messiah is then portrayed as the necessary and only possible solution. In this regard, Scholem's claim that for Jews the consequence of messianism was – and, indeed, has been – a "life lived in deferment," however forceful and dramatic, is counter-intuitive. Admittedly, the case on both sides of the issue remains to be demonstrated, but it is at least questionable that Jews who adhered to some sort of halakic practice would have advocated, much less understood, an ideology that in principle declared their religious behavior nugatory.

In the past quarter century, the established consensus about the messiah in ancient Judaism has begun to break down, and there now are powerful reasons to ditch it altogether. Careful word-studies, fresh and disciplined readings of well-known texts, and a new appreciation of ancient writings as social products and cultural constructions have revealed religious worlds of ancient Jews (and Christians) considerably more diversified and complex than was hitherto imagined.[34] The new agenda requires that we reverse the procedures of earlier scholarship. Instead of treating the literary sources as reflections of a preconceived and synthetic Judaism, or as segments of a hypothetical (and, frankly, fictive) uniform and linear tradition, we must employ them as the context out of which a critical description of Jewish religion must be constructed. It is no longer possible to justify the standard, homogenous reading of the varied Jewish writings or to assume that different Jewish groups, even within Palestine, shared a single outlook, social experience, or religious expectation simply because they were Jews. The evidence in this book shows that preoccupation with the messiah was not a uniform or definitive trait, nor a common reference point, of early Jewish writings or the Jews who produced them. As a speculum for the analysis and understanding of early Jewish religious life, the category "messiah" probes less obliquely, and with rather less precision and discernment, than we have come to suppose.

NOTES

My thanks for generous assistance and good advice are due to Professors Beverly Roberts Gaventa, Jonathan Z. Smith, Gary G. Porton, Burton Mack, Richard Horsley, Elizabeth Fox-Genovese, C. Clifton Black II, and Philip Wexler. I owe a special debt on this project to Professor Jacob Neusner for warm collegiality, critical insight, and exceptional patience.

1 Michel Foucault, *Language, Counter-Memory, Practice,* ed. Donald F. Bouchard, trans. Donald F. Bouchard and Sherry Simon (Ithaca: Cornell University Press, 1977), p. 114.

2 Sigmund Mowinckel, *He That Cometh: The Messiah Concept in the Old Testament and Later Judaism,* trans, G. W. Anderson (Nashville: Abingdon Press, 1956), p. 3: "In later Judaism the term 'Messiah' denotes an *eschatological* figure. . . . To use the word 'Messiah' is to imply eschatology, the last things."

   Joseph Klausner, *The Messianic Idea in Israel: From its Beginning to the Completion of the Mishnah,* trans. W. F. Stinespring (New York: Macmillan, 1955), p. 9, defines belief in the messiah as "The prophetic hope for the end of this age, in which a strong redeemer, by his power and his spirit, will bring complete redemption, political and spiritual, to the people Israel, and along with this, earthly bliss and moral perfection to the entire human race."

3 Gershom Scholem, "Toward an Understanding of the Messianic Idea in Judaism," in *The Messianic Idea in Judaism* (New York: Schocken, 1971), p. 1 [Italics mine].

4 Franz Hesse, "*Chrio,* etc.," *Theological Dictionary of the New Testament* (hereafter *TDNT*) 9 (1974):496–509.

5 Ibid., p. 505. When used in connection with a royal figure, the term occurs in the construct state. The king is "the Lord's anointed." It occurs as an indefinite noun only in Daniel.

6 Morton Smith, "What is Implied by the Variety of Messianic Figures?" *Journal of Biblical Literature* 78 (1959):66–72; M. de Jonge, "The Use of the Word 'Anointed' in the time of Jesus," *Novum Testamentum* 8 (1966):132–48; idem. and A. S. van der Woude, "*Chrio,* etc.," *TDNT* 9 (1974):509–27; James H. Charlesworth, "The Concept of the Messiah in the Pseudepigrapha," *Aufstieg und Niedergang der Römischen Welt* II/19.1 (1979):189–218; A. E. Harvey, *Jesus and the Constraints of History* (Philadelphia: The Westminster Press, 1982), pp. 78–82. Richard A. Horsley, "Popular Messianic Movements around the Time of Jesus," *The Catholic Biblical Quarterly* 46 (1984):471–95.

7 J. H. Charlesworth, "From Jewish Messianology to Christian Christology," this volume.

8 John J. Collins, *The Apocalyptic Imagination* (New York: Crossroad, 1984).

9 Smith, "Variety," p. 68.

10 Collins *Apocalyptic,* p. 123, notes that the "messiahs" in the Qumran texts "imply a definitive change in the historical process, but . . . not . . . an end of the historical process." Also see S. J. Talmon, "Waiting for the Messiah: The Spiritual Universe of the Qumran Covenanters," this volume.

11 Smith, "Variety," p. 69.

12 Raphael Patai, *The Messiah Texts* (Detroit: Wayne State University Press, 1979), p. xxvii.

13 Klausner, *Messianic Idea,* p. 13.

14 Mowinckel, *He That Cometh,* p. 3.

15 Barnabas Lindars, *New Testament Apologetic: The Doctrinal Significance of the Old Testament Quotations* (Philadelphia: The Westminster Press, 1961), especially pp. 251–9.

16 See Howard C. Kee, "Christology in Mark's Gospel," this volume.

17 How Jesus, either before or after his death, came to be called *christos* is a matter of incessant speculation. On the basis of Isa. 61:1 ("The Spirit of the Lord is upon me, because he has anointed me"), Harvey offers a plausible and efficient hypothesis that avoids the inevitable difficulties of supposing "messiah" an eschatological term with royal connotations (*Jesus and the Constraints of History,* pp. 136–53). Most recently, see E. P. Sanders, *Jesus and Judaism* (Philadelphia: Fortress Press, 1985), in which the category "messiah" plays almost no role in the reconstruction of the historical Jesus. Sanders observes that the Davidic Messiah "is one of the least frequent themes in Jewish literature" (p. 117), and conjures up a circumstance in which disciples might have applied the title to Jesus. On p. 306 he argues: "Jesus and his close followers understood that he was entering [Jerusalem] as 'king', but there was no large public hue and cry about it. It fits into Jesus' last symbolic acts: he entered as 'king', demonstrated the destruction of the present temple, and had a meal with his disciples which symbolized the coming 'banquet'." He doubts (p. 307) that Jesus ever called himself messiah, but suggests (p. 308) that "If Jesus said to the disciples only 'there will be a kingdom', 'you will have a role in it', and 'I will share the banquet of the new kingdom with you', the disciples would naturally have been as willing as the Romans to think that he considered himself 'king', and they would equally naturally have found the title 'Messiah' an appropriate one." On the use of *christos* in Paul, see George MacRae, "Messiah and Gospel," this volume.

18 See D. Moody Smith, "The Use of the Old Testament in the New," in *The Use of the Old Testament in the New and Other Essays: Studies in Honor of William Franklin Stinespring,* ed. James F. Efrid (Durham: Duke University Press, 1972), pp. 3–65; and Hugh Anderson, "The Old Testament in Mark's Gospel," in ibid., pp. 280–306. Rowan A. Greer, "The Christian Bible and Its Interpretation," in James A. Kugel and Rowan A. Greer, *Early Biblical Interpretation* (Philadelphia: The Westminster Press, 1986), pp. 134–7, draws a helpful distinction between promise-fulfillment and prophecy-fulfillment.

19 Hos. 11:1 (Matt. 2:15); Jer. 31:15 (Matt. 2:18); Isa. 9:1–2 (Matt. 4:14f.); Isa. 53:4 (Matt. 8:17); Zech. 11:12–13, Jer. 32:6–15, 18:2–3 (Matt. 17:9).

20 Jaroslav Pelikan, *The Christian Tradition: A History of the Development of Doctrine,* Part I, *The Emergence of the Catholic Tradition* (Chicago: The University of Chicago Press, 1971), p. 14.

21 Ibid., p. 13.

22 Gerhard Von Rad, *Old Testament Theology,* Vol. II, *The Theology of Israel's Prophetic Traditions,* trans. D. M. G. Stalker (New York: Harper & Row, 1965), p. 319; also see James Samuel Preus, *From Shadow to Promise: Old Testament Interpretation From Augustine to the Young Luther* (Cambridge, Mass.: The Belknap Press of Harvard University Press, 1969).

23 Joachim Becker, *Messianic Expectation in the Old Testament,* trans. David E. Green (Philadelphia: Fortress Press, 1980), p. 96.

24 See Robin Scroggs, *The Last Adam: A Study in Pauline Anthropology* (Philadelphia: Fortress Press, 1966).

25 Hesse, "Chrio," p. 504.

26 Geza Vermes, *Jesus the Jew: A Historian's Reading of the Gospels* (New York: Macmillan, 1973), p. 130. On the basis of seven passages, drawn from the Psalms of Solomon, the Dead Sea Scrolls, rabbinic literature, and Philo, only four of which employ the term "messiah," Vermes concludes (p. 134) that "ancient Jewish prayer and Bible interpretation demonstrate unequivocally that if in the inter-Testamental era a man claimed, or was proclaimed, to be 'the Messiah', his listeners would as a matter of course have assumed that he was referring to the Davidic Redeemer. . . ." He then demonstrates (pp. 135–40) that at least four non-Davidic understandings also were possible.

27 Mowinckel, *He That Cometh,* p. 8.

28 Emil Schürer, *The History of the Jewish People in the Age of Jesus Christ,* Volume II, rev. and ed. Geza Vermes and Fergus Millar (Edinburgh: T&T Clark, 1979), p. 492. In the preface, p. v, the editors claim to "have felt free, indeed obliged, . . . to introduce new evidence unavailable to Schürer, and to replace those of his views and opinions which appear untenable in the light of contemporary knowledge." Schürer's statement, originally written at the end of the nineteenth century, remains substantially unchanged in the revised version. Apparently, the editors judged it still tenable.

29 Hesse, "Chrio," p. 509.

30 Becker, *Messianic Expectation* pp. 93–94.

31 Mowinckel, *He That Cometh,* pp. 449–450.

32 Klausner, *Messianic Idea,* p. 10, his italics.

33 Scholem, "Messianic Idea," p. 35, his italics.

34 In particular, see Richard A. Horsley and John S. Hanson, *Bandits, Prophets, and Messiahs: Popular Movements at the Time of Jesus* (Minneapolis: Winston Press, 1985), especially pp. 88–134, and Jacob Neusner and Ernest S. Frerichs, eds., *To See Ourselves as Others See Us: Jews, Christians, and "Others" in Late Antiquity* (Atlanta: Scholars Press, 1985).

2

Wisdom Makes a Difference: Alternatives to "Messianic" Configurations

BURTON L. MACK

Jacob Neusner has challenged a long tradition of scholarship by the addition of a single letter to the magical word messiah. Messiahs it now is. And the singular notion of "the" messiah is disclosed for what it always has been – a scholarly assumption generated by the desire to clarify Christian origins. It matters not that biblical scholars have learned long since to contrast Jewish "backgrounds" with the Christian designation of Jesus as the Christ, thus regarding the many diverse "messianic" figures in Judaism primarily as partial precursors to the new and comprehensive configuration. The definitive notion given with the Christian configuration has been the lens through which most studies on "the messiah in Judaism" have nonetheless been undertaken. Neusner has, in effect, asked us to set that lens aside.

With the shift from singular to plural the alternative approach is also given. With plurality noted, differences among exemplary texts are highlighted as of significance for understanding any particular configuration. This particularity of a given configuration, moreover, indicates at least two further, fundamental considerations appropriate to the understanding of a text. One is to see each text as a creative product of the imagination. The other is to see that product placed in some context within which its particularity can be assessed. There are two con-texts with which scholarly discourse is familiar – the social history that provides the setting for a text's composition and address, and the literary-cultural tradition within which a text takes its place. Neusner's challenge is to work out an approach to texts that can position them at the intersection of these two contexts. The analytical approach called for rides on some theory of "intertextuality," i.e., the way in which a given text relates to its contexts as systems of meaning already in place. The significance of the text itself will be some kind of reflection on the relationship between the two contexts.

15

But what now of the notion "messiahs" at all? Once the differences have been noted among configurations normally included in the set of "messianic" texts, the principle of similarity that made comparison possible needs to be rearticulated and justified. Once the notion of "the" messiah has been questioned, the phenomenon under investigation needs to be reconceived.

As an example of the problem as I see it, I take a statement from Anders Hultgard's excellent essay on "The Ideal 'Levite,' the Davidic Messiah, and the Saviour Priest in the Testaments of the Twelve Patriarchs." Hultgard's study is a fine example of the discriminating scholarship called for as we move away from definitions of "the messianic" determined by the Christian lens. He succeeds in delimiting three separate, ideal figures in the Testaments, placing them at particular junctures in redactional history, and clarifying their correspondence to views in general of a carrier group at different points in its own social history. Thus the "saviour priest" of Testament of Levi 18:2–14 can be accounted for without any direct appeal to Christian messianology or interpolation. And yet, the conclusion Hultgard draws is that " . . . the saviour priest of the *Testaments* must be ranged among the great messianic figures propagated by the Judaism of the late Second Temple period: the royal messiah in the Psalms of Solomon 17, the figure of Melchisedek in 11Q Melch and the Son of Man figure in the similitudes of Enoch."[1]

Hultgard has given his reasons for this inclusion. They are based on the judgment that "The presentation of the saviour priest reveals a development of the messianic concepts in the way that the importance given to the saviour figure has been considerably enhanced."[2] The first enhancement is that the figure has attracted and combined a rich cluster of elements – "priestly, royal and angelic." The second major enhancement is that the appearance of this figure "has a universal bearing" making him a "world-saviour" with a "favorable attitude to the Gentiles." The third is that of his "uniqueness," self-sufficiency, and importance as " . . . a key-figure for ushering in the eschatological era."[3]

It is possible that these judgments about the importance of just these characteristics, and about the greatness of these messianic figures, could be justified in some form amenable to scholarly debate. But Hultgard does not tell us what it is that makes uniqueness, universality, and comprehensiveness the marks of a "great" messianic figure. So we are left with the suspicion that these figures are important for Hultgard insofar as they approximate some notion of "the" messiah that he assumes as definitional. Judging from the characteristics he lists as important, that notion may still be the Christian definition.

Our problem, therefore, is that the very notion of "the messianic" is too closely tied to the assumption of a singular profile of specific characteristics, and that the singular profile is too closely tied to a certain, traditional notionality about "the messiah." How to break out of the sense of self-evidence this creates is the challenge. If we relinquish the convenient (but inadequate) method of Christian–Jewish comparison and contrast, what approach shall we take even to get started?

Centering on a Social Anthropology

I propose to begin with a simple reflection on the traditional notion of the messiah, noting that it relies heavily on a certain pattern of characterization that, if raised to formal status, can be used to expand the set of texts available to us for comparative studies. The notion of the messiah actually is a composite characterization won from the set of texts traditionally designated as messianic. This profile usually runs somewhat as follows: The messiah is a figure of high office (usually royal), of exemplary virtue (including gifts of superlative strength, righteousness, and wisdom), appearing at some (future) time of need to execute judgment (if not destruction) upon the enemies of Israel, rescue (or gather) the (righteous) survivors, and (re)establish a perfectly right society in (and for) the world over which he would rule. We can begin to revise our point of departure for a study of messianic figures by making two observations about this profile.

The first observation is that this profile is the product of a certain selection of texts and figures held to be comparable expressions of a single notion. But as the parentheses indicate, significant differences do occur even among those texts so selected. It is also true that no single characteristic given with this profile can be regarded as a feature found only in these texts, attributed solely to "messianic" figures. This means that the principle of selection for texts held to be comparable needs to be reviewed. One recent approach to this problem has been to subsume the so-called messianic texts under the larger set of texts composed during the Second Temple Period in which "ideal figures" occur.[4] This expansion of the set of texts for comparison does appear to be justified. By expanding the set in just this way, the questions we might ask of any of these texts will focus upon the function of the imaginative labor invested in the process of idealization. Comparative studies among figures of different profiles should enhance any particularities discovered, not erode them. But we could be left with the classification of "messiahs and other ideal figures." So something more needs to be said at the point of their characterization. Can a common pattern of characterization be discerned?

The second observation that can be made about the traditional profile of the messiah is that descriptive categories have been preferred over more formal ones. The profile is actually an uneven mixture of both more specific and more general attributions. The very designation "messiah" is a case in point. Anointing is only one of many ways to express legitimation. Other ways of attributing legitimation are the mention of election, appointment, or the covenantal aspect of an office, as well as certain kinds of special endowments and a variety of mythological imageries that link a figure's office to divine initiative, selection, and purpose. Thus the scholarly concern to comb the literature for specifically messianic texts has privileged a particular attribution as distinctive and definitional for a type. The same is true for the adjectival qualifiers frequently appended in scholarly discourse, i.e., "priestly," "royal," and so forth. The particular office attributed to an ideal figure may in fact be a very significant characteristic, more significant than the particular form of its legitimation. But the formal category that makes comparison possible is not that of a particular office, but of the notion of office itself. If office were to be recognized as a basic category among others in a general pattern of characterization, it might be possible to determine the outline scholars actually have had in mind when constructing the profile of the messiah, as well as broaden the set of texts that could be considered comparable.

Taking our lead from considerations such as these, I suggest the use of a formal pattern of characterization that can be used to control comparative studies of the so-called messianic texts with other ideal figures of high office imagined during our period. The pattern includes Legitimation, attribution of Office, Special Endowments, (Dis)Placement relative to social history, and the Execution of Deeds and Institutions fundamental to social structuration and maintenance. One can see immediately the value of such a construct for comparative studies. Courage to suggest such a pattern is given with its recognizably close relation to explicitly formulated theories of characterization in the Greek traditions of literature, rhetoric, and educational handbooks, traditions with which Jewish authors of the period will have been acquainted in some way. But the proposal is made mainly in the conviction that many of the ideal figures appearing in the Jewish literatures of the time do present particular configurations of this general pattern. Jewish nuance and concern may be seen in the peculiar emphasis placed upon the divine legitimation and endowment of these figures of high office, as well as in the particular ways in which these offices and attributions are construed. If we keep this Jewish nuance in mind, note the tightly knit cluster of specifically institutional functions, and anticipate the ways in which a given formal category might come to expression in texts of this time, we can see that a very special kind of anthropological characterization is at hand.

These ideal figures appear to be expressions of a kind of imaginitive effort that was energized with some exuberance and passion by Jewish authors during the Second Temple period. The emergence of marvelous figures populating fantastic worlds was, as we know, an important mark of Jewish reflection precisely during this period. By noting that many of them can be regarded as ideal officials, we can already chart the direction our investigations may take. In the context of a social history marked by tremendous efforts to establish a stable sovereignty in Judaea in the face of foreign powers, by the eruption of internal conflicts over how best to conceive of that sovereignty and go about achieving it, and by the emergence of alternative social formations both in Judaea and in the Diaspora, a period of effort that did not succeed in its designs for Jerusalem, these figures were the poetic means by which Israel could be reimagined. They provided the focus for a serious contemplation on the "state" of Israel: the grounds for its legitimation, the shape of its social orders, and the locus of its authorities.

My thesis will be that these figures functioned as symbols to center essentially social anthropologies. They were not put forth as heroes of achievement, mimetic ideals, or saviors.[5] Neither were they merely idealizations of religious and ethical values common to Jewish culture. They were not set forth to invite aspirations of individuals for virtue or religious identity. And they were not invested with ontological significance as objects of faith or veneration. They were, instead, intellectual investments in the hard work of rationalizing social and political structures. They were images of the human under specifically institutional garb.

Thus these figures collected characteristics that in effect were functions and qualities essential for the social formation of Israel. This can be seen by noting the selection of endowments and functions attributed to these figures. They are exactly and only those that were poignantly under discussion throughout this period as problematic, given the political and social realities. Piety (all of our authors agree that some form of piety was definitive for Israel), power, place among the nations, guarantee of social justice, system of governance, legal basis or constitution, and what to do about internal diversity – all were issues needing resolution in the struggles to conceptualize, actualize, and defend the notion of Israel in the many forms of Judaism attempted during this time.

The formal pattern of characterization was filled in by selecting just that combination of carefully nuanced features that could be integrated in a single configuration. Such a configuration solved imaginatively certain political issues of consequence. A particular slant to the definition of office, a careful selection from among the many notions of legitimation, the mode of power proposed and its constraints, perspectives on piety, definitions of justice, and stance toward conflict, enemies, and the law or traditions – all reflected decisions made about imagining Judaism and its constitution in the midst of Greco–Roman times. An ideal figure could serve as a point of intellectual leverage for gaining perspective on the situation from an ideal viewpoint. In the construction of an ideal figure theoretical analysis of the situation would have been as important as the imaginative projection of fantasy or desire. Real issues with which some group was struggling can often be discerned in the background. Thus the imaginative labor involved must have been in the interest of understanding and facilitating a particular social mode of being in the world. It would be wrong to think that these figures were investments in an ontology of the ideal. They were, instead, rationalizations concerned with the social history of Israel.

It is, then, that moment of rationalization that should be the object of our quest to understand the phenomenon of ideal figures in the literatures of this time. These figures were studies in the disparity between traditional models for the social structuration of Israel on the one hand, and the authors' experience of the present form of Jewish society on the other. I suspect that the phenomenon of exaggerated idealization was the result of such a disparity experienced as no longer tolerable. That the ideals were cast as singular figures does not hinder their function as symbols for a social order. It actually enhanced the intellectual objective; i.e., to work out schematically the interrelationships among the essential factors, qualities, and functions requisite to social formation. Thus, the figures are peculiarly social configurations, loci for the imaginative study of the intracate nexus of social forces specifically relevent to Jewish social history. They encapsulate and facilitate very tough thinking about the exigencies of actual social history in the light of given norms and models held to be definitive for Jewish social identity. They are investigative, experimental, visionary, and programmatic in their conception, intended to reflect back upon the actual labor of social ordering in which authors and readers found themselves.

The present essay is an experimental reading of three texts that cast ideal figures of the official kind. One of them is a classical "messianic" text, but two of them are from literatures in the tradition of wisdom, a tradition considered not to have produced messianic figures, embedding its anthropological ideals in some cosmic order of reality rather than in some historical or eschatological future. Thus, the selection of texts exemplifies the inclusion of messianic texts in a larger set of texts with ideal figures. The examples chosen for this study span the period from the beginning of the second century B.C.E. to the middle of the first century C.E., and include both Palestinian and Diaspora authors, those partial to Second Temple institutions, and those party to severe critique of certain forms those institutions took. The approach to each will be to seek that intersection of literary history and social history at which idealization occurred. The attempt will be to understand each imaginative labor as a cogent rationalization of structural problems and possibilities in Jewish social formation. In a concluding reflection the measure of their cogency as examples of intellectual effort will be assessed. The objective will be not only to demonstrate their function as critical reflection upon social history, but to show that the so-called messianic text functions no differently than the others. All are configurations enabled by the same Jewish "wisdom."

Those "Anointed" by Wisdom

The High Priest in Sirach

Ben Sira's book of wisdom may be dated ca. 180 B.C.E., shortly after the transition in hegemony from Ptolemaic to Seleucid rule and the death of the high priest Simon (d. 198 B.C.E.). Ben Sira's attitude with regard to the political situation in general is known. He was decidedly pro-Second Temple institutions, participating as priest and scholar-sage in some school setting supportive of the cultus, gerousia, Torah, courts, and other structures of public life. His conservative posture with regard to Jewish traditions and institutions was balanced by a decidedly open stance toward Hellenistic culture, appropriating a great deal of its *paideia*. We have evidence for this in his employment of Greek literary forms, philosophical notions, and pedagogical methods. His book approximates a Greek handbook for teachers. And his mentality was cosmopolitan.

He was, however, quiet on the topic of foreign rule. He acknowledged the existence of "kings and rulers" both within Israel's history and as a phenomenon that continued to exist in his own time. But he refused to take sides in the Ptolemaic–Seleucid struggle, apparently willing to accommodate either as long as the institutions of the Second Temple were not forced to bow before another nomos. His depiction of Simon as high priest includes functions that, according to Ben Sira, were royal – i.e., benefactions for and defense of Jerusalem (50:1–4). So it appears that Ben Sira understood Second Temple institutions, symbolized in the office of a high priest, to be a sufficient social structure for the realization and cultivation of Jewish identity as a nation.

His book of wisdom can be understood as the product of a profound imaginative labor in the interest of rationalizing this social model as the locus of divine intention for Israel from the beginning. The idiom was wisdom, the available notion for conceptualizing the sense or logic of the order of things in the world. But in order to achieve a wisdom rationale for a society centered in the figure of a high priest, Ben Sira faced two imposing challenges. One was that the task of using wisdom thought to rationalize such a social system was one for which the traditions of wisdom were unprepared. The other was that wisdom thought itself had come under severe critique by those skeptical or cynical with regard to any claim at all about knowing what was best for humans in a world of uncertainty (Job, Qohelet). Both challenges stemmed from the crisis in wisdom occasioned by the failure of the monarchies and the experience of the exile.

That crisis had produced a deep self-reflection that resulted in the (mythological) notion of wisdom itself. Though absent in society, except as a call from without, wisdom was imagined nevertheless to exist – with God and in the natural orders of his creation (Prov. 1–9). It was this wisdom myth, and its daring affirmations about the potentiality for making sense of things again, that Ben Sira used to rationalize a new societal order. We cannot trace out here the many intellectual efforts of Ben Sira requisite to such an achievement. But scholars will know that he managed to imagine the myth in ways that could bridge the gap between God and his creation on the one hand, and the history of Israel and its culmination in Second Temple institutions on the other. He buttressed the myth with Hellenistic schemata, traced correlations between cosmos, polis, and anthropos, and worked out an anthropological epistemology that rationalized the perception of wisdom in the new social order. In course, the wisdom of God in creation could now be "located" as well in Israel's history, the Torah, the temple, the work of the scholar sage, the institutions of instruction, the assemblies as courts and liturgical gatherings – i.e., the entire social system as patterned life. This achievement, the correlation of the mythical notion of wisdom with some actual social order found worthy of wisdom's blessing, i.e., capable of sustaining social well-being, answered both challenges at once. It reinstated wisdom in the real world, thus overcoming the purely mythological status of the postcrisis object of despair and desire. And it answered the cynical critique by using wisdom thought to justify a concrete social etiquette within which sound judgments could again be made.

For the purposes of this essay, however, it is the treatment of the figure of Simon the high priest in Chapter 50 that requires explication. The depiction comes at the end of a fine poem in praise of the pious, the poem that concludes Ben Sira's book of wisdom. The poem appears at first glance to be a series of independent units, each devoted to the glorious achievements of some figure from Israel's epic history, but recent studies by Thomas Lee and myself have discovered that it possesses a remarkable rhyme and reason.[6] The units follow a pattern of characterization formally analogous to the Greek encomium, but with a specifically Jewish twist. This pattern includes 1) a designation of Office, 2) a notice about Election or divine approval, 3) a mention of Covenant, 4) a mention of the figure's Piety, 5) an account of Deeds, 6) a reference to Setting, and 7) an ascription of Reward. The Jewish twist can be seen in the emphasis upon Covenant, Election, and Office, as well as in the specific ways the Piety, Deeds, and Rewards are cast. Piety and Deeds are typed in ways appropriate to a person's office, and the Reward is simply the glory inherent in the Office itself. Thus it is that the notion of Office determines the characterizations throughout.

There are five offices in play: Father, Judge, Priest, Prophet, and King. By means of a highly selective reading of Israel's epic and historiographic literature, a rich intertexuality drawing upon patterns in Hellenistic historiographic, biographic, and encomiastic literatures, and the employment of an overall narrative pattern taken from the wisdom myth in Chapter 24, Ben Sira structured this series of official figures as an etiology for Second Temple Judaism. This cannot be demonstrated here, but some observations relevant for our interest in Simon can be given.[7]

The poem falls into three main sections and two transitional moments. The first section is composed of seven figures (Noah, Abraham, Isaac, Jacob, Moses, Aaron, and Phineas) and constitutes the primeval establishment of the system of covenants and offices. Then follow the judges and the moment of transition into the land. In the land, the history of the prophets and kings is played out as a struggle *(agon)* to establish a societal order in human history in keeping with the divine intentions. This concludes with the kings and their kingdoms coming to an end, and the prophets announcing a confident hope. After the second transition (three figures of the restoration), the poem concludes with a singularly brilliant and celebrative account of the whole congregation gathered at the temple, Simon surrounded by his brothers, the sons of Aaron, and his pronouncement of the blessing of the Lord on the people on the great Day of Atonement.

A careful study of the poem shows that this moment is climactic, fulfilling the divine intentions for Israel given with the covenants, the promise of blessing, and the structure of its offices as outlined in the primeval epoch. Simon stands in the covenant of Phineas (high priesthood), surrounded by the Sons of Aaron (priests and teachers), having entered into the sanctuary, the presence of God (as only Moses before him is said to have done), and announces officially the blessing (promised to Abraham) on the whole congregation of Israel (i.e., the inheritance of Jacob).

It is not said that Simon was "anointed." But in the poem "anointing" is one of the several ways in which Ben Sira marks a figure's legitimation or election. For Ben Sira, anointing is something prophets do, and Moses, a composite figure combining characteristics of prophets, priests, and kings "before" these offices were separately established, is said to anoint Aaron on the occasion of the establishment of the office of priesthood by covenant (45:15). Within this office Phineas marks the special case of high priesthood, and is said to be "third in line" from Moses (45:23). Simon continues the covenant of Phineas (50:24), and thus is acknowledged to be legitimate.

It is also the case that Simon's "glory" is highly accentuated. This term functions in the poem throughout as a powerful linguistic sign for the correlation of Greek and Jewish manifestations of human and divine excellence, honor, and presence. It functions, plausibly, as a sign for wisdom's presence in the mythic history as well. Thus Simon's depiction as one who appears glorious can be understood as the sign of his divine legitimation (50:5,6–10,11,20). It is also his endowment for the performance of that act which, according to Ben Sira, constitutes Israel as Israel. We might say that Ben Sira "anointed" Simon with the glory of divine wisdom.

I begin the set of studies with this anthropological reflection in order to demonstrate the significance of such an ideal depiction for an essentially social-political concern. Simon is in the center of the picture. But the entire social order Ben Sira had in mind is at stake. Here, in distinction to later reflections on priestly and royal figures, displaced from social history and depicted without names, an actual person of the very recent past has been eulogized. But he has been eulogized only in terms of his office, and only in terms of certain specific characteristics of that office held to be constitutive. And the mode of that eulogy is mythic. What Ben Sira claimed for that moment was nothing less than the full realization in his time of the divine intention for Israel toward which all history had been moving. Cosmos and history collapsed then, and nothing more need be hoped for than that that office, covenant, glory, and blessing would continue for Israel in that social order thereby constituted (50:22–24).

I begin with this study for another reason as well. This is because it is possible to see something here of the "imaginative labor" invested in this kind of mythologization. I have cast this labor as an intellectual achievement in the interest of finding a social order where "wisdom" could make sense again, as well as rationalizing that (new) order in terms of (older) Jewish traditions. But that hardly completes the picture of Ben Sira's investment in this ideal figure. We must note now that, in the troubled times that began with Simon's death, his robes and office became the bones of contention around which a terrible conflict raged. The next high priest, Onias III, was pro-Tobiad, i.e., part of a party politically partial in a way Ben Sira was not. At first pro-Ptolemaic, then swinging precipitously over to the Seleucids with their program of structural Hellenization for Jerusalem, the Tobiads helped set the stage for the politicization of the high priestly office and the unhappy history of 167 B.C.E. and beyond. Ben Sira cannot have been unaware of the threat such factionalism posed for his ideal vision, any more than he was unaware of the actual threat that any hegemony was to a religious order not in full control of the city and land where its temple had to be. So his vision was more than a pious poetic. It was the conception of a political idea, a program, a call to see and remember how precious the traditions were, and what glory would be tarnished should the "covenant of Phineas" be sold.

With Ben Sira we stand at the headwaters of that period of Jewish history in which politics and religion clashed, models and institutions failed to mesh, and ideal figures were imagined dislodged from their rightful place in the center of things. Though we cannot be sure, Ben Sira's intellectual efforts may have had a legacy. Popular leaders may have wanted to start over again with Ben Sira's Joshua in mind. The Hasmonean leaders may have sought to claim his high priest's glory. And others still, worried about the lack of fit, may have wanted to take the ideal with them, away from the city, to prepare for a restoration. For all of these the Second Temple was the way to think "Israel." But others came up with brand new reflections, projecting ideals quite different. It is with two of these intellectuals that we find ourselves now to be engaged.

The Righteous One in the Wisdom of Solomon

The Wisdom of Solomon puts us at the end of the Second Temple period. Dates have been suggested from the last half of the first century B.C.E. into the first half of the first century C.E. Troubled times are in view, probably combining texts and memories from the Maccabean and Hasmonean periods with events more recent having to do with Roman indignities in Palestine and growing Greek hostility in the Diaspora (Antioch? Alexandria?). Our inability to be more precise about this is indicative of the author's own stance toward the situation. He wrote with a certain sense of distance, piling up images of "testing" from throughout Israel's history, and he generalized political issues at the level of theological and ethical rationale that cover over a particular, recent history. His text is also unclear, perhaps purposefully so, about the identity of those addressed – the "righteous," the "wicked," the "enemies," and the "rulers." But he does appear to have been especially concerned about the fate of "the righteous" in the world, and to have struggled to understand how it could be that lawless men could "despise," "oppress," "persecute," and "take them captive" (2:10–20; 17:2; 18:4). He knew that their history and destiny bespoke another ordering of things, an ordering within which the righteous were to be the rulers of the world. He must have had some class of fellow Jews in mind.

Social anthropology is thus the burning question. And the mode of its meditation is again the ideal figure. Most of the traditional offices appear in some form in the book, but it is clearly the figure of the king that dominates the imagination. The book is addressed to kings (1:1; 6:10); the righteous ones in Section I (Chapters 1–5) are destined to judge and rule (3:8; 4:16; 5:1–2); the first-person prayers for wisdom of Section II (Chapters 6–9) are those of a king who will rule wisely and righteously because of wisdom (8:14; 9:2–12); wisdom's function in Section III (Chapter 10) is to rescue the righteous man and lead him to kingship (10:2, 10, 14; cf. 6:20); and in the midrashic rehearsal of the Exodus story (Section IV, Chapters 11–19), the Lord is depicted as sovereign over all, teaching the sons of God how to rule, and preparing them for their destiny, which is to make known the light of the law to the world (cf. 12:12–22; 18:4).

Nevertheless, there is no clear picture of what the requisite social order should be. In spite of the author's preoccupation with the history of Israel, no clear prototypes seem to be drawn from it. Neither does there appear to be a claim implicit for some model oriented to Second Temple institutions. And no eschatological ideal is sketched out even for the righteous king. So the notion of the kingdom of the righteous is vague. As a notion it cannot be forfeited. But to imagine it in any realizable form seems to be beyond the capacity of the author. The problem appears to be that things have gotten that bad. Not only is there no contemporary society where "the righteous" are or can be imagined to be in power. Their very existence as the sons of God is threatened by those who are in power. Thus there is no society within view where "wisdom" may be said to "dwell." It is therefore all the more noteworthy that the author's concern is to affirm the existence and availability of wisdom in the world and to the righteous.

As one who has petitioned for wisdom and received the insight of wisdom's ways in the world, the author promises to share his knowledge of the secret things with his readers (6:21–25; cf. 7:15–21). He does this by means of an extremely powerful poetry that manifests a very high intertextuality. Classical texts were selected from the traditions of Hebrew literature. There is acquaintance with the wisdom literature and myth, as well as a wide range of postbiblical Jewish literatures.[8] And the author was also well versed in the popular philosophy and Middle Platonism of the time,[9] as well as in imagery from the practice and mythologies of Hellenistic religions. We should not underestimate the significance of this erudition. The author's "wisdom" was surely won from a passionate preoccupation and profound "reading" of these resources. His "secret wisdom" is just that he found it possible to create from them an imaginative solution to the problem of justice that exercised him.

His startling claim was that the structure of the natural world as cosmos and creation is actively engaged in the support of justice – the rescue and vindication of the righteous, and the punishment of the wicked (cf. 1:14–15; 4:1–2; 5:17–23; 16:24–25; 17:20–18:1; 19:6, 18). Thus, the miracles of the Exodus story show the natural order effecting the deliverance of the righteous, and the spirit of wisdom in the created order "rescued from troubles those who served her" (10:9). The marvelous poems and depictions of wisdom as beneficent spirit giving structure and purpose to the created order in Chapters 7–9, as well as the philosophical topoi illustrative of harmony and trasformation throughout Chapters 11–19, are intended to make this secret wisdom imaginable for the reader.

There are, however, two problems with the author's vision of the hidden structure of the world as a resolution to the social issue he set out to tackle. One problem that is not noticed by him is just that the imagination of a humane *social* order in history is not facilitated by the location of such a dynamic principle of purposive justice solely in the order of creation. In the schema of cosmos-polis-anthropos, the polis has been elided. All of the functions characteristic and necessary for the structuring of a just, humane society have been transferred to the level of cosmic potentiality. Thus the reader is hardly allowed to see, much less contemplate, any recognizable vehicle for the realization of a society of the righteous in actual history now or later.

The second problem, one that the author does acknowledge and attempts to resolve, is the fact that, in the real world, human events do not match up with his cosmic claims. Real kings and real ungodly men in power do manage to have their way, a way that runs contrary to the way things should go. And the righteous, who know that this is wrong, are unable to do anything about it. Thus, the cosmic support of justice is not readily manifest.

One approach to the second problem was to emphasize the "secret" or "hidden" aspect of cosmic wisdom. Yet the author frets about this in Chapter 13, wondering how it could be that others have missed seeing it, since the greatness, beauty, and power of the created order is readily obvious. The second approach the author takes to the disjunction between cosmos and social history is to affirm for the righteous an eventual success. We see the author at work on this approach to his problem most clearly in Chapters 2–5.

In Chapters 2–5 the figure of the Righteous One is introduced as the persecuted one. He knows that he is a *pais kuriou* (2:13), and expects deliverance and a happy ending (2:16, 20). The ungodly think that "might is right" (2:11), and that there is no deliverance at the end (2:1). Conflict arises when the Righteous One opposes the ungodly, and accuses them of "sins against the law" (2:12). They decide to get rid of him as inconvenient, and do, making a "test of his forbearance" by condemning him to a shameful death (2:19–20). That, however, is not the end of the story, either for the Righteous One, or for the ungodly. That is because, the author tells us, the ungodly were mistaken about the "secret purposes of God" (2:22). The righteous do not really die (3:12). And there will be a "time of their visitation" when the tables are turned. Then they will govern (3:7–8), and the ungodly will be confronted and condemned by them (4:16; 5:1ff.) and punished by the Lord (3:10; 4:19–20).

In order to grasp the full significance of the Righteous One in wisdom of Solomon 2–5, we need to note the way in which the author created his ideal figures throughout the book. He did not focus on a singular figure to represent the social anthropology of Israel. There is, instead, a fragmentation not only of Israel's offices as a coherent set of functions, but of the "powers," which should be concentrated in any systemic grasp of a theocratic vision. Thus "wisdom," *"dikē,"* "virtue," "logos," God's "hand," and "power," can all be imagined separately even though they function similarly. As powers in support of the righteous order of the world, moreover, they can be imagined in various anthropomorphic images of the cosmos at work as agent, then phased into anthropological images that build upon recognizably human figures from the epic history.

On the other hand, however, it is quite possible to align the ideal figures in the several sections of the book, noting their similarities, and arrive at a fairly comprehensive image of the Righteous One the author had in mind. It is possible to do this because the designation "Righteous One" occurs throughout, and none of the figures so designated are called by their names. This elision of all attributions of personal names in the book is one of the ways in which the Righteous One as a type-figure is achieved. The most obvious and significant evidence for this is the poem about the seven righteous ones in Chapter 10. But it alerts us also to the significance of the anonymity of the first-person characterization of "Solomon" in Chapters 7–9, and to the lack of clear reference to the many biblical figures taken up for comment in Chapters 11–19 as well. If we stack these figures up, making of them a composite characterization, a remarkable profile is given.

The Righteous One is pious, gentle, blameless, and so forth, even though he finds himself in straits that threaten his destiny as one who is to rule. He knows that he is chosen and therefore expects a reversal of the circumstances. But it is a mark of his piety that he takes no action, except to pray, keep the law, appeal to the covenants, and affirm his special status as a servant or son of God. In this circumstance he is rescued by means of an active intervention of God's creative powers, and raised to the position of rulership. Reminiscences of the functions of prophet, priest, and warrior are used to tell the story. But it is his capacity as judge over and against his erstwhile enemies, and his function as righteous and wise ruler over the nations, that are highlighted. We can see that all aspects of our pattern of characterization are included in this profile. We can also see that the profile is a study in the social embodiment of Israel in the author's own time. The fragmentation of leadership images and societal functions corresponds to the actual loss of institutional supports for that group which, for the author, represents Israel. The reduction of characteristics to piety, patience, and the refusal to relinquish claim to represent Israel correspond to the limited possibilities of such a group for recognizing social identity.

Legitimation is attributed by means of the special, divine wisdom that this figure possesses as an endowment. Office is attributed, even though it cannot be exercised until after the event of reversal. Displacement is achieved both by idealization of the type-figure and by the assignment of actualization to some future moment of cosmic significance. The deeds are those appropriate to the office – the exercise of judgment and rulership. The consequences are the usual – victory for the oppressed, righteous judgment upon the enemies, and a universal kingdom of justice.

It has been customary to regard the Wisdom of Solomon as a protreptic that recommended Judaism to the Hellenistic world. I find it impossible to read it that way. Hellenistic logics and genres have been marshalled, but the issues addressed are thoroughly Jewish concerns. And the argumentations that are set forth are certainly matters that pertain to a debate internal to the Judaisms of the time. The address to the "rulers of the world" does present a problem. Those who regard the book as a protreptic see in "the rulers" an expression of its intended Hellenistic audience. Can such be the case?

A much more interesting reading would result were it possible to regard the address (1:1; 6:1) as an allusion to the Jerusalem establishment. The painful problem elaborated in Chapters 1–5 appears on the surface to be a philosophical difference of opinion. But the contrast between the two philosophies, though not unimportant as a preparation for the kind of wisdom under discussion in the rest of the book, merely sets the stage for the story of the Righteous One who is violated by the "ungodly." This violation, rationalized to be sure by the false philosophy, is actually triggered by something else. That something else turns out to be a serious difference of opinion about the law. I see no reason not to read this as a troubled polemic against the Hasmonean-Herodian establishment as those who should have known better.

The key passage is 2:12–16, the rationale for the persecution of the Righteous One, put into the mouth of the ungodly. As the author tells the story, the Righteous One reproached the ungodly for "sins against the law," and the ungodly took "offense" at this. The point of view is certainly that of the author, seeing events through the eyes of those who actually were the "offended" ones. But the problem was probably real, and the law under discussion is surely the Jewish law. This becomes more clear in the next line ("He accuses us to sins against our training") and a following notice ("He avoids our ways as unclean"). The combination of law, training, and the clean–unclean categories makes the point.

That the righteous oppose the actions of the ungodly (2:12) is additional evidence for our thesis. The actions enumerated do not have to do only with ethical behavior unacceptable to a conservative Jewish piety – they include the "oppression," "persecution," and execution of the righteous. These are exactly the charges against the Hasmoneans found in other pietistic literatures of the time, and they are hardly conceivable except as actions of those with political power. This means that the "ungodly" and the "rulers" may be the same persons. This suspicion is supported by a statement in 6:4–5, addressed this time to the rulers: "Because as servants of his kingdom you did not keep the law, nor walk according to the purposes of God, He will come upon you terribly and swiftly." So the story cannot really work unless we see in the ungodly rulers an allusion to the Jerusalem leaders. This narrows the social history under review. It also means that the author is writing in sympathy with a popular, or perhaps sectarian, view of events that have taken place there.

But is the author partial to a sectarian form of Judaism? There is no indication that he is. He writes from a distance, as we have observed. He explores the rationale for the ungodly with exceptionally fine poetry. He works out a theodicy that "punishes" them with just that oblivion they themselves expect when life is done. His book is actually an intellectual experiment, an effort to build a case for bridging the gap between power and righteousness. He is troubled about the fate of these righteous ones, and attempts to work out a happy ending for them. But his own position is safer somewhere in the middle, no doubt in the Diaspora.

If so, if the author was surveying the whole ecumenical scene from afar, it is remarkable that he took up the issue in just this way. He did not do justice to the question of what to do about or expect from Jerusalem for Judaism. But neither did he find a way to recommend the Diaspora synagogue as an alternative locus for that wisdom and righteousness that could provide sufficiently for the social identity of Jews, at least not the "Righteous Ones" he had in mind. So he may have been battling on two fronts, viewing events in Jerusalem with alarm, but seeking a rationalization that Diaspora Jews might understand. His accomplishment may be that he worked out a rationale for a quietistic obedience to some canon of Jewish piety. It may be also that, if some group or class was in mind, patience was recommended in the face of impossible circumstances. But he did not find an answer to the question he set out to answer – the (social) nature and destiny of Israel. He did not relinquish the image of kingdom. And he could not give up the notion of Israel as a people. But the kingdom was only imaginable any longer in some vague order of God's cosmic designs. And the righteous ones were, in his depiction, dangerously close to losing their identity.

Caught outside the structures of empowerment and social stability, the only wisdom left to these righteous ones was a secret knowledge, a gift from God, a "revelation" of the hidden purposes of God for Israel. One should notice, however, that given the author's assessment of Second Temple society, devoid of rationality, sense, legitimacy – i.e., wisdom – his refusal to deny the disenfranchised Righteous One some knowledge of wisdom was a remarkable intellectual feat. It amounts to a recognition that, unless one can locate wisdom somewhere, the game really is up. That social sense which remained for the righteous was just the knowledge that they belonged to a people for whom God had purposed something other. This sense of identity is a social datum, and, since that was all there was left of redeemable social significance, *that* is what the author worked with, *that* became the locus of wisdom for him. That wisdom was "hidden" is an acknowledgment, not of some interest in deep, dark mysteries of the mind or soul, but of the fact that manifestations of a *society* for the righteous simply were nowhere to be seen.

Scholars have frequently read the statements about finding or receiving this secret knowledge as references to special revelation or some moment of profound insight or deep religious experience. But these statements are merely the necessary narrative devices for bringing a nonmanifest wisdom-in-Israel into the picture – as a study of the extreme social situation. The righteous do not need revelation to know that they are Jews. What they need is to imagine how it could be so that, knowing they belong to Israel, their social supports are gone. And the answer does not lie in some mystic vision of cosmic penetration. All of that is the mechanism of idealization to gain leverage, perspective, and to bridge the gap between the present time and the ancient promises. So the answer is given in the rest of the book as wisdom midrash on the epic! If the righteous can see themselves there, under the signs both of erasure and rescue, some sense can be derived for the present as well. So the "secret wisdom" is actually made manifest in a rereading of Torah. And that is made possible by showing that the classical moments of Israel's social formations have all happened in accord with a well-known motif from the mythology of wisdom: the rescue and vindication sequence. So again it is a correlation of Torah, wisdom, and society that has made the study possible exactly as in the case of Sirach's vision. That it focuses on the isolated Righteous One is not a sign that wisdom sociology is not underway. Making social sense of an intolerable situation was the very reasons for the study in the first place.

If this interpretation is correct, the author of the Wisdom of Solomon knew what he was doing. He knew that the conception of Israel as a social entity was at stake, that imaginative labor was called for, and that the creation of ideal figures was one way to go about it. But in spite of his effort, wisdom was actually dislodged again from the social orders of Jewish history. Other times and sages would be required to bring her back to earth again.

The Anointed of the Lord in Psalms of Solomon 17

We turn now to one of the classical "messianic" texts. It occurs at the end of a collection of psalms dated in the last half of the first century B.C.E. The collection can be divided roughly into two sets, each of which brings to expression the reflections and concerns of some religiously oriented group at different stages of that group's history.[10] The earlier set builds upon the Psalms 1, 2, 8, and 17, which form a solid narrative and thematic frame for the inclusion of the others. The earlier set probably included Psalms 4, 7, 9, 11, and 12 as well. They are mainly a series of laments that veil thinly a report of events in Jerusalem surrounding Pompey's conquest of the city in 63 B.C.E., but here and there throughout the laments are to be found petitionary prayers for remedial intervention. As the collection now stands, these petitions culminate in our "messianic" text in Psalms of Solomon 17:23–51. Because Pompey's death in Egypt is alluded to in 2:30–35, this set of psalms is born of a reflection that encompasses at least the period from 63 B.C.E. through 48 B.C.E., the year of Pompey's death.

The second set of psalms appears to be an addition to the collection, born of subsequent meditations on the issues of righteousness, theodicy, and piety. These issues had been raised by the earlier events and their interpretation in the first set of psalms, as well as by subsequent experience and perspective. Evidence from both sets will help us place the messianic text in its social and literary contexts.

The history under review may be recalled as follows:[11] The Hasmonean Aristobulus II was the high priest and, in keeping with Hasmonean tradition since Aristobulus I (104 B.C.E.), claimed as well the title of king. According to Josephus, Aristobulus II had gained this position through the military defeat of his elder brother, Hyrcanus II, who had assumed the office upon the death of their mother, Queen Alexandra, in 67 B.C.E. Both had called upon Pompey in Damascus in order to gain Roman support for their causes, Hyrcanus having become the front man for the Idumaean Antipater as well, a man who sought to exploit the rivalry for his own political interests. As Josephus tells the story from this point on, the sequence of events is difficult to trace. What seems clear is that 1) Alexander and parties favorable to him decided to resist, and some ended up occupying the temple as its defenders; 2) Hyrcanus and his supporters opened the city to Pompey and aided him in his siege of the temple; and 3) some of the "people" were outraged by the actions of both leaders. Pompey took the temple, slaughtering the defenders and priests at their sacrifices, according to Josephus.[12] Aristobulus was deposed and taken captive to Rome. Hyrcanus was reinstated as high priest, but without the title of king, and the lands of Coele-Syria were taken away from Jerusalem and constituted as a Roman province.

Thus, the history of overt Roman hegemony began, marked by the division of offices between the Hasmonean high priests in Jerusalem, and (eventually) the Herodian kings in Syria. The sorry history of intrigue, rivalry, and bloodshed within Palestine, and of the precipitous shifts from hostile to fawning attitudes toward Rome which followed, mark the troubled times in which our psalms were composed.

In the first set of psalms a very definite attitude is taken toward some aspects of those events. Toward other aspects the position of the authors is not as easily discerned. We can be clear about the following: The Roman entrance into Jerusalem was regarded both with horror and dismay. Pompey is said to have been the great dragon, insolent one, and alien sinner (2:1, 29; 17:9, 13–16), and his later death was regarded as God's judgment upon him in answer to the psalmist's prayer that he receive his recompense (2:24–35). This rationalization was achieved by combining two traditional topoi. One was the fundamental notion that God hears the cry of the righteous in distress (2:24–29). The second was the wisdom schema about the high and mighty who will be brought low (2:33–35). But these were interwoven with yet another notion, namely, that of the judgement of God upon Israel that could be discerned in defeat at the hands of a foreign power (2:20–29). This means that the set of events in 63 B.C.E. and following triggered a searching and painful reflection on the reasons for the disaster, not only in terms of the insolence of Roman power, but in relation to weaknesses that might be discerned in the constitution of Israel as well. It was in any case not Rome, but the Jerusalem establishment that bore the brunt of the psalmist's wrath. In two psalms there is an enigmatic use of the singular to indicate one who was particularly despised (4:12). Though sitting in "the council of the pious," he is profane (4:1). And the mark of his wickedness and lawlessness was a deceitful way with words by which he decrees harsh judgments, violates oaths, persuades house after house to join him in some desire that succeeds only in generating strife, betrayal, warfare, and the "scattering" of those houses. He is, finally, a "hypocrite." One is tempted therefore to think that some particular figure may be in mind, just as Pompey is clearly the reference in mind for singular designations of the foreign ruler. But the descriptions in Psalms 4 and 12 are so general that any or all of the Hasmoneans or even Herodians could be intended. Since that is so, the collective singular may indicate that the psalmist characterized the leadership in Jerusalem from 63 B.C.E. until his own time in keeping with his views on those who were in power then.

In most descriptions of the sinful princes in Jerusalem, however, the reference appears to be those who were in power in 63 B.C.E., the Hasmoneans Aristobulus and Hyrcanus. In 8:18–19, for instance, the plural is used ("Princes of the Land"), even though the deed recorded ("They opened the gates of Jerusalem") befits especially that of Hyrcanus, according to Josephus' accounts. So the "Sons of Jerusalem" have been lumped together as those whose sins are the real cause of the disastrous events. The psalmist elaborates on these sins. They include adultery, unnatural intercourse, defilement of the sanctuary and Jerusalem, personal cultic impurity, deceit, insolence, lack of mercy, failure to rule in righteousness, failure to defend the city, and accommodation to the alien nations and gentile sinners. There is a good dose of pious wrath heaped upon these leaders. But the overall impression is that some rather specific charges are made about legitimacy, service, and actions that do not accord with standards held dear by those in the psalmists' tradition.

Nevertheless, these princes are taken to be representative of the population of Jerusalem in some inclusive sense. A plural "they" is used to expand the description of those who were sinners in Jerusalem (2:8–9, 14; 8:11, 23). This inclusiveness occasionally spills over into reflection upon the events as God's chastisement of Israel itself, and allows for the few places in which the psalmist includes "the people" or even himself in the defilements that caused this humiliation (e.g., 8:34; 17:6, 22). But that is the rare exception. The rule is to locate the cause exclusively with the Hasmoneans as unrighteous rulers, and to exempt "the pious," who saw themselves victimized by the whole affair, from the judgments brought upon them. Thus the group to which the psalmist belongs has distinguished itself from the Hasmoneans.

We do run into difficulty when trying to be more precise about some social reconstruction of this group, its particular attitudes toward Second Temple institutions, parties, and history subsequent to those events, as well as its own markers for social identity and piety. The conceptual problems may be grasped by noting that the psalms locate the identity of "Israel" in three overlapping, but distinguishable social images. The first is that of the leaders under review, the "princes" and "sons" of Jerusalem whose deeds and dishonor certainly have something to do with the nature and destiny of Israel. The second is the image of Jerusalem, which, though devastated in the events occasioned by the sinful leaders, stands for something independent of them and can be mourned and imagined repopulated as a symbol for Israel's restoration. The third is the class designation of the pious or righteous among whom, as a class, both the chastisements and the deliverance of Israel can also be imagined without recourse to the other two foci. We need to explore this curiosity before considering the function of the messianic figure for the authors of these psalms.

That the notion of Israel suffered a tripartite division is already evidence for the intellectual vitality of the psalmists. The problem was to re-conceive Israel in the light of recent social-political history as they had experienced it. The "princes of the land" were cast as Israel under the sign of failure to achieve its destiny. They attracted to them in the minds of the authors all of the traditional topoi of the threat of judgment upon Israel, as well as the traditional topos of the judgment of destruction upon "sinners." This latter attribution was wishful thinking, since the establishment was probably in power at the time these psalms were written. But it was very important to the authors to see things that way. The complete destruction of these sinners is described similarly to that of Pompey, thus making the point of the double attestation of God's will in the matter, and underscoring the finality of that solution to the problem. What they represented must vanish forever. This is emphasized repeatedly, both as having happened to those sinners, and as a pronouncement of what must happen to the "profane man in the council of the pious" (Psalm 4).

We should pause to take note of the significance of this view of the matter, because it is possible that what the leaders represented were in fact the Second Temple institutions, not just their administration of them. Among the castigations of the sins of these leaders there are, to be sure, a few charges that reflect ideological nuances, as if the question were mainly one of legitimacy. The charges of their cultic impurity and their defilement of the "holy things" and "offerings" (1:8; 2:3) is the clearest example. It does show that the psalmists had a high regard for cultic purity, and that they were or had been deeply troubled by the improper Hasmonean performance of priestly offices. But there is no indication anywhere in the collection that the pious were engaged, actively or imaginatively, with a remedy for, or a restoration of cultic institutions and offices. So the possibility must be left open that this group had already found a way to think the thought "Israel" independently of the Second Temple model.

The image of Jerusalem, however, is still very much in view. There is a lovely poem in which Jerusalem is seen standing on the height, watching her children return to her from the four quarters of the earth, donning once more her glorious garments. This occurs in keeping with "what the Lord has spoken concerning Israel and Jerusalem" (11:1–9). The picture is important because it lets us see that the psalmists were at work on some alternative social conception for Israel. They could not imagine that the righteous who found themselves in separation from the temple society constituted an adequate embodiment. To think Israel one had to imagine (a new) Jerusalem. And the new Jerusalem was expressly set in contrast to the Jerusalem once dishonored (2:20–22), evidence for the conceptual distinction which had been made between the actual and the ideal. But thought had not proceeded very far. The picture had apparently not been filled in. Nowhere in the collection are there any indications of what the structures were to be, save in the messianic poem. So the image of the new Jerusalem served as a symbol for that substitution yet to be imagined, yet to be actualized. It held the space left empty by the thought of the end of Jerusalem under the sinful princes.

So we have a rather fully rationalized negative social model imagined in the past, an almost empty ideal image projected for the future, and a group that actually knew itself to be Israel in the present. But the group had not yet rationalized a new social formation of its own as a legitimate claim to continue Israel's presence in the world. It still thought in terms of Jerusalem at the center, even though the Judaism centered there at the moment had been under the sign of destruction. A very tenuous position, indeed. But it hardly describes a happenstance. Strong loyalties and tough thinking had apparently positioned these righteous where they were. We need to see more clearly what those loyalties were, and where in social-political history this group actually found itself.

Our problem is that we really know very little about the social configurations of movements, groups and classes during this period. We are somewhat better informed about institutions and groups that consciously institutionalized alternative societies (e.g., Qumran) or complementary assemblies in the Diaspora (e.g., Philo's school and house of prayer), but the righteous ones of the psalms fit neither of these patterns. Scholarship has toyed with the idea that the psalms reflect early Pharisaism. Neusner has cautioned us, however, about imagining Pharisees during this period either as a social group with its own institutions, or as a social role with specific status or authority vis-à-vis the society as a whole. Pharisees were, rather, a class or type of individual concerned mainly about Jewish piety, especially focused for them in codes of cultic purity applicable to the normal round of daily life.[13] So we cannot place these psalms in some Pharisaic "circle," and gain thereby a social setting that can help us with the question of the psalmists' notion of the righteous as a distinct class, or satisfy our own suspicion, given the evidence for a textual history, that some group produced them.

Nevertheless, with this aporia fully acknowledged, the psalms do seem to fit somewhere into the larger picture of that type of piety that runs from the early Hasidic movements through Pharisaism and into Rabbinic Judaism. There is much in them that corresponds with Neusner's reconstruction of the history and concerns of Pharisaism. The one thing that is new is that these psalms reflect a very popular piety and appear to gather up the memory, experience, and reflections of a definite group.

There are two attitudes about other social institutions expressed in the psalms that may be important. One is that the events of 63 B.C.E. came as a surprise (1:1–8). The psalmist puts himself imaginatively in the place of

Jerusalem. He had thought that the wealth and prosperity of Jerusalem and her children throughout the world indicated Israel's righteousness and glory. When the alarm of war sounded, he expected the Lord to deliver the city. He had no idea of the secret sins that stood in the way, sins that had to be punished. Now he knows, a remarkable admission of that consternation that set the whole process of reflection on its way. These pious ones were not sectarian.

The other attitude of significance is revealed in mentions made of the synagogues. Even in the earlier layer of the tradition there is a positive reference to "the synagogues of the pious" (17:18). And in the later additions one sees that the pious will be found in the assembly of the people giving praise and glorifying the name of the Lord (10:7–8). Here also, in the later additions, one finally comes upon two clear references to the Torah. One treats the "testimony" as the "eternal covenant," which documents the Lord's mercy to Israel (10:5). The other treats the Torah as "His commandments, the Law which he commanded us that we might live" (14:1). So this group has had no problem with the synagogue. It appears to be the case, in fact, that this group has discovered in the synagogue a social formation that could embody the traditions of Israel apart from the temple, and that in spite of what might happen to Jerusalem.

If this history is correct, a rather momentous series of rationalizations are documented in these psalms. The events of 63 B.C.E. were read as the point after which certain assumptions had to be given up about the Hasmoneans, the Second Temple model for Israel, of naïveté about righteousness and the intentions of the epic traditions, and of the significance for Israel of the assemblies. Laments, theodicies, petitions, judgments, and the crafting of arguments to justify the new notions of righteousness abound. And in the process distinctions tore some things asunder that once had been joined: power and piety, nation and people, authority and judgments, law as constitution and law as commandment, leaders and the powerless poor, and so forth. Serious dislocations occurred that divided things up in the wrong places, and marked off the righteous, the sinners, the nations, Jerusalem, the land (referred to in the psalms as Israel's "inheritance"), and the scattered children, all from one another. Given the social models shared by all Jews for the preceding three or four hundred years, what was a pious poet to do?

At some point in this group's history, one of its sages crafted the poem about the son of David who would "reign over Israel" at a time when God should decide. The familiar text need not be rehearsed. It is enough to recall that this king will purge Jerusalem both of its unrighteous rulers and of the nations that trample it. He will gather, then, the holy people whom he shall lead in righteousness. The emphasis from that point on is upon the manner of his rule and its consequences. His wisdom and righteousness will be such that he can exercise absolute power both over the nations and over the people by his word alone. An absolutely pure and perfect kingdom will result that encompasses the whole world, the glory of which will attract all eyes and hearts forever.

So the imagination has found its way. Jerusalem is no longer empty, desolate. The picture is now full, and centered. What has this poet achieved? He has in the first place offered a perfectly contrastive vision of Jerusalem to that negative image described by the sinful rulers. In the place of their impurity, this shepherd is holy. In the place of their defilements, this one will cleanse. In the place of their oppressions, this one will not suffer any to stumble. In the place of their councils of war, this one will bring peace. And so on. So the contrast serves to support the critique of those sinners the group found it necessary to lodge. It does so merely by setting them in its contrastive light.

But the new image achieves more, even as a contrastive statement against the negative image. That is because the contrasts extend even to matters that have to do with institutional structures and their legitimation. Thus, the most striking features of the contrast are just that this figure is not a priest, but a king, and that the city he cleanses does not require that a temple stand at the center. The only possibility for catching sight of the temple at all is in the statement that "He shall glorify the Lord in a place to be seen of all the earth" (17:37). But the next line focuses on purging the city Jerusalem. And the following line shifts the focus onto the anointed one himself as the one whose glory all the nations will come to see. From that point on it is the ideal king who occupies the center of the picture. So it is a king who sets things right, even to the cleansing requisite to reoccupation, and his perfect reign is imagined with priests and sacrifices and councils and treasuries and the temple nowhere in sight. If the poet can make that stick as the legitimate ideal, he will have found a telling argument in favor of having done with the Hasmoneans.

The legitimacy of this ideal is strongly emphasized in the poem. It is the primary reason for designating the king as the anointed of the Lord, as well as the son of David. Covenant, legitimate selection, and divine approval, if not initiative, are all marshalled. Triple attestation no less. And it is all conceived according to models, promises, and manifestations of Israel won from the ancient traditions. The picture is, in fact, archaizing in its depictions of this kingdom. Even the tribes will be divided upon the land, and the king will judge them in their separate assemblies (17:28, 30, 48)! This is an evocation of epic ideals from the pre-Davidic period of Israel's establishment in the land according to tribes, and it is combined with the Zion theme in a very attractive image. As the nations come to see the glory of this king's reign in Jerusalem, they will bring with them Jerusalem's sons "who have fainted" as their gifts (17:34)! One can hardly imagine a better solution to the contrary history recently experienced. And it is all done by rearranging the old traditions to show how they fit together better this way. Bracketed and cancelled out is the entire history of the temple. From that history and its imagery the notions of Zion, glory, holy hill, etc., have all been deinstitutionalized and reassigned to the righteous king. An argument has been made to the effect that the Second Temple claims to Israel's legacy were not legitimate. An alternative is in place, and it was always there as the intentional and legitimate legacy for Israel.

But what about the alternative model? By crafting it the group's judgment on the Hasmoneans has been justified. Has the poet offered anything more? Indeed he has. He has allowed his readers to see all of the pieces that were ripped apart by the logics of divisiveness put back together. Everyone is back in the picture, all division overcome, except for the "unrighteous rulers." But even they are merely "shattered," "thrust out," "removed," not destroyed. One has the impression that they are removed from positions of power in Jerusalem, then included among the nations and those who will (finally) return to Jerusalem as loyal subjects, perhaps as the "sons who had fainted." Merely to imagine this would be helpful, healing, constructive. But there is more.

The "social anthropology" on the basis of which such a constructive picture could be imagined at all was carefully thought through. The conceptual problems having to do with social forces and functions, at impossible odds with one another in the aftermath of the group's confrontation with its own, earlier naïveties, have been addressed. Authority has been traced back to God's knowledge of the king, and the king's knowledge that all the people are "sons of their God" (17:30, 47). The troublesome question of power has been "solved" by concentrating it solely in the exercise of persuasion. Persuasion that works, moreover, must be instructive and constructive, i.e., the articulation of a wisdom that manifests righteousness as the sole reason for its employment. And righteousness, that axial notion for the alignment of all aspects of Jewish societal ideals, the social notion fundamentally threatened by the groups' failure to see it manifest anywhere anymore except in divine punishments and chastisements, is redeemed. It is redeemed by wisdom. It can be taught. A social order structured on the basis of a certain kind of knowledge can align all of the functions requisite to a complete picture, from God on down, perfectly, forever.

The displacement of the king and his reign is into the future. One might have wondered whether such a projection reflected a political program. There is, however, no indication anywhere in the collection that this group might constitute a pro-Davidic-king party vying for control of Jerusalem, no indications of interest that could generate a popular messianic movement. Perhaps, then, an apocalyptic desire, an eschatological hope? The problem with this approach is that the poetry is exuberant, even celebrative. It does not express longing or expectation.

Perhaps it is an imaginative labor after all, the casting up of an ideal image to work out a social notionality in a time of new social formation. The figure is singular, but the study is social. An ideal king is imagined, but mainly as a figure appropriate to the collection, intersection, and rearrangements among qualities and functions that need to come together constructively again. "Appropriate" because of the given social models, both archaic and contemporary – but not determinative. And that is the most amazing thing about the imaginative efforts we have been following. Ideals constrained by their appropriateness to tradition and imaginability are nonetheless appropriated by means of a remarkable freedom to address and reconstruct the real world.

In the vision of the king it is not royal authority or power that has given the picture coherence. It is the peculiar notion of wisdom and righteousness that does that, qualities the psalmist's group may very well be willing to reflect more about. And as for the king, though his place of glory is on top of the hill, his place of service is precisely in the synagogues of the tribes. In 17:48 there is a mention of the king speaking "in the assemblies (*en synagōgais*)." Gray (in Charles) suspects an error (בְעֵרוֹת for בְּעֵרוּת). The Hebrew original would have read "by means of the testimony," i.e., the law. However, judging from the later additions to this collection of psalms, it is most probable that "law" and "assembly" were becoming closely associated for this group, and that it was there, in the assemblies, where it understood Israel to be constituted. The psalmist had not yet rationalized this social configuration, and still imagined Israel as a nation-state centered in Jerusalem. But he also knew a social formation for the practice of Judaism at a distance. The poet has given the reader the chance to see that social formation in the picture of the perfect kingdom. And the king? Is he not cast essentially in the role of sage and teacher?

It is true that the king is the anointed of the Lord. That takes care of the legitimacy question and justifies the Davidic nuances. But that is all. The characterization actually is derived from another kind of "anointing" altogether: It is the special endowment of the "spirit of understanding." It is very important to see that this attribution of wisdom is absolutely essential to the construction of this figure. It is the axial notion that made it possible to unite otherwise disparate or even contradictory functions. Wisdom has qualified every single aspect of this king's character and effectiveness. It transforms the way in which he will thrust sinners from the inheritance ("wisely, righteously"). It determines the way in which he will take care of the foreign powers ("by the word of his mouth"). He will gather together a holy people, "for he shall know them, that they are all sons of their God." He shall organize the "tribes" and distribute the land "in the wisdom of his righteousness." His glory, which will cleanse Jerusalem and attract all nations to it, lies just in the fact that he is "taught of God." Then he will bless the people "in wisdom and gladness." And he will rebuke, correct, judge, and rule by precious words because he is wise, endowed with the spirit of understanding. Take wisdom out of the picture and everything falls apart again.

The notion of wisdom employed here is, mythologically conceived, that of her universal reign. This reign can be imagined as her own. Or it can be imagined as that of the king she blesses and exalts (cf., e.g., Wisd. of Sol. 7–9). The profile of the teacher that can be discerned is not necessarily an additional characterization. Both wisdom and wisdom's king rule by instructing. The image has been used, moreover, to re-read the epic accounts and derive from them a coherent, archaic idealization. As we have seen, certain aspects of the social experience of the psalmist's group of righteous ones have been painted into the picture. So Torah, wisdom, and contemporary social configurations have been merged in this ideal as well. Another way to imagine social formation has been achieved. The power and authority of words uttered in the assemblies by a teacher who is wise can do quite well. One can even imagine Israel's place in the scheme of universal history by projecting such a synagogue scene into the eschatological future of God's own time.

It is not yet said in the psalms that Israel's wisdom is its law and that its law is the basis for an institution of the people without a king. It is not yet seen that the new and sufficient authority could be that of the teacher and sage alone. But reflected in the ideal image is a kind of wisdom fully appropriate for a group experimenting with such notions. Should they work it out, kings and their kingdoms could come to their end. The "sense" of the image then, is simply that a society could now be imagined on the basis of wisdom, righteousness, instruction, memory, praise, and blessings in the assemblies of the people of Israel.

The Wisdom of Those Anointed

Texts and times belong together. Our texts span that time during which ideal figures focused a certain effort of the Jewish imagination. Effort was called for: Hegemonies and Hellenism impinged from without; critique and conflict emerged from within. The temple-state stood, and the loyalties were strong. But ideals vied, interests clashed, and the political history was bumpy. At the end of the time the temple was gone. Judaism, however, was ready to be born. Alternative social formations and critical reflection on the nature and destiny of the Jewish people had prepared the way. The phenomenon of the ideal figure belongs to the history of

that critical reflection, an intellectual effort that filled the time with experimental fabrications. In this final section of the essay we want to assess the
cogency of these fantastic images as studies in Israel's political and social
options for that time.

Ideal figures and idealistic authors go together. The bite in every case
was the sense of some disparity between contemporary social history and
the traditions received from the past. The need was to account for the
disparity. The process was to recast traditions in such a way as to offer
critique on threatening or untenable social factors and formations and/or
offer a rationalization for new social roles and formations. The result was
the construction of ideal configurations, arising from the promises of the
past, hovering over the present, and anchored in some way to the God of
creation and/or history. The effect was to rethink "Israel."

The past was available mainly in the form of the Hebrew epic, a literature that had itself been recast many times in the course of Israel's history.
Each of those earlier recastings also was the result of imaginative labor in
the interest of getting Israel's social institutions and anthropology straight.
As our period opens, however, recasting by means of rewriting was no
longer practiced. Self-consciousness about authorship had occurred, probably learned in cultural exchange with Hellenism, and with it the notion
that the epic also was authored. Now it happened that recasting was
achieved by means of another "reading" of the epic, written down in
another authored writing. Ben Sira's hymn in praise of the pious is an
excellent example of an authored text in a genre different from that of the
epic, a text that was nevertheless a "reading" of the epic in the interest of
its recasting. Thus the epic and the models derived from it piled up as a
corpus of potentially competitive readings of that past by means of which
alternative social formations and ideologies were rationalized. Thus the
consciousness about authorship and authority contributed to the plurifi-
cation and experimentation of the time.

But now it was the case that every author, every group producing a
written "second reading" of the epic had two texts on its hands. And all
groups had the one text in common. Thus the epic could be used, where
differences occurred and readers were wont to debate them, as the text of
appeal for adjudications. In every case reviewed the epic history of Israel
was reread in such a way as to support or recommend a certain view of
Jewish society in the author's own time. The significance of these appeals
to the charter documents of the past should not be overlooked as we
attempt to assess the cogency of these intellectual endeavors.

To do a second reading of the received traditions in the light of contemporary social patterns and history required considerable thought. Sorting out essentials, reflection on discrepancies, making comparisons and
contrasts – all that would be involved in the discriminating study of a

culture's legacy, values, and societal structures would come into play. The goal was to work out a new "arrangement," a conceptual grasp of how things could be seen to fit together. If the author succeeded, a construct would be the result that could be called idealistic.

For our purposes it does not matter where in time and space (history or creation) the image was placed. With Ben Sira the epic history was idealized and brought right into his own time. Wisdom of Solomon lifted the patterns delineated in the epic history up into a cosmic ever-presence. The author of Psalms of Solomon 17 projected an ideal future. But formally each used the same strategy. Each made of the epic a golden age, contrasted it with the recent past of memory and the author's present time, then "placed" the newly crafted image in some ultimate order of (God's) reality, an order other than the golden age of the past, in an order of things available to imagination in his time. So the first thing that can be said about the cogency of these ideal figures is that critical thought was invested in them, and the second is that the product carried at least the weight that any ideal configuration does if it is done well.

Well done would be a construct that 1) lifted up the essentials from the epic tradition without appearing to criticize the epic itself, alter it essentially, or leave it behind, 2) anchored the image in some trans-historical authority (reason, promise, power, creation, etc.), then 3) placed it in such a way as to bracket the recent past and the present between the image as ideal and the more remote traditions it claimed to articulate. Thus Ben Sira encompassed the history of prophets and kings as well as the Hellenistic temple-state (Ptolemies, Seleucids, and all, though he purposely left them out of the picture) by idealizing the primal history, then bringing the ideal forward to hover above and upon the reign of Simon. He could do this because he was comfortable in rationalizing the Second Temple model, and decided against overt, critical comparison with the state of hegemony. But the claims he made for the temple society were mythic nevertheless. These claims could (and did) get dislocated from social reality, once disparity vis-à-vis the ideal was no longer bearable.

In the case of Wisdom, the Hasmonean/Roman history was bracketed by lifting from the scriptural traditions of the past an ideal figure that could be imagined to survive the devastating conflicts. It represented the royal ideology of a disenfranchised, divided religious people. The Psalms of Solomon placed contemporary history between the archaic image of David's Kingdom and its promises on the one hand, and a yet to be realized idealization of it on the other. In this case, as with the Wisdom of Solomon, the ideal functioned both as a critique of competitive ideologies, and as rationalization for a group's own separatist piety.

The logic involved in idealization of this sort is narrative. Three scenes are cast. The first (archaic traditions) is "promising." The second (recent

past and present) is a study in struggle, conflict, and the threat of failure.
The third (ideal) imagines the perfect resolution in keeping with the
promises. This narrative pattern has occurred time and again whenever a
cultural epoch or group felt itself to be different with respect to the immediately preceding epoch of social history. It appears to be standard for what
might be called the (repeated) remythologization of cultural history.

So we have gained yet another perspective on the cogency of these figures. Insofar as an ideal figure invited rethinking about the dynamic factors involved in social formation, and succeeded in making it possible to
imagine certain relationships constructively combined, we may say that
the "study" was persuasive. But there is more. For each of the figures we
have reviewed, some relation to "wisdom" was intended to be seen. And
it is this relationship of the ideal figures to notions about wisdom with
which we may conclude our study. For with the attribution of wisdom to
an ideal figure, the claim has expressly been made that a rational social
order is intended. This we need to understand better.

In the traditions of Hebrew literature, "wisdom" could refer to a very
broad spectrum of human skills, thought, and discourse. It also came to
refer to abstractions that objectified and mythologized the sense in
things – abstractions frequently pictured as a figure transcending human
capacity to discern, a figure imagined known only by God. Thus, we have
tended to think of "wisdom" as a particular capacity of individuals, or a
body of knowledge with specific content, or a symbol for mysterious
meaning. But between the extremes of simply sane behavior on the one
hand, and privileged insight on the other, wisdom actually referred in
general to the "sense" that might be made of human society and the
world. This broad middle ground of wisdom as a term for reasonableness
in general needs to be emphasized. It was the Jewish analogue to Greek
paideia and philosophy. That it was mythologized in a way not usual for
"philosophy" in the Greek tradition was simply a result of Hebrew political history, the exile in particular. For Israel the possibility of making
sense of things was made critical by the radical dissolutions of social structuration experienced. This was quite different from anything experienced
by the Greeks. The naming of an objectified "wisdom," no longer in the
world, occurred just at that time. So the absence of wisdom was acknowledged in the situation of the absence of a stable, rationalized society.

This being the case, our understanding of the wisdom tradition may
need to be questioned, insofar as we have thought of it primarily in indi-
vidualistic terms. I have emphasized the elision of society and social history in the later literatures, which imagined wisdom in the ordering of
the world as a creation, then as special revelation or endowment to gifted
ideal figures. But now it appears that wisdom in the tradition of Israel and
Judaism may always have been predicated on a social notion. Sense may

have been possible only as social sense. And the elision I have noted may not be a product of the failure of the imagination at all, but a realistic assessment of the social state of things as experienced.

That the naming of wisdom occurred just at the moment of its absence, and its absence was noted just at the moment when Hebrew society had been dismantled, is a telling consideration (Prov. 1–9). Its imagination as an object of thought dislodged from human society may in fact be the first effort in idealization of the very kind we have been tracing. As a mythological notion the figure of wisdom had its fantastic heyday precisely during this period. It may be our sense of things that determines the judgment about its lack of content, precision, reference, practical engagement of concrete realities, or well defined concepts, i.e., its apparent distance from Greek thought. Instead, its logic may actually have been derived from serious and sane reflection upon society as society. And its idealizations may have been fanciful, focused, but essentially empty just because, without the con tent that a society's sense supplied, wisdom *could* not function except as the articulation of desire, experimentation, and quest for a new "house."

Striking, to say the least, is the fact that wisdom's cosmic and epic adventures took place just during the period of party conflict and uncertainty about the stability and legitimacy of the Jewish polis-society. And the similarities between the figure of wisdom and the ideal figures we have reviewed are very strong. Both kinds of figures are imagined dislodged from social history, idealized, located in trans-social orders of reality, theologized, then storied in such a way as to suggest availability. But the story always marks out the gap as well, and seeks to overcome it by various devices that reveal its conditionality, mere potentiality, future actualization, or dependence upon the continuance of the human quest itself.

This attempt to relocate wisdom in the social world has often considered a more belabored, more arbitrary, and less definitive aspect of the poetries of mythologized wisdom than the marvelous flights of fancy that delighted in picturing wisdom up and out in the first place. The attempt to bring wisdom down may indeed be more belabored, more arbitrary. But it is possible that it is not less, but more definitive of the object of wisdom thought than we have suspected. Ben Sira's belabored and arbitrary relocation of wisdom in his society may have been exactly what the rationality of wisdom required. It may even have been enabled by the social sense actually achieved by the early Second Temple structures. From this perspective, the extravagance and incredibility of the Wisdom of Solomon would not be due to delight in mystic anthropology or speculative cosmology, but to a second crisis in wisdom thought caused by the failure of Second Temple institutions to sustain a society that made sense.

We may even go one step step further. Staying for a moment with the mythological metaphor of "relocating" wisdom in the social world, two loci appear to have been favorites. One was the anthropological figure. The other was the "identification," as we say, of wisdom with Torah. There may be more logic to the selection of just these two loci than we have suspected. If a wisdom anthropology turns out to be a study in social anthropology, and if the identification of wisdom with Torah turns out to be based upon a recognition that tradition and constitutional "law" are fundamental for social constructions, Jewish sages cannot be charged with a poetry only of fantasy and desire.

We can focus these considerations quite nicely now with a final glance at each of the figures we have studied. What we want to suggest as a summary statement of our theoretical reflections about ideal figures and Jewish wisdom is the following: 1) In each case some notion of wisdom has been attributed to the ideal figure. This attribution is not cosmetic, but essential to the idealization. Without it the figure would not have been imagined. 2) The wisdom of these figures represents a social notion, thus supporting the thesis that the figures themselves are studies in a social anthropology. 3) The imagery that gives content to these singular characterizations of the wise society is drawn in each case from the epic traditions. In each case it is also the extent to which the epic may reflect wisdom, i.e., configurations of forces required for the ordering of society, that has been researched. Thus a wisdom reading or hermeneutic of Torah is basic to the process. The corollary is that Torah is (implicitly) the locus of Israel's wisdom. 4) The method for the construction of these figures is determined by a simple, logical device. The profile must reflect recognizable and distinctive characteristics of Jewish society from a) contemporary social configurations, b) models available from the Torah, and c) some notionality of wisdom itself. By means of the logic of analogy alignments can be made. If an image can comprehend Torah, wisdom, and (some contemporary) model for society, the case will have been made. The Greeks also would be impressed. To correlate cosmos, nomos, physis, polis, and anthropos in a single configuration!

Several notions about wisdom occur in our texts. Each can be related to mythologies of wisdom in one way or another. Each tends to emphasize what might be called a narrative moment. Ben Sira, for instance, imagined wisdom's quest for a home, and her entrance into the temple in Jerusalem as that home (Sir. 24:8–12). In the Wisdom of Solomon the emphasis is upon wisdom's rescue and vindication of the one selected to be king. In the Psalms of Solomon it is the universal, righteous, and beneficent rule of wisdom and her king that is employed. But all of these motifs, though mythological, have not erased the fundamental relationship of wisdom to social orders. The thesis still stands that all of these references to wisdom is the same as making sense of society.

These ideal figures were not the only way in which Jewish thought and practice addressed the problems of societal experimentation and change in an era of uncertainty. Nor have the figures we have traced provided a complete picture even of this kind of contribution to the rethinking of Israel. The impression should not be left that any of the circles behind these figures played essential roles in the discovery of that solution which finally proved successful. Once the Rabbinic solution was in place, moreover, the fanciful poetries of cosmic wisdom and heavenly kings could subside. Another rereading of Moses would bring his wisdom into the daily round by yet another path.

But the present study may be valuable, nonetheless, for it reveals a kind of intellectual effort even in the most fantastic constructions that diverse groups placed upon their ideals. Some of this fantasy would border on madness, were we not able to see its cogency. But a certain toughness of the intellect marks the limits to which the flights were allowed to go. A realism about the way things were going in actual social history was never denied. It was in fact that acknowledgment which placed the questions and generated the energies that produced these marvelous visions. If we see them constrained both by a painful analysis of social events – the careful sifting of the epic traditions and ideals – and studied reflection on the options available for remedial or alternative social formations, this imaginative labor had not lost touch with reality. It was marked, in fact, by a stubborn capacity not to give up the archaic ideals even in the face of events and circumstances that could only be seen to reflect them in the furthest stretches of the imagination.

NOTES

1 Anders Hultgard, "The Ideal 'Levite,' the Davidic Messiah, and the Saviour Priest in the Testaments of the Twelve Patriarchs," p. 105. In *Ideal Figures in Ancient Judaism*, pp. 93–110, ed. George W. E. Nickelsburg and John J. Collins (Chico, Calif.: Scholars Press, 1980).

2 Hultgard, "The Ideal 'Levite,'" p. 104.

3 Hultgard, "The Ideal 'Levite,'" p. 105.

4 George W. E. Nickelsburg and John J. Collins, eds., *Ideal Figures in Ancient Judaism. Profiles and Paradigms.* Society of Biblical Literature Septuagint and Cognate Studies 12 (Chico, Calif.: Scholars Press, 1980).

5 See the important, recent study by Richard Horsley, "Popular Messianic Movements around the Time of Jesus," *Catholic Biblical Quarterly* 46:3 (1984), pp. 471–95. Horsley makes the point that the popular movements were generated by circumstances and folklore, not the depictions of ideal images produced by intellectuals, i.e., the texts available to us.

6 On Ben Sira's literary achievement see Thomas Robert Lee, "Studies in the

Form of Sirach (Ecclesiasticus) 44–50" (Ph. D. diss., University of California, Berkeley, 1979) and Burton L. Mack, *Wisdom and the Hebrew Epic. Ben Sira's Hymn in Praise of the Fathers,* Chicago Studies in the History of Judaism (Chicago: University of Chicago Press, 1985).

7   For a demonstration of the thesis that Sirach 44–50 functioned as an etiology for Second Temple Judaism, see Mack, *Wisdom.*

8   See C. Larcher, *Etudes sur le livre de la sagesse.* Etudes bibliques (Paris: Gabalda, 1969).

9   See David Winston, *The Wisdom of Solomon. A New Translation with Introduction and Commentary.* Anchor Bible 43 (Garden City, N.Y.: Doubleday, 1979).

10 See Joachim Schüpphaus, *Die Psalmen Salomos. Ein Zeugnis jerusalemer Theologie und Frömmigkeit in der Mitte des vorchristlichen Jahrhunderts.* Arbeiten zur Literatur und Geschichte des hellenistischen Judentums 7 (Leiden: Brill, 1977).

11 Based on Josephus, Antiquities XIV. The Loeb Classical Library. (Cambridge, Mass.: Harvard Univ. Press; London: William Heinemann, 1966).

12 Josephus, Antiquities XIV, 69–72.

13 Jacob Neusner, *From Politics to Piety. The Emergence of Pharisaic Judaism* (Englewood Cliffs, N.J.: Prentice-Hall, 1973).

3

Salvation without and with a Messiah: Developing Beliefs in Writings Ascribed to Enoch

GEORGE W. E. NICKELSBURG

It is axiomatic in modern biblical studies that variety was a salient feature of early Jewish eschatology. As a probe into this variety, I shall discuss the corpus known as 1 Enoch. In this self-contained body of literature we can trace the development and transformation of certain eschatological traditions over the course of perhaps 350 years. In keeping with the theme of this volume, my focus will be on the Messiah. The topic is not to be taken for granted since this figure is explicitly mentioned only in the latest stratum of the Enochic tradition, the Book of Parables (Chaps. 37–71). My intention, however, is to show how the messianic figure of the Parables assumes functions the earlier strata attribute to other figures.

Dominating the action in the Book of Parables is a transcendent figure, who is the agent of eschatological judgment and salvation. He is known variously as "the Chosen One," "the Righteous One," "the Son of Man," and, on two occasions, "the Anointed One." In the first part of the paper, I shall take up the themes of judgment and salvation in the earlier strata of 1 Enoch, focusing on the following issues: What are the authors' circumstances? That is, what is the nature of the predicament that calls forth judgment and salvation? Who is the agent of judgment and salvation? What is this agent's relationship to God? What is the specific function of the agent and how does the agent mediate judgment and salvation? Against this background, I shall turn in the second part to the messianic soteriology in the Book of Parables.

Agents of Judgment and Salvation in the Early Strata of 1 Enoch

Two myths dominate the Enochic corpus, both of which are set in primordial times but are also closely related to the end-time. The first

49

myth recounts how the patriarch Enoch was escorted through the cosmos, where he learned the secrets of heaven and earth, which he wrote down for the benefit of his children who would be living in the end-time. The second myth describes the fall of the heavenly watchers in ancient times and its consequences in the Deluge. The actions of the watchers and their sons, the giants, as well as the Deluge, have counterparts in the evil of the end-time and its eradication in the great judgment.

The Astronomical Book (Chapters 72–82)

Chapters 72ff. are probably the oldest stratum in the Enochic corpus.[1] Here Enoch recounts how the angel Uriel escorted him through the heavens, showing him the created order in the activity of the heavenly bodies. Although the compositional history of this section is uncertain,[2] we can draw several tentative conclusions about the earlier form of the tradition. The alleged author was Enoch, who transmitted his writing to his son, Methuselah. It is uncertain whether the text was composed as a polemic against people who disagreed with the author's astronomical and calendrical observations and speculations.[3] The use of the apocalyptic form and its claim of revealed authority may imply such a polemic. In any case, as parts of Chapters 80–82 indicate, and as the Book of Jubilees confirms, the Astronomical Book came to be used for such polemical purposes. In that context, the Enochic writing served a salvific function. It transmitted cosmic revelations that had been given to Enoch for the benefit and salvation of the latter generations. The astronomical laws were a Torah that governed the proper observance of the religious calendar.

Myths about the Rebellion of the Watchers (Chapters 6–11)

Chapters 6–11 are the next oldest stratum in the corpus. They tell the story of the rebellion of the heavenly watchers and its consequences. Actually, two myths are recounted and there is probably another level of redaction.[4] The first myth is an interpretation of the cryptic verses in Genesis 6:1–4 about the mating of the sons of God and the daughters of men.[5] In the Enochic version, the angelic chieftain, Šemiḥazah, and his companions, marry mortal women and beget belligerent giants, who devastate the earth and obliterate life. According to the second myth, the angelic chieftain ʿAśaʾel reveals heavenly secrets about metallurgy and mining, which enable men to forge the weapons that devastate the earth and to make the jewelry and cosmetics that facilitate sexual seduction. In yet another version, the watchers reveal the magical arts and astrological forecasting.

In the present composite form of the story, the angelic intercessors hear the prayer of dying humanity and plead its case before God, who commissions these angels to enact judgment. Although the story is set in primordial times, the description of the salvation that follows the judgment transcends the account in Genesis 9 and takes on the character of an eschatological scenario. Thus, the whole story presumes an Urzeit/Endzeit typology. The primordial giants are prototypes of warriors in the author's own time. In my view, these were the Diadochoi, who claimed divine parentage and waged continual warfare, as they battled for Alexander's crown.[6] Certain of the demonic revelations correspond to aspects of contemporary culture.

In these myths, the evils of the author's own time are not simply the accumulation of the evil deeds of human beings. They derive from a radical evil, which came into being through an act of rebellion that took place in a realm beyond human access. The real perpetrators of evil are not flesh and blood, but principalities and powers. The warrior kings are the personification of an evil that the watchers bred into the world. Magicians and soothsayers are possessors of forbidden knowledge and the agents of malevolent spirits. And the human race, as a whole, is their helpless victim.

Since evil derives from supernatural sources, it must be overcome by divine intervention. Different from Genesis 6–9, this heavenly deliverance is enacted by angelic agents of judgment and salvation.

The words of commissioning and the specific functions of the angels are pertinent to our topic. The son of Lamech is the prototype of the righteous person in the end-time. In words reminiscent of a prophetic commissioning, God dispatches Śariel: "Go to Noah and say to him in my name, 'Hide yourself'" (10:2–3). The angel is the revealer, the teacher, who warns of the coming judgment, from which Noah must flee and hide if he is to be preserved (cf. Isa. 26:20–21) as the plant whose seed will provide a new start for the human race. Salvation results when Noah obeys the revealed word of the divinely commissioned messenger. We shall meet this motif frequently in 1 Enoch.

Raphael, the second angel, is sent against 'Aśa'el. The demon who has revealed how to bind with spells is himself bound and cast into the pit, and God's healer cures the earth from the plague that has afflicted it.

Representing the divine Warrior, Gabriel is dispatched against the *gibborîm,* whom he sends against one another in a war of mutual extermination.

Michael's tasks parallel those of Raphael and Gabriel. He is to destroy the giants and restore the earth. But at least one nuance is different. He does not heal the earth; he "cleanses" it. The term has priestly connotations, and the action is reminiscent of Noah's sacrifice.

To summarize, a myth set in primordial times explains the demonic origins of evil in the present time and promises its extermination. The agents of that judgment and the salvation that will follow are transcendent figures from the heavenly realm, who are commissioned with functions that parallel those of human agents: prophet, healer, warrior, high priest. Each of these roles reflects a particular model of salvation, which is here construed in eschatological dimensions.

Enoch's Ascent to Heaven (Chapters 12–16)

The myths in Chapters 6–11 never mention Enoch or suggest that he is their author. Chapters 12–16, on the other hand, are a first person account in which Enoch describes his ascent to the heavenly throneroom and his subsequent interaction with the rebellious watchers. This section does not *narrate* the events in Chapters 6–11, but it does presuppose the story and makes repeated reference to it. Nevertheless, although the judgment of the watchers and the giants is often in focus, the angelic agents of this judgment, who are so prominent in Chapters 6–11, are never mentioned.

This silence is a reflex of Enoch's centrality in the narrative, which, in turn, is related to the genre of these chapters. They recount a series of commissionings, preeminently Enoch's prophetic commissioning.[7] First, Enoch is commissioned by angels to indict the rebel watchers and announce their coming judgment. Then the watchers commission Enoch to intercede for them. When he does so, he is summoned to the heavenly throneroom, where God commissions him to repeat the verdict of the heavenly court. Enoch does this by writing down the indictment and verdict and reading them in the presence of the rebel watchers.

Thus these chapters mirror Chapters 6–11 in some interesting ways. The heavenly intercessors, who plead for humanity in Chapters 6–11, are replaced by Enoch, who pleads ineffectively for the rebel watchers – the fallen heavenly priests.[8] The heavenly agents of judgment have also been replaced by Enoch, who is the agent of judgment because as a prophet of doom he bears the irreversible message of that judgment. Thus these chapters focus not on the actual events of judgment and punishment in primordial and eschatological times, but on the message and the messenger who announces that judgment and the punishment that follow it. When God speaks and God's word is conveyed, the act has, in effect, taken place.

The relationship between primordial and eschatological time is essential here. The words of heavenly judgment that Enoch wrote down in ancient times are the words of the text of the book of Enoch. Chapter 14 begins with this superscription, "The Book of the Words of Truth and the Reprimand of the Watchers who were from Eternity." Enoch is important in his role as prophet and scribe, and he describes how God created him and destined him (y^{c}hab, 14:2, 3) to be the revealer of the heavenly reprimand. Thus, judgment is bound up with the word that reveals that judgment. The author of these chapters is an agent of judgment in that he reveals the irrevocable sentence of condemnation.

The Journeys of Enoch (Chapters 17–19 and 20–36)

Chapters 17–19 and 20–33 provide a locative affirmation of the message of the previous sections. They recount two cosmic journeys to the places where the judgment already spoken of will be dispensed to the fallen watchers and to the righteous and sinners of the human race.[9] We learn little about the agents of this judgment, although God is mentioned once (25:3). As in Chapters 12–16, revelation is central here. The mediators of this revelation are the angels, who escort Enoch and interpret the meaning of his visions, as well as Enoch himself, who reveals what has been revealed to him.

The Oracular Introduction to 1 Enoch (Chapters 1–5)

Chapters 6–36 are introduced by a prophetic oracle that announces the eschatological theophany and the final judgment and its consequences. In the superscription, Enoch introduces his book with language drawn from the Blessing of Moses and the prophecies of Balaam (1:1–2; Deut. 33; Num. 24).[10] The theophany is described in 1:3c–9. The heavenly warrior will appear with the myriads of his angelic army. The rebel watchers will quake, and the whole cosmos will react. Judgment will be executed on the human race. The wicked will be punished for their impious deeds and blasphemous words. The final section of the oracle contrasts the blessings and curses that will come to the righteous and the wicked (5:6–9). The righteous and chosen will be forgiven and receive mercy and peace. They will be the recipients of wisdom, which will enable them not to sin in word and deed and thus to avoid divine judgment.

Different from the previous sections, here the eschatological appearance of God is central, and God, not his angels, is the primary agent of judgment. As in Chapters 12 and following, Enoch remains an important figure; he is the revealer of the coming judgment, and he speaks in the idiom of biblical prophecy. The wisdom that will lead to the salvation of the righteous is possibly related to the Enochic revelation of the judgment (see the next section).

The Epistle of Enoch (Chapters 92–105)

Chapters 92–105 of 1 Enoch purport to be an Epistle from Enoch to his spiritual descendants who would live in the last days. Its primary themes are familiar: righteousness and sin and their reward and punishment in God's judgment. The Epistle differs from Chapters 6–9 in that it makes almost no reference to the primordial angelic rebellion. Like Chapters 20–33 and especially 1–5, it focuses on the judgment of the righteous and the sinners who live in the latter days.[11]

Two types of sin parallel their counterparts in the early chapters. Parallel to the blasphemies and hard and proud words in 1:9; 5:4; 27:2 are idolatry and deceit and false teaching (especially in 98:9–99:10).[12] The wicked *deeds* of the rich and powerful sinners include preeminently their oppression and murder of the righteous (cf. 22:5–7 and the sin of the giants).[13]

The Epistle consists primarily of alternating series of admonitions and woes. Enoch admonishes the righteous to endure in the face of oppression and to resist the temptation to sin, promising them the rewards that are written on the heavenly tablets that he has inspected. In the woes he threatens the sinners with damnation for their sins of word and deed.

Intermingled with the admonitions and woes are several passages that describe aspects of the judgment, employing motifs familiar from the early chapters of 1 Enoch. These and a few other passages provide some information on the nature of the judgment and the divine agents who will execute it. As in Chapter 9, the prayer of the righteous will reach the angelic intercessors, whose intervention will catalyze the judgment (97:3–6; 99:3; 103:14–104:3). One aspect of the judgment will be a familial war of mutual self-destruction reminiscent of the *gigantomachia* (10:9–10). Two descriptions of the judgment allude to the theophany described in Chapter 1 (100:4–5; cf. 1:7, 9; 102:1–3). God's angelic entourage will serve as his agents, dragging the wicked from their hiding places and keeping the righteous and pious safe until the divine fury has spent itself.

But the executors of the judgment are not limited to God and his angels. Two new motifs enter the picture. The heavenly bodies and cosmic forces, mentioned in 2:1–5:3 as paragons of obedience to God's commandments, function in the Epistle as witnesses of human sin and agents of the judgment (100:10–101:9). Moreover, the righteous themselves – whose previous participation in the judgment has been through the prayer for vengeance – will take part in a holy warfare against the wicked (95:3; 96:1; 98:12; cf. 93:10; 91:11–12).[14]

Our discussion of the earlier parts of 1 Enoch noted the important salvific role played by revealer figures: Sariel the angel sent to Noah; Enoch the seer; and the real author of these revelatory texts. This divine activity, which prepares one for the judgment, is crucial in the Epistle. According to the Apocalypse of Weeks (93:9–91:11), the seventh week will be characterized by a generation that perverts truth into falsehood. It will be overcome when the chosen are given the sevenfold wisdom and knowledge that will undermine the violence and falsehood of the perverse generation (cf. also 94:1–2). In 104:12–13 this wisdom and knowledge is identified, at least significantly, with the Enochic literature, which will be the property of the righteous community of the end-time. They, in turn, will instruct the sons of the earth in this salvific wisdom.[15]

These texts direct us to the premise that governs the literary genre of the Epistle and endows it with divine authority. This is a book of divinely revealed wisdom, mediated through the anonymous sage who has taken the name of the primordial seer, Enoch. The revelatory aspect extends to the corpus as a whole. The descriptions of primordial sin and punishment and Enoch's revelations of the cosmos and of the future are the presupposition for the message of the Epistle. The corpus as a whole is a deposit of revealed wisdom directed to the people of the end-time, providing the divine means to endure judgment and receive salvation. Thus, through his book the sage functions as the indispensable divine agent of salvation.[16]

The Animal Apocalypse (Chapters 85–90)

1 Enoch 85–90 is an apocalypse that recounts in allegorical form the history of the world from Adam to the end-time. Human beings are depicted as animals, the rebel watchers are fallen stars, and the seven archangels are human beings.

This extended allegory has many points of similarity with the earlier strata of 1 Enoch. Angels function as agents of judgment and as mediators between beleaguered humanity and its God. In the end-time Judas, the champion of the pious, leads them in a holy war against the wicked, mainly the gentiles. Final judgment takes place in connection with a theophany.

Idiosyncratic to this text is the figure of the great white bull of the eschaton. Scholars have often identified him as the Davidic Messiah – mainly because they suppose that an eschatological scenario demanded a Davidic Messiah.[17] While this great eschatological beast may, indeed, be a symbol for such a Messiah, several points are worth noting. The only identifiable eschatological human agent of judgment is the ram, Judas Maccabeus. He, if anyone, corresponds to a militant Messiah. The great bull of the eschaton is important not for what he does, but for what (or who) he is. He is born after the judgment has taken place and is a reversion to the white bulls of primordial times – the Sethite line from Seth himself to Isaac. He is, moreover, the first fruits of a humanity returned to primordial purity and vitality.[18] His importance lies in this patriarchal status and not in any explicit messianic function. Indeed, different from all the divine agents we have discussed, this figure receives no commission or delegation of authority, nor is he the recipient of revelation.

The Book of Parables (Chapters 37–71)

For explicit reference to the idea of a Messiah, we must turn to the latest stratum in 1 Enoch, Chapters 37–71, the so-called Book of Parables. Here, motifs previously ascribed to men, angels, and God are attributed to a figure whom the texts described as "the Lord's anointed." However, as we shall see, he is not the kind of Messiah described in texts that await a Davidic king or a Levitic priest. He is a transcendent heavenly figure with titles and functions drawn from several biblical eschatological scenarios.

Relationship to the Enochic Corpus

The Parables are a creative reformulation of the Enochic tradition. Its contents are an account of Enoch's ascent to heaven and his journeys across the earth, where, guided by interpreting angels, he sees in a series of tableaux the events related to the final judgment.

Two related features distinguish the book from the rest of the extant Enochic literature, and they constitute the core of the book's soteriology and theology of judgment. First, the book centers on events in the divine throneroom, where God is preparing his judgment. Second, the agent of this judgment appears nowhere else in the extant Enochic tradition; his pedigree is to be found in non-Enochic texts. Thus a tradent of the Enochic tradition or a group of such sages have drawn materials from outside this tradition and created a composite figure to serve the judicial and salvific functions that the earlier Enochic traditions ascribed to men, angels, and God.

The Setting

The Sinners. Before turning to this figure and the judgment that he executes, we must look at the circumstances that precipitate the judgment. Two groups of villains dominate the scene in the Parables. Between them they divide the sins ascribed to the watchers in Chapters 6–11. The rebel angels in the Parables, whose leader is Azazel, are uniformly accused of the sin that chapters 6–11 attribute to the angelic chieftain 'Aśa'el.[19] They have revealed forbidden secrets to humanity (Chap. 64) and thus led them astray (54:5–6; 56:1–4; 64; 65:6–11; cf. Chap. 8).

The second, more prominent group of villains in the Parables are "the kings and the mighty who possess the earth (*or* the Land)." Their violent and bloody oppression of the righteous is reminiscent of the activity of the giants in Chapters 6–11 and the deeds of the rich and powerful sinners in the Epistle.

Several factors characterize the conduct of the kings and the mighty (46:5–8). They refuse to acknowledge that they have received their kingship from the Lord of Spirits. Conversely, their faith is in the gods that they have made with their hands (i.e., their idols), and thus they deny the name of the Lord of Spirits.[20] Moreover, they persecute the houses of his congregations, the faithful who depend on the name of the Lord of Spirits. The author refers to gentile kings and rulers who are persecuting pious Jews. Their sin is characterized by means of the myth about the arrogant rulers who are the agents of the demon who storms heaven and assaults the divine throne.[21] To persecute the righteous clients of the Lord of Spirits is to assault God and deny God's ultimate sovereignty.

The Righteous. The counterparts to the sinful kings and the mighty are "the righteous" and "the chosen" and "the holy." These three titles appear sometimes singly and sometimes in various combinations, but they are never explicitly defined. The text never states why they have been chosen or what deeds or characteristics make them righteous or holy. We are told only that they "have hated and despised this unrighteous age . . . and all its deeds and ways" (48:7). Nonetheless, the author does mention a few characteristics of the righteous.

Of primary importance is their sad lot in life. The kings and the mighty persecute them (46:8). For this reason, presumably, they grieve (48:4), their faces are downcast (62:15), and they await their rest (53:7). Persecution, moreover, has led to the death of the righteous (47:1, 2, 4).

Repeatedly mentioned is the faith of the righteous. If the nature of their righteous deeds is not described, we are told that these deeds are dependent (lit., "hang on") the Lord of Spirits (38:2), and they themselves are "the faithful, who depend on the Lord of Spirits" (40:5; 46:8; cf. 58:5). In a similar idiom, they rely on (lit., "lean on") God and the "staff" that is the Son of Man (48:4; 61:3, 5; cf. "hope," 48:4).

Central and constitutive to the faith of the righteous and chosen is their knowledge of the heavenly realm and specifically the Son of Man.[22] God chose the Son of Man and hid him in his presence, but he has revealed him to the holy and righteous and chosen (48:6–7; 61:13; 62:7: 69:26).

In a formal sense this revelation is a defining characteristic that distinguishes the righteous from the sinners. As we shall see, the Son of Man is the vindicator and savior of the righteous, and, in that capacity, he is the judge of the kings and the mighty who persecute them. With respect to this issue, the author establishes a specific contrast between the two groups. To the righteous has been revealed the one who will enact God's righteous judgment in their behalf. The sinful, kings and mighty, who persecute them deny God's sovereignty and the possibility of his retributive justice.

Whether the righteous and chosen represent a particular, sociologically and religiously defined group of Jews is uncertain. The terms "righteous," "chosen," and "holy" are generic expressions that need not imply that certain other Jews are not part of the community of the saved. Similarly, the expression "the houses of his (God's) congregation" (46:8; cf. 53:6) indicates only that they gathered in groups and not that they did so in intentional separation from other Jews.

The Messianic Figure in the Parables

The messianic figure in the Parables, who is to be the executor of divine judgment against the rebel angels and the kings and the mighty, is designated by four names: most frequently "the Chosen One"; twice "the Righteous One"; twice "the Anointed One."[23] Several times he is called "Son of Man." However, since this term is almost always qualified ("this Son of Man," "that Son of Man," "the Son of Man who . . ."), we must be cautious in calling it a title.[24] The names of the exalted one are derived ultimately from three types of scriptural texts. "Son of Man" has been drawn from Daniel 7.[25] "Chosen One" and "Righteous One" are titles of the Deutero-Isaianic Servant of the Lord. "Anointed One" is a messianic title strictly speaking.

The major references to the exalted one occur in a series of heavenly tableaux that describe events leading to the enthronement of the Chosen One. In addition to these scenes of dramatic action, there are a number of anticipatory allusions to the functions of the Chosen One. My discussion will draw mainly on the tableaux.

The first major text is Chapter 46. In form it is typical of a certain kind of revealed vision: vision, seer's question, answer by the interpreting angel. Enoch's vision is based on Daniel 7:9, 13:

> And I saw there one who had a head of days
> and his head was like white wool.
> And with him was another, whose face was like the
> appearance of a man;

and his face was full of graciousness like one of the holy
angels.
(1 Enoch 46:1)

The author introduces the two principal figures from the Danielic vision.
The second of these is clearly a transcendent figure. His humanlike face is
glorious like that of an angel.

When Enoch inquires about "that Son of Man," the interpreting angel
responds:

This is the son of man who has righteousness,
and righteous dwells with him.
And all the treasuries of what is hidden he will reveal;
for the Lord of Spirits has chosen him,
and his lot has surpassed all before the Lord of Spirits in
truth forever.
(1 Enoch 46:3)

This explanation uses or implies three of the descriptive terms applied to
the transcendent figure. He is "Son of Man." His "righteousness" implies
the title "the Righteous One." As the one whom the Lord of Spirits has
chosen, he is "the Chosen One." Moreover, he is the highest functionary
in the heavenly court – thus surpassing in rank even the four archangels,
Michael, Raphael, Gabriel, and Phanuel. The righteousness of this Son of
Man is the quality by which he will judge (cf. e.g., 62:3; 63:3, 8–9). The
hidden treasuries he will reveal most likely contain the hidden sins of
those whom he will judge (cf. 49:4; 50:2; 68:5). The rest of Chapter 46
anticipates the judgment scene in Chapter 62 (see below).

Chapter 47 returns to the Danielic source (7:9, 10, 22): The Head of
Days is seated on his glorious throne in the midst of his angelic court, and
the books of the living are opened. Judgment will be executed on behalf
of the righteous. The event that catalyzes this session of the heavenly
court is extraneous to Daniel and is typically Enochic: It is the intercession
of the angels, who relay to God the prayer of the righteous whose blood
has been shed (47:1, 2, 4; cf. Chap. 9).

Although the session of the heavenly court, described in Danielic language, leads us to expect that God will exact judgment on the kings and
the mighty, as the Ancient of Days does in Daniel 7, here this judgment
does not happen straightaway. Instead, the author recounts the commissioning of that Son of Man, which in Daniel takes place only after the
judgment.

This commissioning is described in two lengthy poetic stanzas (Chaps.
48–49), which draw their imagery and language from the call and presen-

taion of the Servant in Isaiah 49 and 42 and from royal passages in Psalm 2 and Isaiah 11.[26] According to 48:2–3, at this moment in the session of the court, that Son of Man is named in the presence of the Lord of Spirits. Actually, the text goes on, his name was named before creation, and he was chosen and hidden in God's presence at the time (v. 6). In contrast to the Deutero-Isaianic Servant, the naming and hiding of the servant figure precede not a human birth, but the creation of the universe. The functions of this Son of Man are described in language from Isaiah 49:

> He will be a staff to the righteous,
>   that they may lean on him and not fall.
> He will be a light to the nations,
>   and he will be a hope to those who grieve in their hearts.
>
> (1 Enoch 48:4)

Moreover, he has preserved the portion of the righteous, and he is the vindicator of their lives (48:7).

The narrative switches to an anticipation of the coming judgment. In those days, the faces of "the kings of the earth" will be cast down (48:8). This title for the kings, which occurs in the Parables only here, introduces an allusion to Psalm 2:2: These kings will be judged "because they have denied the Lord of Spirits and his Anointed One" (48:10). Although this judgment is a function of the Chosen One, it will be executed against the kings also by the chosen ones.

The second stanza of this pericope brings us back to the scene in the heavenly court (Chap. 49). The Chosen One has taken his stand before the Lord of Spirits. His qualifications are divine wisdom and righteousness:

> He is mighty in all the secrets of righteousness . . .
> And in him dwell the spirit of wisdom and the spirit of
>   insight,
>   and the spirit of instruction and might,
>   and the spirit of those who have fallen asleep in
>   righteousness.
> And he will judge the things that are secret,
>   and no one will be able to speak a lying word in his
>   presence.
> (1 Enoch 49:2–4)

This passage draws its motifs from Isaiah 11:2–5, which stresses the judicial functions of the Davidic king, primarily the divinely given wisdom that enables him to penetrate the human facade and judge human deeds righteously and with equity. Into this allusion is added reference to the persecuted righteous, whose vindicator the Chosen One is.

The motif continues in the final lines of the Enochic stanza. He can so judge, "because he is the Chosen One in the presence of the Lord of Spirits, according to his good pleasure."

Here the allusion is to the presentation of the Servant in Isaiah:

> Behold my servant, whom I uphold,
>   my Chosen One in whom my soul delights;
> I have put my spirit upon him,
>   he will bring forth justice to the nations.
>   (Isaiah 42:1)

This Deutero-Isaianic text itself parallels the passage in Isaiah 11.

The unfolding drama of judgment reaches its climax in Chapters 61–63. In 61:6–13, we are again in the heavenly courtroom, among the angelic hosts. God now seats the Chosen One on his glorious throne. First, he judges the angels.

Then, in Chapters 62–63, he judges the kings and the mighty. This lengthy scene reflects a traditional reworking of the last Servant Song of Second Isaiah, which is attested also in Wisdom of Solomon 4–5.[27] Crucial to this interpretation of Isaiah is the conflation of the Servant Song with the description of the fall of the King of Babylon in Isaiah 14.[28] Through this conflation, the kings and the nations of Isaiah 52–53, who have been neutral spectators of the Servant's suffering, are not identified with the demonic anti-God figure, who strives to storm heaven and is thrown down to Sheol. In Wisdom 4–5, these royal figures (or at least the wealthy ungodly) are judged by the Servant figure himself, the righteous one whom they have persecuted. In 1 Enoch 62–63, they are judged by the Chosen One, who is the heavenly champion of the chosen ones whom they have persecuted.

This close relationship between the Chosen One and the chosen ones is expressed in two ways in this passage. First, it is a special quality of the chosen ones that the Chosen One who had been hidden was revealed to them (62:6–7; cf. 48:6–7). In contrast to this, the kings and the mighty face their judgment with astonishment. Implied from the parallel in Wisdom of Solomon 4–5 is an element of unexpected recognition: In the exalted Chosen One they recognize the chosen ones whom they have persecuted. Moreover, in their confession (Chap. 63) they acknowledge what they had previously refused to acknowledge: the sovereignty of the God whose chosen they have persecuted. There is a second aspect in the relationship of the Chosen One and the chosen. This relationship does not end with the judgment. The Chosen One is not only their heavenly champion and vindicator. He will be their companion in the eternal life that is now bestowed on them.

We have seen how the Parables describe the exalted one as the agent of divine judgment. One final set of passages describes this figure in language reserved elsewhere in 1 Enoch for God. After the superscription and introduction in Chapter 37, which correspond to 1:1–3b, the text of the Parables opens with reference to an epiphany (37:1–5), which corresponds to 1:3c–6. However, different from Chapter 1, which describes how God will appear to judge, the Parables speak of the appearance of "the Righteous One." A further reference to this epiphany occurs in Chapter 52. The mountains and hills will melt like wax at the appearance not of God (cf. 1:6–7), but of the Anointed One and Chosen One (cf. also 53:6–7 for the appearance of the Righteous and Chosen One).

The Transformation of Traditions in the Parables

The Parables make use of a number of Enochic motifs of significance to us. 1) The author's principal concern is the persecution of the righteous by kings and rulers who are the embodiment of demonic forces. 2) As judge God will adjudicate this gross inequity. 3) Angels will be agents of this judgment. 4) The persecuted righteous also share the prerogative of executing this judgment. 5) The author of the Parables describes his book as revealed wisdom that Enoch received and transmitted for the benefit and salvation of those who would live in the end-time (Chap. 37).[29]

The Parables are remarkable, however, for their transformations of these traditional motifs. These transformations are bound up with the figure of the Chosen One, which itself represents a transformation of other, non-Enochic traditions about divine judgment.

The transformations of the Enochic materials are as follows. 1) Theophany is replace by "huiophany." The righteous Son of Man appears to judge and is seated on God's glorious throne. Corresponding to the royal status of the persecutors, he is God's own king. His relationship to God is denoted both by the messianic term, "Anointed," and the servant term, "the Chosen One." 2) Although the angels carry out punishment on the hosts of Azazel who have led humanity astray and the kings and the mighty who have persecuted the righteous and chosen, their presence is much less dominating than in Chapters 6–11. The preeminent agent of judgment is the high functionary of the heavenly court, whose face shines like an angel, but who surpasses all others in the heavenly court. 3) The participation of the persecuted righteous in the judgment of their enemies is primarily through the activity of the champion of the righteous and the chosen, the Righteous One and Chosen One. 4) The focus of this author's revelation is on visions of the Chosen One, the heavenly figure whom God had hidden but has now revealed to the righteous and chosen.

The other side of the issue is the Enochic transformation and fusing of non-Enochic traditions. Three traditional figures of exalted status have become one figure who is both similar to, and notably different from, the prototypes. The Danielic Son of Man, the angelic patron of the people of the holy ones of the Most High,[30] here appears in the heavenly court not after the judgment, but in order to enact that judgment. The counterpart to the exalted Servant figure of the Wisdom of Solomon is not the vindicated righteous one himself, but the transcendent heavenly patron of the righteous and chosen. The Anointed One of the Lord, who will execute God's justice on the kings and rulers of the earth, is not a human king born of the line of David, but a member of the heavenly court.

This last point relates in particular to the theme of this volume and requires a little more elaboration. During the Greco-Roman period, when the Davidic throne was vacant, earlier royal texts from the prophets and the Psalms were read as prophecies of a ruler yet to come. Psalms of Solomon 17 employs a remarkable pastiche of language drawn from Psalm 2, Isaiah 11, and Ezekiel 34 to describe the future son of David who will oppose the unrighteous Roman rulers who have overrun the land. A fragmentary *pesher* on Isaiah from Qumran Cave 4 interprets Isaiah 11 (4QpIs[a]). The Florilegium from Cave 4 quotes both the oracle of 2 Samuel 7 and Psalm 2. The Testimonium quotes the Balaam oracle (Num. 24:15–17) with reference to the Davidic king. Running through all these texts is the king's function as the exector of God's judgment. The Testament of Levi 18, which I take to be pre-Christian in essential points,[31] ascribes to the eschatological priest attributes appropriate to the Davidic king.[32]

These texts, among others, testify to a live messianic hope in the two centuries B.C.E. The theologies that informed that hope anticipated variously a Davidic king, an anointed priest, or both. Some even ascribed quasi-divine attributes to these human figures. However, what distinguishes the Parables from these texts is the Parables' identification of the messianic figure with traditional transcendent exalted figures. The central figure of the Parables is God's *heavenly* vice-regent. For whatever reason, the author of the Parables believed that the biblical promises about the future king and the traditional messianic function of the judgment had to be fulfilled by a transcendent savior – one he found described in other traditions. Furthermore, in conflating these traditions, the author allowed the Servant title, "the Chosen One," to dominate the messianic title, "the

Anointed One." Later texts from around the year 100 C.E., which also make use of Daniel 7, change this emphasis and designate the transcendent judge of the kings and rulers and the savior of the righteous primarily as "the Anointed One."[33]

Although I have stressed the transcendent character of the Chosen One, it has often been argued that this heavenly figure is an exalted persecuted righteous man. Two data appear to support this position. First, the present conclusion to the Parables identifies the Chosen One with the exalted Enoch (cf. especially 71:14 with 46:3). Secondly, the Servant traditions in the Parables are most closely paralleled in the Wisdom of Solomon, which cites Enoch as the example of the righteous one par excellence (4:10–15) and uses language from Psalm 2 to describe the interaction between the righteous one and his rich and royal persecutors (4:18; 6:1). This impressive evidence gives one pause, but it falls short of certain proof. Chapter 71 may well be a later appendix to the book. In such a case, the original form of the Parables construed the relationship between the Chosen One/ Righteous One and the chosen and righteous ones as that of patron and clients rather than as a one-for-one identification. Nevertheless, the form of the Parables that identifies the exalted figure with Enoch and the closely related tradition in the Wisdom of Solomon testify to a situation in Judaism that may well have facilitated the claim of primitive Christianity that a particular persecuted righteous one had been exalted as the unique Chosen One, Son of Man, and Messiah.

Summary

In the first part of this chapter we worked through the early strata of 1 Enoch, looking at texts that describe God's judgment, its agents, and their functions. In the earliest narrative strata (Chaps. 6–11), angels, described first as heavenly intercessors, are commissioned variously as eschatological revealer, healer, warrior, and high priest. Later they will continue to appear as intercessors and as members of the entourage of the Divine Warrior, whose theophany precipitates the judgment. In Chapters 12–16, Enoch assumes functions ascribed earlier to angels: intercessor for the defunct intercessors and the prophet who announces doom on the watchers. This revelatory function underlies the whole of the Enochic corpus. One's salvation or damnation at the judgment hinges on one's response to the revelations mediated by Pseudo-Enoch, the anonymous seer. Finally, functions of divine judgment are given to the elements of nature and to the righteous of the end-time, including Judas Maccabeus. In perhaps one of these texts we may have a single reference to a Davidic king; in none of them does the word "anoint" appear.

In the Parables of Enoch, the subject of the second part of this study, the execution of judgment is partly in the hands of the angels and the persecuted righteous. For the most part, however, the agent of judgment is a transcendent heavenly figure, who assumes functions that the other strata in 1 Enoch attributed to the angels, the righteous, the elements of nature, and God. The author of the Parables describes his protagonist through the use of biblical traditions that originally described the "one like a Son of Man" in Daniel, the Servant/Chosen One of Second Isaiah, and the Davidic king in Isaiah 11 and Psalm 2. In this reformulation of the tradition, two things are noteworthy. First, the messianic traditions are subordinated to those about the Son of Man and, especially, the Chosen One. The title "Anointed One" occurs only twice. Second, by conflating the messianic tradition with the other two, the author depicts the Messiah not as the human son of David, but as a transcendent figure. This type of Messiah continued to appear in Jewish works written shortly after the fall of Jerusalem in 70 C.E.

Finally, we have seen in the Parables the continued importance of the role of revelation. The reality of the Chosen One and the judgment that he will execute are revealed to the righteous, but hidden from their enemies. The book of Parables is the embodiment of this revelation, and through it the author calls the righteous to the faith and faithfulness that will enable them to be saved at the time of the judgment. In this sense, the apocalyptist and his apocalypse play a key role in the drama of judgment and salvation.

The findings of this paper have at least two general implications for the study of early postbiblical Judaism. First, belief in a Messiah was not a *sine qua non* for Jewish theology in the Second Temple Period. Other savior figures of nonroyal status had ascribed to them attributes and functions that are traditionally called "messianic." In such cases, however, the use of this adjective may be deceptive, because it may wrongly imply that these attributes and functions derived from speculation about a divinely appointed king. Second, speculations about such a king, where they do occur, often differ greatly from one another. The king is not always thought of as a human being descended from the Davidic line.[34] He may be an exalted transcendent figure. He may be described in language drawn from speculation about nonroyal figures. The title "Anointed One" may or may not be prominent in the descriptions of the figure.

These findings are also of crucial significance for the study of Christian Origins, both with respect to our understanding of the development of christology and our interpretation of the early interaction of Christianity and Judaism. But that is the subject of another paper.

NOTES

1   See J. T. Milik, *The Books of Enoch: Aramaic Fragments of Qumran Cave 4* (Oxford: Clarendon, 1976) pp. 7–8, and in much more detail, James C. VanderKam, *Knoch and the Growth of an Apocalyptic Tradition* (Catholic Biblical Quarterly Monograph Series 16, Washington, D.C.: The Catholic Biblical Association of America, 1984), pp. 79–88.

2   The Qumran Aramaic fragments of this section indicate that the Ethiopic version is a compilation of several documents that have been severely abbreviated by a later editor. See Milik, *Enoch,* pp. 271–97; and Otto Neugebauer, "The 'Astronomical' Chapters of the Ethiopic Book of Enoch (72–82). With Additional Notes on the Aramaic Fragments by Matthew Black," in Matthew Black, *The Book of Enoch or 1 Enoch: A New English Edition with Commentary and Textual Notes,* Studia in Veteris Testamenti Pseudepigrapha 7 (Leiden: E. J. Brill, 1985), pp. 386. See also VanderKam, *Enoch,* pp. 76–79.

3   VanderKam, *Enoch,* pp. 90–1.

4   For the various options, see Paul D. Hanson, "Rebellion in Heaven, Azazel, and Euhemeristic Heroes in 1 Enoch 6–11," *Journal of Biblical Literature* 96 (1977): 195–233; George W. E. Nickelsburg, "Apocalyptic and Myth in 1 Enoch 6–11," *Journal of Biblical Literature* 96 (1977): 383–405; John J. Collins, "Methodological Issues in the Study of 1 Enoch: Reflections on the Articles of P. D. Hanson and G. W. Nickelsburg," in Paul J. Achtemeier, ed., *Society of Biblical Literature 1978 Seminar Papers* 1, pp. 315–22; Hanson, "A Response to John Collins' Methodological Issues in the Study of 1 Enoch," in Achtemeier, *1987 Seminar Papers,* pp. 307–9; Nickelsburg, "Reflections upon Reflections: A Response to John Collins' 'Methodical Issues in the Study of 1 Enoch,'" in Achtemeier, *1978 Seminar Papers,* pp. 311–14; Devorah Dimant, "1 Enoch 6–11: A Methodological Perspective," in Achtemeier, *1978 Seminar Papers,* pp. 323–39; Carol A. Newsom, "The Development of 1 Enoch 6–19: Cosmology and Judgment," *Catholic Biblical Quarterly* 42 (1980): 310–29.

5   Although the author of this section reflects Genesis 6, this does not exclude the possibility that he also knew an older and fuller form of the tradition that appears in evidently compressed form in Genesis.

6   See Nickelsburg, "Apocalyptic and Myth," pp. 389–91; see also Rüdiger Bartelmus, *Heroentum in Israel und seiner Umwelt* (Abhandlungen zur Theologie des Alten und Neuen Testaments 65; Zürich: Theologischer Verlag, 1979): 174–87.

7   H. Ludin Jansen, *Die Henochgestalt* (Oslo: Dybwad, 1939), pp. 114–17; George W. E. Nickelsburg, "Enoch, Levi, and Peter: Recipients of Revelation in Upper Galilee," *Journal of Biblical Literature* 100 (1981): 576–82.

8   Nickelsburg, "Enoch, Levi, and Peter," 584–7.

9   George W. E. Nickelsburg, *Jewish Literature Between the Bible and the Mishnah* (Philadelphia: Fortress, 1981), p. 54.

10   VanderKam, *Enoch,* pp. 115–19.

11   George W. E. Nickelsburg, "The Apocalyptic Message of 1 Enoch 92–105," *Catholic Biblical Quarterly* 39 (1977): 309–28.

12   George W. E. Nickelsburg, "The Epistle of Enoch and the Qumran Literature," *Journal of Jewish Studies* 33 (1982: *Essays in honour of Yigael Yadin*): 334–40.

13   Nickelsburg, "Riches, the Rich, and God's Judgment in 1 Enoch 92–105 and the Gospel according to Luke," *New Testament Studies* 25 (1978–79): 324–32.

14   Nickelsburg, "Apocalyptic Message": 317.

15   Nickelsburg, "Epistle,": 340–5.

16   On this issue, see Nickelsburg, "Revealed Wisdom as a Criterion for Inclusion and Exclusion: From Sectarian Judaism to Early Christianity," in J. Neusner and E. S. Frerichs, eds., *"To See Ourselves as Others See Us": Christians, Jews, "Others" in Late Antiquity* (Chico, Calif.: Scholars Press, 1985), pp. 73–91.

17   E.g., R. H. Charles, *The Book of Enoch or 1 Enoch* (Oxford: Clarendon, 1912), pp. 215–16,

18   See Jonathan A. Goldstein, "How the Authors of 1 and 2 Maccabees Treated the 'Messianic" Promises," this volume.

19   The Parables are extant only in Ethiopic. In Chapters 6–11 this same name occurs in the Ethiopic text, where the Aramaic reads 'Aśa'el. On the relationship, see Nickelsburg, "Apocalyptic and Myth," pp. 401–4.

20   It is uncertain whether the author has other opponents in mind when he refers to undefined sinners who deny the dwelling place of the holy and the name of the Lord of Spirits. Possibly he has in mind other persons who deny divine retribution or in other ways disagree with the theology of the author and his group. However that may be, the focus and emphasis is clearly on the gentile kings and rulers whose opposition to the righteous is construed as an act of hubris that demands the divine retribution that will affirm God's ultimate sovereignty. See the next note.

21   George W. E. Nickelsburg, *Resurrection, Immortality, and Eternal Life in Intertestamental Judaism* (Harvard Theological Studies 26; Cambridge/London: Harvard University Press/Oxford University Press, 1972), pp. 74–5.

22   See the discussion by John J. Collins, "The Heavenly Representative: The 'Son of Man' in the Similitudes of Enoch," in John J. Collins and George W. E. Nickelsburg, eds., *Ideal Figures in Ancient Judaism* (Society of Biblical Literature Septuagint and Cognate Studies 12; Chico, Calif.: Scholars Press, 1980), pp. 111–33.

23   "Chosen One": 39:6; 40:5; 45:3, 4; 49:4; 51:3, 5: 52:6, 9; 55:4; 61:5, 8, 10; 62:1. "Righteous One": 38:2; 53:6. "Anointed One": 48:10; 52:4.

24   The term occurs in: 46:2, 3, 4; 48:2; 62:5, 7, 9, 14; 63:11; 69:26, 27, 29; 70:1. It occurs in absolute form only in 62:7 and 69:27. The literature on this figure is, of course, legion. For a good discussion and bibliography, see Carsten Colpe, *"ho huios tou anthropou," "Theological Dictionary of the New Testament* 8 (1972) and for an updated bibliography, Gerhard Friedrich, ed., *Theologisches Wörterbuch zum Neuen Testament* 10:2 (1979), pp. 1283–6.

·25   See Johannes Theisohn, *Der auserwählte Richter* (Studien zur Umwelt des
      Neuen Testaments 12; Göttingen: Vandenhoeck & Ruprecht, 1975), pp. 14–
      23, who argues that the author of the Parables is dependent on Daniel 7 rather
      than on a source behind that text.

26   For the best exposition of the the messianic material in the Parables, see ibid.,
      pp. 68–99.

27   Nickelsburg, *Resurrection,* pp. 70–74, and the literature cited in nn. 87, 88.
      See also Theisohn, *Richter,* pp. 114–26.

28   See Nickelsburg, *Resurrection,* pp. 62–78.

29   See Collins, "Son of Man."

30   For the Danielic Son of Man as the archangel Michael, see John J. Collins,
      The Apocalyptic Vision of the Book of Daniel (Harvard Semitic Monographs 16;
      Missoula: Scholars, 1977), pp. 146.

31   See George W. E. Nickelsburg and Michael E. Stone, *Faith and Piety in Early
      Judaism* (Philadelphia: Fortress, 1983), p. 199, nn. 2, 3.

32   Jonas C. Greenfield and Michael E. Stone, "Remarks on the Aramaic Testa-
      ment of Levi from the Geniza," *Revue Biblique* 86 (1979):223–4.

33   2 Apoc. Bar. 39–40 interprets the Danielic vision about the four kingdoms.
      Chap. 72 bears interesting resemblances to the judgment scene described in
      Matt. 25:31–46, which, in turn, is related to 1 Enoch 62–63; see David R.
      Catchpole, "The Poor on Earth and the Son of Man in Heaven: A Reappraisal
      of Matthew xxv.31–46," *Bulletin of the John Rylands University Library of Man-
      chester* 61 (1979): 378–83. 4 Ezra 12–13 is a reinterpretation of Daniel 7. On
      the complex history of traditions, see Michael E. Stone, "The Concept of the
      Messiah in IV Ezra," in Jacob Neusner, ed., *Religions in Antiquity. Essays in
      Memory of Erwin Ramsdell Goodenough* (Supplements to Numen 14; Leiden:
      Brill, 1968), pp. 303–10; see further, Stone, "The Question of Messiah in 4
      Ezra," this volume.

34   The complexity of this situation is illustrated by the Qumran text about "The
      Chosen One of God." For a lengthy discussion, see Joseph A. Fitzmyer, "The
      Aramaic 'Elect of God' Text from Qumran Cave 4," *Catholic Biblical Quar-
      terly* 27 (1965): 348–72; reprinted in Joseph A. Fitzmyer, *Essays on the Semitic
      Background of the New Testament* (London: Chapman, 1977; reissued as Society
      of Biblical Literature Sources for Biblical Study 5; Missoula: Scholars Press,
      1974), pp. 127–60. 1:1–4 suggests that this "Chosen One" would be a human
      being. However, certain of his characteristics mentioned in 1:5–10 are remi-
      niscent of parts of 1 Enoch 49 and 63 that draw on Isa. 11. This may be of
      special significance, since no manuscript evidence for the Parables has been
      found at Qumran. Fitzmyer (ibid., pp. 149–50) minimizes the possibility of
      Isaianic influence on the Qumran text, noting rightly that the latter (very
      fragmentary) text gives no indication that its protagonist was a scion of David.
      However, the force of this argument is considerably lessened by the certain
      Isaianic influence of the Parables, a complete text that certainly does not envi-
      sion a Davidic origin for the Son of Man/Chosen One/Anointed One.

4

How the Authors of 1 and 2 Maccabees Treated the "Messianic" Promises

JONATHAN A. GOLDSTEIN

Great were Jacob and Moses and Balaam and the prophets of Israel for their prophecies, which were fulfilled in history down to the fifth century B.C.E. In many ways, greater still have been the same prophets and the seers of the books of 1 Enoch and Daniel for the impact of their prophecies that were still unfulfilled in the second century B.C.E. and even later. Those unfulfilled prophecies each promised one or more of the following: the permanent liberation of the Jews from exile, from foreign rule, and from all mishap; the erection at Jerusalem of a temple more magnificent than Solomon's, which God Himself would choose as His own place, glorifying it and making it secure from desecration and destruction; the rule over the Jews of a great and just king from the dynasty of David; their exaltation to imperial primacy among the nations; the conversion of the gentiles to follow the ways of the true God; the coming of a permanent era of peace; the resurrection of the righteous dead; and the punishment of all the wicked, past and present. Many of those prophecies omitted any mention of a king, but already Isaiah displayed the tendency to focus the fulfillment of such promises upon the coming of a single royal figure.[1] From Isaiah on, prophets might predict that that king would accomplish some or all of the great things promised by God. On the other hand, some religious spokesmen might hold that God himself or other persons would fulfill all or most of the promises before the coming of the royal figure; then, that king would at least henceforth be the good ruler of a great restored Israel.

Beginning with some writings of the first century B.C.E. and perhaps earlier,[2] that royal figure came to be called "the Lord's anointed," "the Messiah" (Hebrew and Aramaic: *mšyh;* Greek: *christos*). This eschatological meaning of "Messiah" cannot be found in the Jewish Bible. Scholars have struggled with the problem of explaining how the usage could have evolved.[3]

The prophetic books of the Hebrew Bible all date either from the time of the kings of Israel and Judah or from the exilic and postexilic periods. It is not surprising that most if not all of the aforementioned promises of the canonical prophets (like Zech. 1:12–13) essentially have to do with a coming time of God's favor that will put an end to the effects of the wrath of God that was kindled in the time of the kings of Israel and Judah.

The first centuries of the postexilic period could only have been puzzling for faithful believers: The glorious prophecies of restoration uttered by the true prophets were not being fulfilled. Yet a believer could hardly conclude that those inspired utterances were false. Fulfillment would come, but later. There had to be some explanation for the delay; usually, the faithful found it in present or past sin. That solution, too, posed difficulties: Moses, Isaiah, Jeremiah, and Ezekiel predicted that in the Age of Mercy after the end of the exile God would never again let his wrath fall upon Israel; indeed, in that age the Chosen People would never again come to sin. The evidence from the period after the return from the exile shows the Jews' peculiar predicament. Despite the joyous proclamations of the postexilic prophets, despite the return of many exiles to the Promised Land, despite the completion of the Second Temple, it was clear to believing Israelites that they were still living in the "Age of [God's] Wrath."[4]

The First Temple, in accordance with Deuteronomy 12:5–14, had been God's Chosen Place so as to bar the offering of Jewish sacrifices at any other location. The miraculous fire from heaven that was said to have attested God's election of Moses' tabernacle (Lev. 9:24) and Solomon's temple (2 Chron. 7:1–3) never came down upon the altar of the Second Temple. Also lacking from the Second Temple were the ark and Moses' tabernacle and its sacred furniture, which were reported to have been placed in Solomon's sanctuary (1 Kings 8:4, 2 Chron. 5:5) and which had never been recovered after its destruction in 586 B.C.E. The absence of those objects, too, might imply that the Second Temple was not the Chosen Place. For long centuries it remained inferior to Solomon's, and it was as vulnerable as the Jews themselves, though no one desecrated it until Antiochus IV sacked it in 169 B.C.E. Even so, many Jews held the Second Temple to be God's Chosen Place, equal in this respect to the First Temple. However, many other Jews – indeed, entire sects – held the Second Temple to be incompletely holy or even completely unfit for the offering of sacrifices. If it was not God's Chosen Place, Deuteronomy 12:5–14 would no longer forbid the existence of other Jewish sacrificial shrines. Jews might be free to recognize the legitimacy of other holy places, such as the Samaritan shrine on Mount Gerizim.[5]

More disappointments tested the faith of the Jews in the Age of Wrath. Taught by their tradition to expect that their God would perform miracles for them, they found none in their own time; knowing that God sent His true prophets to reveal His will to their ancestors, they themselves found fewer and fewer true prophets and finally none at all.[6] From lessons preached by Jeremiah, Ezekiel, and the book of Chronicles, they learned that God Himself had set over them their foreign rulers and would punish them severely if they rebelled. Accordingly, Jews for centuries were loyal to their pagan kings.[7] If the signs of the times should indicate that the delay was coming to an end, Jews would infer that the complete fulfillment of the prophecies was imminent, and some of them might rise in revolt while others might expect that God by Himself would accomplish all.

The events of the years from the 170s down to 134 B.C.E., narrated in 1 and 2 Maccabees, were epoch-making in the history of the Jews and in the development of Jewish eschatology. In particular, a series of disasters came upon the Jews, contrary to God's promises through the true prophets that nothing of the kind could happen after the return from the Babylonian exile:[8] In 169 B.C.E. King Antiochus IV sacked the temple and Jerusalem;[9] in 167 his commander Apollonius perpetrated a massacre in the Holy City and took large numbers of Jews captive;[10] later in 167 Antiochus IV imposed upon the Jews an idolatrous cult and made death the penalty for obeying the Torah and for refusing to observe the imposed cult.[11]

The response of most believing Jews to those disasters was to search the scriptures for guidance. Surely they were part of God's plan. Surely the true prophets must have foreseen them and given instructions how to respond. But no prophet had predicted that Israelites in their own land would be forced to worship idols! Nevertheless several prophets had predicted a time of terrible troubles during the Last Days before the Great Redemption.[12] Pious Jews were quick to assume they were living in that penultimate time of troubles.

In the period between 167 and 161 B.C.E. pious Jews made up for what the true prophets had failed to do: They produced texts in which the disasters of their own time were "predicted" and in which God's spokesmen gave counsel for the present and hope for the future.[13] Two sets of these texts thereafter exerted profound influence on the evolution of messianic figures in the beliefs of Jewish and Christian sects: Daniel 7–12 and 1 Enoch 85–90.[14] In both sets, the real author's present closely reflects events from the times of Judas Maccabeus.[15] In both we find the belief expressed that the present sufferings of the Jews are the last climactic stage of seventy periods of punishment imposed by God for heinous sins committed before the destruction of the temple (Dan. 9:24, 1 Enoch 89:56–67). If the authors by skill or luck had an accurate chronology, the sins occurred ca. 654 B.C.E., in the reign of Manasseh, archsinner among the kings of Judah. If the persecutions were part of a sentence imposed by

God, what could the pious do but endure them until God's appointed time for their release? The authors tried to predict the coming of that time.

In Daniel 7:13–14, 22, appears the prediction that imperial power will come to the grievously persecuted righteous Jews ("the Saints of the Most High"). The collectivity of those "Saints" is there symbolized by a figure described as like a "human being" or "Son of Man." A Jew (or Christian) who thought of deliverance as coming through superhuman beings and of power as being exerted by kings could easily take that figure to be a superhuman savior (despite the descriptive epithet, "human being") or a king. Nowhere in the book of Daniel is there an allusion to David. Daniel 12:2–3 is the earliest Jewish text to predict in absolutely unambiguous fashion a resurrection of the righteous dead for glory; it also predicts a punishment of the wicked. Daniel 7 reached its final form in 167, and one can demonstrate that Daniel 7:25 means that the prediction would be fulfilled with the coming of the sabbatical year in Tishri, 164 B.C.E.[16] Daniel 12:2–3 can be shown to have been written before Antiochus IV marched eastward in June, 165, and Daniel 12:11–12 predicted that the great fulfillment would be complete by August 12, 163, 1,335 days after the desecration of the temple altar on 25 Kislev, 167. Throughout Daniel 7–10 the Second Temple is held to be God's Chosen Place.[17]

I shall demonstrate elsewhere that 1 Enoch 90:6–39 is the result of a series of rewritings of a text first composed at the end of the third century B.C.E.; the rewritings all occurred in response to events in the career of Judas Maccabaeus before his death in 160 B.C.E.[18] The writer's sectarian beliefs were different from those of the author of Daniel, and the passage is largely, if not completely, independent of Daniel.[19] The messianic elements of the extant text may (or may not) all go back to the earlier original. In any case, the passage as it stands is a remarkably early example of bringing together around a single royal figure the fulfillment of most if not all of the messianic prophecies. The text does not contain the word "Messiah," and there is some doubt that 1 Enoch 90:33 refers to a resurrection of the dead rather than to an ingathering of the living exiles.[20] Unlike the book of Daniel, 1 Enoch 90:6–39 contains a figure demonstrably connected with David.

The commanding figure of 1 Enoch 90:37–38 is surely royal and rules over Jews and gentiles after the great fulfillment, after all wickedness has been defeated and all pagans converted and humanity restored to the longevity that characterized the patriarchs (symbolized in Enoch's vision by the sheep and other animals turning into bulls).[21] We are thus entitled to speak of him as a Messiah. His person and those of the remiss angelic shepherds of God's flock in 1 Enoch 89:59–90:25 are derived from Ezekiel 34, where "David" will rule over the Chosen People after God delivers them from evil and brings retribution on the bad shepherds. Both in Ezekiel and in 1 Enoch, the great king comes after the great miracles and divine judgments have occurred. He has no role in accomplishing them. From the fact that 1 Enoch 89:59–90:25 is derived from Ezekiel 34, we can infer that at least one can call this Messiah "David." Did the writer of that text think it was a mere matter of the king's bearing that name? The writer was at least a spiritual (and perhaps a physical) ancestor of the Qumran sect, who certainly believed in a Messiah descended from David. Accordingly, we may assume that the Messiah of 1 Enoch 90:37–38 also is descended from David.[22] The writer holds that all offerings at the Second Temple were unclean (89:73) and predicts that it will be replaced by another, which will descend from heaven (90:28–29).

The authors of Israelite prophecy were seldom if ever interested in the remote future, and the audiences who preserved their works were chiefly interested in the present and in a future that included little if any more than their own lifetimes. For Isaiah, the "end of days" or "days to come" (*ʾaḥărīt hayyāmīm*) of his Chapter 2 were probably no more remote than that.[23] Certainly the writers of the predictions in 1 Enoch and Daniel believed they were living in the last days before God's great intervention.

Thus, signs of the times could lead Jews of the second century B.C.E. to expect imminent fulfillment of the glorious prophecies, and Daniel 7–12 and 1 Enoch 85–90 as well as other texts attest that Jews who lived in the times narrated in 1 and 2 Maccabees had such expectations. Nevertheless, the word "Messiah" (whether in transliterated Hebrew or in Greek) does not occur in either book of Maccabees. The writers who produced them certainly knew the predictions of the Torah and the Prophets. One can demonstrate that they knew Daniel 7–12 and perhaps also 1 Enoch 85–90.[24] The writers believed that important aspects of the Age of Wrath had run their course and were now past. Yet the books contain no hint of the expected coming of a wonderful king descended from David or of a figure called the "Son of Man." This surprising fact demands explanation. The causes can be found in the character of the content of the two books.

1 Maccabees is a history written to demonstrate the right of the Hasmonaean dynasty, descended from the zealous priest Mattathias and his son Simon, to be hereditary high priests and princes ruling the Jews.[25] Never does the author write anything that would suggest there was doubt among Jews concerning God's election of the Second Temple. From clues in the book and from other evidence one can establish that it was written ca. 90 B.C.E., in the reign of the Hasmonaean king, Alexander Jannaeus.[26] We shall refer to the author as the "Hasmonaean propagandist."

2 Maccabees is composite. It begins with two letters, each written to induce the Jews of Egypt to observe the festival commemorating the purification in 164 B.C.E. of the temple of Jerusalem. The first letter (2 Macc. 1:1–10a) contains nothing connected with messianic figures; we shall not

consider it further. Let us call the second letter (2 Macc. 1:10b–2:18) "Epistle 2" ("Ep. 2"). Epistle 2 is an important document for our study. It purports to have been sent by the Jews of Jerusalem and Judaea and by Judas Maccabaeus to Aristobulus, the Jewish philosopher of priestly stock, and to the Jews of Egypt; in fact, it was forged late in 103 B.C.E., long after Judas' death in 160. The bulk of the letter (1:18–2:18) serves to prove that important aspects of the Age of Wrath have ended forever, especially some which had cast doubt on God's election of the second temple. The letter concludes with a vigorous expression (2:17–18) of confidence in the present situation of the Chosen People and of hope that God will speedily fulfill his promises and put an end to all aspects of the Age of Wrath.[27] It also contains a prayer for the end of the Age of Wrath (1:24–29). Obviously, the author believed that Age had not yet completely ended.

We shall call the remainder of 2 Maccabees the "Abridged History." Demonstrably it was originally separate from the two letters. It is an anonymous abridgment of a history by one Jason of Cyrene of the wars of Judas Maccabaeus and his brothers. Nothing further is known of the unabridged work or of its author or the abridger. One purpose of the Abridged History is to oppose the dynastic claims of the Hasmonaeans. Another is to demonstrate that although the Second Temple is not yet the exclusive location for sacrifical worship demanded by Deuteronomy 12:5–14, there are important senses in which it is now God's Chosen Place. From the content of the abridgment and other evidence, one can infer that the unabridged work was written by 86 and the abridgement by 63 B.C.E.[28]

1 Maccabees

The predictions of Daniel and Enoch are never mentioned in 1 Maccabees, but the attitude of the Hasmonaean propagandist toward them is clear. He knew that the course of history had proved them false: There had been no miraculous manifestations of God and His power after the coming of the sabbatical year in 164 B.C.E. and during the lifetime of Judas Maccabaeus. The Hasmonaean propagandist was intensely hostile to the following fundamental teachings of the book of Daniel: (1) that God Himself decreed the persecution of the Jews by Antiochus IV as the last stage of their punishment for sins committed some 490 years before (Dan. 9:24); (2) that therefore Jews ought to accept the divine decree and suffer torture and death as martyrs until the appointed time for God's intervention, at most a few years away (Dan. 7:21–27, 9:24, 11:33, 35, 12:10–12); (3) that those pious Jews who perished would be resurrected and rewarded (Dan. 12:2–3); and (4) that the Hasmonaean revolt at best was a "small help," and it was an act of "slippery treachery" *(hălaqlāqōt)* for pious Jews to join forces with the Hasmonaeans (Dan. 11:34).

The Hasmonaean propagandist held, on the contrary, that the recent sins of Hellenizing Jews had provoked God into using Antiochus IV as His punishing instrument; unresisting martyrdom was disgraceful and brought the martyrs no reward but only their own deaths.[29] False, in his view, was the belief in the resurrection, which served to compensate the martyrs for their suffering.[30] He went out of his way to contradict the mistaken predictions in Daniel 7–12 and wrote barbed parodies of their words to point up their falsity.[31]

The Hasmonaean propagandist had less reason to hate the revelations in 1 Enoch 90, which endorsed the career of Judas Maccabaeus. But he resented their falsity: God did not perform His great intervention while Judas Maccabaeus still lived. He also seems to have resented the effect those revelations must have had on Judas, inspiring him to believe he would not be killed but would live to see that great intervention, so that he went into battle against overwhelming odds and lost his life. The barbed remarks at 1 Maccabees 9:27 may well allude to the falsity of 1 Enoch 90.[32] Moreover, the seer of 1 Enoch 90:37–38 reiterated the prediction of a Messiah descended from David. The Hasmonaean propagandist, on the contrary, wrote to prove that God's instrument for bringing permanent victory to the Jews was the Hasmonaean dynasty,[33] and he took care at 1 Maccabees 2:57 to hint that God's election of David's dynasty might not be permanent.[34] At the very least, he quoted the resolution of the Jews, that the Hasmonaeans had the right to be princes and high priests over the Chosen People "Until a true prophet shall arise."[35] Writing in the reign of King Alexander Jannaeus, the author of 1 Maccabees knew of the strong claims of the king's father, the Hasmonaean prince John Hyrcanus, to be a true prophet.[36]

The Hasmonaean propagandist could not deny the authority of the glorious predictions that constituted so important a part of the words of the accepted "true" prophets. Indeed, as a believing Jew with high hopes for the future, he had no desire to cast doubt on those predictions. One might expect him to make every effort to prove that they were being fulfilled through the Hasmonaeans.

The predictions of how God after the end of the Babylonian exile would bring about a great restored Israel in a perfected world can be divided into two classes: those that could conceivably be fulfilled by Jewish mortals (e.g., conquest of Moab, Ammon, and Philistia; military security for Judaea),[37] and those that could be fulfilled only by a supernatural power (e.g., creation of new heavens and a new earth, resurrection of the dead, streaming of the gentiles of their own free will to Jerusalem to learn the ways of the God of Jacob).[38] The Hasmonaean propagandist does not touch the predictions that could be fulfilled only by a supernatural power,[39] but he exploits some of his opportunities to suggest that Hasmonaeans fulfilled those possible for mortals, as we shall see, and one could go on to trace the efforts of Hasmonaeans to fulfill them after the times narrated in 1 Maccabees.[40]

Interesting, however, is the fact that the Hasmonaean propagandist abstains from using many of his opportunities to portray the members of the dynasty as fulfilling prophecies. Let us give a brief survey of what he might have done and what he actually did.

For the Hasmonaeans and their propagandist, the first decisive step in ending the Age of Wrath was Mattathias' act of zeal: He refused to obey the king's edict to observe the imposed cult, slew a Jew who was about to comply and killed the royal official enforcing compliance, and called upon all Jews loyal to the Torah to follow him into rebellion. Thus, he broke with the doctrine Jews had followed during the centuries of the Age of Wrath, that the Chosen People must not rebel against their foreign kings because God had placed those kings in power and would punish rebellion.[41] The next decisive steps were the mighty deeds of Judas Maccabaeus and his men as they battled the armies of Seleucid kings. And next were the similar mighty acts of Judas' brothers, Jonathan and Simon. The Hasmonaean propagandist gives all these due prominence. The Hasmonaeans' acts of insubordination against the kings brought the Jews, not punishment inflicted through the wrath of God, but liberation. For the Hasmonaeans and their propagandist, these facts proved that the Age of Wrath was at last approaching its full end, though the miserable deaths of Judas, Jonathan, and Simon and the vicissitudes of Simon's heirs strongly suggested that God's wrath still had a few more years to act upon the Jews.

The Jews called the Seleucid empire of Antiochus IV "Greece" *(Yāwān)*.[42] A prophecy of God's great final intervention predicted that He would "make the sons of Zion mighty against the sons of *Yāwān*" (Zech. 9:13), and there can be no doubt that this prophecy was being read in Mattathias' lifetime, because there is an allusion to Zechariah 9:8 at Daniel 11:20.[43] The author of 1 Maccabees repeatedly echoes the wording of the Hebrew Bible as he narrates the exploits of his heroes. Would not one expect him to echo Zechariah 9:13 at least once, in telling of Mattathias or Judas or Jonathan or Simon or their followers as "might against *Yāwān*"? Not once does he do so! Indeed, relatively infrequent are the Hasmonaean propagandist's allusions, in telling of his heroes, to the books of the Writing Prophets. His most audacious echoes of those books occur in connection with Judas Maccabaeus. In the "Ode to Judas" with which he introduces the great Maccabaeus' career, he says, "His renown spread to the end of the earth, as he gathered together those who were astray"

(1 Macc. 3:9). The second half of the verse certainly echoes Isaiah 11:12; the first half may well echo Isaiah 12:5. God is the subject of the verbs in both verses in Isaiah. Surely the Hasmonaean propagandist is portraying Judas as God's agent in the fulfillment of Isaiah 11:12 and probably of Isaiah 12:5 as well.[44] Less certain[45] but similarly audacious is the probable allusion to Isaiah 52:12 at 1 Maccabees 5:53: Judas is God's agent in fulfilling His promise to be the rear guard gathering up the stragglers.[46] At 1 Maccabees 4:58 we read, "The shame inflicted by the gentiles was removed." "The shame inflicted by the gentiles" probably is an echo of Isaiah 25:8 and Ezekiel 36:4, so as to suggest that God has fulfilled those verses through the dedication of the new temple altar by Judas and his men.

Many of the sects of pious Jews could agree that Judas Maccabaeus was the Lord's agent.[47] More controversial were his brothers, first Jonathan and finally Simon, real founder of the Hasmonaean dynasty.[48] Would not one expect the Hasmonaean propagandist to apply the language of biblical prophecy to Simon? In fact, in his "Ode to Simon" (1 Macc. 14:4–15), he does use at 14:8 the words of Leviticus 26:4, Ezekiel 34:27, and Zechariah 8:12; at 14:9 he uses the words of Zechariah 8:4;[49] and one might think he uses at 14:12 the words of Micah 4:4 and Zechariah 3:10.[50]

In telling of Simon's climactic achievement, the liberation of Israel from tribute-paying bondage, the Hasmonaean propagandist may have echoed prophecies, but more likely he avoided doing so. At 1 Maccabees 13:41 we read that "the yoke of the gentiles was lifted from Israel." In fact, what was lifted was the "yoke" of the Seleucid empire, the latter-day Assyria.[51] No Jewish Bible-reader could fail to think of Isaiah 10:27 and 14:25, but there is rather good reason to think that the Hasmonaean propagandist deliberately avoided writing an exact echo of those verses. Explainable is the omission of a word corresponding to the Hebrew *subbolo* ("his burden") of Isaiah 10:27 and 14:25. The Greek of both verses shows that Jews of the Hellenistic period did not know the meaning of the word. But the word $\dot{\eta}\rho\theta\eta$ ("was lifted") in the Greek text of 1 Maccabees 13:41 probably indicates that the Hasmonaean propagandist used a Hebrew verb from a root different from the one *(sūr)* employed at Isaiah 10:27 and 14:25, for at both places in Isaiah the Greek renders the Hebrew word by $\dot{\alpha}\rho\alpha\iota\epsilon\theta\dot{\eta}\sigma\epsilon\tau\alpha\iota$, not by a form of $\alpha\dot{\iota}\rho\epsilon\iota\nu$, the verb which $\dot{\eta}\rho\theta\eta$ is the first aorist passive.[52]

In most instances, the author of 1 Maccabees in writing of his heroes, the Hasmonaean brothers, seems deliberately to have departed from or to have avoided the wording of biblical prophecies. Repeatedly he tells of the victories they won in the land of the Philistines, and he also tells of their victories in Ammon, Moab, and Edom, but not once does he echo the prophecies of conquests there.[53]

One can understand the Hasmonaean propagandist's failure to put into his narrative of Jonathan's exploits allusions to prophecies of dynastic glory. The author of 1 Maccabees was a partisan of Simon's heirs, and Jonathan had descendants who might contest their claims to rule.[54] But the Hasmonaean propagandist takes pains to identify Jonathan as a judge (1 Macc. 9:73). Biblical judges were not dynastic princes whose sons inherited their power. And even so, the Hasmonaean propagandist does not echo Isaiah 1:26 at 1 Maccabees 9:73.

Indeed, though, most believing Jews facing the persecution under Antiochus IV probably thought they were living in the prophesied time of troubles immediately before the final Great Redemption, the Hasmonaean propagandist regarded that response to the dreadful challenge as disastrously wrong. He displays how such beliefs brought only disappointment and death to those who bravely refused to violate the Torah and waited for God's supposedly imminent fulfillment of the prophecies. He was aware how Judas Maccabaeus' belief that he was living in the time of fulfillment of prophecies misled him to go into hopeless battle and to perish, and he may well have thought similar beliefs led Jonathan to his doom.[55] More than one generation had elapsed by the time he wrote. It was therefore obvious to the Hasmonaean propagandist that the troubles had not been the prophesied prelude to the Last Days.

I do not think that the way he portrays his heroes is entirely due to hindsight. They never ask for the fulfillment of prophecies and never say they are fulfilling them. Yet a Jewish response to the persecution had to be based on scripture. The Hasmonaean response as portrayed in 1 Maccabees has a consistent character and fits the known conditions of the time. In all probability it is not a mere creation of the author but reflects the actual ideology of Mattathias and his sons.

From the beginning, the Hasmonaean doctrines were so audacious that many pious Jews viewed the party as wicked and opposed it.[56] The Hasmonaeans were ready to engage in acts of war against the royal army, a step that required breaking with the long-held Jewish belief that rebellion would bring disastrous divine punishment. Old Mattathias dared to act on the assumption that a king who commanded Jews to violate the Torah could no longer be ruling Jews by divine right. No prophecy predicted that God's requirement to obey the pagan kings would be repealed before the miraculous end of the Age of Wrath. In Zechariach 9:9–13, before Jews fight Greeks, the Jews have their own king in Jerusalem. Far from having ended at the time Mattathias dared to act, the Age of Wrath was continuing! The old man was a priest, perhaps from a family of some distinction,[57] but he made no claim to have received a new revelation from God either through prophecy or through priestly oracles.

To judge by the account in 1 Maccabees, Mattathias differed from many of his contemporaries in explaining how the persecution fit into God's plan. According to 1 Maccabees, the persecutions were not troubles belonging to the Last Days, nor were they the climactic end to the punishment for preexilic sin. Rather, in origin they were an ordinary punishment brought on by the recent sins of Hellenizing Jews, but Antiochus IV, God's punishing instrument, had exceeded his divine mandate as Assyria in days of yore had exceeded hers (Isa. 10:5–34).[58] We may imagine Mattathias as theorizing that a Jew might dare to resist a pagan ruler who had overstepped the mandate of God. If the persecution was merely an excessive act of God's unruly whip, it would do no good to study prophecies of the Last Days. If the present persecution posed unprecedented problems, it would do no good to look in the laws of the Bible for solutions. But the heroes of the biblical narratives had also had to face problems that for those heroes were unprecedented. Mattathias' religious approach as presented by the Hasmonaean propagandist was revolutionary in its time: Follow the glorious *examples* of the heroes of the past!

No law, no prophecy justified rebelling against Antiochus. If Mattathias had based his acts upon a scriptural law or prophecy, the careful author of 1 Maccabees surely would have quoted it. Instead, the author does everything possible to portray Mattathias' act of zeal as equivalent to Phineas' act of zeal in Numbers 25. Just as Phineas showed "zeal" and acted on behalf of the "anger" of the Lord (Num. 25:11) and stabbed the sinful couple in their illicit bedroom,[59] the place of their sin (Num. 25:8), so Mattathias was "filled with zeal and anger" and slew the idolater on the altar, the place of his sin (1 Macc. 2:24–26).

The Hasmonaean propagandist pushes the principle of following the examples of the heroes of scripture far beyond the point of justifying Mattathias' act of zeal: He has old Mattathias on his deathbed urge his sons (1 Macc. 2:51–61) to note the examples of how God rewarded the brave and righteous conduct of Abraham, Joseph, Phineas, Joshua, Caleb, David, Elijah, Hananiah, Azariah, Mishael, and Daniel. The implication is that by emulating the conduct of those heroes, the sons will earn similar rewards: God will regard them, like Abraham, as righteous; they will be raised to high office under kings, like Joseph; they will found a high priestly dynasty, like Phineas; they will hold judgely power, like Joshua; they will receive territory of their own, like Caleb; they will become kings, like David. They may even aspire to have God perform for them miracles as he did for Elijah, Hananiah, Azariah, Mishael, and Daniel.

Throughout the rest of his book, the Hasmonaean propagandist echoes the language of biblical stories of heroes, from Judges, 1–2 Samuel, and 1–2 Kings, in order to base the dynastic claims of the Hasmonaeans on the fact that their accomplishments equaled those that earned such rewards for those heroes.[60] At 1 Maccabees 5:62 the author is at his most audacious in asserting for the Hasmonaeans the prerogatives reserved for David's line in earlier Jewish tradition.

Indeed, he there calls Mattathias and his descendants "that seed of men to whom had been granted the deliverance of Israel through their agency."[61] The expression is strange both in the Greek and in the reconstructed original Hebrew *(ăsher lāhem nitt^enāh y^ešū⟨at yisrā⟩ēl b^eyādām)*. The use of the passive voice is simply an instance of the Hasmonaean propagandist's habitual avoidance of speaking directly of God, but "deliverance of Israel through their agency" is an unnatural way of saying "that they would be the deliverers of Israel." The strange syntax can have come only from 2 Samuel 3:18, " . . . The Lord hath spoken of David saying, 'Deliverance of [*hōshīa⟨*] My people of Israel is through the agency of David My servant. . . .'" The verse in 2 Samuel refers to David, yet the Hasmonaean propagandist uses its language to refer to the Hasmonaeans.[62]

Thus the echoes in 1 Maccabees from the biblical histories far outnumber the allusions to the Writing Prophets. By this procedure, the Hasmonaean propagandist avoided two dangers. In the first place, Jews had been disastrously wrong in identifying their own time with the predicted End of Days. If the reigns of the Hasmonaeans should prove to be that very time, well and good, but their claims should not depend upon any particular interpretation of prophecies the meaning of which was a matter of bitter controversy. In the second place, there were predictions about the great postexilic dynasty of kings that could not possibly be dissociated from the line of David, to which the Hasmonaeans did not belong.[63] Hasmonaean claims to have fulfilled any of those predictions would immediately be rejected as illegitimate.

The Hasmonaean propagandist did not wish to give up completely the possibility of leading his readers to believe that Mattathias' sons fulfilled the words of the prophets. Without echoing the words of the prophecies, he could tell of the deeds of his heroes that looked as if they were fulfillments and he could then leave it to Jewish Bible-readers to infer the point. He seems to have done so repeatedly.[64] Caution thus led the Hasmonaean propagandist to base his case for the rights of the dynasty upon their achievements and how they equaled those of earlier heroes of scripture; for the most part he avoided making direct claims that they were the fulfillers of the glorious prophecies. His cautious procedure did not suffice to protect Alexander Jannaeus from the dilemmas posed by the words of the prophets for anyone who claimed to be a postexilic king of the Jews. True prophets had promised that the postexilic king would be invincible, winning victories over all neighboring peoples. If Jannaeus did not try to make the predicted conquests, Jews would be quick to regard his rule as illegitimate. In fact, he did attempt to make those conquests. As a result, with every defeat of the king who prophecy predicted should be invincible, Jews regarded him as an impostor with no right to be king and rebelled against him. His long series of wars against foreigners and against his own people shows how he was, in effect, a prisoner of the prophecies.[65]

In another respect the Hasmonaean propagandist was incautious. Although the defeats and deaths of his heroes made it impossible for him to hold that the Age of God's wrath was over, he still believed that the worst part of that Age was past. He had no doubt that Jews now had the right if not the duty to rebel against the pagan kings ruling over them. He held that in the reign of Simon God had lifted the yoke of subservience to the gentiles that He had imposed upon His sinful chosen people.[66] He asserted that God had chosen the Hasmonaean dynasty to bring permanent victory to Israel.[67]

The Hasmonaean propagandist never found an answer to the difficult question, "Precisely what aspects of God's wrath still operate today upon the Jews?" He thus was left without any easy theological explanation for the deaths of his heroes – Judas, Jonathan, and Simon. He tells of the aftermath of Judas' death in language appropriate for narrating an Age of God's Wrath (1 Macc. 9:23–27), but he portrays the aftermath of Jonathan's fall only as a time of wicked gentile plotting (1 Macc. 12:53) (gentiles can plot against Israel even in an Age of God's Favor). Hardest of all to explain was Simon's death, and the Hasmonaean propagandist tells of it without any theological comment. Jannaeus was trapped by the implications of the title "king." But even if a descendant of Simon refrained from assuming the royal title, the theology of the author of 1 Maccabees left the member of a dynasty supposed to bring permanent victory with no easy way to explain a defeat.

The Second Letter at the Head of 2 Maccabees

To understand the content of Epistle 2 one must know something of its background. Late in 163 or early in 162 B.C.E., the regime of Antiochus V, to which Judaea was subject, passed over Onias IV, rightful heir of the Zadokite–Oniad line of high priests, and gave the high priesthood instead to Alcimus, who was not a member of that line. Thereupon, Onias IV left Judaea for Egypt. There, through good service, he earned the favor of King Ptolemy VI and eventually won royal permission to build at Leontopolis in Egypt a Jewish temple where sacrifices were offered to the Lord. Although this schismatic rival to the temple of Jerusalem might seem a violation of the prohibitions at Deuteronomy 12:5–14 against offering sacrifices in any place except the one chosen by God, surviving texts show many Jews believed that God in 586 B.C.E. had revoked His election of

Jerusalem when He allowed the temple to be destroyed. God had never given the sign to prove He had chosen the Second Temple of Jerusalem.[68]

Onias IV and his Oniad family became leaders of the Jews of Egypt and stood loyally by the dynasty of Ptolemy VI and his wife, Cleopatra II. Later, in 107 B.C.E., civil war broke out between Cleopatra III (the daughter of that royal couple) and her own son, Ptolemy IX. In the time of this civil war, the chief Oniads were Chelkias and Ananias, sons of Onias IV. They served Cleopatra as commanders. In 103 B.C.E., when Ptolemy IX from Cyprus invaded Palestine and attacked Judaea, which was then under the rule of the Hasmonaean king and high priest Alexander Jannaeus, Cleopatra III and her Jewish commanders marched into Asia and beat Ptolemy off. Chelkias died in the course of the fighting, but Oniad Ananias himself endorsed Jannaeus' dynastic claims and convinced Cleopatra not to annex Judaea. Trumped in Judaea, Ptolemy saw that if he could seize control of Egypt, he still might decisively defeat his mother, who was in Asia with her army. In the second half of 103 he invaded Egypt. The Jews of Egypt, so strongly identified with the cause of Cleopatra III, had much to fear from the hostility of Ptolemy IX. His invasion confronted them with clear and present danger.[69]

The author probably was in Egypt when he forged Epistle 2 in late November or early December, 103 B.C.E. He meant to preach the following messages to the Jews of Egypt in their hour of danger. First, that they should observe the festival now called Hanukkah, in honor of the purification of the temple of Jerusalem by Judas Maccabaeus and his followers. That observance would be a symbolic expression of the writer's more fundamental second message: that the temple of Jerusalem was still God's Chosen Place, so that the Jews of Egypt were sinning in accepting or even tolerating the temple of Leontopolis. Third, God's promised salvation for the Jews was being realized in Judaea through the Hasmonaean dynasty of high priests, princes, and kings. Epistle 2 thus endorses the dynastic claims of the Hasmonaeans, but its emphases and arguments are very different from those of 1 Maccabees.

In the meager narrative in Epistle 2 telling of the supposed events culminating in the death of Antiochus IV in 164 B.C.E. (2 Macc. 1:11–17), God is the sole power named as active against the enemies of the Jews; nothing is said of the victories of Judas Maccabaeus and his brothers and their followers. The fact may well reflect the nature of the audience of Egyptian Jews in 103 B.C.E., who, it seems, tended to favor the Oniads and to regard the Hasmonaeans as usurpers. It would have been bad tactics for the author to begin the letter by rousing the hostility of his audience. But all Jews of Ptolemaic Egypt would hear with pleasure of God's victory over the wicked Seleucid king, Antiochus IV.

In the very first verse after the salutation, Epistle 2 implies, in agreement with 1 Maccabees, that the Jews are now permitted to rebel against their foreign king. The requirement of the full Age of Wrath, that Jews be loyal even to oppressors, has passed away. The bulk of Epistle 2 (2 Macc. 1:12–2:15, 18) serves to prove that despite the shortcomings of the Second Temple of Jerusalem, it is indeed the Chosen Place. God brought gruesome death upon the king who had made war upon the Holy City (2 Macc. 1:12–17). God made possible the purification of His temple (1:18, 2:18). The Second Temple did not need to have the Lord's election of it attested by miraculous fire from heaven, because its fire was in fact the wondrously preserved fire of the First Temple (2 Macc. 1:19–36). True, the Second Temple lacked ark, tabernacle, and incense altar, but that fact was God's will; the missing sacred articles would be restored in His own Time of Mercy (2 Macc. 2:1–8). The present status of the Second Temple itself marks an important abatement of God's wrath.

The Days of Purification were a rite celebrating a victory of the Hasmonaeans, however much one might try to minimize the connection between the observance and the dynasty.[70] To ask that those Days be observed was therefore to give some endorsement to Hasmonaeans, at least to Judas Maccabaeus, whose generalship led to the victories that made possible the purification of the temple. At 2 Maccabees 2:17, the author of Epistle 2 went much further in supporting the Hasmonaeans. If my restoration of the original text is correct, he there presents Judas Maccabaeus and the pious Jews as asserting confidently in 164 B.C.E., "God, Who saved His entire people and restored the heritage to us all will also restore the kingdom and the priesthood and the sanctification."[71]

The writer has just demonstrated that the Second Temple is God's Chosen Place. Hence, when he employs the word "heritage," he alludes primarily to its occurrence in Deuteronomy 12:9–14: if Jews possess the heritage, i.e., the Promised Land, they are not permitted to offer sacrifices except at that Chosen Place. One therefore cannot tell whether the author is alluding also to Isaiah 57:13, 58:14, Jeremiah 3:18–19, 12:14–15, 49:8, Zechariah 8:12, which predict restoration of the heritage. In any case, he greatly exaggerates the extent of the Jews' recovery of promised territory in 164 B.C.E. Only Jannaeus' vigorous territorial achievements and aspirations could bring anything like literal truth to a claim that the heritage had been restored.

As for "the kingdom and the priesthood and the sanctification," those words are taken from Exodus 19:6 as read in the second century B.C.E., a verse promising those three attributes to the Chosen People.[72] If my reconstruction of the text is right, the writer correctly refrained from having Judas Maccabaeus and his contemporaries claim that in their time God had restored the three attributes promised at Exodus 19:6. Rather, he made them express their confidence, using the future tense, that the attributes would be restored in the near[73] future. For an author writing in 103 B.C.E., only in the reigns of the Hasmonaean kings, Judas Aristobulus I and Alexander Jannaeus, could the Jews have a claim to have recovered the complete triad of kingdom, priesthood, and sanctification, and there is good reason to believe that the Hasmonaeans in the time of Judas Maccabaeus did not yet have such audacious aspirations.[74] Consequently, the author of Epistle 2 here reflects and endorses the achievements and aspirations of Alexander Jannaeus.

We have admitted the possibility that the word "heritage" in 2 Maccabees 2:17 is an allusion to passages in the Writing Prophets, but that is far from being a certainty. The allusion there may be only to Deuteronomy 12:9. If it is, the author of Epistle 2, in making assertions about the present sanctity of the Second Temple and about the achievements and aspirations of the Hasmonaeans, has refrained as conspicuously as the Hasmonaean propagandist from echoing the words of books of the Writing Prophets (the author of Ep. 2 at 2 Macc. 2:7–8 did fabricate unambiguous utterances of Jeremiah to drive home important points).

On the other hand, in contrast to the writer of 1 Maccabees, the author of Epistle 2 does not hesitate to specify what has not yet been accomplished, i.e., what aspects still continue of the Age of Wrath. He quotes in full the prayer (2 Macc. 1:24–29) that, he says, was recited on the Day of the Fire,[75] when the wondrously preserved fire from the first temple was ignited upon the altar of the second. He could have had only one reason to quote the passage: He wanted the Jews of Egypt to use it as part of the observance of the Days of Purification.[76] The prayer asks that God guard Israel and make her holy; that He gather the dispersed exiles and free those who are enslaved among the nations; that He be mindful of the Jews, whom the gentiles despise and abominate; that He take vengeance upon the oppressors; and that He plant His people in His Holy Place as Moses said (Exod. 15:17).

This prayer, in alluding to still unfulfilled promises and to continuing aspects of the Age of Wrath, does echo words of the Writing Prophets.[77] Though the great prophetic forecasts for the postexilic era had predicted a prompt ingathering of the exiled Jews[78] and a prompt punishment of their oppressors,[79] the author of Epistle 2 concedes the obvious truth, that those promises were still unfulfilled in 164 and even in 103 B.C.E. Despite the successes and aspirations of Jannaeus, Judaea in 103 B.C.E. obviously still lacked complete sanctification: It still was vulnerable to gentile attack. Nevertheless, the author of Epistle 2 ends with the hope that the last remnants of the Age of Wrath will *speedily* pass away, with the renewed fulfilment of Exodus 15:17, i.e., a new Exodus by which the exiles will return to be planted again in God's Holy Place.

As a supporter of the dynastic claims of the Hasmonaeans, the author of Epistle 2 passed over in silence the prophecies that predicted a king descended from David. Like the Hasmonaeans, he also passed over in silence the revelations of 1 Enoch 85–90 and Daniel 7–12 and with them the belief in the resurrection. We may infer that he rejected both the revelations and the belief.

The Abridged History

We do not possess the original work of Jason of Cyrene. All we have of it is the anonymous Abridged History. Although I interpret the abridger's preface (2 Macc. 2:19–32) as a promise that the abridgment faithfully reflects the original,[80] skeptics may not accept my interpretation or may not choose to believe the abridger kept that promise. I shall use "our writer" in order to have a convenient brief expression, meaning "Jason of Cyrene or the abridger," so as to designate the person responsible for the views expressed in the Abridged History.

Our writer knows that the glorious predictions of the canonical prophets and Daniel were at best incompletely fulfilled, but he keeps his faith that they are true. Furthermore, he knew of the shortcomings of the second temple, but he kept his faith that it was holy. He believed that some aspects of the Age of Wrath had run their course and reached their end. Indeed, unlike the Hasmonaean propagandist, he maintained that truly supernatural miracles had occurred in the Present Age. For our writer, this and other abatements of the Age of Wrath did not mean that all aspects of that Age had passed away. Writing in the first half of the first century B.C.E., he knew (like the Hasmonaean propagandist and unlike the seers of Daniel and 1 Enoch) that the troubles of 169–164 B.C.E. had not been those of the Last Days. Unlike the Hasmonaean propagandist, our writer defined the conditions of the Present Age as falling far short of the predicted period of Israel's unending bliss. Israel can still sin and, on sinning, will bring upon herself and even upon the temple the calamitous wrath of God. Even so, paradoxically, our writer finds it possible to assert that God's promise at Isaiah 54:10 is already fulfilled, "God never lets His mercy depart from us. Rather, though He teaches us by calamity, He never deserts His people" (2 Macc. 6:16).

On the other hand, our writer is no more successful than the Hasmonaean propagandist in finding a theological explanation for some of the misfortunes of his heroes. Why should pious Onias III have had to face the plotting of wicked Simon and Menelaus, and why should he have been murdered (2 Macc. 3:4–6, 4:1–6, 33–34)? Why should Razis have been driven to suicide (2 Macc. 14:37–46)? Like the Hasmonaean propagandist, our writer in these instances tells the difficult truth without theological comment.

The Abridged History shows great interest in the sanctity of the Second Temple. Near the very beginning of the narrative, our writer may well be claiming that prophecies of Isaiah concerning the Second Temple were fulfilled in the time of the high priest Onias III, for 2 Maccabees 3:2–3 probably draws on Isaiah 60:3, 7, 10. Our writer then turns to tell the story of the thwarting of Heliodorus (2 Macc. 3:4–39), the first miracle attested for the Second Temple. It constituted the first important break in the manifestations of the Age of Wrath (2 Macc. 3:30 probably draws on Isa. 60:7). God had at last ended His centuries-long abstention from giving supernatural aid to His Chosen People.[81] The thwarting of Heliodorus is a fulfillment of Zechariah 9:8. It is likely that 2 Maccabees 3:39 contains a paraphrase of Zechariah 9:8.[82]

Our writer agreed with the Hasmonaean propagandist in holding that the sins of the Hellenizing high priest, Jason the Oniad, and of his followers provoked the wrath of God and caused Him to use Antiochus IV as His punishing instrument.[83] Our writer also agreed that thereupon Antiochus IV in his arrogance exceeded his mandate and went on to persecute the Jews and their religion.[84] In these points, Jason of Cyrene departed from the views of the seers of Daniel and 1 Enoch, who say nothing of present sin as the cause of God's wrath and regard the persecution as the climactic stage of centuries of punishment for sins committed in the time of the First Temple. Our writer, however, need not have felt that there was any conflict between his own theological explanation of Antiochus' hostile acts and the views of Daniel and 1 Enoch, for he surely agreed that the Age of Wrath had begun in the time of the First Temple.

Allusions in the Abridged History to 1 Enoch are faint and questionable,[85] but it is clear that our writer believed in the revelations of Daniel 7–12. He quotes from them and writes his narrative in a manner that shields them from challenge.[86] His strongest allusions to Daniel (2 Macc. 7:9, 14) are to the verse predicting the resurrection (Dan. 12:2).[87] After 162 B.C.E. believers in Daniel 7–12 faced difficult problems. The revelations had been correct in predicting that the suffering Jews and their temple would win vindication and that the persecuting king would perish, but many other details in the predictions had proved to be false. The Seleucid empire did not fall in the 160s B.C.E., contrary to Daniel 7:11. Jews did not gain imperial or cosmic power, contrary to Daniel 7:13–14, 27, 12:3. The aftermath of the death of Antiochus IV did not fit Daniel 12:1. The chronology of the events was far from fitting Daniel 7:25, 9:24–27, 12:7. There was no resurrection, contrary to Daniel 12:2.

The procedure of believers ever after was like that of Christian Jerome in his *Commentary on Daniel:* The predictions in Daniel 7–12 that had not yet been fulfilled would be fulfilled at some time in the future. But the wording of Daniel 7–12 made it difficult for anyone who knew the history of the times to dissociate many of those predictions from the years 169–162 B.C.E. Moreover, the time for the future fulfilment of the flagrantly unrealized predictions of the end of pagan empires and of imperial and cosmic power for the Jews was obscure, even where the meaning was otherwise clear. It was best to say as little as possible of the predictions. However, Daniel 12:2, the sole unequivocal prediction of the resurrection in the literature of Jewish revelation, was too precious to give up or pass over in silence. One could read the text in such a way as to believe that the resurrection would indeed come after the death of the impious Antiochus IV, King of the North, but would not necessarily follow that event immediately. Accordingly, our writer loudly echoes Daniel 12:2 to preach belief in the resurrection.

Our writer admired Judas Maccabaeus and strove to discredit all other Hasmonaeans.[88] He knew that the terrible events of the 160s B.C.E. had not been the trials of the Last Days, predicted by the Writing Prophets. But the words of those prophets had done much to determine the actions of the embattled Jews of the 160s, shaping especially their expectations and the form of the supernatural apparitions they perceived. These recognizable effects of the words of the Writing Prophets Jason of Cyrene took over from his sources.[89] Our writer, however, chooses the words of his narrative very carefully. Much as he admires Judas Maccabaeus, in telling of that hero's achievements he abstains from echoes of the Writing Prophets.[90] No Hasmonaean, including Maccabaeus, is to be viewed as fulfilling those words!

Perhaps the most striking scriptural allusion in the Abridged History (2 Macc. 8:27) comes from the Book of Samuel (2 Sam. 21:10), the favorite source for the Hasmonaean propagandist. Characteristically, that allusion in its context refers more to God's appreciation of the merit of the martyrs, than to the achievements of Maccabaeus and his men.[91]

In telling of the atrocious sufferings that came upon Israel, our writer shows deep concern to console his pious readers (2 Macc. 6:12–17). He also presents the martyrs as uttering theatrical speeches to encourage themselves and exhort posterity (2 Macc. 6:24–28, 7:6, 9, 11, 14, 16–19, 22–23, 27–38). Furthermore, he sought to discredit the Hasmonaean dynasty, which by his time had "usurped" the high priesthood and the kingship.[92] To encourage the pious readers and to discredit the Hasmonaeans, one procedure would seem to have been obviously effective: allude to the glorious messianic promises attached indissolubly to the dynasty of David, as is done in Psalm of Solomon 17. Our writer could have argued:

Though martyred Israel has to face the tyrant, Antiochus IV, at some time in the future the Chosen People will live secure under the glorious rule of David's heir! Whatever their achievements, the Hasmonaean usurpers have no claim to be fulfilling those glorious prophecies!

The Abridged History, however, contains nothing of the kind. Nowhere does our writer mention David. One would like to know why. Did Jason of Cyrene have evidence that David's line was extinct or had been disqualified by sin? If our writer could predict a resurrection, why could he not predict the coming of a righteous king from the dynasty of David or of David himself? His failure to do so suggests that his sect of Jews, unlike the sect of the seer of 1 Enoch, no longer even thought of a Davidic king. If that possibility seems strange, let us note how there is no mention of David in the book of Daniel and how the Hasmonaean propagandist could hint that David's line received the kingship only "for ages," not forever.[93] True prophets had promised eternal rule to the line of David and had predicted a glorious Davidic "Messiah." How could many Jewish sects have come to the conclusion that those prophecies were void? We do not know. But the evidence seems to show that important Jewish sects of the second and early first centuries B.C.E. disagreed with the seer of 1 Enoch 85–90: They did not believe in the coming of a Davidic Messiah.

ABBREVIATIONS

CD	Document of the Damascus Covenanters, published in Chaim Rabin, *The Zadokite Documents*, (2d ed.; Oxford: Clarendon Press, 1958)
CHJ	*The Cambridge History of Judaism*, ed. W. D. Davies and Louis Finkelstein (Cambridge: Cambridge University Press, forthcoming)
EM	*Entsiqlopediah miqra)it* (Jerusalem: Bialik Institute, 1955–82)
Goldstein, *I Maccabees*	Jonathan A. Goldstein, *I Maccabees* ("Anchor Bible," Vol. 41; Garden City: Doubleday, 1976)
Goldstein, *II Maccabees*	Jonathan A. Goldstein, *II Maccabees* ("Anchor Bible," Vol. 41A: Garden City: Doubleday, 1983)
Nickelsburg, *Literature*	George W. E. Nickelsburg, *Jewish Literature between the Bible and the Mishnah* (Philadelphia: Fortress Press, 1981)
PAAJR	*Proceedings of the American Academy for Jewish Research*
RE	*Realencyclopaedie der klassischen Altertumswissenschaft*, ed. A. von Pauly, G. Wissowa, et al. (Stuttgart: Metzier, 1894–1980)

TDNT   *Theological Dictionary of the New Testament,* ed. Gerhard Kittle (Grand Rapids and London: Eerdmans, 1964–74)

NOTES

1 Isa. 9:1–6, 11:1–10; in this paper I follow Jewish tradition and treat Daniel not as one of the books of the Prophets but as one of the Writings (Hagiographa).

2 Writings of the first century B.C.E.: Psalms of Solomon 17–18 (see Nickelsburg, *Literature,* pp. 203–4, 207–9, and J. H. Charlesworth, "From Jewish Messianology to Christian Christology, this volume). For the Qumran texts containing the word *māshîaḥ* in this sense, see ibid. As for possible earlier use of the word in this sense, one should take note of the messianic passages in the Testaments of the Twelve Patriarchs. Part or even most of the Testaments of the Twelve Patriarchs may go back to the first quarter of the second century B.C.E.; see Elias Bickerman, *Studies in Jewish and Christian History,* Part II ("Arbeiten zur Geschichte des antiken Judentums und des Urchristentums," Band IX; Leiden: Brill, 1980), pp. 1–15, 19–23, and the third paragraph from the end of George W. E. Nickelsburg, "Salvation without and with a Messiah," in this volume. But the messianic passages of the Testaments may well be Christian interpolations. See Bickerman, *Studies,* Part II, pp. 6–8; de Jonge, "*Chriô ktl.* C III. Apocrypha and Pseudepigrapha," TDNT, IX (1974): 512–13; and Charlesworth, "Jewish Messianology."

    The "Parables of Enoch" (1 Enoch 37–71) are difficult to date, but I think the mention of 1 Enoch 56:5 of the Parthians as a menace to Judaea excludes their having been written before the first century B.C.E. (see Nickelsburg, *Literature,* pp. 214–23). Moreover, the "anointed one" of the Parables is a heavenly being (see Nickelsburg, "Salvation") and nothing is said there about his being born on earth to the dynasty of David. True, the language used to describe him and his actions is taken from Isa. 11 and Ps. 2. Isa. 11 is indissolubly connected with the line of Jesse and David. The anointed king of Ps. 2 is not necessarily descended from David, but he certainly is said to be king on Mount Zion. The figure in the Parables may indeed receive the epithet "anointed" because it was used to refer to the Davidic kings (2 Sam. 19:22, 22:51, 23:1, etc.). On the other hand, the heavenly being of the Parables, like the Persian king, Cyrus, is a power from outside Judaea who brings vindication to the suffering righteous, so that his epithet "anointed" may be taken from the description of Cyrus at Isa. 45:1. See also Charlesworth, "Jewish Messianology."

3 On the use of *mšyḥ* in the Jewish Bible, see Hesse, "*Chriô ktl.* B III. *Māshiaḥ* in the Old Testament," TDNT, IX (1974); 501–5, and Jacob Liver, "*Māshîaḥ,*" EM, V (1968): 508–9. As examples of scholarly efforts to explain the evolution of the eschatological term, see Hesse, "*Chriô ktl.* B IV. The Development of Messianic Ideas in Israel," TDNT, IX (1974), 505–9, and Liver, "*Māshîaḥ,*" 507–26.

4　Prophecies about the Age of Mercy: Deut. 30:6, 8, 10, Isa. 54:9–10, Jer. 31:30–39, Ezek. 11:17–20, 36:24–29, 37:21–28. The expression "Age of Wrath" is found at CD 1:5–6; cf. Ezra 9:7–9, Neh. 9:30–37. Some of the relevant texts pretend to have been written in the time before the return from the exile: Dan. 9:12–19, 24, 1 Bar. 2:4–3:8, 1 Enoch 89:58–90:8. On the date and purpose of 1 Baruch, see Jonathan A. Goldstein, "The Apocryphal Book of 1 Baruch," PAAJR 46–47 (1979–80), 179–99.

5　Goldstein, *II Maccabees*, pp. 14–16.

6　Goldstein, *I Maccabees*, pp. 12–13.

7　Goldstein, *II Maccabees*, pp. 150–1; 1 Bar. 1:1–12, 2:21–4; and cf. Rom. 13:1–7.

8　E.g., Isa. 51:7–8, 22; 55:4–10; Jer. 30:23–40, 32:37–44.

9　1 Macc. 1:20–28, 2 Macc. 5:1–23; see also Goldstein, *I Maccabees*, pp. 49–51, 207–9, and *II Maccabees*, pp. 246–61.

10　1 Macc. 1:29–40, 2 Macc. 5:23–7; see also Goldstein, *II Maccabees*, pp. 261–6.

11　1 Macc. 1:44–64, 2 Macc. 6:1–11.

12　E.g., Isa. 24–7, Ezek. 38–9, Zech. 12–14, Mal. 2:2–4.

13　On the Testament of Moses, 1 Enoch 85–90, and Dan. 7–12, see the discussion at Goldstein, *I Maccabees*, pp. 39–46, and *II Maccabees*, pp. 90 (n. 34), 92–4, 106–9.

14　I speak of "sets" because the sections of Dan. 7–12, though they may well all be by the same author, were written at various intervals between 167 and 163 B.C.E. The same is true of the rewritings that produced the present text of 1 Enoch 90:6–39 (see n. 18).

15　See Goldstein, *I Maccabees*, pp. 40–4.

16　Ibid., p. 42.

17　Ibid, pp. 42–4.

18　In my book *Chosen Peoples* (forthcoming). See for the present Goldstein, *I Maccabees*, pp. 41–2, esp. n. 12.

19　Ibid., p. 42; I hope to treat elsewhere the problem of the relationship of 1 Enoch 85–90 to Dan. 7–12.

20　One would expect so miraculous and so longed-for an event as the resurrection to receive more elaborate treatment (contrast Dan. 12:2–3) and to be narrated in less ambiguous language. Nevertheless, if 1 Enoch 103–4 comes from the first half of the second century B.C.E. (see Nickelsburg, *Literature*, p. 150), the expectation of a resurrection there would suggest that the writer meant one in 90:33.

21　Cf. Jubilees 23:26–31 (by an author who shares the views of the seer of 1 Enoch 90).

22　On the connections of 1 Enoch with the Qumran sect, see for the present the cautious remarks of Nickelsburg, *Literature*, pp. 53–4, 90–4, 149. For the Qumran texts referring to a Messiah descended from David, see van der Woude, TDNT, IX (1974): 517–20.

　　John J. Collins, "Messianism in the Maccabean Period," this volume, has challenged my assertion here, that the person of the commanding figure of 1

Enoch 90:37–38 and those of the remiss angelic shepherds in 1 Enoch 89:59–90:25 are derived from Ezek. 34. Collins finds my assertion "far too simple." "The imagery," he writes, "of the *Animal Apocalypse* is not simply derived from Ezekiel 34 or any one source. The white bull, specifically, does not figure in the imagery of Ezekiel at all, and even if it did, we could not automatically assume that it had the same meaning in its new context."

I never asserted that the *imagery* of the "Animal Apocalypse" was derived from Ezek. 34, although in part it surely was. The imagery by which the Israelites' superior ancestors, the patriarchs, are portrayed as bulls and the hostile nations by various wild beasts and birds – that imagery is the original creation of the author of the "Animal Apocalypse." On the other hand, his portrayal of the Israelites, beginning with Jacob's sons, as sheep is a scriptural commonplace.

But where else but from Ezek. 34 did that author derive his idea (1 Enoch 89:61–90:17) that *remiss* shepherds would tend the Lord's flock, letting them be scattered among the wild beasts (1 Enoch 89:75; Ezek. 34:5–6) and abandoning them to be destroyed and devoured by predators (1 Enoch 89:61–90:17; Ezek. 34:5–8), while, moreover, the shepherds themselves kill, destroy, and eat the sheep (1 Enoch 89:69–70; Ezek. 34:2–3, 10)? Where else but from Ezek. 34 did he derive his idea that thereafter God would put an end to the shepherds and would Himself take charge of the sheep, gathering together the dispersed (1 Enoch 90:20–33; Ezek. 34:9–16) to a good pasturage (1 Enoch 90:20; Ezek. 34:13–14), while also punishing any evil members of His flock (1 Enoch 90:26–27; Ezek. 34:16–22), and thereupon would place in power over them a shepherd/protector of patriarchal character (a white bull in 1 Enoch 90:37; "David" in Ezek. 34:23)? If the whole scheme of shepherds plus ruler is taken from Ezek. 34, surely the great white bull is a Davidic Messiah. Parenthetically, we may note that Zech. 11:3–7, too, probably depends on Ezek. 34.

23 Jermiah's use of)*aḥărīt ḥayyāmīm* shows that its meaning is relative to what the speaker had in mind: "At the end of the predicted course of events," which might be relatively brief (as at Jer. 23:20) or (as at Jer. 30:25) a matter of many years (though not of centuries). It may well be that Isaiah himself meant the events of Chap. 2 to be taken as following immediately upon the purging of Israel described in 1:24–31.

24 On Daniel, see Goldstein, *I Maccabees*, pp. 42–52, and *II Maccabees*, pp. 63–9, 305–6. On 1 Enoch, see Goldstein, *I Maccabees*, pp. 95–6 (through line 2), 374; *II Maccabees*, pp. 495, 499.

25 Goldstein, *I Maccabees*, pp. 1–21, 62–78.

26 Ibid., pp. 62–78; Goldstein, *II Maccabees*, pp. 71–83.

27 Goldstein, *II Maccabees*, pp. 157–67.

28 Ibid., pp. 3–24, 71–83.

29 See Goldstein, *I Maccabees*, pp. 4, 12, 226, 227–8, 231–2, 235–6.

30 Ibid., pp. 12, 227.

31 Ibid., pp. 45, 47–8. I am puzzled why Collins, "Messianism," should say that my detection in 1 Maccabees of parodies of the words of Daniel is

overly ingenious. Let others decide whether he is right after reading my arguments.

32   Ibid., p. 48.

33   Ibid., pp. 4–12, 63–78.

34   Ibid., pp. 240–1. Collins, in "Messianism," finds insecurely based my assertion that there is a hint at 1 Macc. 2:57 that God's election of David's dynasty
might not be permanent. I here restate the basis. At 1 Macc. 2:57 David is
said to inherit the throne *eis aiônas*, an expression which usually means only
"for ages," but on my own showing (*I Maccabees*, p. 240) in some contexts
means "forever." Not I alone, but also ancient scribes who believed in the
eternal royal rights of the dynasty of David took *eis aiônas* at 1 Macc. 2:57 to
mean only "for ages" and therefore altered the text to make it say "forever";
see my *I Maccabees*, p. 241. Further confirmation for my inference that the
propaganda of the Hasmonaeans denied the permanence of the royal rights
of the house of David can be found in the bitter complaint at Psalms of Solomon 17:4–6 that the Hasmonaean usurpers denied those rights.

35   1 Macc. 14:41; see Goldstein, *I Maccabees*, pp. 507–8.

36   Josephus, *War* i.2.7.68–69; *Antiquities* xiii.10.3.282, 7.299–300; *Tosefta Soṭah*
13:5 and parallels.

37   Isa. 11:14, Mic. 4:5.

38   Isa. 65:17, Dan. 12:2 (and Isa. 25:8, 26:14, 19), Isa. 2:3–4.

39   One might regard, as a pale allusion to and partial fulfillment of the predicted
resurrection, the temporary suspension of the power of death that may be
claimed at 1 Macc. 5:54; see Goldstein, *I Maccabees*, p. 304. But in telling of
it, the Hasmonaean propagandist does not use his opportunity to echo the
language of the prophecies. There is only indirect evidence in 1 Maccabees
on voluntary conversion of gentiles (see Goldstein, *I Maccabees*, pp. 347, 349–
50). Though Hasmonaeans may have encouraged the process, the Hasmonaean propagandist makes no claim that they did.

40   See Jonathan A. Goldstein, "The Hasmonaean Revolt and the Hasmonaean
Dynasty," in CHJ, Vol. II, Chap. 8.

41   1 Macc. 2:1–26; see Goldstein, *I Maccabees*, p. 5.

42   C. C. Torrey, "'Yawan' and 'Hellas' as Designations of the Seleucid Empire,"
Journal of the American Oriental Society 25 (1904):302–11.

43   Goldstein, *II Maccabees*, p. 197.

44   Goldstein, *I Maccabees*, p. 245.

45   Because the allusion, if present, involves only the single word *episynagôn*
(Hebrew *mᵉasseph*).

46   Ibid., p 304.

47   The numerous sects are attested by the irreconcilable character of the surviving pieces of literature emanating from them: the Testament of Moses, Dan.
7–12, 1 Enoch 85–90, and 1 and 2 Maccabees. See Goldstein, *I Maccabees*, pp.
1–34, 39–52, *II Maccabees*, pp. 12–19. Not the least of Judas' achievements
was his ability to unite under himself forces from so many irreconcilable
groups (1 Macc. 3:9, 13; 2 Macc. 8:1, 1 Enoch 90:10; Goldstein, *I Maccabees*,
pp. 65, 504, *II Maccabees*, pp. 323–4). See also the beginning of my treatment
of Judas Maccabaeus in my forthcoming study in CHJ, Vol. II, Chap. 8.

48   Goldstein, *I Maccabees,* pp. 65–66.

49   Cf. Goldstein, *I Maccabees,* p. 491

50   But see n. 60.

51   Goldstein, *I Maccabees,* p. 210.

52   The inference is only probable, not certain, because the Greek verb αρειν renders the *hiph⟨īl* of the Hebrew root *sūr* at Gen. 35:2 and Isa. 5:23 and its *huph⟨al* at Isa. 17:1.

53   Prophecies of conquests: Num. 24:17–18, Isa. 11:14, 25:9–12, Jer. 49:1–6, Amos 9:12, Obadiah (esp. 19), Zeph. 2:4–10. There are also prophecies that predict that the Lord will smite Philistia, Moab, Ammon, or Edom but say nothing of Israel as the agent (Isa. 15–16, Jer. 48:1–47, 49:7–22, Zech. 9:5–7); nothing in those texts, however, would prevent a searcher of prophecies from suggesting that the Lord used the Hasmonaeans as his agents in fulfilling them. Hasmonaean victories: 1 Macc. 3:41 with 4:12–22, 5:1–23, 55–68, 10:67–89, 11:60–62.

54   Goldstein, *II Maccabees,* p. 31.

55   Mistaken beliefs of the pious martyrs: see Goldstein, *I Maccabees,* pp. 227, 235–6, 273–80, 331–2, 371, and cf. Dan. 11:33–35; on Jonathan's death, see Goldstein, *I Maccabees,* pp. 468–9; on Judas', ibid., p. 374, and in text.

56   Goldstein, *I Maccabees,* pp. 64–6.

57   Ibid., p. 231.

58   Goldstein, *I Maccabees,* p. 239 (note on 2:49), and compare 1 Macc. 6:12 with Isa. 10:7. In 1 Enoch 85–90, too, the angelic shepherds exceed their mandate from God, but there the sin to be punished is Israel's ancient sin, not the recent sin of Hellenizers, and the punishing instruments are superhuman beings.

59   Here one must render the obscure Hebrew word in Num. 25:8 according to interpretations current in Mattathias' time. I follow the Septuagint (and the Vulgate).

60   Judas Maccabaeus' feats are narrated in words echoing the stories of Joshua, Jephthah, Gideon, Samuel, Saul and his son Jonathan, and especially David; see Goldstein, *I Maccabees,* pp. 244, 246, 247, 248, 251, 260, 261, 263, 264, 265, 266, 270, 284, 296, 298, 300, 304, 305, 320, 342, 374, 375. The Hasmonaean propagandist is careful to have his narrative of Jonathan echo stories only of Joshua and the Judges and Joab, not of royal or princely heroes, because he does not want to imply that Jonathan's descendants deserve a share of royal power; for the passages, see ibid., pp. 377, 381, 384, 393, 395. The narrative on Simon echoes stories of Elijah and especially of Solomon; see ibid., pp. 472, 490, 491–2. 1 Macc. 14:12 certainly echoes Mic. 4:4 (cf. Zech. 3:10), but the Hasmonaean propagandist probably was most intent on the fact that Simon has equaled the example of Solomon (1 Kings 5:5).

61   "Seed of men" here means "family," but in the Hebrew Bible the expression is used only by Samuel's still childless mother, Hannah, of the child she longs to bear, as she prays to God that she conceive and bear him (1 Sam. 1:11). Samuel grew up to become the prophet and judge who brought about the salvation of Israel in his time (1 Sam. 7:8–16); see also Goldstein, *I Maccabees,* p. 305, notes on vv. 60–62 and 63.

62 I give the reading of the Masoretic text of 2 Sam. 3:18, which has the noun-expression *hōshīa⟨* (an infinitive construct), where the Greek of 1 Macc. 5:62 has a noun, *sōtēria*. There is another example in Samuel of such use of an infinitive construct, at 1 Sam. 23:20; cf. also Jer. 10:5, and see *Gesenius' Hebrew Grammar*, ed. E. Kautzsch (2d English ed., rev. A. E. Cowley; Oxford: Clarendon Press, 1910), sec. 114a, p. 347. Most scholars have rejected the Masoretic reading at 2 Sam. 3:18, following Keil's judgment, "*Hōshīa⟨* is an evident mistake in writing for *⟩ōshīa⟨*, which is found in many mss. and rendered in all the ancient versions" (C. F. Keil and F. Delitzsch, *Biblical Commentary on the Books of Samuel* [Grand Rapids, Mich.: Eerdmans, 1950], p. 303). With the reading *⟩ōshīa⟨* the passage would mean, "Through the agency of David My servant I shall deliver My people Israel." The Hasmonaean propagandist's habitual avoidance of speaking directly of God could easily have turned even the reading *⟩ōshīa⟨* into the strange noun-expression at 1 Macc. 5:62. Nevertheless, the noun in the allusion at 1 Macc. 5:62 would seem to attest the infinitive construct of the Masoretic reading at 2 Sam. 3:18. The author of Psalms of Solomon 17:5–6, who wrote at least 42 years after the Hasmonaean propagandist, had good reason to complain that the Hasmonaeans had usurped the prerogatives of the (hidden or extinct) dynasty of David. Collins, "Messianism," does not say why he is skeptical about my suggestion that 1 Macc. 5:62 echoes 2 Sam. 3:18.

63 2 Sam. 7:16 (cf. 1 Chron. 17:12), Jer. 33:19–26, Zech. 12:8. Pro-Hasmonaean exegesis might twist other passages. E.g., in Isa. 9:6 (cf. 16:5) one might say that only the throne was David's but that members of another worthy Jewish dynasty would sit upon it. Of Ezek. 34 one might say that the king would need only to take for himself the name "David."

64 Goldstein, *I Maccabees*, pp. 261 (note on 1 Macc. 3:44–45), 298, 301, 304, 310, 415, 442, 443, 465, 472 (where I should not have spoken of echoes), 473, 474.

65 See the discussion of the reign of Alexander Jannaeus in my forthcoming study in CHJ, Vol. II, chap. 8.

66 1 Macc. 13:41.

67 1 Macc. 5:62; the word "permanent" does not occur in that verse, but prophets had promised that God's postexilic Age of Mercy and Vindication for Israel would be permanent (e.g., Isa. 54, Jer. 31:31–40).

68 Goldstein, *II Maccabees*, pp. 14–16.

69 Hans Volkmann, "Ptolemaios 30," RE, XXIII[2] (1959), 1740–42; Alan E. Samuel, *Ptolemaic Chronology* (München: Beck, 1962), pp. 148–51; Goldstein, *II Maccabees*, p. 162.

70 In the Abridged History there is an effort to discredit all Hasmonaeans except Judas Maccabaeus and to minimize the connection.

Collins, "Messianism," calls "unfounded" my theory that the letter in 2 Macc. 1:10b–2:10 contains implied opposition to the temple at Leontopolis and holds that it is especially incongruent with the setting I propose, "Since the Oniads of Leontopolis supported Alexander Jannaeus." See rather my *II Maccabees*, pp. 25–6, 158–60. The paradoxical position of the Oniads and their temple is a fact of history which no one would have suspected if our sources did not tell us about it. Onias IV surely respected the temple at Jerusalem yet founded a schismatic sanctuary at Leontopolis. The Oniads regarded their own high-priestly line as the legitimate one, yet Ananias of that line refused to exploit an opportunity to depose the Hasmonaean Alexander Jannaeus, for which the price would have been the subjection of independent Judaea to Ptolemaic Egypt. The authorities whose views are preserved in the Mishnah surely believed in the exclusive legitimacy of the temple at Jerusalem but still conceded limited validity to vegetable sacrifices offered at Leontopolis. See my *II Maccabees*, pp. 162–3, and my review of Robert Doran's *Temple Propaganda*, *Jewish Quarterly Review* 75 (1984), 80.

71 For the correct reading at 2 Macc. 2:17, see Goldstein, *II Maccabees*, p. 187. I emended the text in order to give it good Greek syntax. Without my emendation, the case for regarding 2 Macc. 2:17 as pro-Hasmonaean propaganda from the reign of Alexander Jannaeus becomes even stronger, for the verse then asserts (supposedly in 164 B.C.E.) that God has already restored to the Jews the kingdom, the priesthood, and the sanctification – at a time when no Jew aspired to be king (least of all, Judas Maccabaeus); when the high priests were appointees of the Seleucid kings, first the impious Menelaus and then the pious Alcimus (who, however, was bitterly opposed by many pious Jews); and when the pagans and apostates, who occupied the citadel of Jerusalem and parts of Judaea, were always able to commit acts of desecration! Jewish claims that the kingdom, priesthood, and santification had all been restored were impossible before the accession of the first Hasmonaean king, Judas Aristobulus I. His brief reign (104–103 B.C.E) was troubled and was too early to have produced some of the allusions in Ep. 2. The combination of allusions and claims thus fits only the reign of Alexander Jannaeus (103–76 B.C.E.).

72 Goldstein, *II Maccabees*, p. 188.

73 Cf. "speedily" *(tacheôs)* in 2 Macc. 2:18.

74 Goldstein, *II Maccabees*, pp. 160–1.

75 See 2 Macc. 1:18.

76 Cf. ibid.

77 2 Macc. 1:25 contains echoes of Isa. 14:1, 41:8, 44:1–2; 2 Macc. 1:25 and 27 draw on Ezek. 37:28; 2 Macc. 1:25 and 28 draw on Jer. 2:3; 2 Macc. 1:27 looks to Isa. 49:7; 2 Macc. 1:27–28 draws on Isa. 49:25–26. See also Goldstein, *II Maccabees*, p. 179.

78 Ingathering: Isa. 27:12–13, 43:3–8, 49:8–12, 22, 60:4, etc. Punishment: Isa. 41:11–12, 49:23, 26, 60:4, 66:14–16, etc.

79 Collins, "Messianism," questions my inference that the author of the letter in 2 Mac. 1:10b–2:18 rejected the belief in the permanent royal rights of the dynasty of David. My inference is based not only upon the author's "remarkable reference" (Collins' expression) to the restoration of *the* kingdom (i.e., the promised kingdom, par excellence), but also on the absence of any reference to David's dynasty in the author's prayer for the fulfillment of those divine promises still unfulfilled. The author of the letter makes clear just what those promises are.

80 Goldstein, *II Maccabees*, pp. 190–2.

81 Goldstein, *I Maccabees*, pp. 12–13, 28, 49.

82   Goldstein, *II Maccabees,* p. 215. Dan. 11:20 certainly alludes to the same event and draws on Zech. 9:8; see Goldstein, *II Maccabees,* p. 197.

83   Macc. 4:10–17.

84   2 Macc. 5:17, 21–22, 7:31, 34, 9:4, 8, 10–18.

85   Goldstein, *I Maccabees,* pp. 96–97 (through line 2), *II Maccabees,* p. 501.

86   Ibid., pp. 63–70, 305–6.

87   Ibid. pp. 305–6. On his allusions to Dan. 8 and 11, see ibid., pp. 306–7, 351, 353, 355.

88   Goldstein, *II Maccabees,* pp. 17–18.

89   Ibid., pp. 293, 295–6, 298, 354–5, 386, 392–5, 397–9, 403, 405–6, 442, 495, 501.

90   In the passages cited in n. 89, from my *II Maccabees,* I was not always careful to distinguish a literal echo of the words of the Writing Prophets from a recognizable effect of those words, taken over by our writer from his sources.

91   Goldstein, *II Maccabees,* pp. 336–7. On the possible allusion to 1 Sam. 2:1–10 at 2 Macc. 6:30, see Goldstein, *II Maccabees,* pp. 287–8, but in writing my comments there I wrongly believed that the great figure at 1 Enoch 90:37–8 was not a messianic king. Otherwise, I still stand by them.

92   The abridger in his epilogue might seem to value the Hasmonaean achievement of keeping the Holy City out of the hands of gentiles (2 Macc. 15:37), but in the context of the whole Abridged History that achievement is at best small: The same situation prevailed almost throughout the period of the Second Temple, even under the wicked high priest, Jason. It was interrupted only by the atrocities that began with the sack by Antiochus IV in 169 and ended with the defeat of Nicanor in 162 B.C.E. Thus, in our writer's view, conditions under the Hasmonaean high priests need not have been any better than under wicked Alcimus after the death of Maccabaeus in 160 B.C.E.!

93   At 1 Macc. 2:57; see above, n. 34. In a paper limited to the writers in 1 and 2 Maccabees, I refrain from surveying the opinions on the dynasty of David in the other Jewish sources which survive from the late fourth to the first century B.C.E. I have just shown how peculiar is the silence in 2 Maccabees on a coming Davidic king. There might be nothing strange, however, about the absence from Daniel of allusions to David. The writers in Daniel might have taken for granted that the imperial power predicted for the Jews would be exercised by a Davidic king. No one can read the mind of those writers, but in my forthcoming book *Chosen Peoples* and in my commentary on Daniel I shall demonstrate that the traditions that shaped the revelations in Daniel had nothing to do with a Davidic king. Collins, "Messianism," questions my inference that the writer of the abridged history in 2 Maccabees "no longer even thought of a Davidic king." Again let me point out that my inference is not a mere argument from silence, but from a silence where one would expect an assertion of the rights of the dynasty of David. Throughout this entire volume we run the risk of relying upon mere arguments from silence, so incomplete is our evidence. But if there is a silence where demonstrably there should be a statement, the silence becomes eloquent indeed.

5

Messianism in the Maccabean Period

JOHN J. COLLINS

The Terminology

The terms "Messiah" and "messianism" are used in various ways in modern scholarship. Sometimes "messianism" is used very broadly for any eschatological tableau that involves the salvation of Israel, whether or not an individual Messiah is involved. So Schuerer's classic *History of the Jewish People,* in its recently revised edition, offers "a systematic outline of messianism based on all the inter-Testamental sources, including the Dead Sea Scrolls, but presented according to the pattern emerging from the Apocalypses of Baruch and Ezra, since it is in these two late compositions that eschatological expectation is most fully developed."[1] However useful such a synthesis may be as a collection of motifs, it surely distorts the historical picture by retrojecting a pattern from the late first century C.E. on the preceding centuries, and blurs the boundaries of actual messianic expectation. Even when the discussion is restricted to the expectation of an individual figure, the term Messiah is still used in various ways:

1. Perhaps the simplest criterion for determining messianic references is the use of the term *māšîaḥ* or its equivalents (*christos, unctus,* etc.).[2] The modern scholarly usage of "Messiah," however, does not simply correspond to the usage of the ancient texts, since it is restricted to anointed figures who have eschatological significance. Allusions to an anointed king in 2 Samuel, to God's anointed in Ps. 2, to an anointed prince in Daniel 9 or the prophets as anointed ones in the Qumran scrolls are not usually regarded as "messianic." The eschatological use of Messiah still involves considerable variety. The anointed one may be a king or a priest, or even a supernatural figure as in the Similitudes of Enoch.[3]

2. The term is sometimes restricted to the specifically Davidic Messiah.[4] This restriction, however, risks losing sight of the variety of messianic figures attested in the texts.

97

3. Many scholars extend the concept of Messiah to include passages that do not use the term but refer to an agent of salvation in a definitive sense. Schuerer's discussion includes Sibylline Oracles 3:49 and 3:652–56, which refer to kings who are to come but do not use the term "anointed," and it is not unusual to speak of the Messiah of Levi in Testament of Levi 18, where, again, the term is not used. This broader usage also blurs significant distinctions, but it does draw attention to the wider context in which Jewish messianism must be seen.

We have no instance of *māšîah* or its equivalents in an eschatological context that can be dated with certainty to the second century B.C.E., although the Qumran usage may well have originated in that century. There is relatively little textual evidence from that period for the hope that the Davidic line would be restored. Instead, we find a range of figures who are viewed as agents of salvation by different groups.

Messianism in the Second Century

The wisdom book of Ben Sira reveals the views of a pious scribe in Jerusalem at the beginning of the second century B.C.E. As is well known, Ben Sira had little interest in eschatology of any sort. The prayer for divine intervention in 36:1–17 is so different in tone from the rest of the book that its authenticity must be questioned. Yet even there we find no reference to a Messiah. Ben Sira praises David at some length (47:1–11) but does not use the occasion to speak of the restoration of his line. The statement that God exalted his horn forever (47:11) does not necessarily imply that the dynasty will last forever.[5] In 49:4–5 Sirach states that the "horn" of the Davidic kings was given to others because all but three were sinful. Only in the Hebrew psalm inserted in chapter 51 between verses 12 and 13 do we find the hope for the restoration of the Davidic line (line h), but this psalm is almost certainly a later addition. For Sirach himself the glory of David belongs to the past. Moreover, Ben Sira 45:25 contrasts the Davidic covenant with that of Aaron, and suggests that it is inferior in some respects.[6] The covenant with Aaron is elaborated at far greater length than that of David (45:6–22). There is no doubt that Sirach viewed the High Priest Simon as the main mediator of God's blessing in his own time (50:1–21). The sage's lack of interest in Davidic messianism is a consequence of his satisfaction with the priestly theocratic regime.

Most scholars agree that Sirach has no interest in a Davidic Messiah.[7] By contrast, the Third Sibylline Oracle is often cited in discussions of messianism.[8] The chief passage in question is Sibylline Oracles 3:652–56: "and then God will send a king from the sun who will stop the entire earth from evil war, killing some, imposing oaths of loyalty on others;

and he will not do all these things by his private plans but in obedience
to the noble teachings of the great God." This king, however, is not said
to be of the line of David, or even Jewish. Elsewhere the sibyl repeatedly
says that the turning point of history will come in "the seventh reign,
when a king of Egypt, who will be of the Greeks by race, will rule" (Sib.
Or. 3:193, compare 318, 608) – i.e., the seventh king of the Ptolemaic
line, either Ptolemy VI Philometor (if Alexander the Great is counted) or,
more probably, his anticipated successor, Ptolemy Neos Philopator. Sibylline Oracles 3:652–56 most probably refers to the same king. The phrase
"king from the sun" is rooted in Egyptian mythology and is also found in
an Egyptian eschatological prophecy of the Hellenistic period, the Potter's
Oracle.[9] I have suggested elsewhere that Sibylline Oracles 3 was composed by a follower of Onias IV, the heir to the Jewish High Priesthood
who became a general in the army of Ptolemy Philometor.[10] In any case,
the oracle expresses the views of Jews who looked to the military and
political power of Egypt to deliver Judea from the threat of the Syrian
Seleucids. Here again we find a political perspective that had no place for
a Jewish Messiah and even ignores the historical reality of the Maccabean
revolt.[11]

The attempt to find a messianic reference in Sibylline Oracles 3:265–
94 must also be rejected.[12] This passage refers to the restoration of "a certain royal tribe whose race will never stumble," but the reference here is
to the Jewish people, not to the Davidic dynasty. The context is the restoration of the Jews from the Babylonian exile. The king who is sent by
the heavenly God (Sib. Or. 3:286) must be identified as Cyrus of Persia.[13]
If this passage has any bearing on the eschatology of the sibyl it suggests
that the final restoration of the Jews will also be mediated by a gentile
king.[14]

It is generally agreed that the apocalypses of the Maccabean era have
little interest in the restoration of the Davidic line. For many centuries
Jews and Christians alike identified the "one like a Son of Man" in Daniel
7 as the Messiah,[15] but that interpretation is only rarely defended today.[16]
The problem with the messianic interpretation is that Daniel never refers
explicitly to a Davidic Messiah or indicates any interest in the restoration
of the dynasty.[17] The only agent of salvation explicitly identified is
Michael the archangel, who arises in victory before the resurrection (Dan.
12:1). The view that the "one like a Son of Man" in Daniel 7 is a supernatural figure is supported by analogy with Michael's explicit role in chapters 10–12, as well as the imagery of chapter 7 itself.[18] This figure is said
to be *like* a human being or Son of Man, just as the angelic interpreter in
Daniel 8:15 is said to have the appearance of a man or as the figure in
Ezekiel's vision had "a likeness as it were of a human form" (Ezek. 1:26).

(Angels are referred to simply as "men" in Dan. 10:5 and 12:6–7). The heavenly "one like a Son of Man" in Daniel is the forerunner of the Son of Man figure in the Similitudes of Enoch, who is also called "Messiah," but is not given a messianic title in Daniel. The only "anointed" ones to whom Daniel refers are the "anointed prince" at the time of the restoration (probably the High Priest Joshua) and the anointed one who is cut off after sixty two weeks (the murdered High Priest Onias III).

Daniel's lack of interest in the promises to David must be seen in relation to the aspirations of the wise teachers or *maśkîlîm* with whom the author seems to identify. In the pre-Maccabean stage of the Daniel tradition preserved in Daniel 1–6, Daniel and his friends are loyal servants of the gentile kings. In Daniel 2, the stone cut by no human hand, which became a great mountain, is presumably a Jewish kingdom, but the emphasis of the story falls on Daniel's ability to reveal mysteries rather than on the expectation of that kingdom.[19] In chapters 7–12 gentile rule is more directly rejected. In chapter 7 we are told that a kingdom shall be given to the people of the saints of the Most High, which, again, is a Jewish kingdom of universal scope. The nature of this kingdom is not elaborated, however. The fact that it is associated with "holy ones" or angels[20] suggests that Daniel is interested in its heavenly rather than its earthly dimensions. Daniel is privy to the conversations of "holy ones" (Dan 8:13–14) and the recipient of angelic revelations. The climactic revelation of the book is the promise of resurrection and exaltation to the stars in Daniel 12. It would seem that the primary aspirations of the *maśkîlîm* were to live lives of purity (11:35) and heavenly wisdom and to be exalted after death. The campaign of the Maccabees was little help, if any, for these people, and a Davidic Messiah may have been irrelevant too.

I do not suggest that the aspirations of Daniel were incompatible with the expectation of a Messiah, but only that they did not require it. The Enoch tradition was no less interested in the heavenly world than Daniel. Yet the Animal Apocalypse endorses Judas Maccabee and envisages some kind of leader in the eschatological period. Whether the "white bull" in 1 Enoch 90:37–38 is a Davidic Messiah, is, however, difficult to decide. Goldstein contends that he is "surely royal and rules over the Jews and Gentiles."[21] All the text says is that "all the wild animals and all the birds of heaven were afraid of it and entreated it continually" (1 En. 90:37), and it is not apparent that this necessarily implies royal status. Goldstein infers that one can call this "Messiah" David because "his person and those of the remiss angelic shepherds of God's flock in 1 Enoch 89:59–90:25 are derived from Ezekiel 34, where 'David' will rule over the Chosen People after God delivers them from evil." This is far too simple. The imagery of the Animal Apocalypse is not simply derived from Ezekiel 34 or any one source.[22] The white bull, specifically, does not figure in the imagery of Ezekiel at all, and even if it did we could not automatically assume that it had the same meaning in its new context. It is *possible* that this figure is a Davidic Messiah, but his Davidic affiliation is not demonstrable, and George Nickelsburg's cautious treatment of the passage must be commended.[23] As Nickelsburg notes, the white bull is not the agent of salvation. That role falls to Judas Maccabee ("that ram"), who receives angelic and ultimately divine assistance.

The primary interest of the Enoch tradition for the subject of messianism lies in the development of the transcendent Messiah of the Similitudes, as Nickelsburg rightly observes. Although this figure is called "Messiah," he does not represent the restoration of the Davidic line, and only part of his profile has Davidic associations.[24] The most striking aspect of this figure is surely his transcendent character, which owes much to Daniel 7. The development of this transcendent king and judge must be related to the general lack of interest in traditional Davidic messianism in the Enoch and Daniel traditions, and to their speculative and mystical tendencies.

Transcendent Savior Figures

The notion of a transcendent savior figure under God is perhaps the most significant development in Jewish messianism (broadly defined) in the second century B.C.E. Such figures play an important part in the Qumran scrolls. The Community Rule (1QS) speaks of the Prince of Lights who stands over against the Angel of Darkness. In the War Scroll the Prince of Light is contrasted with Belial (13:10–12, cf. CD 5:18) and is apparently identical with the archangel Michael (17:7). In 11QMelchizedek, Melchizedek appears as a heavenly figure *(elohim)* who stands over against Belial. This dualism of supernatural figures appears already in developed form in the Testament of Amram, which is dated palaeographically to the mid-second century B.C.E. If the editor, J. T. Milik, has reconstructed this document correctly, it contrasts two figures, one called Michael, Melchizedek, or Prince of Light and the other Belial, Prince of Darkness, and Melchireša'. Only the name Melchireša' is preserved in the extant fragments, but it is obviously a counterpart to Melchizedek.[25]

The dualism of Qumran is widely and plausibly believed to have been shaped in part by Persian influence, especially in its imagery of light and darkness and the balanced contrast of the two angelic figures.[26] Its origin, however, remains obscure. A tendency toward dualism can already be found in the Book of the Watchers in 1 Enoch, where Michael and the good angels stand in contrast to the rebellious Watchers and in the opposition of the angel of the presence and Mastema in Jubilees, although there is no dualism of light and darkness in these documents. Already in the early postexilic period we find Satan set over against the angel of the Lord in Zechariah 3 (where some Persian influence is also possible). In Daniel, Michael appears as the heavenly savior figure, but his adversaries are the angelic "princes" of Persia and Greece, not a Prince of Darkness or evil.[27] Michael's role in Daniel recalls the "prince of the army of the Lord" who appears to Joshua as a man in Joshua 5:13–15, and, in a more general way, the traditional "angel of the Lord" *(mal)ak YHWH)*.[28] In short, the notion of an angelic savior figure or of an exalted angel had roots in older biblical tradition. Nonetheless, such figures become much more prominent and important in the Hellenistic period, when they acquire explicit names and more elaborate roles in the context of apocalyptic speculation.

The development of interest in angelic savior figures had enormous importance for later tradition. It is an important factor in the Christian identification of Jesus as the "Son of Man"[29] and in early descriptions of the glorified Christ.[30] Within Judaism we find the development of such figures in the Similitudes of Enoch, in Jaoel of Apoc Abraham, and ultimately in the Metatron of 3 Enoch, who is even called "the lesser YHWH."[31] Even some Jewish documents that have a more traditional picture of the Messiah integrate some transcendent features: e.g., 4 Ezra, which states clearly that the Messiah will die (7:29), also represents him as a man rising on clouds from the heart of the sea (4 Ezra 13).[32]

Later, rabbinic, Judaism attests extensive controversy on the subject of "two powers in heaven." One aspect of this controversy concerned the idea of a principal angel or mediator arising from the interpretation of Daniel 7 and other passages.[33] There is little evidence of controversy on the subject in the Maccabean period. There is, however, a striking statement in Jubilees:[34]

> for there are many nations and many peoples, and all are his, and over all hath he placed spirits in authority to lead them astray from him. But over Israel he did not appoint any angel or spirit, for he alone is their ruler, and he will preserve them and require them at the hand of his angels and his spirits and at the hand of all his powers.
> (Jub. 15:31–32)

This passage reaffirms Deuteronomy 32,[35] but seems to contradict the book of Daniel, where Israel has a prince, Michael, just as Persia and Greece do. Despite this, Jubilees is not reticent about the role of angels, and the Angel of the Presence intervenes to thwart Mastema in the sacrifice of Isaac (Jub. 18) and again at the Exodus (Jub. 48). Jubilees, then, does not exclude the exalted angel, counterpart of Mastema or Belial, but denies him the rank of Prince of Israel, in conformity to Deuteronomy.

Some tension is also evident in the Qumran War Scroll, col. 13, which states:

> Thou [hast redeemed us] for Thyself [O God], that we may be an everlasting people. Thou hast decreed for us a destiny of Light according to Thy truth. And the Prince of Light Thou hast appointed from ancient times to come to our support . . .[36]

The scroll goes on to ask: "O God of Israel, who can compare with Thee in might? Thy mighty hand is with the poor. Which angel or prince can compare with Thy [redeeming] succour?" It has been suggested that this question stands as a correction to the allusion to the Prince of Light, which is itself regarded as an interpolation.[37] Yet the document as it stands does not deny the role of the angelic prince, but puts it in perspective: He is clearly subordinate to God himself. Similarly in the War Scroll (1QM 17:7) God will raise up "the kingdom of Michael in the midst of the gods and the realm of Israel in the midst of all flesh." Here again Michael has a role, but the primary agent is God.[38] Needless to say, the "Son of Man" figure is also subordinate to God in Daniel and the Similitudes, as even Metatron is in 3 Enoch.

We should note that the transcendent angelic figure coexists with the expectation of human messiahs in the Qumran scrolls, even in individual documents such as the Community Rule (1Q5) and the Damascus Document (CD). Whereas the two kinds of messianism (transcendent and earthly) are different in origin and function, they are not mutually exclusive.[39]

The Hasmoneans

The question of the fulfillment of the hopes for the Davidic line was raised in a new way by the rise of the Hasmonean dynasty, as Jonathan Goldstein has discussed in this volume. Although we may not accept Goldstein's characterization of the "fundamental teachings" of Daniel or his ingenious detection of "barbed parodies" of Daniel in 1 Maccabees, we can grant that there is a fundamental difference between the viewpoint of the apocalypses and that of the "Hasmonean propagandist." The author of 1 Maccabees is no more interested in the Davidic line than is Daniel, but for fundamentally different reasons. He views the Hasmoneans as adequate agents of salvation. As Goldstein and, earlier, Arenhoevel[40] point out, 1 Maccabees 5:62 is most revealing: The family of the Maccabees is "that seed of men to whom had been granted the deliverance of Israel through their agency." It is not necessary to see here an allusion to 2 Samuel 3:18, which promises deliverance through the hand of David in a specific historical situation, but it is clear that the author did not wait for a Davidic descendant to gain the salvation of Israel.

It is also clear that 1 Maccabees stops short of claiming that the messianic prophecies were fulfilled in the Maccabees. The reasoning and motivation behind this reticence are less clear. Goldstein attributes to the author an extremely subtle strategy of suggesting that Mattathias' sons fulfilled the words of the prophets, without actually saying so. Such a thesis is very difficult to prove. The issue here is whether 1 Maccabees sees the Hasmonean dynasty as a full-fledged replacement for the Davidic dynasty. Goldstein suggests that such an understanding is implied and finds a preparatory hint at 1 Maccabees 2:57 "that God's election of David's dynasty might not be permanent." The "hint," however, is that David is only said to inherit the throne of the kingdom *eis aionas*.[41] Goldstein argues that the plural form (in Greek or Hebrew) does not necessarily mean "forever," although it frequently does. Since he admits that the phrase *can* mean forever, his inference that 1 Maccabees intended a less permanent meaning is unsubstantiated. It is quite possible that the author of 1 Maccabees affirmed the traditional hope of the restoration of the Davidic line, but assigned it to the eschatological future. The Davidic Messiah need not be an agent of salvation in history, any more than the white bull in the Animal Apocalypse. Unlike the Apocalypse, however, 1 Maccabees is not greatly concerned with the eschatological future and does not expect it with any urgency. In the meantime, the Hasmoneans can achieve the salvation of Israel, and their rule is legitimated by analogies with biblical precedents such as that of Phineas, who received an eternal priesthood.

In the case of 2 Maccabees, Goldstein's thesis that the author of the second letter supported the Hasmonean dynasty is well founded on the remarkable reference to the restoration of kinship, priesthood, and consecration of 2 Maccabees 2:17. Whether this necessarily involved rejection of the Davidic promises is not clear, in view of the brevity of the letter.[42] The Abridged History in 2 Maccabees clearly does not entertain any messianic pretensions for the Hasmoneans, or address the question of messianism at all. This, again, does not necessarily imply the rejection of the promises to David, but only that the author's interest lay elsewhere.

Qumran

Expectation of a Davidic Messiah emerges vigorously in the Qumran scrolls, often in the context of a dual expectation of messiahs of

Aaron and Israel.[43] The expectation of two messiahs, which is also reflected in the Testaments of the Twelve Patriarchs, is widely thought to express opposition to the Hasmonean combination of royal and priestly titles by insisting on the separation of the two offices.[44] It is noteworthy that the most elaborate expression of Davidic messianism in the first century B.C.E. is found in a document which is also very critical of the Hasmoneans – the Psalms of Solomon.[45]

Yet the messianism of Qumran can also be seen as a development of traditions that were alive, although not prominent, in the early Maccabean period. The notion of two messiahs, with the priest in the primary role, derives from the structure of the postexilic community, attested in Zechariah 1–6. For most of the postexilic period the High Priest stood alone as the leader of the community, and as we have seen this was the situation reflected in Sirach. The Aramaic Levi apocryphon from the Cairo Geniza, which is also attested by Qumran fragments, applies royal terminology to Levi and fails to mention Judah on occasions where both patriarchs appear in the Greek Testament of Levi. This suggests that the expectation of an ideal priest preceded that of two messianic figures in the tradition of the Testaments.[46] However, in Jubilees 31 we read that the spirit of prophecy came to Isaac and he blessed Levi and Judah. Significantly, Levi received the first blessing. Then Judah was told:

> a prince shalt thou be, thou and one of thy sons, over the sons of Jacob . . . Then shall the Gentiles fear before thy face . . . in thee shall be the help of Jacob and in thee shall be found the salvation of Israel.

This passage is at least implicitly messianic, and lays the foundation for the expectation of the two messiahs. Yet Jubilees was most probably written before the Hasmoneans appropriated either royal or priestly titles.[47]

Davidic messianism is also implied in "The Words of the Heavenly Luminaries," a document found at Qumran but lacking distinctively sectarian motifs.[48] Since the manuscript has been dated to the middle of the second century B.C.E., it may be a traditional document preserved in the Qumran library rather than a distinctively Essene composition. God is reminded that "Thou hast chosen the tribe of Judah and hast established Thy Covenant with David that he might be as a princely shepherd over Thy people and sit before Thee on the throne of Israel forever." This document seems to attest an ongoing tradition that looked for a restoration of the Davidic line. The renewed prominence of messianism in the scrolls may have been prompted by opposition to the Hasmoneans, but it also drew on these traditional expectations.

Conclusion

There are some traces of messianism in the Maccabean period. It is evident, however, that messianism was neither widespread nor prominent in this period and that there was no one "orthodox" notion of "the Messiah." The traditions on which Davidic messianism was based were preserved, but these in themselves did not ensure any lively expectation. The presence or absence of messianism was primarily determined by the political attitudes and circumstances of the different groups within Judaism. Those who placed their hopes in the institutions and leaders of their day, whether the High Priests, the Ptolemies, or the Maccabees, had little interest in messianism. Apocalyptic groups developed the idea of a transcendent savior figure, either as an alternative or as a complement to earthly messianism. Only with the rise of the Qumran community do we find a group with a strong and developed interest in messianism, and then again in the first century B.C.E. in the Psalms of Solomon.[49]

NOTES

1   Emil Schuerer, *The History of the Jewish People in the Age of Jesus Christ,* rev. and ed. Geza Vermes, Fergus Millar, and Matthew Black (Edinburgh: Clark, 1979), Vol. 2 p. 514.

2   This criterion is followed by J. H. Charlesworth in "The Concept of the Messiah in the Pseudepigrapha," *Aufstieg und Neidergang der Römischen Welt* 2.19.1 (Berlin: de Gruyter 1979): 188–218. Charlesworth surveys the corpus of Pseudepigrapha attributed to Old Testament figures rather than a specific historical period.

3   See A. S. van der Woude and M. de Jonge, "Messianic Ideas in Later Judaism," *Theological Dictionary of the New Testament* 9(1974): 509–27.

4   Schuerer, *The History,* pp. 518–19: "Pre-Christian Judaism – in so far as its messianic expectations can be conclusively documented – regarded the Messiah as a fully human individual, a royal figure descended from the house of David." "The Messiah," here, is evidently distinguished from the priestly and prophetic messianic figures attested in the Dead Sea Scrolls.

5   See A. Caquot, "Ben Sira et le Messianisme," *Semitica* 16(1966): 55. See also H. Stadelmann, *Ben Sira als Schriftgelehrter* (Tübingen: Mohr, 1980), p. 160.

6   The Greek text notes the limitation of the royal covenant, which is transmitted from son to son, whereas the priestly covenant applies to all the descendants of Aaron. The Hebrew, *naḥalat)iš lipnê kᵉbôdô* is probably a corruption of *naḥalat ʾiš libnô lᵉbaddô,* "the inheritance of a man is for his son alone." (B. Vawter, "Realized Messianism," *De la Tôrah au Messie* [Mélanges Henri Cazelles; Paris: Desclés, 1981], p. 270.)

7   See Caquot, "Ben Sira et la Messianisme." See also T. Middendorp, *Die Stellung Jesu Ben Siras zwischen Judentum und Hellenismus* (Leiden: Brill, 1973), p.

174; Stadelmann, *Ben Sira,* p. 164. A few scholars nonetheless find Davidic messianism here: G. Maier, *Mensch und freier Wille. Nach den jüdischen Religionsparteien zwischen Ben Sira und Paulus* (Tübingen: Mohr, 1971), p. 57; R. H. Lehmann, "Ben Sira and the Qumran Literature," *Revue de Qumran* 3(1961): 103–16.

8   For example, Schuerer, *The History,* Vol. 2, p. 501: "In the oldest Jewish Sibylline Oracles of around 140 B.C., the flow of messianic prophecy is rich and abundant."

9   See further J. J. Collins, *The Sibylline Oracles of Egyptian Judaism* (Missoula: Scholars Press, 1974), pp. 40–4; *Between Athens and Jerusalem. Jewish Identity in the Hellenistic Diaspora* (New York: Crossroad, 1983), pp. 68–70. On the Potter's Oracle see L. Koenen, "The Prophecies of a Potter: A Prophecy of World Renewal Becomes an Apocalypse," *Proceedings of the Twelfth International Congress of Papyrology* (Ann Arbor: University of Michigan Press, 1970), pp. 249–54.

10   "The Sibylline Oracles," *The Old Testament Pseudepigrapha,* ed. J. H. Charlesworth (New York: Doubleday, 1983), pp. 355–6.

11   A. Momigliano, "La Portata Storica dei vaticini sul Settimo Re nel Terzo Libro degli Oracoli Sibillini," *Forma Futuri,* in Studi in Onore del Cardinale Michele Pellegrino (Torino: Bottega d'Erasmo, 1975), pp. 1077–84. The author finds support for the Maccabean revolt at verse 194 – "and then the people of the great God will again be strong" – but the reference here is to a future time and does not specify any link with the Maccabees.

12   J. Nolland, "Sib. Or. III.265–94, An Early Maccabean Messianic Oracle," *Journal of Theological Studies* 30(1979): 158–67. See my critique in *Between Athens and Jerusalem,* p. 67.

13   See also Schuerer, *The History,* Vol. 2, p. 501.

14   Sib. Or. 3:49, which occurs in an oracle from the Roman period, refers to a "holy prince" who will rule the whole earth. This may refer to a Jewish king, but may possibly refer to God himself.

15   For a survey of the history of interpretation of the "Son of Man" figure, see A. J. Ferch, *The Son of Man in Daniel 7* (Berrien Springs: Andrews University Press, 1979), pp. 4–36.

16   For a recent defense of the messianic interpretation, see G. R. Beasley-Murray, "The Interpretation of Daniel 7," *Catholic Biblical Quarterly* 45(1983): 44–58.

17   Compare the remarks of J. A. Goldstein, "How the Authors in 1 and 2 Maccabees Treated the 'Messianic' Promises," this volume.

18   For the arguments, see J. J. Collins, *The Apocalyptic Vision of the Book of Daniel* (Missoula: Scholars Press, 1977), pp. 123–52; id., *The Apocalyptic Imagination* (New York: Crossroad, 1984), pp. 81–3. The angelic interpretation is also defended by A. Lacocque, *The Book of Daniel* (Atlanta: John Knox, 1979), p. 133; C. Rowland, *The Open Heaven. A Study of Apocalyptic in Judaism and Christianity* (New York: Crossroad, 1982), pp. 178–82; and Ferch, *The Son of Man,* p. 174.

19   J. J. Collins, *Daniel, with an Introduction to Apocalyptic Literature*, Forms of Old Testament Literature 20 (Grand Rapids: Eerdmans, 1984), pp. 46–53.

20   Compare Dan 8:13, where "holy ones" are clearly angels.

21   See his article in this volume.

22   On the imagery of the Animal Apocalypse, see P. A. Porter, *Metaphors and Monsters. A Literary-critical Study of Daniel 7 and 8* (Lund: Gleerup, 1983), pp. 46–60; J. C. VanderKam, *Enoch and the Growth of an Apocalyptic Tradition*, Catholic Biblical Quarterly Monograph Series 16 (Washington, D.C.: Catholic Biblical Association, 1984): 164–7.

23   See Nickelsburg, "Salvation without and with a Messiah," this volume.

24   J. Theisohn, *Der auserwählte Richter* (Göttingen: Vandenhoeck & Ruprecht, 1975); Collins, *The Apocalyptic Imagination*, pp. 142–54.

25   J. T. Milik, "4Q visions de Amram et une citation d'Origene," Revue Biblique 79(1972): 77–97; id., "Milkî-sedeq et Milkî-reša dans les anciens écrits juifs et chrétiens," *Journal of Jewish Studies* 23(1972): 95–144. See also P. J. Kobelski, *Melchizedek and Melchireša*, Catholic Biblical Quarterly Monograph Series 10 (Washington, D.C.: Catholic Biblical Association, 1981): 24–36. Melchireša also occurs in 4Q280, where he is the object of cursing.

26   See Kobelski, *Melchizedek*, pp. 84–98. P. von der Osten-Sacken, *Gott und Belial* (Göttingen: Vandenhoeck & Ruprecht, 1969), focuses instead on the Israelite background.

27   See J. J. Collins, "The Mythology of Holy War in Daniel and the Qumran War Scroll. A Point of Transition in Jewish Apocalyptic," *Vetus Testamentum* 25(1975): 596–612, contrasting Daniel's use of Canaanite myth with the adaptation of Persian dualism in the War Scroll.

28   See the discussion of "The development of an exalted angel in apocalyptic literature," by Rowland, in *The Open Heaven*, pp. 94–100.

29   B. Lindars, "Re-enter the Apocalyptic Son of Man," *New Testament Studies* 22(1975–76): 52–72.

30   Rowland, *The Open Heaven*, pp. 100–1; 112–13, à propos of Rev. 1:13–17. Note also how the Epistle to the Hebrews defines the status of Christ in relation to the angels.

31   Rowland, *The Open Heaven*, pp. 102–3; 110. See also I. Gruenwald, *Apocalyptic and Merkavah Mysticism* (Leiden: Brill, 1980).

32   M. E. Stone, "The Concept of the Messiah in IV Ezra," in *Religions in Antiquity: Essays in Memory of E. R. Goodenough*, ed. J. Neusner (Leiden: Brill, 1968), pp. 295–312; also U. B. Mueller, *Messias und Menschensohn in jüdischen Apokalypsen und in der Offenbarung des Johannes* (Gütersloh: Mohn, 1972), pp. 107–53.

33   A. F. Segal, *Two Powers in Heaven: Early Rabbinic Reports about Christianity and Gnosticism* (Leiden: Brill, 1977), pp. 149–51.

34   This passage was brought to my attention by Prof. Jean-L. Duhaime of the Université de Montréal.

35   Deut. 32:8–9, reading "sons of God" with LXX and 4QDeut^q.

36   1QM 13:9–10, *The Dead Sea Scrolls in English,* trans. G. Vermes (Harmonds-
     worth: Penguin, 1968), p. 141.

37   J.-L. Duhaime, "La Rédaction de 1QM XIII et l'Evolution du Dualisme a
     Qumrân," *Revue Biblique* 84(1977), pp. 210–38.

38   Duhaime also regards this passage as secondary.

39   For the classic contrast of two kinds of messianism, see S. Mowinckel, *He That
     Cometh* (Nashville: Abingdon, 1955), p. 281. On the coexistence of both
     kinds at Qumran, see Collins, *The Apocalyptic Imagination,* p. 139, and D.
     Dimant, "Qumran Sectarian Literature," *Jewish Writings of the Second Temple
     Period* (Compendia Rerum Iudaicarum ad Novum Testamentum, ed. M. E.
     Stone [Philadelphia: Fortress, 1984]), pp. 538–42.

40   D. Arenhoevel, *Die Theokratie nach dem 1 and 2 Makkabäerbuch* (Mainz: Mat-
     thias–Gruenwald, 1967), pp. 40–4.

41   J. A. Goldstein, *I Maccabees, Anchor Bible* 41 (Garden City: Doubleday, 1976),
     p. 240.

42   Goldstein's theory that the letter implied opposition to the temple at Leon-
     topolis is unfounded, and is especially incongruent with the setting he pro-
     poses, since the Oniads of Leontopolis supported Alexander Jannaeus.

43   For discussion of Qumran messianism, see S. Talmon, "Typen der Messiaser-
     wartung um die Zeitenwende," in *Probleme biblischer Theologie,* ed. H. W.
     Wolff (München: Kaiser, 1971), pp. 571–88; A. S. van der Woude, *Die Mes-
     sianischen Vorstellungen der Gemeinde von Qumran* (Assen: van Gorcum, 1957);
     J. J. Collins, "Patterns of Eschatology and Qumran," in *Traditions in Trans-
     formation,* ed. B. Halpern and J. D. Levenson (Winoma Lake, Ind.: Eisen-
     brauns, 1981), pp. 351–75; Dimant, "Qumran Sectarian Literature," pp. 538–
     42. The main references are found in 1QS, 1QSa, CD, 4Q Testimonia, 4Q
     Florilegium, and 4Q Patriarchal Blessings.

44   A. Hultgård, *L'Eschatologie des Testaments des Douze Patriarches* (Stockholm:
     Almquist & Wiksell, 1977), Vol. 1, pp. 60–9.

45   See G. Nickelsburg, *Jewish Literature Between the Bible and the Mishnah* (Phil-
     adelphia: Fortress, 1981), pp. 203–12, and G. Davenport, "The 'Anointed of
     the Lord' in Psalms of Solomon 17," *Ideal Figures in Ancient Judaism,* ed. J.
     Collins and G. Nickelsburg (Chico: Scholars Press, 1980), pp. 67–92.

46   J. C. Greenfield and M. E. Stone, "Remarks on the Aramaic Testament of
     Levi from the Geniza," *Revue Biblique* 86(1979): 219–20.

47   On the date of Jubilees, see J. C. VanderKam, *Textual and Historical Studies in
     the Book of Jubilees* (Missoula: Scholars Press, 1977), pp. 217–24.

48   Vermes, *The Dead Sea Scrolls in English,* pp. 202–5.

49   The roles of Levi and Judah in the Testaments of the Twelve Patriarchs stand
     in some relation to the two messiahs of Qumran, but the historical prove-
     nance of the Testaments remains obscure. See Collins, *The Apocalyptic Imagi-
     nation,* pp. 106–13; id., "Testaments," *Jewish Writings of the Second Temple
     Period,* ed. M. E. Stone, pp. 325–55.

6

Waiting for the Messiah:
The Spiritual Universe of the
Qumran Covenanters

SHEMARYAHU TALMON

The vision of an "Anointed King" – Hebrew *māšīaḥ* and Greek *christos* – who will rise in a diversely determined or altogether undetermined future, was deemed by Martin Buber to constitute "die zutiefst originelle Idee des Judentums,"[1] deeply rooted in the biblical world. The concept emanates from the existential chasm that exists between the actual socio-religious and political human condition and the fervent hope for an immaculate, ideal future age that the "Anointed" will ring in.

The messianic age maintains a focal, although differently accentuated position in the Jewish and Christian faiths. Therefore, "Messianism," its meaning and evaluation, constitutes a credal and intellectual challenge for each generation of Jews and Christians, calling for a separate, internal reassessment at every juncture of history.

The Qumran Discoveries

In our own time an additional factor justifies a reopening of the discussion: the discovery of documents from the turn of the era that contain new information on some configurations of the messianic idea in the critical period that witnessed the parting of the ways for Judaism and Christianity. I refer to the well-known manuscript finds in caves located in the area of Qumran in the Judean Desert, which at first often were and sometimes still are designated by the misnomer "The Dead Sea Scrolls."[2] Restrictions of space prevent me from reviewing here in detail the history of their discovery and from presenting a thorough analysis of the materials salvaged from the caves and the structure of the community that deposited them there. Nor is such a survey required in the present framework. Likewise, the identity of this community, its position vis-à-vis other groups, especially mainstream Judaism of the late Second Temple Period and

111

Christianity, can be touched upon only en passant.[3] However, some intro-
ductory remarks may be helpful in tracing the coordinates of the context
in which a discussion of the Covenanters' Messianism must be set.

In the summer of 1947 two Bedouin shepherds were grazing their flock
in the Judean Desert at a place known by the modern Arabic name of
Qumran, situated near the northwestern shore of the Dead Sea, about
seven miles south of Jericho. While searching for a strayed goat, they
chanced on a crevice in the rocks which upon investigation turned out to
be an opening in the roof of a large cave. Letting themselves down into
it, they found upon its floor eight large oblong earthenware jars, some still
covered with bowl-shaped lids. Seven jars were empty, but the eighth contained one large and two small leather scrolls. Once the find became
known, freelance diggers retrieved from the cave four more scrolls and
several large fragments.

Because of the clandestine character of the discoveries, at first doubts
about their authenticity and antiquity were entertained by some scholars.
The suspicions were allayed, however, when the antiquity of the material
was independently established by E. L. Sukenik of the Hebrew University
and J. C. Trever and W. H. Brownlee of the Albright School of Oriental
Research in Jerusalem. Properly conducted archeological excavations in
the Qumran area between 1951 and 1956 verified the dating of the scrolls
to the last two centuries B.C.E. and the first century C.E. The results
achieved by paleographic analysis were later confirmed by carbon-14 tests.
A search of some 200 caves in the area produced written materials from
an additional 10, the richest find hailing from Cave 4. Pottery similar to
the jars from Cave 1 was found in about 25 other caves.

Not far from the cave discovered by the Bedouins, archeologists laid
bare the ruins of fairly large communal buildings that had been occupied
in several phases between the beginning of the second century B.C.E. and
67 or 68 C.E., when the Roman legions destroyed the settlement on their
march from Jericho to Jerusalem. One may surmise that the inhabitants
of that settlement – "The Covenanters" (see below) – had secreted the
scrolls away before their communal center was stormed by the Roman
soldiers. But the exact nature of that assemblage of written materials and
the reasons for their having been taken to the caves remains under scholarly debate.

The scrolls are long sheets of leather, made by stitching hides together.
The needle marks are still clearly recognizable even where the sinew-
thread has rotted away. The letters were inked on the porous side of the
hide, from which the hair had been shaved off. The writing is predominantly in square Hebrew letters, but there are also fragments written in
the ancient Hebrew alphabet and others in Greek. The scrolls differ in

length; the longest, the "Temple Scroll," may have measured some 30 feet when intact and fully rolled out. They seem to have been made in two standard widths, one measuring about eight inches, the other between eleven and twelve. Two corresponding types of jars served as receptacles, each capable of holding three or four scrolls. Originally, they may have been standing next to one another in rows on shelves, giving the impression of an ancient library.[4] The writings preserved in that collection shed light on the history and the conceptual world of a community that emanated from proto-Pharisaic Judaism at the beginning of the second century B.C.E., gradually diverged, and ultimately completely separated from it. The existence of that group probably came to an end in the first half of the second century C.E. Thus, the Qumran community existed altogether for some three centuries.

The new discovery provided firsthand evidence for trends of religious development that affected Judaism toward the end of the Second Temple Period, that is to say, in the last phase of Jewish political sovereignty, which in part preceded and in part coincided with the emergence of Christianity. The scrolls reflect the credal concepts of a group of dissenters who propounded an extreme Messianism. They indeed parted company with proto-Pharisaic Judaism, but never amalgamated with Christianity. A probe into their socioreligious history should thus provide new, albeit indirect, information on the contempoary messianic concepts of rabbinic Judaism and of nascent Christendom, whether by pointing out similarities the Qumran community shared with either, or else by highlighting views that contrasted with one or the other, or with both.

The first lot of manuscripts turned out to be fairly representative of the three categories under which most of the Qumran writings can be subsumed:

1. Copies of books included in the Hebrew Bible. With the exception of the Book of Esther (and possibly Ezra), all books are represented, some by only a few fragments, others by several, sometimes almost complete manuscripts. Quotations of and allusions to biblical texts abound in the specifically Qumranic works (see below).

2. Copies of Apocrypha and Pseudepigrapha, such as Ben Sira, Jubilees, Enoch, the Testaments of the Patriarchs and Tobit. These works had been preserved in the Bible Canon of the Church in ancient translations. Qumran provides irrefutable proof that originally they had been penned in Hebrew.

It should be stressed that the manuscripts in these categories are not necessarily Qumranian in origin or character. They may have been in the possession of prospective members when they joined the community, and thus represent what may be considered the common heritage of Jewry in the Second Temple Period. Therefore, for example, the many textual divergencies from the Masoretic Text found in biblical manuscripts from Qumran must be taken in part to reflect an all-Jewish tradition. Others may have had their origin at Qumran, where scribes would have copied books for the use of their fellow members.

3. The third category is of an altogether different kind. It contains manuscripts and fragments of literary works that are peculiar to the Covenanters. There are the *pesharim, viz.* actualizing extrapolations of biblical books, especially of prophetic literature and the Psalms. By this method of interpretation, Scripture is shown to foreshadow the history of the Covenanters, which is presented as the fulfillment of preordained processes and divine promises. The picture is rounded out by works (not based on the Hebrew Bible) which provide an insight into the structure of the Qumran community, its particular understanding of Jewish (biblical) monotheism, and the norms of its socioreligious life.

It is to these specific Qumranian writings of the third category that we must turn our attention so as to extract from them information on the Covenanters' conception of "Messianism" and the ideal future aeon.

Terms and Methods

I must make three further preliminary remarks regarding terminology and methodology.

1. For the sake of brevity, I shall refer to the Qumran Covenanters in the ensuing deliberations as *"Yaḥad"*. This term is an apocopated form of the designations *Yaḥad Benē 'Ēl* or *Yaḥad Benē Ṣādōk* – "The Commune of the Divine Ones" (or possibly, "The Followers of Sadok") – which the authors of the Qumran writings employ when they make reference to their own community.

2. Proper methodology requires that Qumran Messianism be discussed first and foremost against the background of information gleaned from the *Yaḥad's* own literature, leaving aside at this state of the investigation any considerations based on comparisons with other groups in Second Temple Judaism. The overly hasty comparative approach leads to a premature identification of this new socioreligious phenomenon with other previously known streams in Judaism of that period of which ancient sources – Hellenistic, Rabbinic, and Christian – supply partial evidence, for none of these is as fully documented as is the *Yaḥad,* thanks to the rich finds that issued from the Qumran caves.

I shall also steer clear of the prevailing identification of the *Yaḥad* with the Essenes. As a matter of fact, if these two entities of dissenters from mainstream Judaism are lumped together, the resulting amalgam should be called Qumran-*Yaḥad* rather than Essenes, since documentation on the former is incomparably more detailed and comprehensive than the latter. Moreover, whereas information about the Essenes comes entirely from retrospective reports written by authors who had never been members of that community – with the possible exception of Josephus, if his claim is taken at face value – our knowledge of the *Yaḥad* is derived from first-hand sources authored by its own members, and is contemporaneous with the events described in them. This gives the latter an edge over the former.[5]

I shall yet have occasion to demonstrate that the specific configuration in which Messianism appears at Qumran, unlike what has been ascribed to the Essenes by any ancient informant, is of decisive importance for my reticence to identify the one with the other.

3. I use the term "Messianism" with some hesitation. The notation of the uniqueness of the messianic savior that inheres in this concept as commonly employed is not compatible with the Qumranians' fervently expected rise of "Two Anointed," one descended from the "House of David" and one from the "House of Aaron." This distinction should be kept in mind when, for the sake of brevity, I shall nevertheless employ the term "Messianism" in the ensuing deliberations.

For similar reasons, I shall avoid as much as possible the employment of the term "eschatology," which bears the stamp of metahistory or is understood to designate "the end of historical time." Rather I shall speak of the "Age to Come," which the Qumranians, like biblical Israel, perceived within the framework of actual history, expecting it to set in at a preordained stage in the progress of history.[6]

The Founders of the *Yaḥad*

The founding members of the *Yaḥad* can best be described as a group of Jews possessed by an ardent messianic vision. Viewed from the angle of typology, they represent the most decidedly millenarian or chiliastic movement[7] in Second Temple Judaism and possibly in antiquity altogether, Christianity included.[8] By extrapolating biblical texts, they had worked out the exact date of the onset of the ideal "Age to Come," and held themselves in readiness to welcome its harbingers, the "Anointed," who would usher it in. However, they did not live to see their hopes materialize, and thus were suspended in limbo between the real and the visionary stage of history. They present to us a prime example of stumped millenarianism. The *Yaḥad* is a godsend for anyone interested in a typology of religious dissent, its internal development and the communal structures and organization in which it expresses itself. The study of "Sectarianism," not alone in the framework of Judaism but as a general phenomenon, could greatly benefit from an expertly carried out sociological analysis of the *Yahad*.[9]

We should be reminded that once before Israel had experienced an almost-realized messianism.[10] The returnees from the Babylonian Exile, led by Zerubbabel, Ezra, and Nehemiah, had conceived of their return and the restoration of a religiopolitical Judean entity, however restricted, as the realization of Jeremiah's prophecy in which he had foreseen for Judah a period of doom and exile that would last for seventy years (Jer. 25:11, 12; 29:10; cf. Zech. 1:12; 7:5; Dan. 9:2; 2 Chron. 36:21; see also Ezra 1:1 = 2 Chron. 36:22). At the end of this preordained span of time, God would reverse his people's bitter fate and restore Judah to her fortunes. The post exilic biblical books bear witness to the fact that the returning exiles took Jeremiah's prophecy at face value, surprising as this may sound to us. They question whether the appointed time indeed had run its course, and whether the stage was set for the rebuilding of the temple, God's time-honored abode, which would signify his residing again in the midst of his redeemed people (Hag. 1:2).

Prophets who were active in those days, Zechariah and especially Haggai, gave divinely inspired sustenance to their contemporaries' conviction that the restoration of Judah's glory of old indeed had set in, nay that the glory of the "New Age" that they would experience would surpass that of the former (Hag. 2:1–9; cf. Zech. 1:16, 2:8–9, 14 [Heb.]; 8:1ff.). Some utterances of these prophets have distinct "messianic" overtones. Zerubbabel, scion of the House of David, figures in them as the "Anointed Who Had Come" (Hag. 2:20–23; Zech. 4:6–10), and traditional Davidic "Hoheitstitel" are assigned to him (e.g., Hag. 2:23; Zech. 3:8; 6:12). The oracles are patterned upon prophetic "latter-day"[11] visions of the First Temple Period and upon descriptions of the "Exodus from [the Egyptian] Exile" and the ensuing "Landnahme," as can be seen from a comparison of, e.g., Hag. 2:5, 21–22 with Ex. 15:4, 19; Zech. 3:10 with Mic. 4:4; Zech. 8:20–23 with Isa. 2:2–3 = Mic. 4:1–2 et al.

In the final reckoning, the returnees' flighty expectations did not come to fruition. The world that had been seen to be in upheaval (Hag. 2:20–22) came to rest (Zech. 1:11). Mundane, real history took over once more. With the fading of Zerubbabel from the scene, the hopes that had fastened upon the "Anointed" came to naught. The actual "Restoration" did not measure up to the anticipated profound remaking of the historical world.

The founding members of the *Yahad* may have thus judged the Period of the Return from the Babylonian Exile. The allusions to and mentions of it in their literature are so scanty that one is inclined to assume that they intended to obliterate it entirely from their conception of Israel's history, and to claim for themselves the distinction of being the first returnees after the destruction. As will yet be elaborated, they conceived of themselves as exiles from Judah who had missed their chance when the edict of Cyrus had made possible the return foreseen by prophets of the First Temple Period. In any case, in their view, the divine promise had not yet been fulfilled and remained open-ended. Now it fell to their lot to close the circle and to assume the preordained task of the Restoration Generation.

Working Presuppositions

The ensuing discussion will be based on the following theses:

1. The Covenanters of Qumran conceived of themselves as the sole true representatives of biblical Israel. While in reality they existed in the Hellenistic and early Roman period, conceptually they lived in the biblical age, which for them, in distinction from mainstream Judaism, had not yet concluded. Viewed from this angle, they could be designated the last *ba'alēmiqrā'*. This characteristic misled some scholars to identify them with the medieval Karaites.[12]

2. More precisely, the *Yaḥad* members viewed themselves as the exclusive *zera' yiśrā'ēl* (CD XII:21–22),[13] the "holy remnant" – *zera' haqōdeš* (Ezra 9:1–2; cf. Isa. 6:13) who in this *qēṣ* or generation, had been favored by God again "to fill the universe" (CD II:11–12) forever and ever (1QH XVII:14).

3. The *Yaḥad* assumes the role that postexilic biblical historiography (Ezra–Nehemiah, 2 Chron. 36:22–23) and prophecy (Haggai, Zechariah, and Malachi) accord to the returnees from the Babylonian Exile in the early Persian Period. The substitution possibly was helped along by contracting the entire Persian Period to a bare minimum, thus linking their own generation "directly" to the post-destruction generation.

4. Any elucidation of Qumran "Messianism" and the Covenanters' concept of the "Messianic Age" must take this historical construct into account. Their notions in these matters were directly bound up with the views reflected in the postexilic biblical literature.

Like their precursors, the returnees under Zerubbabel, Ezra, and Nehemiah, the Qumran Covenanters sought to underpin their claim to the task and the title of the "Saved Remnant" by basing it upon a biblical prophecy. They achieved this aim by focusing on a symbolic act, performed at divine instruction by the prophet Ezekiel in face of the besieged city of Jerusalem: "You lie down on your left side and place the iniquity of the house of Israel on it; for the number of days that you lie on it you shall bear their iniquity. I am converting for you the years of their iniquity into a number of days — 390 days. . . . When you finish these, you shall lie down a second time, on your right side, and bear the iniquity of the house of Judah for forty days; I am converting each year of it into a day for you" (Ezek. 4:4–6). Irrespective of the originally intended meaning of this passage – which at times is interpreted to have a "retrospective," not a "prospective," thrust (see e.g., Rashi *ad* 2 Chron. 36:22)[14] – the Qumranians, in a *pesher*-like fashion, read Ezekiel's symbolic act of woe as an oracle of weal, deftly balancing the explicit threat of exile with an implied message of hope. The account they give of the genesis of the *Yaḥad* opens as follows (CD I:3–8): "For when they were unfaithful and forsook him, he [God] hid his face from Israel and his sanctuary and delivered them up to the sword. But remembering the covenant of the forefathers, he left a remnant to Israel and did not deliver it up to [utter] destruction (cf. Jer. 5:18; 30:11; 46:28; Neh. 9:31). And in the age of wrath (i.e., their own days), three hundred and ninety years after he had given them into the hand of King Nebuchadnezzar of Babylon, he remembered them (cf. CD VI:2–5) and caused the root he had planted to sprout from Israel and Aaron to take [again] possession of his land and enjoy the fruits of its soil" (cf. Zech. 3:10; 8:12; Hag. 2:18–19). Exegetes have found it difficult if not impossible to make head or tail of the figure 390,[15] whereas the unit of 40 days, signifying 40 years, obviously reflects the biblical stereotype that accords this number of years to an average generation. The Covenanters attached realistic values to these figures.[16] It cannot be pure coincidence that by subtracting 390 from 586, when Jerusalem and the Temple were destroyed by the Babylonians, one arrives at the beginning of the second century B.C.E., which scholarly *communis opinio* takes to be the time in which the *Yaḥad* arose.[17] I am persuaded that what we have here is yet another piece of millenarian arithmetics.[18] Ezekiel's oracle of 390 years took on for the Covenanters the very same key meaning that Jeremiah's prophecy of 70 years had for the Judeans who returned from the Exile.[19]

It may be presumed that then and there, the founding members of the *Yaḥad*, "the first men of holiness" [*'an šĕ hagōdeš* [*hari*] *šōnīm*] (CD IV:6), readied themselves for the great event, the onset of the "New Age." In their millenarian calculations, they still had to account for the 40 years that Ezekiel had foreseen as the period of Judah's exile. It would appear that they took care of this matter in several ways.

Telescoping Deuteronomy 2:14, which speaks of the Exodus (from Egypt) generation, with Ezekiel 4:6, the author of CD tells us that "from the day of the 'Teacher of the *Yaḥad*' [probably to be identified with the "Righteous Teacher" of whom I shall yet speak] until all the inimical men [men of war] who sided with the "Liar" [their prominent opponent] will come to an end, [exactly] forty years [will pass]" (CD VIII:52–54; Rabin, XX:13–15).

The same figure is given for the duration of the final war, during which time the Covenanters, "The Sons of Light," will vanquish all their opponents, "The Sons of Darkness," i.e., foreign nations (1Q MI–II) and Jews who had not joined the "New Covenant."

However, of more importance for our present concern is the opening passage of the Zadokite Document to which I already referred. Having elucidated the figure of 390 years, the author goes on to report that as the founding members "perceived their iniquity and recognized that they [still] were guilty men, for twenty years they were like blind men groping for their way. And God observed their deeds, that they sought him with a whole heart, and he raised for them a [or: the] Teacher of Righteousness [or: Righteous Teacher] to guide them in the way of his heart" (CD I:8–11). This passage forms the continuation of the preceding *pesher*-like interpretation of Ezekiel 4:4–6. Therefore, the figure "20" requires an explanation. Two possibilities offer themselves. Either the Ezekiel text on which the author relied contained in 4:6 the reading "20" instead of MT's "40"[20] or (preferably) he divided the stereotype lifespan of one generation into two parts, each amounting to 20 years (cf. the figures given for Samson's "Judgeship" in Judges 15:20 and 16:31). This leads to the following understanding of the passage, which, however, is not explicated in the Covenanters' writings: After the founding members had been "groping for the way" for 20 years, the Righteous Teacher arose to lead them for another 20 years. Assuming that the "Teacher" had himself been one of the "gropers," his association with the group would thus have spanned the life of one generation – 40 years, parallelling the figure of 40 years given for the time that elapsed from the day of his demise to the end of the "Liar's" men (CD VIII:52–54).

The Righteous Teacher

Some attention now must be given to the figure of the *mōrēh haṣedek*,[21] who at this juncture enters the scene and from here on will occupy a prominent position in the Qumran writings. In all likelihood, he was of priestly descent. What is important for our present concern is the role accorded him in the unfolding messianic drama, or rather in its impeded dénouement. The "Teacher" was born out of intense emotional stress, triggered by the profound disappointment that the unrealized hope for an imminent onset of the millenium had evoked in the initial nucleus of Covenanters when the precalculated date passed uneventfully. Thus, emerging in a second stage of the group's history, and not being its initiator,[22] he cannot be defined as a "Founding Prophet" (in the typology introduced by Max Weber), nor has the occasionally proposed identification with Jesus Christ any basis.[23] Rather, he must be seen as an inspired interpreter whose latent inspiration revealed itself in his response to his fellows' despair. It fell to him to find the means for bridging the gap between the unduly protracted *now* and the disappointingly delayed *then*. This he apparently did by transforming the loose group-cohesion of the founding members into a structured socioreligious system. Under his guidance, their utopian millenarianism,[24] which originally had anarchistic overtones, crystallized into a structured order. Before long, the basically antiestablishment millenarians formed a socioreligious establishment of their own which was soon to surpass in rigidity and normative exactitude the system of the mother community from which they had separated.

The vista of the "New Age" was not lost from sight. But it appears that once Ezekiel's vision had failed to materialize for them, the Covenanters could not anymore or would not venture to establish by chiliastic computations the exact date of the onset of the ideal aeon. One wonders why they did not seize upon the apocalyptic 490 years' [7 × 70] vision in the Book of Daniel (Chs. 9–10) for achieving this purpose. To go here into speculations about what caused this abstinence would lead us too far afield, although some explanation could be tentatively suggested.[25] In any case it stands to reason that in this crucial second period of 20 years, the founding members retreated into the Judean Desert, led by the *mōrēh haṣedek*. Reenacting the paradigmatic events that had determined and enfolded Israel's history in the biblical period, life in the arid area of Qumran signified for them the period of Exile – Egypt and Babylon rolled into one. There, they located typologically the "Damascus," beyond which Israel would be exiled, according to the prophet Amos (5:27).

"I shall take you into exile beyond Damascus, says God" (CD VII:13–14; cf. Zech. 6:8). There "they shall escape again in the time of the visitation [or: judgment]," whereas "they that turn away [from God and the Covenant] shall be delivered to the sword when the Anointed of Aaron and Israel shall come" (CD VII:20–21a; cf. Zech. 11:11).

Like the "locust" that usually invades the Land of Israel from the south and represents the "foe from the north" in the visions of the biblical prophet Joel (Joel 2:10; cf. 1:1–2:11), "Damascus" and the "north" in the Qumran writings should probably be understood as cyphers for "exile in the desert of Judah."[26] There, in that "Damascus," they established the New Covenant (CD VI:19; VIII:21). By this token, the loosely knit group of founding members achieved the character of a structured community that set out to attract and initiate an ever-growing number of novices (1QS I:1–II:18, et al.).

It seems that when the Covenanter's millennial expectations consolidated into institutionalized heterodoxy, the authorities of the mother community, who until then appear to have viewed their dissenting concepts with equanimity, took steps to prevent a further solidification of the rebellious community. Led by the "Wicked Priest," they pursued the "Teacher" and his followers to Qumran, his "house of exile" (1QpHab XI:4–8), where the Covenanters had meant to weather out the now uncharted period of time that intervened between their own days and the hoped-for *Age to Come*. Then, they would embark on their march to Jerusalem, regain the Holy City, and make her the kingpin of the established Commonwealth of Israel, thus bringing once again to its climax the historical cycle of biblical days: Exile – Sojourn in the Wilderness – Settlement.[27]

Their ignorance of the (next) *appointed day* brought about the decisive modification in the Covenanters' millenarian stance. In the initial phase they had expected the progress of history toward the divinely ordained onset of the *New Age* to unfold in a smooth process. Just as the Judeans in the Babylonian Exile had *passively* bided their time until the day that would be ripe for the divinely promised return (Jer. 29:1–14), the Qumran millenarians at first adopted a quietist posture in their *Waiting for the Messiah:* Since the date of this rise had been divinely ordained, no human interference was required to bring it about.[28] The changed circumstances engendered a reformulation of this attitude. They began to perceive their own sinfulness (CD I:8–9) as a factor that had contributed to or had altogether caused the retardation of the redeeming event. The need for action was further accentuated by the interference of hostile agents – the "Wicked Priest" and his followers – who obstructed the expected smooth progress of history toward the *New Age*. These inimical forces had to be overcome before the New Jerusalem would be achieved. An apocalyptic battle in which all evil powers would be vanquished was now seen as a *conditio sine qua non* for the aspired transition from the dire *here and now* to the illumined *then and there*. This battle, which was to shake the foundations of the universe, is portrayed in the War Scroll (1QM).[29] It is conceived in the image of Ezekiel's Gog and Magog vision (Ezek. 38–39) and the apocalyptic engagements of which the Book of Daniel speaks. In view of this presumed development of the Covenanters' messianism, the War Scroll probably was produced during a later stage of the *Yaḥad's* existence. However, this assumption rests solely on the evolution of ideas presented here and cannot be substantiated by other evidence gained either from a scrutiny of Qumran literature or from a paleographical analysis of the scrolls.[30]

The Anointed

The victorious termination of the final war, the recapture of Jerusalem, and the rebuilding of the Temple, will pave the way for the assured advent of the *Anointed* as a matter of course. As already said, in Qumran literature this concept develops a distinctive bifurcation: Two figures are seen to appear on the horizon – an *Anointed of Israel,* associated with the royal house of David, and an *Anointed of the House of Aaron.* The doctrine of a priestly Anointed who officiates next to the royal *māšîaḥ* at the head of Israel's body politic is reflected also in some strata of the apocryphal literature.[31] This wider currency proves that it cannot be considered the Covenanters' exclusive legacy, but rather must have been rooted in a common Jewish tradition. However, in the Qumran literature, the doctrine is accorded a much more significant role than in any apocryphal book.

While at times dissent has been voiced on this matter, the opinion prevails that at Qumran the rise of *Two Anointed* was indeed expected.[32] L. Ginsberg's conclusion, which he reached on the basis of the Zadokite Document alone, has lost nothing of its poignancy: "We have to reject the [then] dominant opinion which seems to find references to only one Messiah in our document (CD), who unites both priesthood and kingdom in his person."[33] I fully concur with this view, which can now be buttressed by quotations culled from writings from the Qumran caves.

The following are some of the relevant texts on which a discussion of the issue must be based:

1QS IX:10–11   They shall be judged by the first statutes [or: the statutes laid down by the first/founders][34] by which the *Yaḥad* members were first ruled, until there shall arise [*bw'*] the prophet and the Anointed [*ūmešiḥē*] of Aaron and Israel.[35]

CD XII:22–23   This is the rule of the assembly of the camps who walk in it in the Age of Wickedness [*beqēṣ hāriš'āh*] until there shall arise the Anointed [*'ad amūd mešī/ūaḥ*][36] of Aaron and Israel.

CD XIII:20–22   This is [the rule for] the assembly of the camps during all [the Age of Wickedness – *bekol qēṣ hāriš'āh* – and whosoever will not abide by the]se [statutes] shall not be [considered] worthy to live in the land [when there shall come the Anointed of Aaron and Israel – *be'aḥarīt hayāmīm*].

CD XIX:34 [VIII:21]– XX:1	None of the backsliders . . . shall be counted among the Council of the people and in its records they shall not be entered, from the day of the demise of the Teacher of the *Yaḥad* [*mōrēh hayāḥīd*] until there shall arise the Anointed of Aaron and Israel.
CD XIV:18–19	This is the exact [or: detailed] account of the statutes in which [they shall walk in the appointed period of evil until there shall arise the Anoin]ted of Aaron and Israel who will atone for their iniquity.
CD XIX:9–11 [VII:20–21]	Those who watch for him [or: observe his commands] are the humble of the flock; they shall be saved in the Age of the Visitation [*beqēṣ hapeqūdāh*], whereas the backsliders shall be delivered up to the sword when there shall come the Anointed of Aaron and Israel (cf. 4Q174, II:5:[The Anointed of Is]rael and Aaron).

The duality of the Anointed appears also to be mirrored in the already mentioned opening passage of the Damascus Documents.

CD I:5–7	And in the age of [his] wrath [*beqēṣ ḥārōn*] he remembered them and caused the root he had planted to sprout [again] from Israel and Aaron.[37]

The Duality of the Messiah

I intend to show that the duality of a Davidic lay *māšīaḥ* and an Aaronide priestly Anointed reflects a dependence on a biblical pattern that evolved in the postexilic period.[38] At the same time it underscores the sociohistorical character of the messianic idea in Hebrew Scriptures and in Qumran literature, thus revealing the significance of this concept for both biblical Israel and the *Yaḥad* Covenanters. Also in this matter, the *Yaḥad*'s extreme Bible-directedness to which attention has already been drawn, comes to the fore. The linguistic and stylistic affinities of the Qumran materials with biblical literature, especially the postexilic books, cannot be adequately explained solely by the chronological proximity of these two bodies of writings. They must rather be understood as revealing a striking spiritual consanguinity. The Qumran authors' predilection for depicting their own community, its structure, history, and future hopes, by having recourse to idioms, technical terms, and motifs that are manifestly drawn from biblical writings, discloses the *Yaḥad*'s self-identification with biblical, especially postexilic, Israel and its conceptual universe. From this source, the *Yaḥad* drew also the religiopolitical concept of *Two Anointed* who in the *New Age* would together govern their community, and ultimately the reconstituted polity of the People of Israel.

The roots of this concept can be traced to the world of ideas of the returnees from the Babylonian exile. At that time, the prophet Zechariah had presented to the repatriates a *blueprint* for the organization of the Province of Jahud as a *state in nuce* in the framework of the Persian Empire. It was based on a concept of societal structure that differed quite distinctly from the organization of the Judean body politic under the monarchy in the First Temple Period. Then, the king had not only been in charge of the mundane affairs of the realm, but had also wielded controlling power over the sacred institutions. The proximity of the sanctuary to the palace had enabled the king to exercise close supervision over its affairs (see e.g., 2 Kings 12:7–17 = 2 Chron. 24:4–14; 2 Kings 22–33 = 2 Chron. 34–35; 2 Chron. 17:7–9; 26:16–18; 29–31; 33:15–16). The priesthood was dependent on the king, so much so that the high priests were considered royal officials (2 Sam. 8:17 = 1 Chron. 18:16; 2 Sam. 20:25–26; 1 Kings 4:2, 4–5) whom the king could appoint and depose at will (1 Kings 2:26–27, 35; see also 2 Chron. 24:20–22).

In the early Persian Period the situation changed perceptibly. The loss of political sovereignty with the fall of Jerusalem in 586 B.C.E. had undermined the status of royalty. It was probably further weakened by the Persian authorities' insistence on granting the returnees only a measure of administrative autonomy, restricted, in fact, to the domain of ritual and sacred institutions (Ezra 5:3–5; cf. 1:1–4, and see 4:8–23), at the same time enhancing the status of the priests (Ezra 7:11–26).[39] Moreover, Zerubbabel's position within the Judean body politic seems to have been somewhat tenuous. Being descended not from Zedekiah, the last king of Judah, but from his brother Jehoiachin (1 Chron. 3:17–19), who had been dethroned and exiled by the Babylonians in 597 B.C.E. (2 Kings 24:8–17 = 2 Chron. 36:9–10), his claim to royal authority presumably met with some resistance (contrast Jer. 22:24 with Hag 2:23; and Jer. 22:28 with Jer. 28:4).[40] The combination of these factors enhanced the standing of the priesthood, whose position was further strengthened by collaboration (Hag. 2:10–14;[41] Neh. 13:4–8) and marriage alliances with the upper classes in the Palestinian population that had not been exiled (Ezra 9–10; Neh. 6:18). As a result, the prestige of Joshua the high priest, Zerubbabel's contemporary, rose to an unprecedented height, so much so that he appears to have successfully contested Zerubbabel's supremacy in matters of the body politic.

It is against this background that the prophet Zechariah's intervention must be evaluated. Realizing the changed circumstances, he proposed a plan of "shared responsibilities": the Davidic Anointed and the Aaronide Anointed were to be assigned separate spheres of competence (Zech. 3). Monarchy and priesthood are to complement each other, their mutual relations guided by "a counsel of Peace" (Zech. 6:13), a sign and an example for the entire community (Zech. 8:9–17) and, beyond that, for the family of nations (Zech. 8:20–23; cf. Isa. 2:2–4 = Mic. 4:1–5 et al.). In distinction from the "monocephalic" structure of the Judean realm in the First Temple Period,[42] that of the New Commonwealth of Israel was to be "bicephalic":[43] In his vision, the prophet perceives *two Anointed – šenē benē yiṣhār,* symbolized by "two olives [olive trees/branches] pouring oil through two golden pipes" (Zech. 4:2–3, 11–12) "standing before the Lord of the whole world" (Zech. 4:14; cf. CD XX:1; XII:22; XIV:19 restored).[44]

This duality is given a more realistic expression in a divine word (Zech. 6:9–14; cf. CD I:5–7) that accords a crown to Joshua the High Priest and a throne to the shoot (out of David's root [Zerubbabel]) (cf. 4Q 174, I, 1–2:10–13; 161, 8–10:11 restored), or preferably, a crown and a throne to each,[45] as insignia of their complementary functions.[46]

It cannot be ascertained whether that prophetic concept was indeed realized in the returnees' community. The unexplained disappearance of Zerubbabel, the last scion of the Davidic house, upset the intended balance, turning the scales in favor of the priestly anointed. However, it appears that the *Yaḥad* embraced this plan as the prototype of the political structure and modeled upon it their vision of the future age. Identifying with an idealized Period of Return from the Exile, they discerned in it the *Urzeit* in whose image they conceived the ideal *Aeon to Come.* The *Yaḥad* then were to be established as the axis of a world freed from all tension that had still afflicted the prototypical *Urzeit.* The *New Age* will be a shining creation, healed from all religious blemishes and societal evils which had marred the historical Israel also in the days of that other *Return,* the days of Zerubbabel, Ezra, and Nehemiah.

The character of the *Age to Come* remains largely restorative. It will unfold in the geographical frame of the land of Israel to which the *Yaḥad* returns victorious. The Qumranians expected a new *Landnahme,* culminating in the rebuilding of the temple in Jerusalem, portrayed as an infinitely improved, but nevertheless realistic version, not a spiritualized replica of the historical city. The messianic age will be experienced by the Covenanters as a structured ethnic-national entity – as a renewed People of Israel – not as inspired individuals. This notion again reflects the conceptual universe of biblical, especially early postexilic Israel. However, the

Yaḥad infused into the ascriptive designation *People of Israel* the idea of *elective* association. They are the chosen remnant of biblical Israel (cf. Mal. 3:13–21 [Heb.]; Ezra 9:2 with Isa. 6:11–13) to whom alone out of all Israel God had granted a new lease on life, the right to reconstitute Israel's sovereignty, epitomized in the Twin–Anointed of Israel and Aaron.

The New Age

It needs to be stressed that the Covenanters invested their conception of the messianic age with the same real-historical character which biblical thinkers give to their visions of the future. The new eon was seen by the founding members to be only one step away from their own days. They were standing on the threshold of a new epoch in history, infinitely sublime, but basically not different from preceding stages in actually experienced history.[47] The similarity with the biblical world of ideas shows that in contradistinction to the absence of the historiographical genre from the literature of the Sages, the Covenanters cultivated "historiography," spinning out a literary genre handed down to them as a legacy from the biblical writers who had perfected it.

The progress of history is seen as a succession of *qiṣim*, i.e. blocks of time or circumscribed periods.[48] In keeping with biblical usage, they can also be defined by means of a generation or generations – *dōr/dōrōt* (1QS IV:13, cf. Deut. 32:7; Isa. 41:4 et al.). Beginning with the creation of the world, the series leads up to the *qēṣ/dōr 'aḥarōn*, the initial phase of the *Yaḥad*, and culminates in *'aḥarīt hayāmīm* (see 1QpHab VII:1–2, 7–8, 10–14 combined with II:5–7). This later epoch is not directly designated by the terminus technicus *qēṣ*, but it is referred to as *qēṣ neḥerāṣāh wa aśōt hadāśāh* – "the decreed epoch of new things" (1QS IV:25; cf. Dan. 9:26–27; 11:35–36; Isa. 10:23; 28:22; 43:19),[49] and possibly also by inversion as *'aḥarīt haqēṣ* (4Q 169, 3–4, III:3; 173, 1:5).

A work entitled by its editor *The Ages of Creation* (4Q 180; cf. 4Q 181), in which the *qiṣim* were consecutively enumerated, beginning with the time before the creation of man (cf. CD II:7; 1QS III:15–18; 1QH I:8–12), is preserved in only a few fragments. However, on the basis of data assembled from diverse Qumran writings, the outlines of the *Yaḥad* concept of history can still be recovered.[50] The history of Israel, as of all mankind (1QS IV:15–17), is traced from Creation to *'aḥarīt hayāmīm*, with the destruction of the Temple serving as the main watershed (CD V:20–21; VII:14, 21 VIII:1–3). Events preceding it are reported as having occurred in the days of the *dōrōt ri'šōnīm* (CD I:16–20), i.e., in the predestruction period, which is subdivided into a number of "generations" or *qiṣim*. The postdestruction era is that of the *dōrōt 'aḥarōnīm* (CD I:11–13). It includes the days in which the *dōr 'aḥarōn* (CD I:11–12), i.e., the *Yaḥad*, arose.[51] Becaue of "the wicked" who opposed the Covenanters and persecuted them, it is designated *qēṣ hārešīaʿ, hārešaʿ, hārišʿāh* (CD VI:10,14; XII:23; XV:7,10 restored; cf. XX:23 et al.).[52] This terminology reflects a "relative" – *former* and *later*, not *first* and *last* – chronological system. Events are dated *before* or *after* a middle point – in the case under review, the destruction of the Temple – and not in succession from a primary point of departure, such as the Creation. One is again reminded of a facet in the biblical concept of time that shows up especially in the postexilic literature. Zechariah refers to the prophets of predestruction days as *nebīʾīm riʾšōnīm* (Zech. 1:4; 7:7, 12).[53] Likewise, Haggai speaks of the newly built temple as *habayit haʾaḥarōn* in contrast to *habayit hārīʾšōn* of the First Temple Period (Hag. 2:3–9; cf. Ezra 3:12).

In the present context, the postdestruction era is of focal interest, especially the transition from the *qēṣ/dōr 'aḥarōn*, within the wider setting of *dōrōt 'aḥarōnīm*, to *'aḥarīt hayāmīm*, when the Anointed will arise. Some texts give the impression that initially the age of *'aḥarīt hayāmīm* was considered to be part of the *qēṣ 'aḥarōn*, the positive ending of its negative beginning as *qēṣ rišʿāh* (CD VI: 10–11, 14–15; XII:23; XV:7), *qēṣ 'awlāh* (1QS IV:18), or *qēṣ ma ʿal* (CD XX:23). The basic continuity of these time spans in the Covenanters' view of history shows in passages like the following: "The interpretation of this saying (Hab. 1:4–5) concerns the unfai[thful men] in *'aḥarīt hayāmīm*, the vio[lent breakers of the Cove]nant, who will not believe when they hear all that [is to happen] to the *dōr 'aḥarōn* from the Priest. . . ." (1 QpHab II:5–7); "Its interpretation (Hab. 2:8) concerns the last priests [i.e., the priests of the *dōrōt 'aḥarōnīm*], who amass riches and [illicit] wealth by plundering (the) peoples. But in *'aḥarīt hayāmīm*, their riches and plunder shall be delivered into the hands of the army of the Kittim" (1QpHab IX:4–7).

When the expected smooth shift from the negative phase of the *qēṣ 'aḥarōn (dōr/dōrōt 'aḥarōn/īm)* did not materialize, history was adjusted to the changed circumstances, and *'aḥarīt hayāmīm* was now conceived as a self-constituted *New Age*. The profound disappointment that resulted from the nonrealized transition shows distinctly in the Pesher Habakkuk. The author relates plaintively that "God told Habakkuk to write down (Hab. 2:2) what would happen to the *dōr 'aḥarōn*, but he did not inform him on the termination of that *qēṣ*." This explains the fact "that the *qēṣ ' aḥarōn* shall be prolonged, more than the prophets have [fore]told (cf. Dan. 10:14; 8:19), for God's mysteries are astounding." But "the hands of the men of truth who keep the Torah shall not slacken in the service of truth," even though "the *qēṣ hāʾaḥarōn* is prolonged. For [ultimately] all the divine[ly appointed] ages [*qiṣē 'ēl*] will come in their destined order as he has decreed in his unfathomable wisdom" (1QpHab VII:1–14). If the above argument concerning the proximity of these *qiṣīm* or *dōrōt* to each other can be sustained, it would imply that in the *Yaḥad* view of history, *'aḥarīt hayāmīm* when the Anointed are expected to arise is but a generation removed from the *dōr 'aḥarōn*. Once again, this linguistic-conceptual usage echoes a biblical notion. In the farewell speech of Moses, the phrases *'aḥarē mōtī* and *'aḥarīt hayāmīm* are equated by being juxtaposed in two cola of one and the same verse: "I know that after my death . . . you will turn away from the path that I have enjoined upon you and *be'aḥarīt hayāmīm* [i.e., in the days to come] misfortune will befall you" (Deut. 31:29; cf. 29:21 and Ps. 78:5–6).

All in all it can be said that the Covenanters conceived of the "Messianic Age," *'aḥarīt hayāmīm,* the preordained Period in which the Two Anointed shall ring in the *New Aeon – qēṣ neḥerāṣāh wa 'aśōt ḥadāšāh* (1QS IV:25) – as one further link in the chain of historical epochs. The Anointed will not come at the *end of time,* but rather after a *turn of times,* after a profound crisis in history, marked by tribulations of cosmic dimensions (cf. Hag. 2:20–22). Once these are overcome, the world shall settle down to experience "a time of salvation for the people of God" that is *eo ipso* "an age of [world] dominion for all members of his fellowship," i.e., for the *Yaḥad* (1QM I:5; contrast Zech. 1:10ff.).

The Hierarchy of the Community

The portrayal of *'aḥarīt hayāmīm* in the wider framework in which the (messianic) *Banquet of the Two Anointed* is set reflects distinct characteristics both of the *Yaḥad's* communal structure in historical reality, and of the returnees' community, as described in Ezra-Nehemiah. A comparison of relevant texts discloses their striking congruence. In all three instances there emerges the picture of a tightly knit socioreligious entity, restricted in numbers and spatially compressed. The compactness and smallness make for a high degree of direct participation of the membership in daily communal life and in deliberations and decisions concerning the entire group, notwithstanding the pronounced hierarchical structure of the Qumran commune in practice and theory.

The Rule of the Congregation prescribes the future standing order of members in the assembly:[54]

1QSa I:1–3   *be'aḥarīt hayāmīm* when they will gather [in the *Yaḥad* and con]duct themselves in accord with the ordinances of the *benē ṣādōk* the priests and the men of their Covenant who re[frained from walking in the] way of the people. They are the men of his council who kept his Covenant in the [*qēṣ* of] iniquity, expia[ting for the lan]d [or: world].

This arrangement is foreshadowed in passages that detail the rules by which the Covenanters' life was regulated in actuality (e.g., 1QS V:1ff.; CD XII:22–23). At the same time, it also mirrors the recurring notices in postexilic biblical literature of assemblies in which rules were laid down and statutory acts proclaimed (e.g., Ezra 9:1ff.; 10:7ff.; Neh. 5:1ff.; 8:1ff.; 9:1; cf. also Hag. and Zech.).

Especially striking is the linguistic similarity between the passage in the *Rule of the Congregation* that speaks of the future public reading of the statutes in front of the entire community, and the Reading of the Torah in Nehemiah 8:

1QSa I:4–5   they [the priests] shall convene [*yaqhīlū*] all those who come [including] infants and women, and they shall read in th[eir hearing] al[l] precepts of the Covenant, and shall explain to them [*welahābīnām*] all their stat[tut]es lest they stray in [their] er[ror]s.

Neh. 8:1–8   all the people gather as one man on the square before the Water Gate . . . Ezra the priest brought the Torah before the assembly [*qāhāl*] [consisting of] men, women and all those [children] who understand . . . and he read from it in the presence of the men, the women and those [children] who understand . . . and the Levites explained [*mebīnīm*] the Torah to the people . . . so that the people understood what was read.

Into this *Yaḥad be'aḥarīt hayāmīm* assembly the Anointed are inducted:

1 QSa II:11–17   [This is (shall be) the se]ssion of the men of renown [called to the] [appointed] meeting of the *Yaḥad* Council, when [God] shall lead to them the [Davidic?] Anointed. With them shall come the [Priest] [at the head of the] f[ather (house)s of the] Aaronide priests, the men of renown [called] to the [appointed] assembly. And they shall sit [before him each] according to his dignity and [his standing]. And then shall [come the Anoin]ted of Israel and before him shall sit the head[s of] the [thousands of Israel] each according to his dignity, according to their standing in their camps and marching [formation]s. And all the heads of [clans of the Congrega]tion together with the Wise [of the holy Congregation] shall sit before them each according to his dignity.

The subdivision into priestly and lay leaders that shall obtain in the *Age to Come* once again mirrors the Covenanters' community structure and formal seating arrangements, as the following excerpts indicate. At the same time, both reflect the identical subdivision of the returnees' community (Ezra 1:5; 2:2–39 = Neh. 7:7–42 et al.).

1QS VI:8–9   This is the rule for an assembly of the Congregation, each in his [assigned] place: the priests shall sit first and the elders second, and the rest of the people each in his [assigned] place.

These factions are similarly represented on the *Yaḥad* tribunal of judges:

CD X:4–6   This is the rule concerning the judges [or: court] of the Congregation: A number of ten men selected from the Congregation for a [definite] time [or: for the occasion], four from the tribe of Levi and Aaron, and of Israel six, knowledgeable [*mebūnānīm*] in the Book *hehāgū/ī* and in the tenets of the Covenant . . .

In the biblical sources – Ezra and Nehemiah – the lay leaders always precede the priests. As against this, the inverted order obtains in the Qumran tests: The priests precede the lay leaders, both in reference to the actual structure of the *Yaḥad* and in *'aḥarīt hayāmīm*.

In keeping with this arrangement, and because of the cultic character of that solemn event, in the Messianic Banquet the (Anointed?) Priest takes precedence over the Anointed of Israel in opening the ceremony:

1 QSa II:17–22   And [when] they shall assemble for the common [*yaḥad*] [tab]le [to eat] [and to drink the w]ine, and when the common [*hayaḥad*] table shall be set and [the] wine [poured] for drinking, [no] man [shall extend] his hand to the first [loaf of] bread and the [first (cup of) (wine) before the (anointed?)] Priest; for [he shall] bless the first bread and the wine [and extend] his hand first over the bread. Thereafter the Anointed of Israel [shall ex]tend his hand over the bread;[55] [and then] the entire *Yaḥad* Congregation [shall make a bles]sing [over the food], [each man according] to his dignity. In accord with this statute they shall proceed at every m[eal at which] ten me[n are ga]thered.

Again, the rules foreseen to be operative in the messianic future are effective also in the actual *Yaḥad* community, when no Anointed are yet involved, as explicated in:

1QS VI:3–5   Wherever there are ten men of the *Yaḥad* Council [together], a priest shall be present, and they shall sit before him according to their rank, and thus they shall be asked for their counsel in all matters. And when they lay the table to eat or to drink, the priest shall first stretch out his hand to make a blessing over the first bread and wine.

It has been argued that these texts give the priest and the Anointed of Aaron pride of rank over the lay leader(s) of the Covenanters and the future Anointed of Israel respectively. But this interpretation remains open to doubt. It rather would appear that the precedence accorded to the Aaronides proves the point made above: It is intended to achieve a balance in the standing of the Two Anointed in the community, in contrast to the societal setup of predestruction Israel which patently favored the (anointed) king over the (anointed) priest.

It is probably for this reason that also in the Zechariah passages to which reference has already been made, the High Priest Joshua is mentioned before Zerubbabel, the Davidic scion, when the text speaks of the crown with which each of the *benē hayišhār* (Zech. 4:14; cf. vv. 3, 11–12) – the Anointed – is to be endowed (Zech. 6:12: restored), whereas in respect to the thrones given to them, the Davidic "sprout" precedes the priest (Zech. 6:13).

Conclusion

The above survey points up a striking characteristic of the millenarian–messianic idea at Qumran: The expected *New Aeon* will unfold as an age in which terrestrial-historical experience coalesces with celestial-spiritual utopia. Salvation is viewed as transcendent and imminent at the same time. The New Order to be established by the Anointed is not otherworldly but rather the realization of a divine plan on earth, the consummation of history in history. Qumran Messianism reflects the political ideas of the postexilic returnees' community. It is the *politeia* of the New Commonwealth of Israel and the New Universe.

ABBREVIATIONS

AB	*Anchor Bible*
BJRL	*Bulletin of the John Rylands University Library of Manchester*
BKAT	*Biblischer Kommentar Altes Testament*
BWAT	*Beiträge zur Wissenschaft vom Alten Testament*

BZ	*Biblische Zeitschrift*
CBQ	*Catholic Biblical Quarterly*
CD	The Zadokite Document
DJD	*Discoveries in the Judean Desert*
EJS	*European Journal of Sociology*
HthR	*Harvard Theological Review*
JBL	*Journal of Biblical Literature*
JQR	*Jewish Quarterly Review*
4Q	Qumran Cave 4
1QH	Qumran Cave 1, Hodayoth
1QpHab	Qumran Cave 1, Pesher on Habakkuk
1QS	Qumran Cave 1, Sectarian Manual
1QSa	Qumran, Cave 1, Sectarian Rule
1QM	Qumran, Cave 1, War Scroll
RB	*Revue Biblique*
RQ	*Revue de Qumran*
TWAT	*Theologisches Wörterbuch zum Alten Testament*
ZAW	*Zeitschrift für die Alttestamenliche Wissenshaft*

NOTES

1 M. Buber, *Drei Reden über das Judentum* (Frankfurt: Ruetten & Loening, 1911), p. 91.

2 It is preferable to use the designation *Qumran Scrolls,* since unrelated written materials roughly contemporaneous with some of the documents found at Qumran were found in other locations in the Judean Desert, especially in Wadi Murabba'at. The Qumran Scrolls will be designated by the system of sigla detailed in D. Barthélemy, O. P. and J. T. Milik, *Qumran Cave I, Discoveries in the Judaean Desert* I (Oxford: Clarendon Press, 1955), pp. 46–8.

3 Comprehensive surveys of the Qumran finds are offered inter alia by F. M. Cross, *The Ancient Library of Qumran and Biblical Studies* (New York: Doubleday, 1958, 1961) and G. Vermes, *The Dead Sea Scrolls: Qumran in Perspective* (London: SCM Press, 1982).

4 See F. M. Cross, *The Ancient Library of Qumran.*

5 I have argued these points in previous publications. See "Typen der Messiaserwartung um die Zeitwende," in *Probleme biblischer Theologie. Festschrift für G. von Rad* = "Types of Messianic Expectation at the Turn of the Era," in *King, Cult and Calendar in Ancient Israel* (Jerusalem: Magnes Press, 1986), pp. 202–24, ed. H. W. Wolff (München: Kaiser, 1971), pp. 571–88; "The New Covenanters of Qumran," *Scientific American* 225:5 (1971):72–81; "Qumran und das Alte Testament," *Frankfurter Universitätsreden* 42 (1971):71–83; "The Calendar Reckoning of the Sect from the Judean Desert," *Scripta Hierosolymitana* 4 (1958):162–99.

6 See S. Talmon, *Eschatology and History in Biblical Judaism, Occasional Papers No. 2* (Tantur/Jerusalem: Ecumenical Institute, 1986).

7   A concise discussion of this socioreligious phenomenon and references to rel-
    evant literature may be found in Yonina Talmon, "Millenarian Movements,"
    EJS 7 (1966):159–200; *id.,* "Pursuit of the Millennium: The Relation
    between Religious and Social Change," *EJS* 3 (1962):125–48. By way of con-
    trast one can compare the Samaritans, whose rejection of the Prophets and
    Writings apparently led to their lack of development of any truly messianic
    idea at all.

8   The Judaism at Qumran contrasts starkly with the Judaism of the Mishnah,
    for as Neusner remarks, "the Mishnah presents us with a kind of Judaism
    possessed of an eschatology – a theory of the end – without Messiah, a teleol-
    ogy beyond time" (J. Neusner, "Mishnah and Messiah," this volume.

9   See my paper "The Emergence of Jewish Sectarianism in the Early Post-Exilic
    Period," in S. Talmon, *King, Cult and Calendar,* pp. 165–201.

10 See B. Vawter, "Realized Messianism," in *De la Tôrah au Messie, Études
    d'exégèse et d'herméneutique bibliques offertes à H. Cazelles,* M. Carrez, J. Doré,
    and P. Grelot (Paris: Desclée, 1981), pp. 175–9.

11 Not "last days," as is the prevalent translation. The distinction will be
    explained below. See also *Eschatology and History* (n. 6 above), pp. 8–16 and
    the pertinent literature adduced there.

12 The identification was first proposed by S. Zeitlin in a series of articles pub-
    lished in *JQR* starting with vol. 39 (1948/49) and elsewhere. He was fol-
    lowed by N. Wieder and others. See especially N. Wieder, *The Judaean Scrolls
    and Karaism* (London: East and West Library, 1962).

13 Since the end of the last century this work was known in medieval copies that
    stem from the Cairo Genizah. Fragments of it discovered in Cave IV prove
    its Qumranian provenance. The work (CD) is quoted here according to the
    edition by C. Rabin, *The Zadokite Documents* (Oxford: Clarendon Press,
    1954).

14 See I. Rabinowitz, "A Reconsideration of "Damascus" and "390 Years" in
    the "Damascus" ["Zadokite"] Fragment," *JBL* 72 (1954):33–35.

15 See M. Greenberg, *Ezekiel, 1–20, AB* 22 (Garden City, NY: Doubleday,
    1983); W. Zimmerli, *Ezechiel 1–24, BKAT* (Neukirchen-Vluyn: Neukirche-
    ner Verlag, 1979), ad loc.

16 I have thus reasoned for quite some time (see publications mentioned in n. 5
    above). Recently B. Z. Wacholder arrived independently at the same inter-
    pretation of the opening passage of CD. See his *The Dawn of Qumran. The
    Sectarian Torah and the Teacher of Righteousness. Monographs of the Hebrew Union
    College* 8 (Cincinnati: Hebrew Union College, 1983), pp. 177ff. and the per-
    tinent literature adduced there. Our views differ, though, in the interpretation
    of the socioreligious factors that triggered the emergence of the Qumran
    Community.

17 This was already argued before the discovery of the Qumran writings. See E.
    Meyer, *Eine jüdische Schrift aus der Seleukidenzeit. Abhandlungen der preussischen
    Akademie der Wissenschaften, Phil.-hist. Klass* (Berlin, 1919), pp. 1–65. See also
    E. Täubler, "Jerusalem 201–199 B.C.E.: On the History of a Messianic Move-

ment," *JQR* 37 (1946/47):1–30, 125–37, 149–63; H. H. Rowley, "The History of the Qumran Sect," *BJRL* 49 (1966/67):203–32; B. Z. Wacholder, *The Dawn of Qumran*, pp. 177ff.

18 "Millenarian arithmetics" or "messianic numerology" constitute realistic historical values for those who take them seriously, while outsiders will view them as mere products of religious fantasy.

19 The figure of 390 from Qumran contrasts with the figure 400 used in the book of 4 Ezra for the duration of the Messiah (cf. M. Stone, "The Question of the Messiah in 4 Ezra," this volume). However, the significance of this difference cannot be discussed in the present context.

20 Such a variant is most likely to occur when numerical values are indicated by letters of the alphabet, *mem* standing for "forty" and *kaph* for "twenty." These letters are easily misread for each other, especially in the ancient Hebrew script.

21 See G. Jeremias, *Der Lehrer der Gerechtigkeit* (Göttingen: Vandenhoeck & Ruprecht, 1963) and B. E. Thiering, *Redating the Teacher of Righteousness* (Sydney: Theological Explorations, 1979).

22 This hypothesis is advanced inter alia by B. Z. Wacholder, *The Dawn of Qumran*, especially on pp. 99–119, 135, 140ff.

23 See J. Carmignac, *Christ and the Teacher of Righteousness* (Baltimore: Helicon Press 1962).

24 It may be said that in the, comparatively speaking, subdued messianic hope which obtained in Pharisaic Judaism, the "restorative" orientation prevailed. For Christianity, the "utopian" element, seemingly freed from the fetters of actual history, became the most prominent trait of its Messianism. In the *Yaḥad* concept of the messianic age, one perceives a distinct fusion of those two divergent trends. Utopia and reality have been blended to the almost total obliteration of any demarcation lines between them. In this, as in many other aspects, the *Yaḥad* concept shows strong affiliations with the Hebrew Bible and biblical Israel, possibly more than any other Jewish community of the Second Temple period (see S. Talmon, "Type", note 5 above).

25 Much depends on whether or not the status of the Book of Daniel equaled that of the books of the biblical prophets, such as Jeremiah and Ezkiel. Charlesworth does note that 11Q Melchizedek mentions both the book of Daniel and the "seven weeks," but this does not seem to figure prominently in the eschatological chronology of Qumran (J. H. Charlesworth, "From Jewish Messianology to Christian Christology: Some Caveats and Perspectives," this volume).

26 Scholars are divided about whether "Damascus" stands here for the name of the well-known city or whether it is used as a *topos.*

27 See S. Talmon, "The 'Desert Motif' in the Bible and in Qumran Literature," in *Biblical Motifs, Origins and Transformations*, ed. A. Altmann. *Studies and Texts of the Philip L. Lown Institute of Advanced Judaic Studies* 3 (Cambridge, Mass.: Harvard University Press, 1966), pp. 31–63; id., *"midbār,"* *TWAT* IV (Stuttgart: Kohlhammer, 1983), pp. 660–95.

28 In contrast to this initial quietist attitude, but more in keeping with the *Yaḥad*'s more militant later stance, was the perception of Bar Kokhba, who, as J. Neusner notes, was probably seen in his own day as a "messianic general" and his war "as coming at the expected end of time, the eschatological climax to the drama begun in 70" (J. Neusner, "Mishnah and Messiah," this volume).

29 See Y. Yadin, *The Scroll of the War of the Sons of Light Against the Sons of Darkness,* from the Hebrew, transl. B. and C. Rabin (Oxford: Clarendon Press, 1962).

30 The different outlook and presumed comparative lateness of 1QM may explain the baffling absence of any reference in it to the (Two) Anointed, which is underscored by Yadin (*The Scroll of the War,* p. 227, n. 15.) In contrast, G. Vermes presumes that 1QM and the "Messianic Rule" (1QSa, see below) "were both written during the same period, i.e. in the final decades of the pre-Christian era or at the beginning of the first century A.D." See his *The Dead Sea Scrolls in English* (New York: Penguin, 1972), p. 118.

31 See A. S. van der Woude, *Die messianischen Vorstellungen der Gemeinde von Qumran* (Assen: Van Gorcum, 1957).

32 See inter alia A. S. van der Woude, *Die messianischen Vorstellungen;* K. G. Kuhn, "The Two Messiahs of Aaron and Israel," in *The Scrolls and the New Testament,* ed. K. Stendahl (New York: Harper, 1957), pp. 54–64; K. Schubert, "Die Messiaslehre in den Texten von Chirbet Qumran," *BZ* 1 (1957):177–97; R. E. Brown, "The Messianism of Qumran," *CBQ* 19 (1957):53–82; id., "The Teacher of Righteousness and the Messiah(s)," in *The Scrolls and Christianity,* ed. M. Black (London: SPCK, 1969), pp. 37–44; H. W. Kuhn, "Die beiden Messias in den Qumran-texten und die Messiasvorstellung in der rabbinischen Literatur," *ZAW* 70 (1958):200–8; J. Liver, "The Doctrine of Two Messiahs in Sectarian Literature of the Second Commonwealth," *HthR* 52 (1959):149–85; M. Smith, "What is Implied by the Variety of Messianic Figures?" *JBL* 78 (1959):66–72; W. S. LaSor, "The Messianic Idea at Qumran," in *Studies and Essays in Honor of A. Neumann* (Leiden: E. J. Brill, 1962), pp. 363–4; J. Starcky, "Les quatres étapes du messianisme à Qumran," *RB* 70 (1963):481–505; K. Weiss, "Messianismus in Qumran und im Neuen Testament," in *Qumran-Probleme,* ed. H. Bardtke (Berlin: Akademie-Verlag, 1963), pp. 353–68; R. B. Laurin, "The Problem of Two Messiahs in the Qumran Scrolls," *RQ* 4 (1963/64):39–52; E. A. Wcela, "The Messiah(s) of Qumran," *CBQ* 26 (1964):340–9.

33 L. Ginzberg, *An Unknown Jewish Sect,* updated translation from the German by R. Marcus (New York: Jewish Theological Seminary, 1976), p. 248.

34 The translations offered aim at highlighting the sense of the Hebrew texts rather than rendering them literally.

35 According to Charlesworth, in an older copy of *The Rule,* announced by J. T. Milik, the *locus classicus* for two Messiahs is missing (see J. H. Charlesworth, "From Jewish Messianology to Christian Christology," this volume.

36   As in the following examples, the distributive singular signifies here the plural.

37   A reflection of this duality may be seen in the composition of the *Yaḥad* tribunal which was comprised of "four men of the tribe of Levi and Aaron, and of Israel six" (CD X:4–6).

38   This is very similar to the Mishnah's "blueprint for an Israelite government based on the Temple in Jerusalem and headed by a king and a high priest" (J. Neusner, "Mishnah and Messiah"). Cf. also J. Collins, "Messianism in the Maccabean Period," and H. Kee, "Christology in Mark's Gospel," this volume.

39   See E. Meyer, *Geschichte des Altertums,* 8th ed., IV, 1 (photographic reprint: Darmstadt: Wissenschaftliche Buchgesellschaft, 1980), pp. 88–9.

40   K. Baltzer, "Das Ende des Staates Juda und die Messias-Frage," in *Studien zur Theologie der alttestamenlichen Überlieferungen,* G. von Rad zum 60. Geburtstag, ed. R. Rendtorff and K. Koch (Neukirchen-Vluyn: Neukirchener Verlag, 1961), pp. 38–41.

41   I concur with Rothstein's interpretation of this passage as a simile: The "unclean bread and wine" symbolize the unclean local population. While the priests apparently favored their admission into the returnees' community, the prophet(s) opposed their integration and prevailed upon Zerubbabel to reject them (Ezra 4:1–3). See J. W. Rothstein, *Juden und Samaritaner, BWAT* 3 (1908): pp. 5ff., 29ff.

42   Because of the obvious predominance of the king in the Israelite body politic of the First Temple Period, the later balanced standing of king and priest cannot be traced to those earlier times, as suggested by Baltzer, "Das Ende des Staates Juda," n. 50. See also S. Talmon, "Kingship and the Ideology of the State (in the Biblical Period)," in *King, Cult and Calendar,* pp. 9–38.

43   The emerging picture differs considerably from the still-current portrayal of Judah in the Restoration Period as a religious community whose sole representative was the High Priest of Jerusalem.

44   1QS IX:10–11 refers to "a [or: the] prophet who shall come [arise] with the Anointed of Aaron and Israel." This brings to mind the closing passage of the book of Malachi – in fact, of biblical prophetic literature altogether – where the prophet Elijah is foreseen to precede the advent of the "Day of Yhwh" (Mal. 3:23). Similarly, in a series of Messianic Testimonia from Qumran (4Q 175), biblical prooftexts that refer to "The [future] prophet" (Deut. 5:27–29; 18:18–19), "the [messianic] Ruler" (Num. 24:15–17) and "the [future priest out of the] tribe of Levi" (Deut. 33:8–11) respectively, are adduced in this very sequence. See J. M. Allegro, "Further Messianic References in Qumran Literature," *JBL* 75 (1956):182–7.

45   The passage presents some textual difficulties both in the Masoretic text and in the Versions. The interpretation offered here is based on conjectural restoration.

46   The text was thus (correctly) understood by midrashic exegetes. See Gen Rab 49, 8 *ad* Zech. 4:7–23, ed. J. Theodor and Ch. Albeck (Jerusalem: Wahrmann

Books, 1965), 1212, 1–6; Num Rab 13 *ad* Num. 7:84; Sifra – Torat Kohanim, Ṣaw 18 *ad* Lev. 7:35, ed. I. H. Weiss (New York: Om, 1946), p. 40a; Aboth d'Rabbi Nathan 34, S. Schechter (New York: Phillipp Feldheim, 1945), p. 100 ff. and elsewhere.

47 This contrasts with the Christian Messiah as characterized by Neusner, who says that this Messiah "was the Messiah of the end time, savior and redeemer of Israel from its historical calamity, thus a historical-political figure: King of the Jews" (J. Neusner, "Mishnah and Messiah," this volume).

48 At times, the term is similarly employed in late strata of biblical literature, synonymously with *'et* or *mo 'ēd*, "appointed time." See e.g., Ezek. 7:2–6; 21:25 [Heb. 30], 29 [Heb. 34]; 35:5; Dan. 8:17; 11:40; 12:4, 8–9, 11–13; 8:19; 11:27, 35; cf. 9:26. Cf. 1 QpHab VII:7 *ad* Hab. 2:3 and Ben Sira 43:6–8.

49 In bMeg 3a the messianic age is designated *qēṣ māšīaḥ*. Cf. also Ber Rab 88 *ad* Gen. 49:1, ed. Theodor and Albeck, 1251.

50 See J. Licht, "The Doctrine of 'Times' According to the Sect of Qumran and other 'Computers of Seasons'" *Eretz-Israel* 8, *E. L. Sukenik Memorial Volume* (Jerusalem: Israel Exploration Society, 1967):63–70 (Hebrew).

51 The triad *dōrōt rī'šōnīm – dōrōt 'aḥarōnīm – dōr 'aḥarōn* parallels the same triad in Eccles. 1:11 where, however, the third component is *šeyīhyū la'aḥarōnāh*.

52 This period is also referred to by the term *bhywt 'lh* – i.e., "when these [or: they] were [about]" (1QS VIII:4, 12; IX:3; cf. IV:14, 18).

53 This fixed terminology appears to have developed only after the Return from the Exile. Ezekiel, himself a prophet of the *rī'šōnīm*, refers to prophets who preceded him as those who were active *beyāmīm qadmōnīm* = "in earlier days" (Ezek. 38:17).

54 D. Barthélemy correctly points out the difference in size of the *Community* to which 1QS is addressed and the *Congregation* of which 1QSa speaks (see *DJD* I,28, 1955, p. 108). But these relative differences do not obfuscate the absolute compactness of both of these units, compared with the *Community* of the Essenes and the *Congregation* of the Hasidim (Barthélemy, ibid.).

55 Cf. Ezek. 44:3.

7

Philo and Messiah

RICHARD D. HECHT

The categories "Messiah" and "messianic era" or "end-time" are categories that have been much abused in the history of religions. Scholars in many subfields of the history of religions – as different as for example, Biblical Studies and Native American Studies – have used the categories assuming that they are "normative" categories for religious traditions and without much concern for what the terms might imply about their respective historical data. In many cases, we assume that the "Messiah idea" is the central religious idea, basically the same but with superficial differences in historical manifestation, or that the categories are synonymous (when they should remain distinct, e.g., apocalypticism or millenarian movements).[1] Jacob Neusner has challenged us to revise our understanding of these categories in the Judaisms of late antiquity in his study of the "Messiah idea" in the formative canon of the rabbis. He presents his thesis in this way:

> Does Judaism present a messianism, and may we therefore speak of the messianic idea or doctrine of Judaism? The answer ... is a qualified negative, yielding a flat no. Judaism as we know it contains numerous allusions to a Messiah and references to what he will do. But so far as we examine the original canon of the ancient rabbis, framed over the second through seventh centuries, we find these inherited facts either reformed and reshaped for use in an essentially non-messianic and ahistorical system, or left like rubble after a building has been completed: stones that might have been used, but were not. So Judaism as we know it presents no well-crafted doctrine of the Messiah, and thus its eschatology is framed within the methods of an essentially ahistorical teleology.[2]

Neusner's challenge is to reexamine the variety of Jewish Messiah ideas, the variety of Jewish speculations about what this figure might or might not be, the epoch or time period that he will initiate, and the variety of circumstances in which the Messiah ideas arise from the Persian period to the close of late antiquity. The variety is enormous, from the ideas that emerge in late prophetic literature to the randomly collected messianic and apocalyptic statements in *B. Sanhedrin* 90aff. to the apocalyptic midrashim of the seventh century, reflecting the collapse of Byzantine sovereignty over the Land of Israel, the Arab conquest, and the first centuries of Umayyad and Abbasid rule.[3] The same process of reexamination is taking place in other fields and in other historical periods: There have been new attempts by social scientists to revise the sociological constructs of messianism and millenarianism[4]; renewed interest in the variety of Jewish messianisms in the Renaissance[5]; ground-breaking research on messianism in modern political contexts.[6]

Our focus here is the meaning of Messiah and messianic era in the literary corpus of Philo of Alexandria (ca. 15 B.C.E.–ca. 45 C.E.). This corpus represents the most extensive body of extant materials from the Hellenistic Jewish community outside the Land of Israel or Judea. Nowhere in the corpus does Philo mention the term *christos* ("messiah"), and many have remarked that this absence reflects Philo's lack of concern or interest in this important idea from the Land of Israel. Whatever Philo says or does not say about the messianic figure and time span must be taken seriously as another Jewish formulation in late antiquity. Our discussion is divided into three sections. First, we will summarize the dominant interpreters of Philo, Harry Wolfson and Erwin Goodenough, on the place of the Messiah idea in Philo. Both attempted to interpret Philo on this issue in such a way as to confirm larger ideas about the nature of Judaism in late antiquity. Second, we will examine the texts in which Philo interprets the messianic figure and the new age that accompanies him. Here, we will see that Philo had two different interpretations: one in which he understood the messianic figure to be an allegorical or symbolic designator for the Logos, and a second in which he interpreted the messianic age. Third, we will attempt to determine the social or political contexts of these interpretations. What do these ideas tell us about the political situation or the religious situation of the Jewish community in Alexandria in the first half of the first century?

The Messianic Template

Harry Wolfson and Erwin Goodenough, the two great Philo interpreters of our century, both noted the paucity of discussion or even silence in the corpus about the Messiah. Wolfson wrote that "the solution found by Philo for the Jewish problem of his time was the revival of the old prophetic promises of the ultimate disappearance of the diaspora.

Without mentioning the term Messiah, he deals in great detail with what is known in Jewish tradition as the Messiah and the Messianic Age."[7] Goodenough likewise wrote,

> Philo is usually represented as the complete antitype of the Apoc-
> alyptic writers, a man who found his life in metaphysics and mys-
> ticism, and who was a total stranger to the hysterical hatred of
> Rome that looked for a militant Messiah. . . . He would seem to
> have had too much political sagacity to sign his name to books in
> which the Romans were specifically denounced. He was too large
> minded not to see the value of much in Greek and Roman
> thought. He was no fanatic, and knew that so long as the Messiah
> had not yet come, one must get on with the Romans in the most
> conciliating spirit possible. So Philo kept his Messianism to him-
> self. But one could secretly think, hope and hate. And Philo
> seems to me to be assuring his Jewish friends that he was passion-
> ately doing all three.[8]

These two statements suggest that both Wolfson and Goodenough were convinced of the normative importance of the Messiah in all Jewish think-ers in antiquity. It was constituent of Jewish identity and no Jewish thinker worth his salt could omit it. It was a category that was indispens-able to Judaism and hence both interpreted Philo's silence to accord with an artificially constructed template of Jewish messianism. But how did they argue?

Both located Philo's messianism in his politics and each devoted large sections of their description of the politics to the "silent" issue. Wolfson argued that Philo's description of the Messianic Age in *De Praemiis et Poenis* contains at least three features common in the current Jewish tra-dition, explicit in what he called "native Judaism." First, Philo describes the reunion of the exiled as part of the initial stages of the messianic drama. For example, in *De Praemiis et Poenis* 164–165 he states

> Even though they dwell in the furthermost parts of the earth,
> slaves to those who took them away captive, one signal, as it
> were, one day will bring liberty to all. The conversion [i.e., the
> rejection of polytheism for the Supreme and Single God] in a
> body to virtue will strike awe into their masters, who will set
> them free, ashamed to rule over men better than themselves.
> When they have gained this unexpected liberty, those who but
> now were scattered in Greece and the outside world over islands
> and continents will arise and post from every side with one
> impulse to the one appointed place, guided in their pilgrimage by

a vision divine and superhuman, invisible to others, but manifest only to those being safely restored [to their home].

Second, Philo describes how this ingathering of the exiles will be followed by national prosperity. Here, Wolfson cites additional texts from *De Praemiis et Poenis* (e.g., 168), but also cites a more difficult text from *De Vita Mosis* 2.43–44. Wolfson writes that "in another place, in contrast to the condition of the Jews in his own times, of which he says that 'our nation has not prospered for many years,' (*Mos.* 2.43) he describes the Messianic Age as a time when 'a fresh start is made to brighter prospects' and is 'a period of national prosperity' (*Mos.* 2.44)."[9] This passage is difficult precisely because it does not easily yield the meaning given it by Wolfson. The text appears in Philo's description of the translation of the Septuagint (LXX). Indeed, it is a very important discussion, for it grounds the authority of the Septuagint not as a translation, but, as he writes at *De Vita Mosis* 2.37, the translators "became possessed, and, under prophetic inspiration, wrote, not each something different, but the same, word for word, as though dictated to each by an invisible prompter." He then describes a public festival continued until his own time that marked the completion of the inspired translation process. He notes that Jews and non-Jews attended the festival, meeting on the Pharos Island in the middle of the eastern and western harbors; he also indicates that some set up tents on the shoreline near the royal quarter (perhaps between the Chatby Necropolis and Point Silsileh or Lochias on the contemporary shoreline). The purpose of this festival is, of course, to commemorate the achievement and also to show that the Laws of Moses are "desirable and precious in the eyes of all, ordinary citizens and rulers alike." Here he adds the parenthetical remark that the laws are desired *even though* the nation has not prospered in the recent past. He then muses, I believe, that the lack of success causes people to doubt the worth of the Laws of Moses. But if there were to be a fresh start with prosperity, then everyone would put aside their own native customs and laws, turning only to the Laws of Moses. This seems to be more a general wish for a change than a messianic declaration.

Wolfson continues by indicating a third feature of the Messianic Age according to Philo, a reign of peace (*Praem.* 79–84). The description of the messianic peace is not limited to mankind, but extends to and even begins with the animals. Philo, here, is offering a relatively free interpretation of Isaiah 11:6, 8–9, according to Wolfson. Wolfson also indicates that there is a fourth feature in Philo's description of the messianic time. The unrepentant nations will be punished (*Praem.* 169 and 171) and the description at *De Praemiis et Poenis* 171 suggests to Wolfson "a description in terms of local Alexandrian experience of the War of Gog and

Magog."[10] Wolfson, of course, recognizes that nowhere in these four features does Philo mention the figure of a historical or personal messianic character. He writes "whether Philo believed that the final redemption will take place under the leadership of a particular person such as is known in Jewish tradition as the Messiah is not clear. Nowhere in his writings is there any explicit mention of a personal Messiah. There are two vague statements, however, which may refer to such a Messiah."[11] First, in discussing the blessings that follow from obedience to the Law at *De Praemiis et Poenis* 95–97 he cites the prophecy of Balaam. The Masoretic text of Numbers 24:7 reads "He shall pour the water out of his buckets moistening his seed plentifully, and his king shall be higher than Agag, and his kingdom shall be exalted." However, the Septuagint rendering of the verse is considerably different than either the Masoretic text or some targumic readings of the verse: "There shall come forth a man out of his seed, and he shall rule over many nations; and the kingdom of Gog shall be exalted and his kingdom shall be increased." This rendering of the verse is not necessarily messianic, but Wolfson finds Philo's use of the verse to be in accord with the "native" Judaism of the Land of Israel. He writes, "But inasmuch as in native Jewish tradition this verse in its Masoretic reading, 'He shall pour forth water out of his buckets,' is sometimes taken as referring to the Messiah, there is no reason why we should not assume that Philo has also taken it in this sense."[12] Second, he cites *De Praemiis et Poenis* 165 as another example of Philo's normative reflection upon a personal messianic figure. Here, Philo describes the return of the exiled to their homeland. When the exiles are freed they "will arise and hasten with one impulse from every side to the one assigned place, guided by a vision divine [ϑειοτ;ἐρας]and superhuman, invisible to others, but manifest only to those being safely restored." Although others have interpreted the vision as either the Logos or something like the pillar of smoke and fire that led the Israelites out of Egypt and through the desert, Wolfson sees it as clear evidence for Philo's affirmation of the Messiah of "native" Judaism.[13]

Wolfson acknowledges that Philo describes the Messianic Age in terminology seemingly drawn from the Stoic idea of a universal state at the end of time or at the end of an historical cycle, in short, the classical Stoic formulation of a Golden Age. But, Wolfson argues, this is only superficial, for upon closer examination he sees Philo in clear opposition to the Stoics. First, the universal state of the Stoics has not been established, despite their claims for its existence in the empire of Alexander the Great or of the Romans. Second, the universal law that will govern this state in Philo is only the Law of Moses and nothing else. Third, while the Stoics argued for world-citizenship, Philo argued for citizenship in a divine or holy cosmo-polis. Lastly, in the Stoic state, all national boundaries and historical particularisms will be erased; in Philo's messianic state the various historic states, ethnic and linguistic groups of the world will continue to exist.[14] The differences between Philo and the Stoics are exemplified in Quod Deus 173–75, where Philo describes the rise and fall of the nations. He cites the following empires, which have risen and then been swept away by others: Macedonia, Greece, Persia, Parthia, Egypt, Ethiopia, Carthage, and Libya. For the Stoics, the cycle of growth and degeneration in national states or ethnic groups was the result of fate or chance *(tychē)*. For Philo, it is the Divine Logos that causes the historical growth and decline through the redistribution of material goods throughout the world.[15] He writes at 176

> for circlewise moves the revolution of that divine logos which most call fortune. Presently, in its unending flux, it makes distinction city by city, nation by nation, country by country. What these had once, those have now. What all had, all have. Only from time to time is the ownership changed by its agency, to the end that the whole of our world should be a single state, enjoying the best of constitutions, democracy.[16]

Wolfson sees a striking parallel between Philo and Polybius' *Histories* (38:22.2) in this passage, but once again the similarity is only superficial. For Polybius, the perfect state, Rome, was already present. Philo understands that the Logos has not yet accomplished its purpose, a single state governed by democracy, "the best of constitutions." Most commentators have addressed the question implied by Philo's positive description of democracy here and in other places in the corpus (Agr. 45; Confus. 108; Abr. 242; Spec. Leg. 4.237; Virt. 180). What is the source of his idea that democracy is the best of all constitutions? Colson indicates that it does not come from the Schools, Plato, Aristotle, or the Stoics.[17] However, John Dillon argues that in Philo's usage the term means only a

> constitution in which each is given his due – what Plato and Aristotle would call "geometrical equality," implying a proper weighing of power in favour of the well-to-do. It is probable that for him Augustus' settlement was an establishment of democracy in this sense. . . . On the cosmic level, a world "democracy" will be an order, ruled by the Logos itself, in which each nation, large and small, has its due, and no more nor less than its due. Thus both within the state and on a world scale Philo stands for what Plato and Aristotle would simply term *politeia,* or the constitution *par excellence.* How he arrived at this rather controversial term for it, however, is something of a mystery.[18]

Lastly, while Philo begins this passage with a description of the cyclic motion of history, the Stoics and Polybius understood that these cycles were eternal. This implies that history is driven by only blind, but necessary *tychē*. For Philo, "it is not blind fate, but an intelligent and wise God who guides the destinies of the world and nations. The divine Logos which in this passage he substitutes for fortune or fate is the individual providence of God, and this works according to a certain plan."[19]

In short, Wolfson interprets Philo in accord with the traditions of the native Jewish community of the Land of Israel. There is no radical disjunction between Jewish thinking in Jerusalem or Alexandria, despite the different intellectual forces at work in each place. Philo develops a messianic scenario and a messianic figure that is not substantially different from the biblical texts of the rabbis. Where Philo seems to stray into the Stoic philosophical world, Wolfson argues that Philo only uses the common terminology of his day. Upon closer examination, Philo is seen to reject the political ideas of the Stoics in favor of his own biblical tradition in which, most importantly, God replaces the blind *tychē*.

Goodenough also interpreted Philo as affirming the biblical and rabbinic messianic vision. While keeping his messianism to himself, he does provide clues to his passionate hatred of Roman rule and his hope for the militant Messiah who will put an end to it. Philo's hatred of Rome is, however, not as consistent as Goodenough would like it to be. Indeed, *De Legatione ad Gaium* 143–7 provides an extensive encomium for Augustus, whose "virtues transcend human nature." He wrote that

> This is the Caesar who calmed the torrential storms on every side, who healed the pestilences common to Greeks and barbarians. . . . This is he who reclaimed every state to liberty, who led disorder into order and brought gentle manners and harmony to all unsociable and brutish nations, who enlarged Hellas by many a new Hellas and hellenized the outside world in its most important regions, the guardian of peace, who dispensed their dues to each and all, who did not hoard his favours but gave them to be common property, who kept nothing good and excellent hidden throughout his life. (145–7)

Philo, like almost all intellectuals of the first century, was not immune to the power of Augustus' reign; it was the Golden Age and Philo here describes him as a true messianic figure. Of course, Philo introduces this encomium in order to show the vast disparity between Augustus and Caligula. Nevertheless, Philo's attitude toward Rome lacked the consistency ascribed to it by Goodenough.

While the texts from *De Praemiis et Poenis* are important in Goodenough's analysis of Philo's messianism, he introduces into the discussion an important text from *De Somniis*. Goodenough draws our attention to *De Somniis* 2.61–64, where Philo is juxtaposing those who are driven by vanity in their governing of people and the ruling power of Joseph. At 64 he writes "For just as we find on trees, to the great damage of the genuine growth, superfluities which the agricultural-husbands must purge and cut away to provide for their necessities, so the true and simple life has for its parasite the life of falsity and vanity, for which no agricultural-husband has yet been found to excise and cut away the mischievous overgrowth, root and all." Goodenough argues that this is an indirect description of a messiah-like figure. "The great Husbandman," Goodenough writes,

> has not yet appeared to prune the vine of society by hacking them off at the very roots, but, it is clear, Philo was looking for him to come. His language is strikingly suggestive not only of the pruning of the vine in the Fourth Gospel, but also of Q's account of John the Baptist's messianic announcement that now that the Messiah was about to come, the axe would at last be laid at the very roots of the unfruitful trees. If it is now recalled that much as he felt obliged for the present to propitiate the Romans, he was ready to attack and destroy this power when the opportunity came; it would appear that Philo was not only awaiting the Husbandman, but would swing an axe with him when he came.[20]

Goodenough believed that the allegory of the Agricultural-Husband from *De Somniis* was connected to the other messianic texts in *De Praemiis et Poenis*. This confirmed that the messianic hope was fully integrated into Philo's thought and also was a significant part of what Goodenough described as Philo's "mystical Judaism." At this mystical level, Goodenough argued that the Messianic Era would begin

> when enough Jews who are in political power and responsibility have been transformed into Jews of the mystic goal, then, by the mercy of God and the prayers of the Saints [the Patriarchs], all Jews will suddenly experience the same transformation, and will come out of their present slavery, their political bondage. The world will watch with wonder as they gather from the corners of the earth to return, under the leadership of their Guide, to their own place. Then will come the happy Age, with enemies discomfited, and the Jews in such peace and prosperity as their ancestors have never experienced. The great Ax has indeed laid them low now, but it has not cut the root of Judaism as Philo elsewhere promises it will cut the root of the other "trees." The old Jewish root is left, and from it will miraculously spring up a new and mighty trunk.[21]

Lastly, Goodenough understood that Philo's messianic idea bore directly upon his identity and his role in the Alexandrian Jewish community. He argues that Philo's concern for politics, or rather the manner in which he describes how he was driven into the political world (Spec. Leg. 3.1–6), reflects his understanding of how the divine realities become accessible to the Jews. There must be "Mystic leaders in practical politics for the Jewish people. This may well have been Philo's sense of call. It was truly a despairing ambition to try to live the mystic life in Roman Alexandria. But only as he, Philo, faced this calling with the courage of his embassy to Gaius, could the rest of the Jews hope for the deliverance of the great age to come. He, or men greater than he, must be the political 'saviors' of the Jews."[22]

The interpretations offered by Wolfson and Goodenough have been criticized from any number of perspectives. For example, John J. Collins indicates the Wolfson's attempt to assimilate Philo's messianism to the "native Judaism" must be modified at four points. First, Philo seems most interested in the spiritual triumph of virtue rather than the political victory of a messianic king. Second, throughout much of *De Praemiis et Poenis*, Philo only contrasts the virtuous and the wicked, not the Jews and non-Jews. Hence, the messianic figure of *De Praemiis et Poenis* 95 (Numbers 24:7) does not battle non-Jews, but "some fanatics whose lust for war defies restraint or remonstrance" (Praem. 94). Third, the distinction between the virtuous and the wicked does not fall along national or ethnic lines, Jews and non-Jews (e.g., at Praem. 152 he contrasts the proselyte who has "come into the camp of God" and the nobly born who has profaned his own lineage and birth). Fourth, the physical rewards and punishments are only *symbols* of the spiritual; earthly kingdoms are nothing in themselves but point to another realm. Collins concludes that

> Philo's eschatological tableau is viewed from a very different perspective from the concrete nationalism of Wolfson's "native Judaism." Yet he does speak of a gathering in of the exiles and overthrow of the enemies of Judaism, and the virtuous, while not simply the Jews by birth, are at least the Jews by practice of the law. In view of Philo's insistence on the value of concrete entities and the letter of the law as a basis for symbolism, we may ask whether he did not, after all, expect a visible triumph of Judaism.[23]

However, there is a more fundamental criticism that might be advanced against both Wolfson and Goodenough's interpretation of the place of the Messiah and the messianic time in Philo's thought. Both have committed a religio-historical error in assuming a unified and singular Judaism in late antiquity. Both have placed a template over the corpus, and this has produced a Philo whose messianism is in perfect accord with the "native Judaism" of Wolfson or the mystical Judaism that according to Goodenough contributed so heavily to the formation of early Christianity. Indeed, Goodenough concludes his discussion of Philo's Messiah and the Messianic Era by stating that

> Philo has definitely committed himself to the dream of the Messianic Age familiar to all Jews at the time, an age which will be marked by the complete political rout of all other peoples under the inspired leadership of a Man who will lead the armies and put the axe to the root of the false growth of the Gentiles. And in that Age the dream of the ideal kingship, whether in the person of the Man or in the race, will be realized. That dream of a rulership which can make all society, even the animal and vegetable kingdoms, perfect, can bring universal "salvation," is not vain. Someday the true splendor [σεμνότης] will bring in humility [αἰδώς], impressiveness [δεινότης] will bring fear [φοβός], benefaction [εὐεργεσία] will bring good will [εὔνοια].[24]

For Wolfson, Philo's Messiah is the nationalist Messiah of the "native" Judaism of the Land of Israel; for Goodenough it is a pre-Christian figure who anticipates his full realization in the New Testament.

At a second level, the interpretations of Wolfson and Goodenough overlook a seeming contradiction in the texts themselves that would indicate that the issue is much more complex than admitted by either. Collins seems to recognize this in his criticism of Wolfson. There are extensive texts where Philo describes historical and political processes that are based in the Messianic Era or the Golden Age, or seem to culminate in it. It is here that Philo draws upon the political ideas of the Stoics in order to describe the state of things at the end of time. These texts are contradicted by more fragmentary discussions in the corpus where Philo seemingly allegorizes the process, making it into a spiritualized experience within the individual. This is what he consistently does throughout the corpus, with the Patriarchs, their wanderings, the Exodus experience, and the entire Temple cult. Why should he take the eschatological future any more "realistically" and thereby less spiritually than other elements in his thought? A second look at the texts themselves and their possible contexts will begin to clarify this contradiction and indicate that Philo's messianism is not that of the Jews of the Land of Israel, nor is it in agreement with the Gospels or John the Baptist as Goodenough describes it.

The Messianic Texts

The corpus contains two differing messianic interpretations. First, there are texts that present abbreviated ideas and in which Philo uses his common hermeneutical devices, turning the messianic designators into symbols for the Logos or how virtue is stimulated in the human soul. Second, there is the extensive interpretation of the Messianic Era or end-time presented in *De Praemiis et Poenis* 79–172. This second contains the Stoic political terminology and seemingly overlooks the first interpretation, but not completely. At *De Praemiis et Poenis* 172, the very conclusion of the treatise, he states, "For just as when the stalks of plants are cut away, if the roots are left undestroyed, new growths shoot up which supersede the old, so too if in the soul a tiny seed be left of the qualities which promote virtue, though other things have been stripped away, still from the little seed spring forth the fairest and most precious things in human life, by which states are constituted and manned with good citizens, the nations grow into a great population." Here, after making the case for the messianic time, he momentarily reverts to his dominant interpretive mode in the corpus. The Messianic Era is likened to the tiny seed of virtue in the soul. We can arrange the texts in the following manner:

I	II
Messianic terminology is the allegorical designator for the Logos	Messianic terminology is used to describe historical and/or political processes
De Confusione Linguarum 62–63	De Praemiis et Poenis 79–172
De Virtutibus 75	
De Vita Mosis 2.44	
De Vita Mosis 2.288	
De Opificio Mundi 79–81	

Both categories (I – *Messianic terminology is the allegorical designator for the Logos* and II – *Messianic terminology is used to describe historical and/or political processes*) reflect messianic scenarios in Philo. In the first, the scenario is descriptive of events within the soul or higher functions of the mind. In the second, the scenario is descriptive of events that take place in the world. Let us consider each group in some detail.

The first group of texts has been studied by J. de Savignac, and he argues that these texts are held together as a group because Philo interprets the possible messianic terminology as allegorical designators for the Logos.[25] The single most important example, treated by both Goodenough and Wolfson, is *De Confusione Linguarum* 62–63. Here, Philo states:

> I have heard also an oracle from the lips of one of the disciples of Moses, which runs thus: 'Behold a man whose name is the Rising' (Zech. 6:12), strangest of titles, surely, if you suppose that a being composed of soul and body is here described. But if you suppose that it is that Incorpreal One, who differs not in the slightest from the divine image, you will agree that the name 'Rising' assigned

to him quite truly describes him. For that man is the eldest son, whom the Father of All raised up, and elsewhere calls him his first-born, and indeed the Son thus begotten followed the ways of his Father, and shaped the different kinds, looking to the archetypal patterns which that Father supplied.

Philo introduces the text Zechariah here because the biblical text being interpreted in the discussion of *De Confusione Linguarum* is Septuagint Genesis 11:2, which reads "And it came to pass as they moved from the east [ἀνατολων, lit.: the rising], they found a plain in the land of Shinar, and they dwelt there." Here, Philo clearly takes the messianic title of Zechariah 6:12, *ṣemaḥ* in the Masoretic text and *anatolē* in the Septuagint (LXX), as the Logos: the "eldest son whom the Father of all raised up." This is a classic description of how the Logos works. The Logos is the first generated from the divine mind and brings into creation the discrete elements of the sensible world by following *(mimēsis)* the ideas. The Logos follows *paradeigmata archetypa*, "the archetypal patterns," which at *Di Opificio Mundi* 6 and 25 Philo identifies with the *kosmos noetos*, the intelligible world of the Platonic forms. Savignac underscores the importance of this text by pointing out that it is the one and only biblical text that contains a messianic referent in both the Masoretic and Septuagint texts, without the mediation of an interpretative tradition. This is unlike his interpretation of Numbers 24:7 at *De Praemiis et Poenis* 95. He states that

> *Ainsi, non seulement l'application au Logos du texte messianique de Zacharie (vi 12) établit l'assimilation philonienne du Logos et du Messie, mais le seul texte où Philon traite d'un Messie personnel, loin d'exclure cette assimilation, parait plutôt la supposer; c'est elle qui, semble-t-il, nous en livre le sens. On notera en outre que la désignation du Messie par le terme "homme" devant être séduisante pour Philon car, dans le même traité que celiu où il y fait allusion, il soutient que la perfection consiste à devenir "homme."* (Thus, the application of the messianic text of Zachariah (6:12) to the Logos not only establishes the Philonic assimilation of the Logos and the Messiah, but the only text where Philo talks about a personal Messiah, far from excluding this assimilation, seems more likely to imply it. That is the one which, it seems, reveals the meaning to us. One will note furthermore, that the designation of the Messiah by the term "man" has a certain attraction for Philo because, in the same treatise as the one in which he [uses this] allusion, he affirms that perfection consists of becoming "man" [cf. *De Praemiis et Poenis* 13–14 and *Quod Deterius Potiori insidiari solet* 22–24].)[26]

At *De Opificio Mundi* 79–81 he introduces a similar idea, although by no means as direct as *De Confusione Linguarum* 62–63. Here, he explains why man is created last in the order of creation. The Messianic Era or end-time is an internal experience in which the passions are calmed and extinguished. They are ruled by moderation *(sōphrosynē)*, where wrong is checked by righteousness, where

> the vices and the fruitless practices to which they prompt were to give place to the virtues and their corresponding activities, the warfare in the soul, of all wars veritably the most dire and most grievous, would have been abolished, and peace would prevail and would in quiet and gentle ways provide good order for the exercise of our faculties, and there would be hope that God, being the Lover of virtue and the Lover of what is good and beautiful and also the Lover of man, would provide for our race good things all coming forth spontaneously and all in readiness. For it is easier without calling in the husbandman's [*geōgrikēs*] art to supply in abundance the yield of growths already existing than to bring into being things that were non-existent.

This short text amplifies the "Husbandman" of *De Somniis* 2.64 cited by Goodenough as a messianic figure; both designate activities of the Logos. Likewise, *De Vita Mosis* 2.44, which Wolfson cited as indicative of the transformation of the situation of the Jews during the Messianic Era, is instead a description of an internal transformation reflected in the communal or national destiny. At *De Vita Mosis* 2.288, Philo describes the death of Moses, indicating that God transformed Moses' twofold nature, soul and body, into a single substance, mind. Then at Deuteronomy 33–34, Philo understands that Moses began to prophesy to the individual tribes of Israel rather than the whole nation. He states that the prophecies contain "in particular the things which were to be and hereafter must come to pass. Some of these have already taken place, others are still looked for, since confidence in the future is assumed by the past." Here again the prophecies imply first internal transformation and only then its reflection in the destiny of the tribes. The transformation is again accomplished by the Logos. Lastly, in *De Virtutibus* 75 Philo directly states that God provides exhortations for the future in the Law in order to evoke a sounder mind in man. Here, the Logos is the exhortation. In each of these cases, the texts suggest that Philo spiritualized the figure of the Messiah and the Messianic Era. This conforms to the larger philosophical themes in the corpus and, in short, in this messianic scenario, it is the Logos that brings deliverance, without either the leadership of a human warrior-king or the conquest of the nations. It is a deliverance of the human mind and soul by the quelling of the passions and initiating the ascent to the divine mind. It is a profound noetic experience and thoroughly ahistorical.

The second messianic scenario appears in *De Praemiis et Poenis* 79–172. We should recall that *De Praemiis et Poenis* is the seventh and concluding treatise in Philo's exegetical sequence on the Law. The structure of this sequence is quite simple: He begins with *De Decalogo,* demonstrating that the Decalogue forms the generic categories of the Law. Second, he provides a detailed discussion of the specific laws arranged under these categories in *De Specialibus Legibus* 1–4. He then demonstrates the virtues cultivated by adherence to the Law in *De Virtutibus.* Finally, he indicates the rewards and punishments that follow from obedience and disobedience to the Law in the treatise we are considering. *De Praemiis et Poenis* is divided into two parts. After a brief introduction (1–6) in which he points out that the true athletes of virtue will gain victory and reward in the sacred arena, he presents a list of the rewards and punishments (7–78) and then blessings and curses (79–172). In the first section, he seems to summarize in very abbreviated form materials and lines of argument or thought from *De Abrahamo* and *De Vita Mosis* (and perhaps materials from the lost treatises on Jacob and Isaac). In the second section, he returns to the books of Exodus, Leviticus, Numbers, and Deuteronomy, which are the nucleus of his interpretation in *De Decalogo* and *De Specialibus Legibus.* In this section, the main emphasis is upon the biblical texts of Leviticus 26 and 28, and Deuteronomy 28. The general blessings are victory over human and natural enemies, wealth, happiness, and long life (79–126). The curses include disease, war, famine, cannibalism, slavery, and business failures (127–51).

Recent scholarship has suggested that Philo considered these treatises bound together in a sequence. Indeed, Valentin Nikiprowetzky argued on the basis of Philo's description of the tripartite division of the Law into cosmology, history, and legislation at *De Praemiis et Poenis* 1–2 and *De Vita Mosis* 2.46–47 that he did not even distinguish between the allegorical sequence and the expositional sequence, taken for granted by most commentators since the last century. Instead, Nikiprowetzky argued, Philo used more well-known rhetorical divisions and subdivisions.[27] It might be argued that these concluding sections of *De Praemiis et Poenis* function as a rhetorical conclusion to the lengthy exposition on the Law. Here, we might have something similar to the so-called *Schadenfreude* of *In Flaccum* 121ff, where Philo is not presenting an emotional outburst in which he gloats over the miseries accompanying Flaccus' fall from political grace. Some interpreters have suggested that Philo's hatred for Flaccus and his thorough disgust for the policies of the last years of his rule in Alexandria got the best of the philosopher. Flaccus' fall was the sole result of his mismanagement of Alexandria (although it was probably linked as well with Gaius' efforts to consolidate his power and to remove those who had close contact with Tiberius) and Philo lost the perspective that he wanted to take throughout the treatise. For example, at 159–60 he creates a silent monologue within Flaccus as he arrives at the island of Andros, to which he has been sent into exile. Flaccus says,

> This petty island what shall I call it? My home of exile, or a new fatherland, a hapless haven and refuge? A tomb would be its truest name, for as I journey in my misery it is as though I were bearing the corpse that is myself to a sepulchre. For either through my afflictions I shall break the thread of my miserable life, or even, if I am able to survive, die a long drawn-out death in which consciousness still lives.

Nikiprowetzky argued that in this section of the treatise Philo had not fallen victim to his own passions but had constructed a presentation of the full meaning of divine justice.[28] Here, it might be argued that Philo has once again done the same thing, constructing a portrait of the full meaning of obedience and rejection of the Law.

Ferdinand Dexinger's recent study of post-Herodian Jewish messianism has thrown this rhetorical interpretation of *De Praemiis et Poenis* and the expositional sequence into question.[29] Dexinger's study reveals that Philo's *De Praemiis et Poenis* 79–172 contains a three part messianic scenario. The starting point of the messianic drama is reflected in Philo's description of the enmity between man and beast (85). This situation is the natural state of *status quo* that will be transformed in the initial stages of the Messianic Era. Philo states that "this is the one war where no quarter or truce is possible; as wolves with lambs, so all wild beasts both on land and water are at war with all men" (87). No mortal can alter this situation. Philo is perhaps paraphrasing Isaiah 11:6–9 and uses the conflict between men and animals as a clear sign of the onset of the new time or the transformation of time. In addition to this, the start of end-time is seen in the assault of enemies. Philo writes,

> some fanatics whose lust for war defies restraint or remonstrance come careering to attack, until they are actually engaged, they will be full of arrogance and bluster, but when they have come to a trial of blows they will find their talk has been an idle boast. Win they cannot. Forced back by your [i.e., God] superior strength, they will fly headlong, companies of hundreds before handfuls of five, ten thousands before hundreds by many ways for the one by which they came. (94)

The starting point of the messianic time is, then, the overcoming of the hostility between humans and the animals, and the unsuccessful assault of unnamed enemies.

Here, we already see a major characteristic of Philo's description of the Messianic Era or the Golden Age. He begins immediately by dehistoricizing the human situation. The enemies are unnamed; they are abstractions. Yehoshua Amir describes this dehistoricization as the major characteristic in Philo's reinterpretation of Jewish Hellenistic messianic materials.[30] But Philo also turns the initial conflict with the enemies into a "bloodless" battle. Some commentators indicate that at *De Praemiis et Poenis* 94, Philo is paraphrasing Leviticus 26:7 (LXX "And you shall pursue your enemies and they shall fall before you by the sword") with only the brief phrase "they will fly headlong."[31] Dexinger suggests that the paraphrased text is not from Leviticus but from Psalm 2, where the nations rage against the messianic king and he responds by appealing to God, who tells him (LXX) "You shall watch over them as a shepherd with a rod of iron; you shall break them in pieces as a potter's vessel" (2:9). Regardless of the text in question in Philo's description, the portrayal is not only a dehistoricization, but also an idealization, where the particular qualities of the conflict are covered over for a possible Stoic description of political turmoil.

Second in Dexinger's description of the scenario is the sequence of messianic events. First, without mentioning Israel, he describes its exemplary status (114). Here, Israel provides a model for the nations that imprints itself in their souls. Second, at 95–97, he describes the leadership of "a man" based upon the interpretation in Septuagint Numbers 24:7. This figure will pursue the enemies, subdue populous nations, have courage of soul, be all-powerful, win bloodless battles, have uncontested sovereignty, and bring to his subjects "the benefit which will accrue from the affection or fear or respect which they feel." Third, at 165, he describes the ingathering of the exiles (presumably, of Israel) without mentioning the specific nation. Fourth and fifth, he mentions the passage out of the wilderness accompanied by various divine manifestations (165). Lastly, at 168, he describes the arrival of the people at destroyed and ruined cities. The landscape is one of total destruction. He states that

> the cities which now lay in ruins will be cities once more; the desolate land will be inhabited; the barren will change into fruitfulness; all the prosperity of their fathers and ancestors will seem a tiny fragment, so lavish will be the abundant riches in their possession, which flowing from the gracious beauties of God as from perennial fountains will bring to each individually and to all in common a deep stream of wealth leaving no room for envy.

Third in Dexinger's structure is the transformation of the cosmos or the actual results of the messianic drama. Dexinger indicates that in Philo's vision nature will be transformed in continuity with the first events of the messianic events. At 89–90, Philo states that "when that time comes I believe that bears and lions and panthers and the Indian animals, elephants and tigers, and all others whose vigor and power are invincible, will change their life of solitariness and isolation for one of companionship, and gradually in imitation of their gregarious creatures show themselves tame when brought face to face with mankind." He continues by describing how some animals will be awestruck by their natural master man, and others will become docile in their affection for their master. Scorpions and serpents, he continues, will have no use for their venom. He concludes that man will even be sacrosanct among the most vicious animals such as the crocodiles and hippopotamuses of the Nile. This may be a paraphrase of Isaiah 11:6, but there is nothing in the paraphrase itself which would link it directly to the Septuagint. At 95–97, Philo continues to envision the Golden Age. The peace that reigns between man and animals will also be reflected in the peaceful relations between men and nations. Lastly, Philo describes at 168 the rebuilding of cities as part of the Messianic Era. In short,

> everything will suddenly be reversed, God will turn the curses against the enemies of these penitents, the enemies who rejoiced in the misfortunes of the nation and mocked and railed at them, thinking that they themselves would have a heritage which nothing could destroy and which they hoped to leave to their children and descendents in due succession; thinking too that they would always see their opponents in a firmly established and unchanging adversity which would be reserved for the generations that followed them. (169–70)

The messianic scenario observed by Dexinger is more structured than what appears in the discussion of the very same texts in either Wolfson or Goodenough. However, we note that Philo presents a thoroughly dehistoricized description of the messianic drama when compared to other contemporary visions. The particularism gives way to a general vision of a Golden Age. This very striking dimension of Philo's thought was not given attention by either Wolfson or Goodenough. However, if we compare any element in Philo's vision with that of the so-called "native" Jewish version of the Messianic Era, this becomes more important than simply a difference of style or attitude. For example, if we consider Philo's description of the return or ingathering of the exiles, the *qibbūṣ gāliyyôt*, and three randomly selected examples from the corpus of midrashic literature:

Praemis et Poenis 165
When they have gained this unexpected liberty, those who but now were scattered in Greece and the outside world over the islands and continents will arise and post from every side with one impulse to the one appointed place, guided in their pilgrimage by a vision divine and superhuman unseen by others but manifest to them as they pass from exile to their home.

Mekhilta de-Rabbi Ishmael –
Beshallah 14
Rabbi Nehemiah said: Whoever undertakes one precept in faith is worthy that the *Shekhinah* should rest upon him. Since we find that our ancestors were rewarded for their faith in God by the resting of his Holy spirit upon them, inspiring them to utter song, as it is stated: "They believed in the Lord and Moses his servant" [Ex. 14:31], after which it is written: "Then sang Moses and the Children of Israel . . . " [Ex. 15:1]. Similarly, you find that the ingathering of the exiles is the reward for faith.

Wayyikra Rabbah 7:3
After the destruction of the Temple the sacrifices became invalid. Israel might have argued then: Once we used to offer sacrifice and study their rules and regulations. Now there are no sacrifices and why should we bother to study their rules and regulations? The Holy One, blessed be He, thereupon said to them: Since you are engaged in the study of them, I shall regard it as if you had offered them. Rabbi Huna stated: All the diasporas are only ingathered to the Land of Israel in virtue of their study of Mishnah [containing the rules and regulations of sacrifice]. Why? On the basis of Hosea 8:10 where it is written: "Because they have studied Mishnah among the nations, now I will gather them." [Here, the midrash takes *yitnū*

Yalqut Shemoni – Isaiah 469
"That you may say to the prisoners, Go forth" [Is. 49:9] to those held *in* Sambation. "To them who are in darkness, show yourselves" [Is. 49:9] to those held *beyond* Sambation. But not only those diasporas but wherever there are Jews, they will come together. One who goes on a journey suffers hunger and thirst, but they will not suffer so, as it stated: "They shall not hunger nor thirst; neither shall the heat nor the sun smite them" [Is. 49:10]. Furthermore, the Holy One, blessed be He, will flatten the hills and make them into highways in front of them. The depressions He will elevate in front of them, and make them straight, as it is written, "And I will make all My mountains a way, and My highway shall be raised up" [Is. 49:11].

from the root *TN³*, which implies
Mishnah, and not from the
accepted root here, *TNN,* "to
hire" a prostitute.]

I do not introduce these short texts to demonstrate any historical parallels,
differences, or connections between Philo and the midrashic corpus.
Indeed, these texts span a period of eight hundred to a thousand years.
However, a comparison of the texts on the ingathering of the exiles during the Messianic Era, even if we just lay them out in the above fashion,
reveals some very striking differences. In Philo, the liberation of the exiles
is unexpected and arises because of their conversion *en masse* to virtue,
which "will strike awe into their masters, who will set them free, ashamed
to rule over men better than themselves" (164). The text from the *Mekhilta de-Rabbi Ishmael* suggests that the messianic liberation is not unexpected, but is the direct result of faith. Here, this early midrash does not
even appeal to the idea that the exile is lifted because of "the merit of the
patriarchs," a good theological idea that is commonly read back into sit-
uations such as *qibbûṣ gāliyyôt.* The ingathering of the exiles is as certain
as the biblical case; because the Israelites believed in the sovereignty of
God and the leadership of Moses, they were saved from the army of Phar-
aoh and liberated from Egypt through the miracle at the sea. The text
from *Wayyikra Rabbah* indicates how the rabbinic tradition, like Philo,
found its own values and mythic history in the messianic texts. However,
whereas Philo seems driven to discuss the issue without mention of the
specific people, the particularism of the rabbis' worldview in *Wayyikra
Rabbah* requires the mention of the Temple, Israel, and Mishnah. These
are all givens for them and concrete components of the text's soteriolog-
ical system. Philo's Diaspora is without topography and territory with the
exception of Greece, islands, and continents. The pilgrims may be driven
by an unseen vision, but the short text from *Yalqut Shemoni* (perhaps cod-
ified in the High Middle Ages) indicates that God will ease their journey,
flattening the mountains and filling the valleys. The *Yalqut* also has a specific topography in which the *qibbûṣ gāliyyôt* takes place: The exiles come
from beyond the River Sambation.[32]

The absence of parallels between the Philonic corpus and the rabbis,
even without raising the very difficult question of dating and the historical
development of traditions, is striking given the force of Wolfson's argument. Even the most important distinctions in the rabbinic corpus, for
example between *yemôt hammasiaḥ* and *hāᶜôlam habbaᵓâh,* have not even
an echo in Philo. One might argue that these arise only after Philo; Philo
attests to the "Messianic idea" pre-70 C.E. and, of course, the messianic
nuances of the second century or later are not prefigured or reflected in

the earlier Philo. Yet, if there was similarity, we would expect some definite theme to appear. When the texts of Philo are compared thematically with contemporary or later rabbinic traditions, Philo has almost nothing in common with the "native Judaism" of the Land of Israel. Neusner isolates 76 "principle expressions of the Messiah myth" (50 expressions are of the messianic figure and 26 are of Israel's history and destiny) in the Rabbis' canon.[33] There is not a single parallel in Philo to the expressions for the Messiah and only in the most general way are there some parallels between Philo and the rabbinic corpus around the expressions of Israel's history and destiny (e.g., Expression 10 – "Age of idolatry vs. God's reign"). If we take a theme vital to both, the Temple and sacrifice, we immediately see that Philo does not mention it in his portrayal of the Golden Age. This is not because he is living before the destruction of the Temple, but is the result of his thorough spiritualization of the Temple and its ritual. In this interpretation, he follows a well-defined Middle Platonist tradition in which the authentic ritual is internalized and linked to the soul (Somn. 2.71, 2.34, and 2.217, Det. 21, Ebr. 152, Spec. Leg. 1.201 and 277).[34] This same theme is absolutely essential in rabbinic discussion of the Messianic Age or the World to Come. For example, one central question seen in early midrashic compilations is whether or not the full range of sacrifices will be reinstituted with either the Temple in the Messianic Era or in the World to Come.[35]

Our survey of the messianic texts in the Philonic corpus suggests that Philo had two different interpretations, but not irreconcilable interpretations, of the messianic figure and era. One interpretation transforms the personal figure into an allegorical designator for the Logos. Here, the Messiah referent assimilates into a number of philosophical themes within the corpus, most importantly the wisdom tradition as it was appropriated throughout Hellenistic Jewish intellectual traditions. The second interpretation is a component in Philo's interpretation of the specific laws of the Nomos. Here, Philo's presentation of the Golden Age or Messianic Era is thoroughly dehistoricized and spiritualized. There are no references to an identified national destiny and at the point where this might be introduced, he returns to the spiritualized interpretation. He concludes *De Praemiis et Poenis* by stating,

> for just as when stalks of plants are cut away, if the roots are left undestroyed, new growths shoot up which supersede the old, so too if in the soul, a tiny seed be left of the qualities which promote virtue, though other things have been stripped away, still from that little seed spring forth the fairest and most precious things in human life, by which states are constituted manned with good citizens, and nations grow into a great population. (172)

The Messianic Contexts

The most challenging question is how we account for these two interpretations in the corpus. Amir has argued that they are really two heads of the same coin, so that Philo's "other-worldliness" obliterates the particular historical or national references in the description of the Golden Age.[36] This argument would seem to be negated by underscoring the importance of politics in general in Philo's exegetical concerns and philosophical system. Indeed, the double interpretation of the Messiah and the Messianic Era in Philo might be likened to the double interpretation of Joseph in *De Iosepho* and *De Somniis*. Goodenough argued that *De Iosepho* was intended to demonstrate "by innuendo," to both Greeks and Romans in Alexandria "that the real source for the highest political ideal of the East, the ideal of a divinely appointed and guided ruler, had had its truest presentation in Jewish literature, and highest exemplification at a time when a Jew was, in contemporary language, prefect of Egypt."[37] The small section in *De Somniis* devoted to Joseph's dreams (2.90–109) was intended as a criticism of Roman arrogance in the administration of Egypt and Judea "in code."[38] Goodenough attributed the seeming tension between the Joseph of *De Iosepho* and *De Somniis*, between innuendo and code, as the result of the profound tension in Philo himself over the relationship between philosophy and politics. Indeed, in one of the few autobiographical passages in the corpus (Spec. Leg. 3.1–6), Philo laments that so much of his time is taken by "civil cares" and that he no longer has the leisure to pursue philosophy and to contemplate the universe.

Despite Goodenough's efforts to force Philo's reflections on the Messiah and Messianic Era into a template whose trajectory would culminate in early Christian reflection on the Messiah, his *Politics of Philo Judaeus* stands as a landmark study situating Philo in his social world. The reader concludes with Goodenough that Philo was deeply involved in that world and its politics. The corpus, with the exception of the overtly political and polemical works, is not composed of abstract philosophical or exegetical ideas without a social context. Indeed, I have tried to argue that at many points in the corpus, we cannot fully understand his argument, the way that he reads or allegorizes the biblical text, or the lines of his interpretation without considering his "second exegetical context," the social world of late antiquity and the particular environment of Ptolemaic and early Roman Alexandria. His interpretation of the death of Nadab and Abihu (in Somn. 2.67, Leg. All. 2.57–58, Fuga. 59, Heres. 307, Somn. 2.186, and Mos. 2.158) is a response in part to Manetho's portrayal of the rebellious Israelites in his *Aegyptica*,[39] his interpretation of circumcision (Spec. Leg. 1.1–11), in part a response to the numerous and disparaging interpretations of circumcision found in Greek and Latin authors.[40]

Philo's life spanned a period in the history of Egyptian Jewry when their political status was being quickly eroded. The political rights they had won as a *politeuma* were being challenged by the indigenous Egyptian population and the Greeks in the *chora* and in the city.[41] Their situation worsened with the appointment of Aulus Avillius Flaccus as Prefect of Egypt in either 32 or 33 C.E. Philo tells us that Flaccus ruled well until the death of Tiberius in the year 37 (Flac. 1–6). When Gaius Caligula came to the throne, Flaccus was gradually pushed toward the Alexandrian Greek and Egyptian nationalists, and this initiated a string of events that culminated in the riots of 38 C.E.[42] First, Flaccus showed favor in administration of justice in Alexandria by only hearing the cases of the Greeks. Then Agrippa's visit to the city was exploited in such a way that the popular hostility toward Jews increased with mobs clamoring for the installation of divine images in the Jewish synagogues. Flaccus did nothing, and this only emboldened the mob. When there was no response from the government of the city, the mob rioted and attacked the synagogues. The Jews who were living throughout the city (although at other points both he and Josephus describe them as living only in one quarter) were herded into one of the city's five quarters. There they were set upon: They were mocked, pillaged, and burned (Flac. 56–72 and Leg. 120–31). The members of the *gerousia* were rounded up, and paraded in the streets through jeering crowds to the theater, where many were tortured to death and the remainder imprisoned (Flac. 77–85). The pogrom ended in the fall when Bassus, who had been sent by Gaius, arrived from Italy and promptly arrested Flaccus and began to restore some sense of order in the city. The rioting had gone on for some months, and after the restoration of peace, Philo and other members of the community quickly set forth on their embassy to the Emperor. We know that the situation improved under Claudius, but friction between the communities over limited civil rights continued until the outbreak of the Great Revolt in 66 C.E. Josephus tells us that again rioting broke out and there was severe conflict between Greeks and Jews in the city. The Romans entered the fray on the side of the Greeks (Bel. 2.487–98). The Jewish quarter of the city was quiet during the remaining struggle in Judea and until the revolt of 116–17 C.E. The Roman suppression of this last Alexandria revolt spelled the end of the Jewish community in the city.

This social and political situation in Alexandria provides a fertile context for messianism and apocalypticism as attested to by the *Sibylline Oracles*. Recently, Martin Hengel has attempted to uncover the messianism of the last revolt under Trajan. He notes that the spiritualized messianism of Philo was activated in radical Jewish politics, which began with the destruction of the Temple and continued well into the reign of Hadrian.[43] Hengel had many documents to demonstrate the messianic nature of the last rising and to reconstruct the outline of its religious ideology. This is not the case with the popular messianic movements of Alexandria a century before. Already Tcherikover had argued that messianism had penetrated the worldviews of the "lower classes" at many places within the Jewish Diaspora, but most importantly in Alexandria. However, there is little or no documentary material about it. The papyri hint at its presence, but they are silent about its structure or nature.[44] We may assume that the messianism in Philo's *De Praemiis et Poenis* is a reflection of the ideas of popular messianists. This would begin to explain the differences between his identification of the messianic figure with the Logos and the heavily influenced Stoic portrayal of the Golden Age. The former was intended for those who really understood the Law of Moses and the latter was his effort to include popular rumblings and ideas of political and religious liberation on political radicalism, although transformed by the ever-present spiritualization of history.

However, Philo's transformation of those messianic ideas was more than a translation for a more literate audience or a different social class. Here, we must make reference to an important discussion of messianism in an altogether different historical context. Gershom Scholem argued that modern Hasidism effectively "neutralized" the messianism of both "moderate" and "radical" Sabbatians. He posed this interpretation against those who argued that Hasidism entirely negated messianism (e.g., Martin Buber) and those who argued that Hasidism retained, without substantial alteration, the messianic impulses of the Sabbatians and at the same time was a forerunner of Zionism (e.g., Ben-Zion Dinur and, to a lesser degree, Isaiah Tishby). Scholem concluded that Hasidism had substituted mystical and individual redemption for messianic redemption in the specific doctrine of *devekut* and the new religious community it created. Only the collective actions of the ṣaddikim continued the older interpretations of historical, messianic redemption. Hasidism, like Philo, allegorized messianism, and as Scholem states,

> the one and unique great act of final redemption, "the real thing," if I may say so, was thrown out, i.e., was removed from the sphere of man's immediate responsibility and thrown back into God's inscrutable councils. But let us face the fact: Once this was done, all the mystical talk of a sphere of Messiah in one's own life, wonderful as it may sound, becomes but an allegorical figure of speech ... the Messianism as an actual historical force is liquidated, it has lost its apocalyptic fire, its sense of imminent catastrophe.[45]

Philo's spiritualization and dehistoricization of the Messianic Era accomplishes much the same. The messianism of the community that may have arisen from popular circles is neutralized. Human action is removed to the periphery and it is God alone who moves the people by the collective and unseen vision to give up their places and nations in the Diaspora. No personal figure is needed here, for it is God who will reverse everything that is part of the past and present, beginning with the hostility between man and animal and then moving on to the relations between men and between nations. Unfortunately, there is nothing in this interpretation that would help us to determine a possible date for the latter treatises in his exposition of the Law. One could argue equally well for a date before the riots and pogrom of 38 C.E. or after it, in the first years of Claudius' reign. With the former, one would have to demonstrate that Philo used this interpretation to neutralize and defuse a potentially explosive situation under Flaccus. With the latter, one would have to demonstrate that Philo used this interpretation to neutralize or short-circuit any retaliation following the pogrom motivated by a more active messianism. The relative absence of overt messianism and political disturbances in Alexandria until the revolts of 66 C.E. and 116 C.E. suggest something of the success of Philo's neutralization of messianism.

Conclusion

Our study of Philo's messianism suggests the following: While Wolfson was convinced that Philo's ideas about the Messiah and the Messianic Era were in complete accord with the "native Judaism" of the Land of Israel and Goodenough that Philo was able to conceal his militant nationalism from the Romans, a very different picture emerges from the texts themselves. Indeed, both made the error of creating their portrayal of Philo's Messiah from ideas broken from their textual and social contexts. Wolfson was unable to see variety in the Judaism of late antiquity; Goodenough wanted to construe a secret or "coded" dimension in Philo's messianism that was essential to the mystical Judaism and flowed into early Christianity. Philo's messianism confirms neither view. At best, Philo's messianism might be understood as a "realized eschatology" in which exegetical elements that might be nationalized and identified with specific mythical or historical figures in other systems of Jewish thought or in other Jewish communities became allegorical designators for the Logos in Philo. The first line of meaning for Messiah and Messianic Era was the inner experience in which the soul was transformed. The Logos turns man from the chaos of the senses and pleasure toward the intelligible world.

Philo's neutralization of popular messianism means that he was much more conservative than Goodenough understood him to be. Here, we obviously do not refer to modern political conservatism, but Philo does not appear to hide his true feelings while gritting his teeth in hatred of the cursed Romans. This may well be the most distinctive aspect of Philo's messianism. While other forms of Jewish messianism might have been rejected because of their disastrous results, Philo attempted to accommodate it by transforming its historical and particularistic elements. In neutralizing messianism Philo gave it a new life apart from the particular political energies it might release.

NOTES

I am indebted to my colleague, Professor Birger A. Pearson, for his helpful suggestions in the preparation of this essay. Pearson's "Christians and Jews in First-century Alexandria," in *Christians among Jews and Gentiles: Essays in Honor of Krister Stendahl on His Sixty-fifth Birthday,* ed. George W. E. Nickelsburg and George W. MacRae, S.J. (Philadelphia: Fortress Press, 1986), pp. 206–16 (rpt. *Harvard Theological Review,* 79:1986), is particularly important to the present discussion.

1 One recent and popular example of this is Raphael Patai, *The Messiah Texts* (New York: Avon, 1979), which draws together a great number of different traditions and presents them in English translation. However, Patai seems to assume that the "Messiah idea" is everywhere the same with only superficial and thematic changes or additions. A better collection is George Wesley Buchanan, *Revelation and Redemption: Jewish Documents of Deliverance From the Fall of Jerusalem to the Death of Nahmanides* (Dillsboro: Western North Carolina Press, 1978) where a wider selection is offered with complete translations of texts.

2 Jacob Neusner, *Messiah in Context: Israel's History and Destiny in Formative Judaism* (Philadelphia: Fortress Press, 1984), p. ix.

3 See, for example, Bernard Lewis's study of the short midrash, *The Prayer of Rabbi Shimon bar Yohai,* in "An Apocalyptic Vision of Islamic History," *Bulletin of the School of Oriental and African Studies,* Vol. 13 (1950): 308–38.

4 See, for example, Stephen Sharot, *Messianism, Mysticism and Magic: A Sociological Analysis of Jewish Religious Movements* (Chapel Hill: The University of North Carolina Press, 1982), esp. pp. 3–26 where he attempts to redefine the sociological conceptualization of messianism and millenarianism.

5 See, for example, Shalom Rosenberg, "Exile and Redemption in Jewish Thought in the Sixteenth Century: Contending Conceptions," in *Jewish Thought in the Sixteenth Century,* ed. B. D. Cooperman (Cambridge and London: Harvard University Press, 1983), pp. 399–430.

6 See, for example, Sture Ahlberg, *Messianism i staten Israel: Ein studie om Messiastankens natida förekomst, form och function bland ortodoxa judar,* Vol. 14 of *Stockholm Studies in Comparative Religion* (Stockholm: Institute of the History of Religions of Stockholm University, 1977); David J. Biale, "Mysticism and Politics in Modern Israel: the Messianic Ideology of Abraham Isaac Ha-Cohen Kook," *Religion and Politics in the Modern World,* ed. P. H. Merkl and N. Smart (New York and London: New York University Press, 1983), pp.

191–202; Janet Aviad, "The Contemporary Israeli Pursuit of the Millennium," *Religion,* Vol. 14 (1984): 199–222.

7   Harry A. Wolfson, *Philo: Foundations of Religious Philosophy in Judaism, Christianity and Islam* (1947; rpt., Cambridge: Harvard University Press, 1968), Vol. 2, p. 407.

8   Erwin R. Goodenough, *The Politics of Philo Judaeus: Practice and Theory* (New Haven: Yale University Press, 1938), p. 25. A most important contribution to the history of scholarship on Philo is Deborah R. Sills, *Re-Inventing the Past: Philo and the Historiography of Jewish Identity* (Santa Barbara: Ph.D. Dissertation, 1984), where the author traces the two Philos, Philo Judaeus and Philo Christianus, in the 19th and 20th centuries.

9   Wolfson, *Philo,* Vol. 2, p. 409. The full text of *Philo in the Loeb Classical Library (PLCL)* Mos. 2.43–44 reads as follows:

> Thus the laws are shown to be desirable and precious in the eyes of all, ordinary citizens and rulers alike, and that too though our nation has not prospered for many a year. It is but natural that when people are not flourishing their belongings to some degree are under a cloud. But if a fresh start should be made to brighter prospects, how great a change for the better might we expect to see! I believe that each nation would abandon its peculiar ways, and, throwing overboard their ancestral customs, turn to honoring our laws alone. For, when the brightness of their shining is accompanied by national prosperity, it will darken the light of the others as the risen sun darkens the stars.

10   Wolfson, *Philo,* Vol. 2, p. 411.

11   Ibid., pp. 413–14.

12   Ibid., pp. 414. Wolfson cites Targums Jonathan and Yerushalmi as the evidence for the messianic interpretation of this text. However, David Winston, trans., *Philo of Alexandria: The Contemplative Life, the Giants and Selections* (New York, Ramsey and Toronto: The Paulist Press, 1981), p. 390, n. 696, indicates that the messianic interpretation of the verse is not uniform. Targum Onqelos historicizes the text with a reading intended only to clarify the difficulty of the Masoretic Text (M): "The king annointed from his sons shall increase, and have dominion over many nations." Samson H. Levey, *The Messiah: An Aramaic Interpretation – The Messianic Exegesis of the Targum* (Cincinnati: Hebrew Union College Press, 1974), p. 20, indicates that there are no rabbinic parallels to Jonathan and Yerushalmi's rendering of the text that would suggest a more qualified attitude toward Philo's interpretation of the text.

13   Wolfson, *Philo,* Vol. 2, pp. 415–17. Wolfson sees a parallel to this in Sibylline Oracles 3.702–22, where in the Messianic Era, the non-Jewish nations will only abandon idolatry. However, in Philo, the non-Jewish nations will abandon their peculiar ways, their ancestral traditions, and become full proselytes to the religion of the God of Israel.

14   Wolfson, *Philo,* Vol. 2, pp. 419–20.

15   See David Winston and John Dillon, *Two Treatises of Philo of Alexandria: A Commentary on De Gigantibus and Quod Deus Sit Immutabilis* (Chico, Calif.: Scholars Press, 1983), Vol. 25 of the Brown Judaica Studies, pp. 344 and 354,

for discussion of this well-known theme in Hellenistic tradition and Festugiere's thesis that the origin of Philo's τúχη is to be located in the thought of Demetrius of Phalerum.

16 A parallel idea is seen in Widsom of Solomon 6:3 where God gives dominion to the kings of the earth. However, the source of their sovereignty is from the divine world. See David Winston, trans., *The Wisdom of Solomon* (Garden City: Doubleday, 1979), pp. 151–3.

17 *PLCL,* 3.489.

18 John Dillon, *The Middle Platonists – 80 B.C. to A.D. 220* (Ithaca: Cornell University Press, 1977), pp. 154–5.

19 Wolfson, *Philo,* Vol. 2, p. 425.

20 Goodenough, *The Politics of Philo Judaeus,* p. 25. While Goodenough assumes relatively little ambiguity in Somn. 2.64, other commentators express greater caution. For example, John J. Collins, *Between Athens and Jerusalem: Jewish Identity in the Hellenistic Diaspora* (New York: Crossroad, 1983), pp. 114–15 where he argues that "Philo only says that 'no husbandman has hitherto been found.' We may infer that he expects one, but he does not actually say so. Such a 'husbandman' could be a messianic figure who would put an end to Roman rule, or he might be a reformer who would put an end to corruption."

21 Goodenough, *The Politics of Philo Judaeus,* p. 118. The same interpretation is summarized in his *An Introduction to Philo Judaeus* (1940; rpt., Oxford: Basil Blackwell, 1962), pp. 70–1.

22 Goodenough, *The Politics of Philo Judaeus,* p. 118.

23 Collins, *Between Athens and Jerusalem,* pp. 115–16. Collins also attempts to distinguish Philo's eschatology from many apocalyptic writers and from the majority of Sibylline books, not in terms of concepts and ideas which they hold in common, but in the degree of urgency. The paucity of references to a national eschatology indicates to Collins that it was not at the heart of Philo's thought.

24 Goodenough, *The Politics of Philo Judaeus,* pp. 118–19.

25 J. de Savignac, "Le Messianisme de Philon d'Alexandrie," *Novum Testamentum,* Vol. 4 (1959): 319–24.

26 Ibid., p. 321.

27 Valentin Nikiprowetzky, *Le Commentaire de l'écriture chez Philon d'Alexandrie* (Leiden: E. J. Brill, 1977), pp. 192–202.

28 Valentin Nikiprowetzky, "*Schadenfreude* chez Philon d'Alexandrie? Note sur *In Flaccum,* 121 sq.," *Revue des études juives,* Vol. 127 (1968): 7–19.

29 Ferdinand Dexinger, "Ein 'Messianisches Szenarium' als Gemeingut des Judentums in nachherodianischer Zeit." *Kairos,* Vol. 17 (1975): 249–87.

30 Yehoshua Amir, "The Messianic Idea in Hellenistic Judaism," (Hebrew) *Mahanayim,* Vol. 124 (1970): 54–67.

31 Colson, *PLCL* 8.370 writes "Philo perhaps wishes to avoid the suggestion of actual bloodshed."

32 The River Sambation is an important topographic point in rabbinic and medieval messianic scenarios. It marks one of the farthest points in the exile. L. Ginzberg, *The Legends of the Jews* (1913; rpt. Philadelphia: The Jewish Pub-

lication Society of America, 1968), Vol. 4, pp. 316–17 summarizes the diverse legends concerning the Levites' escape from Nebuchadnezzar:

> At the fall of night a cloud descended and enveloped the Sons of Moses and all who belonged to them. They were hidden from their enemies, while their own way was illuminated by a pillar of fire. The cloud and the pillar vanished at the break of day and before the Sons of Moses lay a tract of land bordered by the sea on three sides. For their complete protection God made the River Sambation to flow on the fourth side. This river is full of sand and stones, and on the six working days of the week, they tumble over each other with such vehemence that the crash and the uproar are heard far and wide. But on the Sabbath, the tumultuous river subsides into quiet. As a guard against trespassers on that day, a column of cloud stretches along the whole length of the river, and none can approach the Sambation within three miles.

See also Vol. 6, pp. 407–9 for a more detailed description of the river in Josephus, where the river runs on Shabbat and hence he deduces its etymology from *sabbatikon;* Pliny, where the river does not run on the Shabbat (in both the river has no messianic connections); and rabbinic and medieval Hebrew literature. The bringing of the Levites from the Sambation was early assimilated into midrashic interpretations of the messianic drama. For example, *Pesiqta Rabbati* (Friedman ed., Vienna, 1880) 146b–47a contains a very early parallel to the *Yalqut* text. Another example is found in *Sefer Eliyahu,* Y. Even-Shemuel, *Midrashe He-Ge'ulah* (Jerusalem and Tel Aviv: Mosad Bialik, 1968), p. 43:

> On the twenty-second of Tishri the First Exile will go out from Babylon with eighteen thousand men and women, and not one of them will be lost. On twenty-fifth of Tishri, the Second Exile which is on the River Sabbation [Sambation] with seventeen thousand, and of them twenty men and fifteen women will be killed. On the twenty-fifth of the eight month [Heshvan], the Third Exile will go out, weeping and crying over their brothers who were killed. They will lament in the desert for forty-five days. They will carry nothing and will live by that which comes forth from the mouth of the Lord. The First Exile will not go out from Babylon until the second reaches Babylon, for it is written in Micah 4:10, "and you shall come to Babylon; there you shall be rescued; there the Lord will redeem you from the hand of your enemy."

For a discussion of how the Sambation is portrayed in Eldad Ha-Dani, is assimilated into the Prester John legends, and was "rediscovered" in the 17th century in New Spain, see Ronald Sanders, *Lost Tribes and Promised Lands: The Origins of American Racism* (Boston and Toronto: Little, Brown, 1978), pp. 45–66 and 363–5.

33 Neusner, *Messiah in Context,* pp. 215–220.
34 Valentin Nikiprowetzky, "La Spiritualisation des sacrifices et le culte sacrificiel au Temple de Jérusalem chez Philon d'Alexandrie," *Semitica,* Vol. 17 (1967): 97–116. Jean LaPorte, *Eucharistia in Philo* (New York and Toronto:

The Edwin Mellen Press, 1983) represents an important example of a thorough study of a single element in Philo's spiritualization of sacrificial ritual. See also Robert J. Daly, *Christian Sacrifice: The Judaeo-Christian Background Before Origen* (Washington: The Catholic University of America, 1978), pp. 389–421, and id., *The Origins of the Christian Doctrine of Sacrifice* (Philadelphia: Fortress Press, 1978), pp. 104–10.

35 For example, *Wayyikra Rabbah* 9:7 and 27:12 argue that all sacrifices with the exception of the Thanksgiving sacrifice will be annulled in the Messianic Temple, while 2:2 indicates that *all* the sacrifices will be reinstituted in the Messianic Era and the world to come.

36 Amir, "The Messianic Idea in Hellenistic Judaism," p. 58.

37 Goodenough, *The Politics of Philo Judaeus*, p. 62.

38 Ibid., pp. 21–41. The most comprehensive study of Philo's politics is Ray Barraclough, "Philo's Politics: Roman Rule and Hellenistic Judaism," *Aufstieg und Niedergang der römischen Welt*, ed. W. Haase (Berlin and New York: Walter De Gruyter, 1984), 2:21.1, pp. 417–553. Barraclough does not have major criticism of Goodenough's interpretation of Joseph (pp. 491–506), and states that his "desire to relate the contents of 'De Iosepho' to Philo's environment is commendable and one needs to remember Philo's experience as a member of the Jewish community in Alexandria. The harrassment of the Jews (climaxing in the pogrom under Flaccus) illustrated the necessity for good rule, otherwise the tyrannical mob, unchecked and unpunished, could wreak the savaging of its hate" (p. 495).

39 "Patterns of Exegesis in Philo's Interpretation of Leviticus," *Studia Philonica*, Vol. 6 (1979–80), esp. 115–28.

40 "Philo's Interpretation of Circumcision," *Nourished with Peace: Studies in Hellenistic Judaism in Memory of Samuel Sandmel*, ed. F. E. Greenspahn, E. Hilgert, and B. L. Mack (Chico, Calif.: Scholars Press, 1984), pp. 51–79.

41 See especially E. Mary Smallwood's description of the erosion of the Jewish political status in *The Jews Under Roman Rule: From Pompey to Diocletian* (Leiden: E. J. Brill, 1976), pp. 220–55 and 364–8. Also, Aryeh Kasher, *The Jews in Hellenistic and Roman Egypt* (Hebrew) (Tel Aviv: Tel Aviv University, 1978) argues that Jewish rights within the *politeuma* were quite extensive on the eve of the Roman conquest of Egypt. The *politeuma* was independent of the Greek *polis,* and this created a major problem for Greek and Roman sovereignty in the city. Both tried to establish only one *politeia* based on the model of Greek kinship. The dynamic set in motion was the abolition of the Jewish *politeia,* reducing the Jews to "aliens" or permanent residents with very limited civic rights under the Greeks and Romans, and recognition of this situation as the status quo.

42 A. N. Sherwin-White, "Philo and Avillius Flaccus: A Conundrum," *Latomus,* Vol. 31 (1972); 820–8.

43 Martin Hengel, "Messianische Hoffnung und politischer 'Radikalismus' in der judisch-hellenistischen Diaspora: Zur Frage der Voraussetzungen des judischen Aufstandes unter Trajan 115–17 n. Chr.," in *Apocalypticism in the Mediterranean World and the Near East,* ed. D. Hellholm (Tubingen: J. C. B.

Mohr-Paul Siebeck, 1983), esp. pp. 679–83. Shim'on Applebaum, *Jews and Greeks in Ancient Cyrene* (Leiden: E. J. Brill, 1979), esp. pp. 201–60 provides a systematic study of the revolt in Cyrene during the reign of Trajan. There, he states, "the spirit of the movement was messianic, its aim the liquidation of the Roman regime and the setting up of a new Jewish commonwealth, whose task was to inaugurate the messianic era" (p. 260).

44   Victor A. Tcherikover, "The Decline of the Jewish Diaspora in Egypt in the Roman Period," *Journal of Jewish Studies,* Vol. 14 (1963): 1–32, and Tcherikover and Alexander Fuks, eds., *Corpus Papyrorum Judaicarum* (1957; rpt., Cambridge: Harvard University Press, 1964), esp. Vol. 1, pp. 1–111.

45   Gershom Scholem, "The Neutralization of the Messianic Element in Early Hasidism" in *The Messianic Idea in Judaism and Other Essays on Jewish Spirituality* (New York: Schocken Books, 1971), pp. 201–2. A recent discussion and application of Scholem's "neutralization" appears in David Biale, *Power and Powerlessness in Jewish History* (New York: Schocken Books, 1986), pp. 40–3.

8

Messiah and Gospel

GEORGE MACRAE, S.J.

Whoever attempts to survey early Christian belief that Jesus of Nazareth was the Messiah of Israel is immediately confronted by a well known but nevertheless major problem. That is the problem of the translation of the Christian proclamation from that of a Palestinian Jewish sectarian group to that of a broader Greco-Roman religious movement, not in intention sectarian, which aimed to appeal to the gentile world at least as much as it did to the Jewish world of the Diaspora. The issue is problematic because, except for a very few isolated words and phrases, the oldest written sources of the Christian movement already reflect the transition. Virtually all efforts to describe the process of the transition are theoretical reconstructions. What we can document most directly are the reflections of either Hellenistic Jewish authors such as Paul or gentile Christian writers such as Luke. The limitations of this situation are obvious. Messianism is essentially a product of Jewish religion, with its roots, if not its most explicit articulation, deeply embedded in the literature of Israel. Our general question must involve this inquiry: How do we recognize the older messianic aspirations in the literature of a movement that expresses itself almost exclusively in Greek and more often than not in Greek categories of thought?

The problem is not merely one of language, though that dimension is not inconsiderable. It has to do equally with categories and patterns of thought. For example, what set of expectations of a messianic figure would be intelligible and natural for a people not nurtured on the hopes of Israel? Or to give an even more concrete example, what would the Dead Sea Scrolls look like in Greek – not merely translated into Greek, but composed in a Greek milieu?

One focus of the problem has to do with how to understand the Greek word *Christos*. The available evidence shows overwhelmingly that this word, undoubtedly originally a translation of the Hebrew *mashiah,* very early was regarded in Greek-speaking circles as a proper name. In the Christian sources, therefore, it is rarely obvious that *Christos* is being used as a title or as a name with no clear allusion to its etymology. The use of the word Messiah is not of course the only way to detect messianic images of Jesus in the tradition; in fact, increasingly it is pointed out that the classical study of christology based on an examination of the so-called titles of Christ is not the best method. Nevertheless, it is difficult to dispense with the titular approach. In what follows we shall devote considerable attention to it, but we shall also endeavor to note some other approaches as well. There have been extensive analyses of the distribution and syntax of *Christos* throughout the New Testament, but in some cases there is little agreement on how to interpret the word in specific contexts. Ultimately the argument is always exegetical, based on the set of factors that comprise exegesis itself. The purpose and scope of this survey do not permit an exegetical study of the many passages, but we shall allude to the issues in some of them.

The place to begin is the Pauline corpus, for two reasons. By widespread agreement the Pauline letters commonly accepted as authentic (Romans, 1 and 2 Corinthians, Galatians, Philippians, 1 Thessalonians, Philemon) are the oldest surviving documents of the Christian movement. There may of course have been earlier ones, such as the letter to which Paul refers in 1 Corinthians 5:9, or perhaps the Synoptic sayings source Q, but we have no direct access to them. Second, the Pauline letters are distinctive in the New Testament as a major body of writings in which the Messiahship of Jesus is simply not an issue. In view of Paul's own Jewish background this situation may seem surprising. Of course we may observe that the letters are addressed to churches made up primarily if not exclusively of gentiles, who might be expected to be less interested than Jews in the messianic identity of Jesus. This is a plausible argument, but two cautions may be offered. First, one should note that other New Testament writers concerned primarily with a gentile Christian audience do not hesitate to emphasize the Messiahship of Jesus – Luke, for example, in both of his books, as we shall note later on. Second, Paul himself shows no general reluctance to presume that his new gentile Christians are interested in and can understand even detailed references to the fulfillment of Jewish or Israelite traditions (see, e.g., the letter to the Galatians, among others). It would indeed be interesting to know how Paul preached to Jewish audiences – that is, whether the issue of the Messiah may have been central to his message, but we have no record of such preaching, and the preaching ascribed to him in the Acts of the Apostles must for a variety of reasons be attributed to Luke rather than to Paul. Thus, the fact that Paul's letters are addressed mainly to gentiles is not without qualification an adequate explanation for the relative absence of messianic issues in them.

No New Testament author uses the name *Christos* more frequently than Paul, who uses it in many different combinations, including Jesus Christ, Christ Jesus (distinctively Pauline), (Jesus) Christ the Lord, the Lord (Jesus) Christ, and of course Christ alone with or without the article. The philological details have often been analyzed and need not be summarized here.[1] One should note, however, that the word *Christos* is never used in Paul with a genitive qualifier such as "Christ of God," "Christ of Israel," or the like. Most of those who have examined the evidence have concluded that *Christos* is never or virtually never used by Paul as a title in the sense of Messiah, but only as a proper name. Even in passages thought to be pre-Pauline and merely used by Paul (e.g., Rom. 1:4; 1 Cor. 15:3; Phil. 2:11) there is no evidence that we are dealing with more than a name. Thus, we may conclude that at a very early date in the development of Christian expression the titular use of *Christos* was in some circles supplanted by its use as a proper name.

One possible exception to this general Pauline usage is Romans 9:5 in which, enumerating the blessings given to the Israelites, Paul says, "and from them is the Christ with respect to what is according to the flesh" (i.e., physical descent; the translation is deliberately over-literal). Here it would be very easy to understand a direct reference to the Messiah, but it must be observed that the statement would be no less clear if Paul were merely using the word as the name Christ. In Pauline usage the presence or absence of the article is not conclusive.

In the later Pauline tradition also there is equally little evidence for the titular use of *Christos.* Again, a possible exception might be Ephesians 5:5, which speaks of an "inheritance in the kingdom of (the) Christ and of God." The association of a kingdom with the Messiah is well known. But here too the statement would make no less sense if the word Christ is merely a name.

Yet it would be wrong to conclude that Paul is unaware of or totally uninterested in the Messiahship of Jesus. There are enough references in his letters to the fact that whether or not this issue formed a part of his original Christian experience, which he describes as a "revelation of Jesus Christ" (Gal. 1:12), he inherited it from the Christian tradition. This fact is apparent, for example, in Romans 1:2–4, which refers to the gospel of God

> which he promised beforehand through his prophets in the holy scriptures, the gospel concerning his Son, who was descended

> from David according to the flesh and designated Son of God in power according to the Spirit of holiness by his resurrection from the dead, Jesus Christ our Lord.

This passage is widely believed to be a pre-Pauline christological formulation which is probably reinterpreted by Paul himself with the contrast between "according to the flesh" and "according to the Spirit of holiness" (though the latter is not a typically Pauline expression).[2] The reference to descent from David is properly understood as a statement of the messianic identity of Jesus, but even here Messiahship is superseded by divine sonship, which in the biblical tradition is not an exclusive property of the Messiah.

That Paul sometimes thinks of Jesus in messianic terms may also be inferred from his use of inherited apocalyptic imagery in such passages as 1 Corinthians 15:23–28, where he says of Christ "at his coming":

> Then comes the end, when he delivers the kingdom to God the Father after destroying every rule and every authority and power. For he must reign until he has put all his enemies under his feet.

The association of Christ with an eschatological kingdom, albeit a temporary one, is strikingly reminiscent of the main lines of Jewish royal messianism, but transformed from the arena of the future of history to that of a transcendent future. A similar messianic reinterpretation, but completely without the kingdom imagery, may be found in Jewish apocalyptic literature in 4 Ezra (e.g., 7:26–31).

Thus there is no question that Paul is aware of the Christian claim that Jesus is the Messiah, and this claim may have formed part of his original preaching, of which we have no direct record. The important point is that he does not discuss the issue in his writings, making no effort to prove or demonstrate the messianic identity of Jesus. For him the Christian message does not hinge, at least primarily, on the claim that Jesus was or is the Messiah. For this reason, in the absence of evidence to the contrary, I do not agree with those scholars who argue that the Messiah issue must have been central for Paul and essential to his gospel.[3] His gospel hinges on the saving death and resurrection of Christ. As 1 Corinthians 15 makes clear, Paul saw the resurrection of Christ as the beginning of God's eschatological act of raising the dead (the "first fruits," 1 Cor. 15:20, 23). As such it grounds the hope of Christians in a fundamental way. In this sense perhaps Paul could envision Christ as a messianic leader, ushering in the final age, but he does so without reference to the limited concept of Messiah as traditionally known.

If we move away from the language of messianism, however, into the broader idea of the function of a messianic figure, there is no doubt that in Paul's understanding Christ fulfills this function. For him Christ is the agent of eschatological salvation.[4] This is so central to his theology that it needs no particular demonstration here. What God has accomplished in Christ for Paul is liberation from the Law – sin, death, and the powers that dominate human life in the world. This is clearly a messianic function, but it is not necessarily the linear fulfillment of the hope of Israel. Instead, it is a Christian interpretation of the messianic function in the direction of transcendence. The Son of God is indeed the Messiah, but for Paul the operative categories go beyond classical messianic ideology. Only in this way can the gospel appeal to the Gentile world at large.

We turn our attention next to the messianic idea in the Gospels and Acts, where the results of inquiry are strikingly different. What we observed in the oldest extant writings of Christianity, Paul's letters, was, among other things, that the issue of Jesus as Messiah was less than pivotal for the proclamation of the gospel. It is also instructive to observe that in the oldest recoverable strata of the written Gospel traditions, the issue of Messiah is either absent or problematic. In the sayings source Q, which underlies the Gospels of Matthew and Luke, Jesus is never referred to as Messiah. And in the oldest of the four Gospels, Mark (in the most common estimation of scholarship), Jesus is indeed Messiah, but the designation is problematic; in fact it is one of the central problems to which this Gospel is devoted. It is an increasingly accepted view of Gospel scholarship that Jesus himself did not historically claim to be the Messiah and did not unequivocally accept attempts on the part of others to identify him as such. The question of the attitude of the historical Jesus to messianic claims is a very complex one that I do not propose to discuss here. As will become obvious, the issue confronts us more immediately at the levels of Gospel tradition and redaction, and it is at those levels that I wish to survey the evidence in summary fashion. I propose therefore to examine each Gospel, as well as the Lukan Acts, for its own understanding of the messianic issue, taking all these writings as later than the letters of Paul though sometimes containing earlier traditions. I shall concentrate mainly on the use of messianic titles, realizing the limitations of such an approach to the general question.

It would be possible to anticipate the evidence in the form of general theses of development within the Christian tradition, though no such development is ever simply rectilinear. The theses would be formulated more or less as follows:

more or less as follows:

1. The earliest recoverable strata of the Christian proclamation of the gospel are aware of the claim that Jesus was (is, or will be; see below) the Messiah of Israel; this claim is not the primary focus of their message.

2. The earliest Palestinian Jewish preaching of the gospel probably emphasized the messianic idea, but there is no adequate evidence to support this probability.

3. The further one gets away in time from the earliest preaching, whether Palestinian or Hellenistic, the more the issue of Jesus as Messiah gains in prominence.

4. This development takes roughly two forms:
   a. a movement away from traditional Jewish understandings of the Messiah and his role, evidenced in the Gospels of Mark and John, and
   b. a movement toward some aspects of the traditional Christian understandings, with an emphasis on the continuity of promise or prophecy and fulfillment, evidenced in the Gospels of Matthew and Luke.

5. These trends are not to be explained simply as diverging views of gentile as opposed to Jewish Christians, for the Gospels of Mark and Luke represent mainly gentile concerns while those of Matthew and John arise out of originally Jewish Christian churches.

We begin with the Gospels of Mark and John. Not only do these Gospels illustrate the movement away from traditional Jewish messianic expectations, but also they are both to some extent critical of the adequacy of the designation Messiah as an understanding of Jesus while unable to reject it because it is an established part of the Christian tradition by the time any Gospel is written. If yet another thesis could be put forward, it would sound like this:

6. The Gospels of Mark and John, and to a certain degree those of Matthew and Luke, illustrate the fact that to the extent that the title *Christos* became progressively more central to early Christian proclamation, to that same extent it departed further from the Jewish understanding of the Messiah.

The Gospel of Mark uses the name or title Christ in fact quite sparingly (seven times), and even if one includes the titles Son of David (used in two passages) and King of Israel (used only in the passion narrative), which are certainly messianic titles, or such expressions as "the kingdom of our father David" (11:10), the designations of Jesus as Messiah are not frequent. One can rapidly narrow down the range of passages relevant to a discussion of Mark's own views. Apart from the incipit of the Gospel (1:1), "The beginning of the gospel of Jesus Christ," the messianic title is confined to the second major division of Mark, from 8:27 (or 8:22) on, which focuses more explicitly on instruction of the disciples than on Jesus' ministry to the public at large and highlights questions of christology. This is what one might expect, but it will appear more significant when the distribution of the title Messiah is seen to be just the reverse in the Gospel of John. If expressions like "the holy one of God" (1:24) or "Son of the Most High God" (5:7) are indeed understood as messianic designations in the first division of the Gospel, it is notable that they are found only on the lips of demonic beings. What the distribution of messianic titles in Mark indicates prima facie is that the question of Jesus' identity as Messiah is a matter of debate within the Christian community itself, since the disciples in the Gospel story represent the Christians of Mark's time. In the incipit, moreover, *Christos* is in any case a personal name, and Mark's acquaintance with it as a name seems to be borne out by the reference to the name of Christ in 9:41.

The last mention of *Christos* in Mark, certainly a titular usage, is placed on the lips of the chief priests and scribes at the scene of the crucifixion (15:32): "Let the Christ, the King of Israel, come down now from the cross." This taunt alludes to the inscription on the cross that identifies the criminal Jesus as "The King of the Jews" (15:26). There can be no doubt historically that the Romans crucified Jesus as a messianic pretender. Whether Jesus himself accepted or, more probably, rejected the title, it is possible that the inscription on the cross lies at the root of the Christian preoccupation with the title.

The use of *Christos* in the apocalyptic discourse of Jesus at 13:21–22 belongs to the apocalyptic tradition, whether Jewish or Christian in its formulation, and refers to a coming future Messiah, not to Jesus himself. In that passage the authentic messianic figure is the "Son of man coming in clouds with great power and glory" (13:26), whom the evangelist undoubtedly understands to be Jesus in his second coming. The preference of Mark for the title Son of Man over Messiah – or perhaps we should say Mark's reinterpretation of the Messiah in terms of the Son of Man – is at the heart of Mark's Gospel. But the triumphant eschatological Son of Man comes to Mark from the apocalyptic tradition; it is not his whole picture of the Son of Man. To complete the picture we must turn to the carefully structured "central section" of the Gospel (8:22–10:52). Here the confession of Peter at Caesarea Philippi, "You are the Christ" (8:29), is followed by the injunction of Jesus to keep this issue secret. The well known motif of the Markan messianic secret is at work here, and, however one understands this motif in detail, it belongs to the level of Markan redaction rather than to that of the historical Jesus. Jesus may properly be confessed as Messiah only when the concept has been invested with the special Markan understanding of the Son of Man as the one who "must suffer many things, and be rejected by the elders and the chief priests and the scribes, and be killed, and after three days rise again" (8:31). The position of this passion prediction right after the messianic confession of Peter clearly shows that it is a corrective to the confession itself. Only in terms of the suffering, dying, rising Son of Man do Christians confess Jesus as the Messiah. Since this corrective is for Mark a summary of the heart of the Christian gospel, it is clear that Jesus is the Messiah only on Christian terms. Mark's purpose is not to emphasize the continuity with the messianic expectations of Judaism.

The same point is made in the scene of the hearing before the Jewish authorities in Mark 14. When asked directly, "Are you the Christ, the Son of the Blessed One?" Jesus replies affirmatively (only in Mark) "I am" (14:61–62). And here too the corrective for understanding Christ is given immediately, in terms recalling the apocalyptic discourse: "And you will see the Son of Man sitting at the right hand of power, and coming with the clouds of heaven." Taken in isolation this understanding of Messiah in Mark implies that it is strictly future, but the interpretation must be balanced against Mark 8:31. For Mark Messiah means both past (or present) and future Son of Man.

Mark is familiar with the Jewish tradition that the Messiah is a descendant of David, but he does not give the title Son of David the prominence that it has in Matthew, for example. The fragment of controversy dialogue about David calling his descendant Lord (via Ps. 110:1: "The Lord said to my Lord") in Mark 12:35–37 and parallels is obscure at best and very difficult to interpret. It probably has its origin in Christian discussion with Jews about Messiah and biblical interpretation in the period after Jesus himself. But as was suggested above, the positioning of the major messianic references in Mark suggests that the debate about how to understand the title *Christos* was for the most part an inner-Christian one. At the very least Mark wished to revise some sort of triumphalist Christology.

The fourth Gospel uses the word *Christos* almost three times as often as Mark, but the distribution of the word, and of the messianic issue behind it, is sharply different. There is an overall structural resemblance between the Gospels of John and Mark in that both have two major divisions, one in which Jesus exercises a ministry to the public at large and one in which he instructs, by word and action, mainly his immediate disciples, who, though slow to understand, show a dogged persistence in their discipleship (the dividing points are at Mark 8:22 and John 13:1). In Mark the use of *Christos* was confined mainly to the second division; in John it is almost exclusively in the first. It appears, to be sure, in John 20:31, the original conclusion of the Gospel: "These things are written that you may believe that Jesus is the Christ," but this passage is clearly a conclusion to the whole Gospel and not just to the second half of it. Elsewhere in the second division of the Gospel it occurs as a name, not a title, in the prayer of Jesus: "And this is eternal life, that they know you the only true God, and Jesus Christ whom you have sent" (17:3). There are good reasons to think this verse may be a late redactional addition to the Gospel in any case.[5] Thus, most of the uses of *Christos* in John are in the public phase of Jesus' ministry and indeed mostly in contexts of controversy with those whom the evangelist calls "the Jews" (only in 1:17 is Christ a name; the other examples are unmistakably titular). One conclusion to draw from the distribution of the title is that the messianic identity of Jesus is not primarily an issue within the Johannine community itself, to whom the second half of the Gospel is ultimately addressed, but an issue between the Johannine Christians and their fellow Jews. Such a conclusion corresponds very well to the judgment of modern Johannine scholarship that the Gospel reflects a profound controversy with the synagogue in the recent past of the community.[6] The clue is often seen in John 9:22 in the story of the man born blind: The healed man's parents are afraid to speak for fear of "the Jews," for "the Jews had already agreed that if anyone should confess him (i.e., Jesus) to be Christ, he was to be put out of the synagogue." Historically this situation best fits the waning years of the first century C.E., but the historical question is not our main concern here.

The Gospel very explicitly reflects the debate with the synagogue in three further passages about how Jesus can qualify as Messiah: 7:25–44; 10:24–25; 12:34–35. In these passages questions are raised about not knowing where the Messiah comes from, the signs that the Messiah performs, Bethlehem as the home of the Messiah and his descent from David, and the necessity of the Messiah remaining forever (as opposed to the death of the Son of Man). We do not know in every instance what source the evangelist had in mind for each of these Jewish expectations of the Messiah, especially the last one, but there is no question about the general thrust of his argument. Jesus is indeed rightly confessed as the Messiah by the Christians, but principally on their own terms. The concept itself is at issue. Jesus comes from the Father; his signs are perceptible only to faith; he is ostensibly from Nazareth, but the Christian may be familiar with the Davidic descent and the Bethlehem tradition, which in any case are not perceived as essential; and the Messiah does remain forever in the presence of the Father beyond death. The Johannine church wants to insist that he is ostensibly from Nazareth, but the Christian may be familiar with the Davidic descent and the Bethlehem tradition, which in any case are not perceived as essential; and the Messiah does remain forever in the presence of the Father beyond death. The Johannine church wants to insist that Jesus qualifies as Messiah without fulfilling the requirements. The concept has become a radically transcendent one.

Yet the situation is more complex still. In the Fourth Gospel not only is the understanding of Messiah reinterpreted polemically over against the Jews, but it also reflects inner-Christian debates. The evangelist also wants to establish an acceptance of faith in Jesus as Messiah on the basis of his revealing word and not his miraculous activity. This presupposes that there are Christians who lay primary emphasis on the latter, and with them John is also in conflict. This side of the Johannine interpretation is shown in two ways, neither of which can be justified in detail here. One is the whole treatment of Jesus' miracles as signs, a special term in John's vocabulary that refers to an insight that goes beyond the miraculous itself into the nature of the miracle worker (see e.g., 2:11; 2:23–25; 3:2–3; 4:48–50; etc.). Signs are an adequate basis for faith in Jesus only insofar as they do not focus on the miraculous alone. No passage links signs and the Messiah directly except 7:31, which is portrayed as the erroneous Jewish view. But there are passages that carefully structure the titles of Jesus in relation to the understanding of him by what he does and what he says. One such is the story of the blind man in which there is a noticeable progression from the acknowledgment of Jesus as prophet (9:17), to Messiah (indirectly in 9:22 and implicitly in 9:33, "if this man were not from God"), to Son of Man (9:35).[7] Other passages could be adduced to show that John, like Mark, prefers to understand Jesus' Messiahship in terms of Son of Man. But unlike Mark, for John the Son of Man title refers primarily to the descent from heaven to reveal the Father and to the return there (6:62 and many other passages).

What is clear from this survey of the Fourth Gospel is that it shares with Mark an uneasiness about the designation of Christ as Messiah unless the term is understood on purely Christian, in this case Johannine, terms. Yet in the context of the Jewish background of the Johannine community, the Gospel will not yield on the issue that Jesus really is the Messiah. The Johannine Messiah, however, shares relatively little with the Jewish and even other Christian concepts of Messiah in that the eschatological dimension of the messianic role is diminished, if not eliminated.

When we turn to the Gospels of Matthew and Luke we discover a very different emphasis. Both are dependent on the Gospel of Mark as their model, according to the Synoptic theory most widely held among scholars today. But both ignore the basic bipartite Markan structure (which is followed by John). In these Gospels there is no mystery gradually to be unfolded. Moreover, both Matthew and Luke have no hesitation about using the designation Messiah and related terms such as Son of David. They have no quarrel with these Jewish categories, even though their understanding of them is not confined to Jewish precedents. In addition, though both these evangelists continue to use the title Son of Man, they see no special christological significance in it as, in different ways, did Mark and John. Indeed, for Matthew the expression sometimes seems to be little more than a substitute for "I" in the sayings of Jesus. It is not itself a special messianic title.

Matthew uses the word *Christos* as a name or a title a little over twice as often as Mark. In fact, the expression Jesus Christ in Matt 1:1, a quasi-title for the infancy Gospel if not for the whole work, is the only time in Matthew or Luke where *Christos* does not have the titular sense. Matthew also gives more prominence than the other Gospels to the title Son of David (e.g., 12:23; 21:9, 15), which is clearly for him a messianic designation. The intention of Matthew to situate the gospel in the line of Jewish messianic expectation is unmistakable; the point is to see how he modifies the traditional expectations.

The main emphasis, or one of the main emphases, of the Matthean genealogy and infancy narrative is to establish that Jesus is the Davidic Messiah, thus asserting for the originally Jewish Christian church of Matthew that Jesus does meet the hope of Israel (1:1, 16, 17). At the same time Matthew wishes to show by the genealogy and the Magi story that Jesus is the son of Abraham (1:1), the one who is destined for a saving role for the gentiles as well. If the beginning of the genealogy uses Jesus Christ as a proper name, as we have suggested, the end of the passage (1:16–17) makes it quite clear that Matthew wishes to remind his readers that behind this name lies the all-important messianic title. The genealogy is of Jesus "who is called the Messiah." The infancy narrative that follows the genealogy is expressly labeled an account of "the birth [or: origin] of the Christ" (1:18). There are good reasons for preferring this reading of the verse to the perhaps more commonly accepted one, which refers to "the birth of Jesus Christ" – again using the name.[8] In a famous article Krister Stendahl has shown convincingly that the first two chapters of Matthew are structured respectively around the answers to the question "Quis et Unde?" or "who and whence?"[9] Chapter 1 demonstrates Jesus' Davidic descent and Chapter 2 his birth in David's city Bethlehem. These are the traditional qualifications that prove he is indeed the Messiah of Israel.

Since Jesus is established by virtue of his birth or even conception as the Messiah, Matthew can go on to write his Gospel as a description of the Messianic Age in which the deeds of the Messiah are visibly present. The relation to Israel is sustained by the typically Matthean emphasis, introduced in the infancy narrative and sporadically repeated throughout the Gospel, on the fulfillment of biblical prophecy (the so-called Matthean formula quotations, e.g., 4:14–17). But for Matthew the Messianic Age does not come to a close with the death of Jesus, for the Gospel ends on the majestic promise of the risen Jesus "Lo, I am with you always, to the close of the age" (28:20). One should compare the use of the name Emmanuel near the beginning of the Gospel (1:23). Only, since this promise is given in the context of the commission to evangelize the gentiles, Matthew is asserting that the Messianic Age is for the gentiles too.

Nevertheless, despite Matthew's insistence on the Jewish messianic identity of Jesus, he interprets the role of the Messiah without reference to the liberation of the Jewish people from foreign domination but only with reference to spiritual qualities. To see this clearly one should highlight passages that are distinctively Matthean, either modifications of his sources or his own composition. Perhaps the most important such passage is the Q passage in Matthew 11:2–6, which Matthew has (certainly) modified by the use of the title *Christos*. It is the story of John the Baptist's embassy to Jesus asking about his identity in messianic terms: "Are you he who is to come, or shall we look for another?" In Matthew's version John is motivated to ask because he has "heard in prison about the deeds of the Christ." What are the "deeds of the Messiah" about which John may have heard? For the reader of the Gospel this would mean Jesus' many healings and exorcisms, his preaching of the presence of the kingdom of heaven and his commissioning of his disciples to heal and preach the same message, and his reinterpretation of Torah in the Sermon on the Mount, an activity which Matthew clearly thought of as messianic. The pericope under discussion gives a quasi-definition of Matthew's understanding of Messiah in Jesus' response to the delegation from John, a passage that has a close parallel in Luke 7:22–23 (Matt. 11:4–6):

> Go and tell John what you hear and see: the blind receive their sight and the lame walk, lepers are cleansed and the deaf hear, and the dead are raised up, and the poor have good news preached to them. And blessed is he who takes no offense at me.

Two other peculiarly Matthean passages need to be mentioned. One is found in Matthew alone, in the context of Matthew's polemic against the scribes and the Pharisees as interpreters of the Law, suggesting that teaching the Law in the Messianic Age is the prerogative of the Messiah alone, as in the Sermon on the Mount: "Neither be called teachers, for you have one teacher, the Christ" (23:10). The other passage is a modification of Mark in the passion narrative in which the opponents of Jesus slap him and offer him the taunt "Prophesy to us, you Christ! Who is it that struck you?" (26:68). With the somewhat savage irony to which Matthew sometimes resorts, this remark implies that the Messiah is in fact the true prophet.

Thus, Matthew defines the functions of the Messiah Jesus in several ways: He is the true Davidic Messiah, though destined for gentiles as well as Jews; he is also the preacher of the eschatological kingdom, the authoritative reinterpreter of the Law, the healer and exorcist par excllence, the teacher and the prophet. He is also the Son of God, which is no small part of Matthew's christology. This emphasis can be seen clearly in Matthew's version of the confession of Peter at Caesarea Philippi, where Peter answers Jesus' question "Who do you say that I am?" with the more elaborate "You are the Christ, the Son of the living God" (16:16). Matthew may have thought recognition of the Messiah relatively normal, given his understanding of messianic functions, but he did not suppose one could recognize the Son of God unaided; that is a matter of revelation. Even before silencing Peter with the Markan command to messianic secrecy, Jesus says: "Blessed are you, Simon Bar-Jona! For flesh and blood has not revealed this to you, but my Father who is in heaven" (16:17). The perception of Christ as God's Son is possible only for faith.

Finally we shall turn to Luke and, as is often customary, group together the Gospel and the Acts of the Apostles, dealing with the latter more briefly. To begin as we have with the other Gospels, we may note that Luke uses *Christos* as a title a dozen times each in the Gospel and in Acts, and frequently also as a name of Jesus in Acts, often in such phrases as "in the name of Jesus (Christ)." What is most distinctive of Lukan usage is that he combines the title with a genitive of God in several instances: the "Lord's Messiah" in Luke 2:26 and Acts 4:26 and the "Messiah of God" in Luke 9:20 and 23:35. This corresponds much more closely to Jewish usage than any other New Testament instances of the titular *Christos.*

That Luke wishes to portray Jesus as the Messiah of the Jews or of Israel is beyond question. The problem is to determine when in Luke's thinking Jesus assumes this role. Because Luke, like the other evangelists, identifies the Messiah with the Son of God, the problem is only compounded. Does Jesus become Messiah at his birth or conception (as implied in Luke 1:32; 2:11, 26), or at his baptism (Luke 3:22, especially if the correct text reads "today I have begotten you," Ps. 2:7), or at his resurrection (Acts 13:33ff.), or at his ascension/exaltation (Acts 2:36), or – finally – at his second coming (Acts 3:20)? Some of these options can be explained, but in any case Luke does not seem confident about the issue. That he originally espoused something like what would later be called an adoptionist christology does not seem unlikely.

The Lukan infancy narrative shares with its very different Matthean counterpart two major concerns: that Jesus is the Messiah expected by Israel, and that as Messiah he is destined to be Savior of the gentiles as well. The first point is made specifically by the Davidic references such as 1:32: "And the Lord God will give to him the throne of his father David." It is reinforced by the general tone of the language, which is consistently and cleverly imitative of traditional biblical language, implying the familiar Lukan theme of promise and fulfillment (see e.g., 2:26). The relevance of the Messiah for gentiles is explicitly asserted in the famous canticle of Simeon which describes the sight of Jesus as "a light for revelation to the gentiles, and for glory to your people Israel" (2:32). It is also implied, I believe, in the collocation of the three titles in the message of the angels: "For to you is born this day in the city of David a Savior, who is Christ the Lord" (2:11). Whatever their precise origin, a much discussed point, the titles Savior and Lord would have their own resonance among the gentile readers of Luke's work.

The fact that the infancy narrative seems to establish the messianic identity of Jesus from his birth or his conception, depending on how one understands the text, runs counter to other typically Lukan ideas, as noted above. It is explained in the minds of many interpreters by the very plausible supposition that the infancy narrative itself was written by Luke after the completion of the Gospel and very likely after the completion of Acts also.[10] Among the reasons for this theory is the fact that there is no allusion to the infancy episodes in the kerygmatic summaries embedded in the missionary speeches of Acts. Luke on this hypothesis seems to have grown in the direction of understanding Jesus' Messiahship as less a matter of adoption than of divine birthright.

Luke gives a quasi-definition of the functions of the Messiah that is not unlike that of Matthew. In the all-important programmatic episode of Jesus preaching in his home town of Nazareth, Luke dramatically portrays Jesus as quoting with reference to himself a combination of Isaiah 61:1–2 and 58:6 (Luke 4:18–19):

> The Spirit of the Lord is upon me,
> because he has anointed me to preach good news to the poor.
> He has sent me to proclaim release to the captives
> and recovering of sight to the blind,

> to set at liberty those who are oppressed,
> to proclaim the acceptable year of the Lord.

The reference to the anointing is clearly an evocation of the etymology of *Christos* or *mashiaḥ*. Since the larger context of this episode in Luke is that of Jesus' turning to the gentiles, it is also a definition of what the Messiah means for gentile readers.

The most distinctive element of the Lukan reinterpretation of the Messiah is the emphasis on his suffering as a necessity imposed by the divine ordering of salvation history: "It was necessary that the Christ should suffer" (Luke 24:26, 46; cf. Acts 3:18; 17:3; 26:23).[11] As suffering Messiah, Jesus provides a sort of role model for the repentance of his followers, a necessary condition for obtaining forgiveness of sins (cf. 24:47).

Acts of the Apostles continues the Lukan understanding of the Messiah Jesus and adds only a few details that are significant for our purposes. Among them is the missionary speech of Peter in Acts 3, which is singular in many of its expressions and seems to portray Jesus as a future Messiah in his second coming (3:19–21):

> Repent therefore, and turn again, that your sins may be blotted out, that times of refreshing may come from the presence of the Lord, and that he may send the Christ appointed for you, Jesus, whom heaven must receive until the time for establishing all that God spoke by the mouth of his holy prophets from of old.

Some scholars have regarded this as a very primitive christology that identifies Jesus with the Messiah only in the eschatological future.[12] This is possible, but other elements in the speech are typically Lukan, such as the phrase "that his Christ should suffer" in 3:18, and, different as it sounds – after all, Luke never repeats things verbatim (see the conversion stories of Paul in Acts 9, 22, 26) – the speech is not clearly un-Lukan. Jesus is the Messiah both in his earthly career and in his future coming, to which Luke was clearly committed.

In the missionary speeches of Acts the messianic identity of Jesus is obviously a central issue, and this may conveniently be observed in such summary passages as 5:42; 17:3; 18:5, 28: "This Jesus, whom I proclaim to you, is the Christ." Yet it is remarkable that the Jewish objections to the apostolic preaching are never phrased in terms of a challenge to this claim (one might contrast the situation of the Gospel of John). Instead, in Acts the Jewish adversaries object to being implicated in responsibility for the death of Jesus, for example (5:28), or they complain that Stephen (6:13) and Paul (25:8) speak against the Temple and the Law, or they especially object to Paul's preaching of the resurrection of the dead (e.g.,

23:6). These latter charges are relatively easy to refute. It is striking that there is no objection to the messianic preaching of Peter and Paul. Perhaps this omission is best explained by some aspect of Luke's apologetic purpose.

To mention one final point about Acts' presentation of the Messiah, one should note the theme that the "anointed one" is to be the eschatological judge. This is made quite clear in Peter's speech before Cornelius: "God anointed Jesus of Nazareth with the Holy Spirit and with power. . . . He is the one ordained by God to be judge of the living and the dead" (10:38, 42; see also, in a more explicitly non-Jewish context, 17:31). This theme is not unique to Acts, however; one need only recall the portrayal of the Son of Man as judge of the sheep and the goats in Matthew 25:31–46.

In summary of the Lukan picture of Jesus as Messiah, two points may be made. Taking Luke–Acts as a whole, the three titles mentioned in Luke 2:11 – Savior, Messiah, Lord – seem in general to be practically interchangeable for Luke. We cannot justify this observation in detail here, but it seems to hold up. It is rooted, as suggested already, in Luke's tendency to universalize the messianic concept so that it is applicable for Gentiles as well as Jews. Secondly, Luke's emphasis on the suffering Davidic Messiah, accepted by God through the resurrection, points to the particular Lukan soteriology of Jesus as exemplar for those who through repentance and faith find access to the forgiveness of sins. They receive the Holy Spirit – a major emphasis of Lukan soteriology – and thus enter into a new relationship to God.

Conclusion

I am somewhat hesitant to conclude with a set of general observations beyond the "theses" set forth earlier in this survey. Given the developments in Christianity after the New Testament period and the common understandings of it that are still prevalent, one may be surprised to observe, not how central the messianic idea is to the gospel, but how it is in a sense peripheral. In Paul and the later Pauline tradition it may be taken for granted, but it is not an issue to be debated or demonstrated. In the Gospels and Acts, on the other hand, it is an issue, but more one of interpretation than of demonstration. The confession of Jesus as Messiah serves to define a Christian only in the Gospel of John (and to a certain extent, but for different reasons, in the First Epistle of John, e.g., 2:22), where the issue arises out of the debate between the Johannine church and contemporary Judaism. In all the Gospels the designation of Jesus as Messiah is subsumed under the categories of Son of Man or Son of God or both understood in specific ways. These categories may be said to be Jewish messianic categories also, but they are not the central ones in the Judaism of the period. It is important in studying the Christian usage to give due weight to the variety of understandings of the Messiah. There is indeed an *interpretatio christiana* of the notion, but it is neither simple nor completely unified.

NOTES

1 See, e.g., Nils A. Dahl, "The Messiahship of Jesus in Paul," in *The Crucified Messiah* (1953; reprint Minneapolis: Augsburg, 1974), pp. 34–47, 170–2; Martin Hengel, "Erwägungen zum Sprachgebrauch von *Christos* bei Paulus und in der 'vorpaulinischen' Ueberlieferung," in *Paul and Paulinism*, Essays in honour of C. K. Barrett, ed. M. D. Hooker and S. G. Wilson (London: Society for the Propagation of Christian Knowledge, 1982), pp. 135–59.

2 Cf. C. K. Barrett, *A Commentary on the Epistle to the Romans* (New York: Harper, 1957), pp. 18–19; Ernst Käsemann, *Commentary on Romans* (Grand Rapids: Eerdmans, 1980), pp. 10–14.

3 Dahl, "Messiahship of Jesus," is more or less of this opinion.

4 On the eschatological character of *Christos* see Dahl, "Messiahship of Jesus," pp. 44–5; Hengel, "Erwägungen," p. 141.

5 See Raymond E. Brown, *The Gospel according to John (xiii–xxi)* (Garden City: Doubleday, 1970), p. 741. The verse is judged to be parenthetical, but not a gloss, by C. K. Barrett, *The Gospel according to St. John* (2nd ed.; Philadelphia: Westminster, 1978), p. 503.

6 See J. Louis Martyn, *History and Theology in the Fourth Gospel* (rev. ed.; Nashville: Abingdon, 1979), esp. pp. 50ff.

7 Cf. Martyn, *History and Theology,* esp. Chap. 7.

8 Cf. Raymond E. Brown, *The Birth of the Messiah* (Garden City: Doubleday, 1977), p. 123.

9 "Quis et Unde? An Analysis of Mt 1 – 2," in *Judentum, Urchristentum, Kirche.* Festschrift für Joachim Jeremias (Berlin: Töpelmann, 1960), pp. 94–105.

10 See Brown, *The Birth of the Messiah*, pp. 239–41.

11 Joseph A. Fitzmyer, *The Gospel according to Luke (I–IX)* (Garden City: Doubleday, 1981), p. 200.

12 E.g., John A. T. Robinson, "The Most Primitive Christology of All?" *Journal of Theological Studies* 7 (1956): 177–89.

9

Christology in Mark's Gospel

HOWARD CLARK KEE

There are two familiar approaches to the subject of Markan Christology – indeed to New Testament Christology in general – that are taken as axiomatic. The first seeks to investigate how Jesus, according to Mark, used the existing messianic titles and the other redemptive categories that were to be found in pre-70 C.E. Judaism. The second seeks to describe the function of the messianic secret in Mark, on the assumption that messiahship was a known category, but that Jesus (as depicted in Mark) wanted to keep his personal identification with the messianic role a secret from the public in general and his antagonists in particular. These christological axioms rest in turn on a pair of historical assumptions: (1) that messianic titles and concepts were fixed entities in Judaism of the Second Temple, and (2) that since there was common agreement as to what messiahship entailed, the difficulty between Jesus and Jewish leaders of his time was his claim that he was the Messiah: A negative corollary of these two assumptions is that, if the use of a title or a concept cannot be documented in Jewish sources of the first century and earlier, then that term or point of view is a later construct of the tradition or the evangelist. It is my considered opinion that none of these axioms and assumptions is valid, and that to pursue the questions of christology on the basis of them results in unintentional ignoring of an important line of evidence.

I should like to propose a pair of hypotheses to replace these well-worn and ultimately fruitless sets of propositions, which have dominated the discussion of the christology of the Gospels since the rise of historical criticism. (1) There was a range of diverse conceptions and titles in Judaism from the postexilic period to the Second Revolt under Bar Kochba for depicting the agent of God who would bring to fruition the hopes of the Covenant people for the achievement of the divine purpose in their behalf or through them. (2) The variations in the conception of that agent or

187

those agents stand in dynamic, functional relationship with the community's understanding of itself as the Covenant people. Phrased differently, the self-understanding of the people of God and their place in the divine purpose is determinative of their conception of God's agent to effect the divine will. Or, epitomized in theological jargon, christology must be understood in direct relationship to ecclesiology. The thrust of this proposal becomes clear when we examine the range of modes of redemptive expectation and community definitions that are discernible in Judaism at the turn of the era. It is to the details of these first century options that we now turn.

In surveying the significance of messianic and redemptive roles in Judaism, the obvious place to begin is with the explicit use of the term *meshiach;* as a verb or in its nominal form. But one must also examine the other titles and images for divinely endowed figures through whom God's purpose is to be accomplished. And finally, the significance of the messianic and related titles must be seen in relation to the self-understanding of the community making the messianic affirmation.

Clearly the overwhelming number of scriptural references to the anointed one do refer to Israel's king, whether in the past or in the future, in both the liturgical and historical lines of tradition. Beginning with 1 Samuel 9:16 – where Saul is anointed as *nagid* rather than as *melek* – the pattern is laid down that the one who rules in God's behalf over his people is chosen, commissioned, and empowered by God for his role.[1] David's refusal to strike out against Saul is grounded on his reluctance to strike "the anointed of the Lord" (1 Sam. 24:10; 26:9; cf. 2 Sam. 1:14–16). Most of the references to the "anointed" in the Psalms concern the king, especially David and his posterity (Ps. 2:2; 20:6; 45:7; 89:20, 38). Although the term "anointed" does not appear in Psalm 110, it is widely and rightly regarded as a Royal Psalm, in which the continuity of the Davidic line, ruling as God's viceregents, is affirmed. As such, it is widely quoted or alluded to in the New Testament (e.g., Mark 12:36 and parallels; Acts 2:34–35; 1 Cor. 15:25; Eph. 1:20; Col. 3:1; Heb. 1:3). But as verse 4 of this psalm tells us, and as Hebrews 8:1 and 10:12 remind us, the role that is being discharged is not only that of ruler (verse 2, "rule," "sceptre") but also that of "priest forever, after the order of Melchizedek," the king-priest.

Zechariah 4:14, with its enigmatic reference to the two olive trees, is widely – and in my judgment correctly – regarded as a prediction of the two messiahs, kingly and priestly, who are to appear in Israel on the day of eschatological fulfillment.[2] Zechariah 6:9–15 confirms this interpretation, with its representation of the chief accomplishment of the eschato-

logical king as the rebuilding of the temple and the restoration of its cultus. Similarly, in Daniel 9:24–25, the term "anointed" is found with
reference to the sanctuary as well as to the appearance of the *nagid,* and to
the one who is "cut off" in connection with the destruction of the sanctuary in the final "week" before the end of the age. In Psalm 84:9, there
is further confirmation of the messianic role of the priest, in that the entire
context of the psalm describes Israel at worship, as shown by the allusions
to "the courts of the Lord" and "the house of God." The "anointed one"
in such a setting is not the king,[3] but the priest. Thus, in Old Testament
tradition the messianic terminology involves both the kingly and the
priestly roles.

It is precisely this phenomenon of dual messianic expectation that is
central in the pseudepigraphic literature of Judaism and at Qumran. In the
Testaments of the Twelve Patriarchs for example, it is Levi and the high
priestly role that have priority in the eschatological scheme. Not surprisingly, in the Testament of Levi the dominant function in the restoration
of the Covenant people in the end time is assigned to Levi, who is the
agent of revelation (18:2), whose star rises from heaven like a king (18:3),
who opens the gates of the New Eden (18:10), and who overcomes the
spirits of evil (18:12). Elsewhere in this chapter he is depicted as recon-
secrating both the Temple and the Covenant people – significantly designated as "the saints" – pouring out on them universal blessing and the
Spirit of holiness. In the Testaments attributed to the other sons of Jacob,
Levi shares authority in the New Age with Judah, the kingly figure, but
Levi is clearly dominant. Indeed, in passages like Testament of Reuben
6:11, Levi is said to be the one through whom God reigns, though Judah
is mentioned in the same context. In the Testament of Naphtali, it is Levi
who seizes the sun, while Judah lays hold of the moon, in this vivid image
of the assumption of eschatological authority. Only in the Testament of
Judah (1:6; 24:1–25:1) is Judah represented as the major figure, with prophetic images seen as finding their fulfillment in him: Star from Jacob,
Sun of Righteousness, Shoot of God, beneficiary of the outpoured Spirit.
In the other Testaments, Levi and Judah share the messianic functions.[4]

In the Testament of Benjamin, however, the promise of the restoration
of the Temple and return from the dispersion of the twelve tribes,
together with representatives of all the nations, is expected to occur at
"such time as the Most High shall send forth his salvation through the
ministration of the unique prophet." This concept, which builds on Deuteronomy 18:15, 18, is developed more extensively in the Qumran documents, to which we must now turn.

In The Scroll of the Rule and the Damascus Document, the stylized
references to the divinely endowed agents for the final redemption of the

Covenant community refer to "the Messiahs of Aaron and Israel," by which are meant, of course, the Anointed Priest and the Anointed King.[5] In the Melchizedek fragment, the importance of that ancient figure for the Dead Sea community is clearly based on the fact that he is depicted as both king and priest.[6] In that portion of the Messianic Florilegium that expounds 2 Samuel 7:10–14, the primary interest is in the restoration of the temple and its purification so that the proper cultus can be reestablished there, although the role of the descendant of David in the defeat of Belial and the hosts of evil as well as the resumption of his monarchic line is also important.[7] A text based on Genesis 49:10 declares the eternal establishment of the throne of David as the agency of God's rule over his covenant people.[8]

Other messianic texts, however, depict the future of the community in terms of (1) the Prophet who is to come, based on Deuteronomy 18, the Star from Jacob (Num. 24:15–17), and (2) the priests and Levites as the guarantors of the purity of the covenant people (Deut. 33:8–10).[9] The prophetic role is highlighted in a fragment sometimes known as "The Wondrous Child." A prophetic reinterpretation of the tradition was carried out by the founder of the Qumran community, who was called "The One who Teaches [the Law] Rightly," as T. H. Gaster has noted. In the Qumran Hymns, the writer (presumably the teacher himself) declares that God has opened a fountain by the mouth of his servant, that the divine mysteries are on his tongue, in order that he might interpret these insights to other creatures of dust like himself. It is he who interprets the community rule in the Damascus Document, and he who expounds the scriptures in the distinctive *pesher* method of the Scrolls. In the messianic texts, it is the teacher whose coming is seen as an eschatological sign, in fulfillment of Deuteronomy 18.[10]

On the other hand, it is the priests in the War Scroll who summon and direct the troops in the eschatological battle, and who offer the benediction at the successful outcome. The troops respond appropriately by purging themselves ritually of the pollution that came on them as a consequence of killing their enemies (War Scroll 13:1–18:15). In the Florilegium section based on Psalm 2, however, it is the king who is the Anointed One, and – as in I Enoch – who is also designated as the Elect One.

What is evident, therefore, is that Messiah is not so much a title in this late prophetic and apocalyptic literature as an epithet used to designate someone in a range of roles whose function is seen to be essential for fulfillment of the divine purpose for the future of the Covenant community. As is the case in the Old Testament texts examined above, the messianic roles are always linked directly with the welfare of the Covenant people, so that one cannot accurately assess the role of the Messiah without under-standing the values and aspirations and norms of the community making that messianic affirmation.

Not only, therefore, is it inaccurate and misleading to assume that Mes-siah was a term with a fixed royal connotation in the Second Temple Period of Judaism, but also it must be recognized that there was a wide range of roles and images that did not use the noun, adjective, or verb forms of *meshiach,* but that described the agents and agencies through whom the eschatological aims were to be accomplished for God's people. Also, terms that we have seen to be linked with *meshiach* – namely, king and prophet – are also found without the explicit messianic designation, but in contexts that point to eschatological fulfillment. The expectation of the king is important in Zechariah (9:9; 14:9, 16–19), as well as in the Royal Psalms, which were interpreted eschatologically, as we have docu-mented from Qumran,[11] and within the New Testament.[12] The return of "the prophet like Moses" and of Elijah are announced in scripture (Deut. 18; Mal. 3:1; 4:5), and both these prophetic figures appear in the pseud-epigraphic literature of Judaism around the turn of the eras.[13] One may note in passing that in 1 Kings 19:16, when Elijah is about to be with-drawn from the scene by being taken up to heaven (2 Kings 2:11), he is instructed to anoint both the king-to-be (Jehu) *and* his successor as prophet, Elisha.

The impossibility of maintaining sharp distinctions among these redemptive figures is evident in both canonical and deutero-canonical lit-erature. The king in Psalms 2:6 is in the next verse referred to as "my son." In 4 Ezra 13 the "man from the sea" (verse 26) is forthwith iden-tified as God's son (verse 32). Under both designations, he is the one cho-sen and reserved by God to defeat the wicked and vindicate the righteous. In the Parables of Enoch, the one chosen by God for roles nearly identical with those of the Man from the Sea in 4 Ezra is variously designated as "the Elect One" (1 Enoch 39:6; 45:4; 40:5), "the Son of Man" (46:3, 62:6–14; 63:11; 67:27–29), and as "Messiah" (52:4). Further complicat-ing the situation is the fact that in both 1 Enoch and Daniel 7, the term "Son of Man" seems at times to refer to a single individual, and at others to be a way of describing the elect community to whom and through whom the divine purpose is to be achieved.[14] The point of these images, which speak of "man" or "Son of Man" or human beings, seems to rest on the biblical picture of Adam as the one given responsibility to rule over the creation in God's way and in his behalf – a divine intention which will be accomplished only in the age to come. Hence both the power and the fluidity of the term "Son of Man" in the Jewish apocalyptic tradition.[15]

The range of divine agents in the apocalyptic tradition includes even the "worthless shepherds" of Zechariah 11–13, whose infidelity to the people Israel is the instrument of God whereby the faithless two thirds of the nation will be destroyed, and the surviving third is purged and purified (Zech. 13:7–9). Similarly, Cyrus, who enables Israel to return from exile, is called Yahweh's "shepherd" (Isa. 44:28), while Nebuchadnezzar is described as Yahweh's "servant" (Jer. 25:9). Yet elsewhere in the prophetic tradition, "servant" is used to refer to Israel (Isa. 41:8; 44:1; 48:20; 65:8–9) as well as to an individual (52:13; 53:11), the "righteous one," whose sufferings work to benefit the many. In Isaiah of Jerusalem, on the other hand, the restoration of the Davidic dynasty is to be accomplished through one designated "the Branch," a motif that builds on Isaiah 11:1 and is developed in Jeremiah 23:5 (cf. 33:15) and especially in Zechariah (3:8; 6:12), where once more the roles of ruler and priest are combined.

Still another facet of messianic-eschatological hope centers on wisdom. What is to characterize the king, according to Isaiah 11, is the "spirit of wisdom and understanding," which in turn leads to righteousness for human existence and renewal of life for the whole created order (11:3–9). The eschatological presence of Yahweh on Zion depicted in Isaiah 33:5–6 will fill the city with justice and righteousness, with wisdom and knowledge. The ideal of the wise king, as represented by Solomon (1 Kgs. 4:29; 10:23) and demonstrated by his rule of justice, is given expression in Psalm 72, which with the cessation of the monarchy became understood as an utterance of eschatological hope. In the apocalyptic tradition, Daniel's divine gift of wisdom is seen as enabling him to possess "knowledge, understanding to interpret dreams, explain riddles, and solve problems" – skills that he draws upon to discern and to interpret the divine purpose for the creation and for God's people as it is unfolding (Dan. 5:11–12). According to Ben Sira (42:19), God "declares what is past and what is still to come, and reveals the depths of hidden things." Wisdom is seen in the later period of postexilic Judaism as not merely a matter of insight and discernment, but as revelation of the future purpose of God. That is the point of Gabriel's message to Daniel, "I have now come to give you wisdom and understanding" (Dan. 9:22), as well as of the message of the heavenly man (Dan. 10:12–14) who tells Daniel that he has come to enable him to "understand what is to befall your people in the latter days."

What this sketch of some of the motifs of messianic, revelatory, and redemptive figures in the prophetic and apocalyptic traditions shows is that the Messiah or redeemer is in every case a mediator between the divine purpose and the aspirations of a community. The values and assumptions of the community are, therefore, always reflected in the image of the redemptive agent. If the communal goal is political independence, then the rhetoric is that of royalty, of dominion, of triumph over foes. But if the chief concern is for purity, the agent is seen as priestly in function, reconstituting the cultic system and purging God's Chosen People. If the group is in despair of the present order of things, the agent is seen as one who radically transforms the present epoch, replacing it with a New Age, in which the helpless are vindicated and the evil powers routed. If the ethos is more intellectual in nature, then the agent is expected to effect, through wisdom, the triumph of order and rationality. In each case, the beneficiaries see their hopes and destiny as corresponding precisely to the qualifications and capabilities of the messianic figure.

The range of these possibilities is evident in Judaism of the late Hellenistit–early Roman period. The book of Daniel speaks for and to those who, disillusioned by the coercive tactics of the pagan powers as well as by the increasing secularization of the Hasmoneans, despair of any political solution to the plight of the Jewish people, and turn instead to a hope for a radical break with the present order, whereby God intervenes directly and gives the rule to the patient, pious remnant. They alone discern the divine plan, and they alone will benefit from its fulfillment. On the other hand, those like the Sadducees, for whom the unbroken continuity of Temple cultus is the essence of Jewishness, will be willing to put up with foreign domination – indeed, to cooperate with it – so long as there is no hindrance to the ongoing worship of God in his dwelling-place on Mt. Zion.

At the opposite extreme are those for whom from time to time national independence has the top priority, and who accordingly cannot rest content so long as their chief city and lands are dominated by a pagan rule. The Pharisees, disheartened by the secularization of the Jewish leadership, begin to develop informal, voluntary meetings for the study of the scriptures, in which they transfer the cultus from the Temple to the table-fellowship of the gathered community. With them begins in the late first century B.C.E. the lay movement that will survive the catastrophes of C.E. 70, and will develop into the rabbinic Judaism known from the Mishnah and Talmud as it emerges in the second to the sixth centuries.[16] Yet another segment of Judaism in the first century B.C.E. will despair of the priesthood and the temple cultus, withdrawing to a refuge of purity and piety near the Dead Sea, where they will await the divine intervention that will destroy their enemies and establish them as the rightful leaders of the worship of the God of Israel. Each of these groups, building on the scriptural tradition (variously defined) begins by defining the Covenant people. The specific form of messianic or redemptive function is correlated with that for which the community hopes or to which it aspires.

In approaching these questions of community definition, the insights of Mary Douglas are of great value, especially in her classic study, *Purity and Danger,*[17] as well as in her more schematic study of religion and culture, *Natural Symbols: Explorations in Cosmology.*[18] Also furnishing valuable insights on the matter of personal identity through religious structures are Hans Mol's *Identity and the Sacred,* and Thomas Luckman and Peter Berger's *The Social Construction of Reality.*[19] These studies in sociology of religion and sociology of knowledge demonstrate persuasively the ways in which the individual receives a sense of identity through a shared view of the world, a common myth or history, and ritual patterns in terms of which internal structures of the society and differentiation of its members from outsiders are drawn. As Mary Douglas phrased it,

> The idea of society is a powerful image. It is potent in its own right to control or to stir men to action. This image has form: it has external boundaries, margins, internal structure. Its outlines contain power to reward conformity and repulse attack. There is energy in its margins and unstructured areas.[20]

After tracing in detail how cultures use the symbolism of the physical body for defining the social body, she notes that "the model of the exits and entrances of the body is a doubly apt symbolic focus of fears for [a group's] minority standing in the larger society." She then suggests

> that when rituals express anxiety about the body's orifices, the sociological counterpart of this anxiety is a care to protect the political and cultural unity of a minority group. The Israelites were always in their history a hard-pressed minority. In their beliefs all the bodily issues were polluting, blood, pus, excreta, semen. The threatened boundaries of their body politic would be well mirrored in their care for the integrity, unity, and purity of the physical body.[21]

We have noted above how ambiguous Jewish identity was during the era of hellenistic and Roman dominance of the land of Palestine. The competing claims and hypotheses about the essence of Jewishness in this period stand in sharp contrast to the clearly defined structure and authority roles as they are described – perhaps in idealized form – in the priestly reworking of Israel's law and history. Mary Douglas's insights are relevant here as well:

> Where the social system is well-articulated, I look for articulate powers vested in the points of authority; where the social system

is ill-articulated, I look for inarticulate powers vested in those who are a source of disorder. . . . The contrast between form and surrounding non-form accounts for the distribution of symbolic and psychic powers: external symbolism upholds the explicit social structure and internal, unformed psychic powers threaten it from the non-structure.[22]

This is wholly appropriate as a formal description of the situation in first-century Judaism, with the priestly structures and the aristocratic collaborationists functioning in the *synedrion* and in the Herodian administration, symbolizing order and power. By 65–67 C.E., the revolutionaries will be at work seeking to develop their own alternative power structure, presumably modeled after the idealized hierocratic structure of the early post-exilic period. Meanwhile, the Pharisees are seeking to develop their own structures of purity and piety, over against and withdrawn from the political structure of their time, while the Essenes respond to what they see as the disorder and defilement of Jewish structures by physical withdrawal to Qumran and the establishment of a society there that can withstand the works of Belial and await the imminent divine vindication. With these perspectives in mind, we must look at Mark's representation, not only of Jesus as the messianic figure, but also of the community by whom that messianic claim is advanced in the midst of other competing schemes within Judaism of the first century.

By the time the reader reaches Mark's first summarizing statement (1:32–34) the central focus of Jesus's words and works as Mark portrays them is clear: the defeat of Satan and the establishment of God's Rule. Jesus' message is not simply an announcement of the nearness of the kingdom: it is also an invitation to enter it or to receive it (Mark 1:14; 4:26–30; 3:24; 13:8; 9:47; 10:23–25; 12:34).[23] The images that depict the kingdom are organic and assume growth over a period of time, with mixed results, as the parables of Mark 4 show vividly. Admission to the kingdom is not based on ethnic origin or ritual purity, but on acceptance of God's Rule as a gift (10:14–15). Mark 10:35–45, with the rebuke of the power-seeking sons of Zebedee, shows that the kingdom does not come as the consequence of military might or exercise of political power, but that it is dependent entirely on divine grace, as shown by the pious passive circumlocution, "It is for those for whom it has been prepared" (10:40). The initiative lies entirely with God.

The second image of community is that of the family, which is radically redefined in Mark 3:20f. and in 10:28–31. In a society steeped in tribal heritage as the ground of present identity and of future hope, Jesus' words are the more shocking: "Whoever does the will of God, that one is my brother and my sister and my mother" (3:35). As I wrote in my book on Mark, "All genetic, familial, and sex distinctions are eradicated in this new concept of the true family."[24] The break with the traditional family and the acceptance of persecutions (10:30) are to characterize the common life of the faithful community.

The image of the community as the scattered flock of God's people appears at two crucial points in Mark: at 6:34, in connection with the story of the feeding of the 5000, and at 14:27 in Gethsemane, just before his arrest. In the latter case, the direct quotation from Zechariah 13:7 fits in well with the whole latter portion of that prophetic writing, with its frequent predictions of the infidelity of those who have taken on leadership roles for God's people, and of the consequent persecution that the faithful must endure.

A similar allusion to Zechariah 10:4 occurs in Mark 6:34, as the scene is set for the first of the feeding stories. The version of this story in John 6:46–51, with its explicit parallels with Moses' feeding of the people Israel, spells out what is implied in Mark: Jesus is summoning and miraculously sustaining the embryonic people of the Covenant. The analogy with the Sinai experience is underlined by Mark, who twice notes that the incident occurs in a desert place (6:32, 35). The covenantal dimensions of this story are amplified by the use of what became the technical language of the eucharist: He took, he blessed, he broke, he gave (6:41).

The direct covenantal language appears again, of course, in the scene of the Last Supper, where Jesus' impending death is represented as the sacrifice that seals the New Covenant and prepares for the coming of God's Rule (14:22–25). The beneficiaries of this sacrifice are referred to broadly as simply "many" *(hyper pollon)*.

The image of the New Vineyard, developed as it is out of the allegorical depiction of Israel in Isaiah 5:1–7, is shifted in Mark 12:1–11 to that of a building. Since the point of the parable of the vineyard has been altered in Mark from that of Isaiah's unfruitful vine to focus on the rejection of the owner's son, not only are the christological implications obvious, but also the corporate nature of God's intention is implicit in the building image and explicit in the quotation from Psalms 118:22–23. Mark leaves his reader in no doubt about the import of this parabolic picture. Jesus is reported as interpreting the parable to mean that the kingdom has been given to a nation other than Israel (12:43). And the religious leaders "perceived that he was speaking about them" (12:45). This prophetic expectation of the replacement of Israel by a new People of God is confirmed from the negative side by the cursing of the fig tree (11:12–14), and from the positive side by the summons to faith uttered as a comment on the withered fig tree (11:20–25). It is expressed even more clearly in the story of the cleansing of the Temple, when the quotation from Isaiah 56:7 declares that God intends his "house" to be a place of prayer "for all the nations" (11:15–19). Thus it is not merely the case that Mark portrays Jesus as linking his messianic role with the destiny of a New Covenant people, but he also implies or directly declares that the people will not be defined by ethnic or ritual boundaries.

We must examine in detail, therefore, the qualities attributed by Mark to Jesus concerning the modes of community definition that prevailed in Judaism of the first century, especially within the emerging Pharisaic movement. In Mark 6 to 8, which form the mid-section of the gospel, there is the pair of feeding stories, one of which presumably takes place in Jesus' native Galilee (6:30) and the other, in Gentile territory (7:24, 31). This inference is confirmed by the use of the symbolic numbers of baskets: twelve, for Israel, and seven, for the gentile mission, as in Acts 6. Thus, Jesus is depicted as laying claim to the Covenant tradition of Israel in such a manner as to include both Jews and gentiles. The stories told between the two feeding accounts strengthen that claim. Not only is the Pharisaic practice of purification from ceremonial defilement rejected, but the setting aside of this strand of Jewish legal tradition is justified by appeal to the scripture (Mark 7:6 = Isa. 29:13). The parable that brings the pericope to a conclusion makes the point that moral relationships rather than ritual requirements are the essence of obligation for his people. We must bear in mind that it was precisely in the first century that Pharisaism was developing and refining its definition of ritual purity as a new way to provide covenantal identity for the Jewish people. The Jesus of Mark seems to go out of his way to defy these boundaries, as we shall see.

As with the ritual purity regulations, Jesus flatly and repeatedly sets aside the sabbath law. In the first instance, Jesus heals the demonic in the Capernaum synagogue on the sabbath (1:21–28), but the comments by the onlookers have to do with Jesus' authority rather than with the sabbath violation. The healings continue on the holy day, however: first Simon's mother-in-law (1:29–31) and then a great crowd of the sick and possessed, whose healing is witnessed by "the whole city" (1:32–34). The first challenge to Jesus' and his disciples' activity on the sabbath is raised in the incident of the disciples plucking grain (2:23–28). This culminates in the justification of their actions by appeal to scripture (1 Sam. 21:1–7) and then the astounding claim that "The Son of Man is lord even of the sabbath" (2:17). In the very next pericope – once more, in a synagogue, the informal gathering place of the pious as the Pharisaic movement is taking its rise – the Pharisees wait to see if Jesus will once again violate the sabbath prohibition against labor. His violation and self-justification so dis-

turb the Pharisees that they form a coalition with the Jewish collaborationists, the Herodians, with whom they would under normal
circumstances have had no dealings. The common concern of this coalition is that Jesus is a threat to the integrity of the Covenant people as
members of both these very different segments of Judaism perceive it.
Jesus' curious response about doing good or harm, killing or saving life,
on the sabbath seems to echo the issue among the Jewish nationalists as
they had to decide whether or not to fight and defend their lives when
attacked by the Romans on the sabbath. Jesus is depicted by Mark, not as
inadvertently or tangentially involved in the sabbath dispute, but as exer-
cising sovereign authority in setting aside the one law above all others that
provided Jews with their distinctive identity.

Similarly audacious is the Markan Christ's pronouncement of the forgiveness of sins. The issue first arises in the Markan modification of the
traditional story of the paralytic lowered through the roof.[25] In the biblical
tradition, the Covenant people had two resources for dealing with sin: (1)
to seek God's forgiveness, as is beautifully illustrated in the Psalms (especially 51, 79, 80, 85); (2) to bring the appropriate sin offering, as detailed
in Leviticus 4–5. Jesus in Mark appeals to neither of these resources, but
with sovereign authority pronounces the forgiveness of sins (2:5); he represents all sins as potentially forgivable, except the blasphemy against the
Holy Spirit, which in the context probably refers to those who attribute
his healing powers to Satan rather than to God (3:23–26). Further, Jesus
declares that those who do not share in the mystery of the kingdom (4:11)
will not obtain forgiveness (4:12). The only other reference to forgiveness
in Mark is simply to note that willingness to forgive others is a prerequi-
site to seeking God's forgiveness (11:25). Here again, by claiming insight
and access to the divine prerogative of forgiveness, Jesus appears in Mark
as one who is redrawing the boundaries of the Covenant people.

Mark also highlights the access to covenant participation by non-Jews,
and by those who would have been on the margins of the holy people.
His activities are concentrated on persons of suspect or clearly deficient
standards of purity: demoniacs; those sick with various diseases, including
such defiling ailments as leprosy and menstrual flow; contact with the
dead, with those in tombs, with swine; eating with masses in Jewish and
gentile territory without raising the question of dietary or ritual purity;
coming to the aid of gentiles, of the blind, of cripples. The Markan picture
is not that of an occasional slip in violation of purity standards; it is rather
of an aggressive, intentional setting aside of these boundaries in the interest of bringing the grace of God to meet human needs. In serving this
aim, Jesus goes into unclean territories (3:7–8; 5:20; 7:24; 8:27), associates
with unclean people, and defies the existing Jewish standards of purity.

His own purity is based on baptism, on divine attestation – at baptism and in the Transfiguration scene – and in his moral demands. He transmits cleanness through his teaching of responsibility to neighbor, through his announcement of forgiveness, and through his own death as experienced "for many" (10:45) and as the seal of the new covenant (14:24–25).

Equally revolutionary in its implications for first-century Judaism is the attitude toward the Temple and its cultus in Mark. The Temple, the courts of which were intended by God to provide access to him for all nations (11:17; Isa. 56:7; Jer. 7:11), is to be destroyed. It is referred to in this context as a "house of prayer," rather than as a place of sacrifice. The only sacrifice mentioned favorably in Mark is that of Jesus himself. From Jesus there is no hint of regret or of ultimate restoration of the Temple and its cultus in Mark. Hence, in these attitudes toward purity and cultus, Mark represents Jesus as over and against Pharisees, Sadducees, and Essenes. For the show of piety in the form of holy garb, Jesus has only scorn (12:37–40). The sole criterion for acceptance into Jesus' newly defined Covenant community is trust in him, or in the authority of his name (8:38; 9:38–41). To identify mistakenly the source of his authority is unforgivable blasphemy, as we have seen (3:29–30). Only those to whom God has granted the insight will recognize in him the agent of God (4:11–12), but those who do respond in faith to the Gospel will come from all the lands of the earth (13:27).

The Pharisees' request for a "sign from heaven" as proof of the divine origin of his undertaking is wholly in keeping with the Old Testament tradition. There Moses (Exod. 4:8), Gideon (Judg. 6:17–23), and Hezekiah (2 Kings 19:29; 20:8) are reassured by signs of divine support in fulfilling their responsibilities. Both Israel's historic deliverance from Egypt and the certainty of future judgment in response to her disobedience to Yahweh are confirmed by divine signs. Nebuchadnezzar (Dan. 4:3) and Darius (Dan. 6:27) are described in Daniel as expressing to their subjects assurance of God's work in behalf of the faithful remnant of his people through signs and wonders. Jesus, however, refuses to give a sign, leaving it to the observers to discern in his acts what the source of his authority is (Mark 3:19–30). Ironically, it is the *unclean* spirits who identify him as the Son of God (Mark 3:11), while the religious leaders with responsibility for the maintenance of the purity of the Covenant people are those who form the coalition with the political powers to destroy Jesus. This irony is compounded in Mark by the claims that Jesus refused to go along with the militant nationalists' resistance to Roman taxation (12:13–17), that he befriended those who collected taxes for Rome (2:13–17), that he was put to death by the Romans on an insurrectionist charge (15:9, 12, 18, 26, 31), and was identified by a Roman officer as "Son of God" (15:39).

Consistently, therefore, Jesus is represented by Mark as standing over against the whole range of options open to Judaism in the first century for identification with the true Covenant community. He appears in Mark as one who declares himself to be the instrument of God to establish the New Covenant people and to prepare them for the coming of God's Rule. It is to the specifics of these explicit and implicit messianic designations that we now turn.

Messiah

The modern interpreter of Christology should take a cue from the Gospel of Mark itself: Of the seven places where *christos* appears in Mark, all but two are uttered by those who do not understand what Jesus' mission is, or who are hostile toward it. The first exception is in the title of the Gospel, Mark 1:1;[26] the second is in Jesus' promise of a reward for those who give aid to his emissaries; that is, to "those who bear the name of Christ" (9:41). Elsewhere, whether it is the declaration of Peter (8:29), the question of the scribes about the relationship of Messiah to David (12:35), the false messianic claimants in the eschaton (13:21), the question of the High Priest (14:61), or the mockers of Jesus on the cross (15:32), the use of the term betrays a misconception of Jesus' role in the purpose of God. In contrast to these erroneous notions of messiahship, the woman with the alabaster flask who anoints Jesus (is it accidental that Mark uses the sensual, secular term, *muridzo,* rather than *chrio?*) perceives that his death is essential to his messianic mision.

Son of God

The importance of the title "Son of God" as a clarification of who Jesus is and what it signifies to call him *Christos* is signaled in the super-scription of the book (1:1). That impression is confirmed both directly and indirectly throughout the Gospel. The private affirmation of divine sonship to Jesus at baptism ("You are my beloved Son," 1:11) is matched by the announcement to the perplexed disciples at the transfiguration ("This is my beloved Son," 9:7). It is also the declaration of the demons, who rightly see in Jesus their conqueror (3:11; 5:7). It is implicit in the descent of the Spirit upon him (1:11), as well as in his being the channel for the Spirit (1:8) and the instrument of God's Spirit, as the charge of blasphemy against those who attribute his exorcistic powers to Satan indicates (3:29). It is likewise to be inferred from the reminder to the cured demoniac at Gerasa "how much the Lord has done for you," although Jesus was the direct agent of his cure (5:19).

Jesus explicitly identifies himself as Son (of God) in the apocalyptic discourse, when he contrasts the limits of his knowledge of the timing of the New Age with that of the Father (13:32), and when he addresses God as "Abba, Father" in Gethsemane (14:36). But the clearest affirmation is in response to the High Priest's question in 14:62. There, however, he does something of profound significance for Markan christology: He combines the acknowledgment of his messiahship and divine sonship with the concept of Son of Man and with the exaltation of the king-priest at God's right hand. This is conveyed through the reference to a Royal Psalm (Psalm 110), that Mark has already quoted (12:36) in response to the scribes' question about Messiah and Son of David. That Jesus' self-identification with Messiah/Son of Man is understood as blasphemy, and therefore as meriting the death penalty (14:63–64; cf. Lev. 24:16) shows the implied kinship of Jesus with God. Yet the fact that, as Mark affirms, the death of Jesus is necessary, not because of a blasphemous claim, but because his death and vindication are essential to the divine purpose, shows that the Markan Jesus has radically redefined what it means to say that he is the Son of God.

Son of Man

Similarly, in the use of the Son of Man title the Jewish tradition is being fundamentally reworked. In Daniel, the Son of Man is the representative figure of the faithful remnant who have resisted the pressure of pagan rulers to compromise or to abandon their devotion to the God of Israel and to his laws, which differentiate his people from other nations. Similarly, the Son of Man in the Parables of Enoch is the one "to whom belongs righteousness and with whom righteousness dwells" (46:3), who hears the petitions of the righteous (47), who preserves them (48:5), and who bestows on them glory and honor, while the unrepentant are judged (50), together with sinners and rulers (53), who are humbled in the presence of the Son of Man (62). In 4 Ezra, it is those who have been fully obedient to the Covenant and its laws who are vindicated in the end-time (5:23–39; 7:46–47), since only a few have failed to violate the Covenant and will be delivered by the Man (Messiah) at the end of the age (7:26–30). The just have patiently and obediently continued in their pilgrimage toward salvation (8:38). The Man from the Sea, who is also the Son of God (13:37, 52), will berate his opponents for their impiety. By contrast with this wicked majority, Ezra is the model for the faithful community, in that he "relinquished [his] own interests and devoted [himself] to God's; [he] explored God's law and dedicated [his] life to wisdom . . . " (13:54).

Obviously the Son of Man, as in Jewish apocalyptic tradition, is for Mark an eschatological agent. This is explicitly stated in Jesus' confession before the High Priest, with its equating of Messiah and Son of Man and its reference to the prediction of Daniel (7:13) about his coming "with the clouds of heaven," a promise offered earlier in the synoptic apocalypse (13:26). But there are two important features in Mark's presentation of the Son of Man that have no counterpart in the Jewish tradition. The first is the necessity of the death of the Son of Man. Daniel and his friends are repeatedly called upon to accept martyrdom rather than to disobey the law of God, but in each case they are miraculously delivered. In 4 Ezra the Messiah and his companions die in their pursuit of righteousness (7:26–29), but are revived in the resurrection (7:32). For Mark, however, the death of Jesus is essential to the establishment of the New Covenant: He gives his life as a ransom "for many" (10:45). He *must* suffer and die (8:31); it is "written in scripture" – though we are not told where – that "he should suffer many things and be treated with contempt" (9:12). The repeated predictions of his death (9:30–32; 10:33–34; 14:17–21; 14:41), as well as his rising from the dead (9:9), all attest to this. As in 4 Ezra, his resurrection will effect the vindication of the faithful community (8:38), or rather, those who abandon the cause of Jesus will be abandoned by him in the last Day.[27]

The other distinctive feature of Mark's Son of Man is that, while he expects fidelity from the members of his community, he sets aside the legal norms by which Jewish covenantal identity was maintained. Instead of announcing the judgment of sinners, as in the earlier Son of Man tradition, Jesus claims the authority of the Son of Man in pronouncing the forgiveness of sins (2:10). Instead of differentiating his followers from those who breach the covenantal obligations, Jesus declares the Son of Man to be Lord of the Sabbath, and the commandment itself subservient to human need (2:28). In Mary Douglas's terms, the people of the Son of Man in Mark are not those who maintain the covenantal boundaries of the Law of Moses, but those who transcend them.

Son of David

The Son of David would seem to have a self-evident meaning; that is, the royal heir of Israel's first true king, who will preside over the affairs of the people of God. This does not apply in Mark, however. Jesus' violation of the sabbath law, or more precisely, his defense of his disciples for such an infraction of the commandment, is justified by appeal to the precedent of David (2:23–27). When one of his potential beneficiaries, Bartimaeus the blind beggar, beseeches Jesus to heal his eyes, the appeal is to the mercy of the Son of David, not to his power as monarch. The complexity of the relationship of the Messiah to David is pointed up in the enigmatic pericope, Mark 12:35–37, where the one descended from David (i.e., his son) is also his Lord, who sits at the right hand of God, as described in Psalm 110:1. The messianic figure does not merely model the Davidic paradigm but surpasses David in a transcendent manner.

King of Israel

Similarly, when Mark uses the title King of Israel it is with connotations radically different from those of Jewish nationalists. The first occurrence of the phrase is in the story of Jesus' entrance into Jerusalem (Mark 11:1–10), at which point is the unmistakable reference to Zechariah 9:9, where the king's advent is in humility, not in triumph. His visit leads to the critique of the official cult center, the announcement of its impending destruction, and his own death at the hands of a coalition of religious and political authorities, Jewish and pagan. He refuses to take a stand of resistance to the Roman taxation practices, but instead urges that Caesar be given his due (12:13–17). When asked if he is King of the Jews, his answer is equivocal, since he surely is not portrayed by Mark as fitting the nationalists' hopes for a politically sovereign Israel. The mockery at his crucifixion is the more poignant, therefore. Hanging on the cross under the sign charging him with claiming to be the king of the Jews (15:26), he is scornfully addressed and given mock deference, while real insurrectionists are crucified on each side of him (15:27).

Not only the role of the king but the nature of the kingdom has also been redefined by Jesus in Mark's gospel. It is no longer a solely future expectation, but has already drawn near (1:14); it is a power already at work in the midst of human affairs (4:26–29, 30–32); it can be said to have "already come with power" (9:1). Unlike a kingdom built on ordinary human values, it is accessible to children (10:13–16), and has no place within it for the power of wealth (10:17–27) or of political ascendancy (10:35–45). The fundamental act by which its coming is guaranteed and by which its covenantal base is established is the death of Jesus (14:22–25). The final touching act of kindness done to Jesus is performed by Joseph of Arimathea, who is said to be "looking for the kingdom of God": the proper burial of Jesus.

Teacher/Prophet

For the most part, these traditional messianic titles and roles are presented by Mark as challenges to Jesus, but there are also indications in

Mark as to how he understood Jesus to have defined his own role. It is as prophet that he presents himself, and as teacher that he is predominantly pictured in Mark. The correlative title of his inner circle of followers is *mathetai* ("learners"). By his followers, his antagonists, and his interrogators he is addressed as *didaskale*.[28] If we add to these eleven passages those three in which he is called Rabbi (twice by the disciples: 9:5; 11:20; and once by a seeker: 10:51), it becomes clear that this is the major role in which he was perceived by his contemporaries, as Mark represents them. An unusual touch is his self-identification as "teacher" when he gives the disciples the instructions for preparing the Last Supper (14:14). As we noted above, the role of the Teacher of Righteousness was perceived by the Qumran community as a central eschatological function, linked with the promise of the prophet like Moses in Deuteronomy 18. In addition to the pervasive details of his preaching[29] and teaching[30] activity, there are at crucial points in the Markan narrative explanations offered by Jesus to the inner core of his followers (3:23; 4:10, 13, 33–34; 10:23; 13:5) in a manner that resembles the method of the Teacher at Qumran. Strikingly, both his instructional and his exorcistic activity are given the general designation of "teaching" (1:22; 4:2; 11:18; 12:38). The most forceful statement along this line is in 1:27, "What is this? A new teaching! With authority he commands even the unclean spirits, and they obey him!" As to his "teaching" in the more usual sense – which is differentiated from that of the scribes (1:22) – he radically reinterprets the law, both by precept and example. He sets aside the purity laws in relation to table-fellowship, eating freely with those who have been ceremonially defiled. He challenges the regulations concerning divorce and marriage, including the principle of levirate marriage (12:18–27). He allows the defiled and the defiling to touch him. He uses spittle as a medium of healing. He associates with a leper, and justifies his eating with sinners. Indeed, he is represented as seeing his role as the convoking, not of the righteous, but of sinners (2:17). Unlike Ezekiel's elaborate vision of the restoration of the Temple, or the Qumran community's variant thereof, he announces its destruction without regret. The only positive comment he makes about the Temple is that it is to be a house of prayer for all the nations (11:17), which builds on an interpretation of the scriptures (Isa. 56:7; Jer. 7:11), as we have noted.

There are clear links in Mark between Jesus' role and that of the prophets, though he by no means conforms to what may well have been the standard expectation of the return of Elijah at the end-time (Mal. 3:1; 4:5). That role is assigned to John the Baptist (Mark 1:2), though wrongly attributed to Isaiah, and later – in Mark's view – wrongly assigned to Jesus (6:14–16). But Jesus' proverbial response in 6:4 ("a prophet is not without honor") clearly implies his own self-identity as a prophet, as does his association with Elijah and Moses in the Transfiguration experience (9:2–8) and the discussion about Elijah's eschatological coming in the pericope (9:9–13).

Messianic/Redemptive Functions

In addition to the variety of ways in which the Markan tradition links Jesus to a range of explicit messianic and redemptive roles, even while differentiating his mission from theirs, Mark's account also uses more general terms to characterize Jesus, and is content even to imply his extraordinary authority in the plan of God without specifying his role or title. John the Baptist, for example, speaks in general terms of one coming after him who is "mightier than I" (1:7). Similar language is used in the Beelzebub pericope, where Jesus explains his exorcisms as part of a larger enterprise in which the kingdom and the dynasty ("house") of Satan are in the process of being taken from him, while he is bound and his goods being plundered. By implication, Jesus is stronger than the "strong man" (3:22–27).

At times the assessment of Jesus' authority is left open-ended in Mark: In 1:38 he explains that preaching the gospel was the reason "why I came out," though he does not say whence. In 1:44 the leper is to show himself to the priest, in keeping with Leviticus 13:49; 14:2–32, "as a proof to the people," though there is no specification of what is to be proved. When Jesus treats the storm on the lake as he does the demons, and controls them by his commanding word, the disciples ask a question for which Mark furnishes no direct answer: "Who is this, that even wind and sea obey him?" (4:41). As we have observed, Jesus refuses to perform miracles as signs of divine attestation (8:11–13) or to identify the source of his authority (11:27–33). Yet he is conscious when *dynamis* leaves him (5:30), and knows the authority that is resident in his name (9:38–41). Among the titles or descriptions assigned to him by the demons is the enigmatic, "holy one of God" (1:24), which is the more strange since neither his mode of life and interpretation of the law nor what he requires of his followers conforms to first-century Jewish standards of holiness.

Perhaps one of the most significant clues as to how Mark perceives Jesus in relation to the expectations about God, the law, covenant obligation, and the future of God's people is given in the parabolic words of 2:21–22. The dual images of sewing a patch of unshrunk cloth on an old garment and the putting of new wine in stiff, old wineskins make the same point: Jesus does not fit the categories of Jewish piety, of covenantal def-

inition, of messianic expectation, of eschatological hopes. To try to force
him into these patterns will tear the fabric; it will split the hide.

In more specific christological and ecclesiological terms, Mark wants his
reader to understand that none of these traditional terms or expectations
has a permanent, self-evident meaning. All must be reassessed in light of
the transformation through Jesus of understandings of the divine purpose
and of God's expectations for his people in the New Age. Each of these
messianic and redemptive terms must be reexamined as to its bearing on
the community's understanding of its origins, its criteria for admission, its
standards for behavior in obedience to God, its mission in the world, and
its expectations concerning the consummation of God's plan for the created order.

Conclusion

Although from the opening of Mark's gospel there are private
disclosures and public hints of Jesus' special relationship to God, his role
is implied rather than defined when, in Mark 8:29, Peter asserts that Jesus
is the Christ. It is clear from what follows in Mark that Peter does not
have a clear notion of what role that title designates. It has to be defined
by what Jesus says and does, including his acceptance of suffering and
death. Peter's so-called confession, therefore, may serve modern interpreters of the Gospels as a paradigm of how not to do it. Indeed to refer
to Peter's statement as a "confession" is almost a contradiction in terms,
since it is clear from what he reportedly says immediately following his
announcement that Jesus is the Messiah that he does not understand who
Jesus is, or what God is doing through him, or who God's people are, or
what their destiny is. Only in light of the resurrection encounter – which
in Mark is merely promised, not described (14:28; 16:7) – will Peter truly
understand the answers to these fundamental questions.

Let us learn from Peter, therefore, not to impose traditional categories
on the Markan representation of Jesus' messiahship or of the intimately
linked corollary consideration, the nature of the New Covenant community. Rather, let us explore how Jesus' redemptive mission is redefined
against the background of the spectrum of Jewish expectations, and how
the Covenant is structured, in kinship with, and in contrast to other competing Jewish views of the time, and what the resources and responsibilities are within that new community. Fully aware that Jesus was not putting new wine in old skins, as Mark portrays him, let us be sure that in
our historical and theological investigation and reconstruction we are alert
to the new skins into which the new wine has been placed.

NOTES

1   In later prophetic tradition (e.g., Isa. 45:1), "anointed" is used of a secular agent through whom the divine will is to be achieved (Cyrus), but also of an unspecified agent through whom the covenant people are blessed and renewed (Isa. 61:1). In Hab. 3:13 the term occurs as a designation for the elect community, since *meshiach* is in parallel with *'am.*

2   The explicit reference is to the two branches of the olive tree through which the oil (that is, the Spirit, cf. 4:6) is poured out on the faithful. The two are identified as "the anointed ones [*bene hayitzhar*] who stand by the Lord of all the earth" (Zech. 4:14).

3   The simplistic assumption that Messiah = "king" is evident in the New English Bible translation here, which renders *magineu* as "king" instead of as "shield," and *meshiach* as "prince," ignoring the meanings required by the context.

4   E.g., Test. Sim. 7:1–3; Test. Issachar 5:7–8; Test. Dan. 5:10; Test. Gad. 8:1; Test. Joseph 9:11a.

5   Cf. IQS 9:11; Covenant of Damascus 7:21a; 12:23; 14:19.

6   T. H. Gaster has reconstructed this material in his *The Dead Sea Scriptures* (New York, 1976, 3rd ed., 433–6).

7   4Q Florilegium.

8   Exposition of Gen. 49.

9   Testimonia 14–20.

10   Testimonia 5–8.

11   4Q Florilegium, where Ps. 2 is expounded messianically.

12   The New Testament writings include a disproportionate number of quotations from and allusions to Ps. 2, 8, 110.

13   The Apocalypse of Elijah and the Testament of Moses have been adapted by Christians down through the third and fourth centuries, but they consist of basically Jewish material from at least as early as the first century C.E. Cf. the introductions to these writings in *The Old Testament Pseudepigrapha*, ed. J. H. Charlesworth (New York: Doubleday, 1983); *The Apocalypse of Elijah*, by O. S. Wintermute, pp. 721–33; and *The Testament of Moses*, by John Priest, pp. 919–25.

14   See note j, p. 43, in E. Isaac's translation of 1 Enoch, in Charlesworth, ed., *Pseudepigrapha.* This distinction is apparent when one compares 1 Enoch 71:14 (= "human being") with 71:17 (= "regnant figure").

15   I conclude, with E. Isaac (on 1 Enoch) and B. M. Metzger (on 4 Ezra), that these documents – though later edited and interpolated by Christians – assumed their basic form in Jewish circles no later than the first century C.E., and that they are therefore documents relevant for the study of the context of the New Testament.

16   These fundamental insights into the rise of the development of Pharisaism, with their revolutionary implications for the study of the origins of both Christianity and of rabbinic Judaism, have been set forth by Jacob Neusner in his *The Rabbinic Traditions about the Pharisees before 70* (Leiden: Brill, 1971),

and in *From Politics to Piety: The Emergence of Pharisaic Judaism* (Englewood Cliffs, N.J.: Prentice-Hall, 1973; 2nd ed., rev., New York: Ktav, 1979). More recently he has spelled out the historical ramifications of these perceptions in a series of collections of essays under the general title *Formative Judaism* (Brown Judaic Studies [Providence: Brown University Press, 1982, 1983]).

17   Mary Douglas, *Purity and Danger: An Analysis of the Concepts of Pollution and Taboo* (London & Boston: Routledge and Kegan Paul, 1966, 1980).

18   Mary Douglas, *Natural Symbols: Explorations in Cosmology* (New York: 1973).

19   Hans J. Mol, *Identity and the Sacred* (New York: Free Press, 1977); Thomas Luckmann and Peter Berger, *The Social Construction of Reality* (Garden City, N.Y.: Doubleday, 1960). See also Alfred Schutz and Thomas Luckmann, *The Structures of the Life-world* (Evanston, Ill: Northwestern University Press, 1973).

20   See Douglas, *Purity*, pp. 94–139.

21   Ibid., p. 124.

22   Ibid., p. 99.

23   Here and throughout this section I summarize what I have set forth in the chapter "Community and Christology in Mark," in Kee, *Community of the New Age*, 2nd ed. (Macon, Ga.: Mercer Univ. Press, 1983).

24   Kee, *Community*, 109.

25   For the interpolation technique, see Kee, *Community*, 54–6.

26   Reading the basic text of Nestle-Aland, 26th rev. ed. (New York: American Bible Society, 1979).

27   Discussed in Kee, *Community*, 133–4.

28   By followers, 4:38; 9:38; 10:35; 13:1; by antagonists, 12:14, 19, 32; by questioners or seekers, 5:35; 9:17; 10:17, 20.

29   Mark 1:4; 1:34; 2:1.

30   Mark 1:22–27; 2:13; 4:1; 6:1; 6:6; 6:30; 8:31; 9:31; 10:1, 32–34; 12:35, 38.

10

The Question of the Messiah in 4 Ezra

MICHAEL E. STONE

The agenda for this volume was set by J. Neusner in a number of communications over the past few years. He puts it in a statement of 7 November, 1982:

> The organizing category is the social group, its world-view and way of life ("Judaism") and the uses and conceptions of the figure of the Messiah within that social group's world-view. The essential issue is the larger conception of Israel's history and destiny expressed within, and by, the group's version of the Messiah-myth (or: expressed without reference at all to that myth).

In what follows I have attempted to look at the way the Messiah is presented in one apocryphal apocalypse, and rather than stressing the detailed analysis of the actual information offered about the Messiah, I have attempted to clarify why Neusner's agenda is very difficult to follow in this case. There is, I think, a good deal to be learnt from that difficulty.[1]

The issue we wish to investigate is how the view of the Messiah in 4 Ezra is related to the way that the community responsible for 4 Ezra sees itself. In order to do this, a number of different questions must be approached.

1. What does 4 Ezra say about the Messiah?

2. From a broader perspective, what role do ideas of redemption play within the thought structure and religious dynamic of the book? How do his views of Messiah function within this context?

3. What can be inferred from this about the author (or his community) and his world view? Methodologically some further issues arise here. Do peculiarities of his views indicate matters of particular interest to him? Perhaps so, but this does not imply that where he utilizes more "traditional" concepts the matter is not important to him, for such traditional

views might well have accorded exactly with his own ideas.[2] On the optimistic (though unrealistic) assumption that answers to the above questions can be determined, what may we extrapolate from them about the views of the person or the community that produced the book?[3]

What Does 4 Ezra Say about the Messiah?

The Messiah is definitely referred to in 7:28f., 11:37–12:1, 12:31–34, 13:3–13, 13:25–52, and 14:9.[4]

In 7:28–29 the Messiah's characteristics and role are clear. He is entitled very specifically "my Messiah" and "my servant the Messiah"[5] He is said to be revealed together with his company, suggesting preexistence. After 400 years he is to die together with all people, a specific tradition almost unparalleled (only 2 Apocalypse of Baruch 30:1 can be said to be similar to it).[6] He is given no role in the events ushering in the messianic kingdom and his appearance seems to be part of the "wonders" that the survivors will see (7:27). He is said merely to make those who remain rejoice for the duration of his kingdom, and then to die.

In the *Eagle Vision,* Vision 5, the Messiah plays a significant role. In the symbolic dream he appears as a lion who indicts and sentences the eagle (11:37–46); the eagle disappears and the earth is greatly terrified (12:1–3). In the interpretation the lion is said to be the Davidide, reserved for the end (12:32), who rebukes and destroys the last empire (12:33). He will deliver the rest of the people in the land of Israel and rejoice with them until the end and the day of judgment (12:34).

The utilization of the lion symbol in the dream suggests the Messiah's Judahite descent (cf. Gen 49:9–10). The interpretation of the dream identifies the lion as the Davidic Messiah, preserved for the end (12:32). Yet, in spite of this, his activity both as judge and as leader in the subsequent period is not talked of in royal terminology. Moreover, the text clearly implies that he is preexistent, intensifying his cosmic role and function.

His activities have to do first and foremost with the fate of the Roman empire. While in the dream he is described as indicting the eagle, the interpretation says "he will first set (the last of the four world empires) up in judgment while they are alive, and it shall be when he will have rebuked them he will destroy them" (12:33). Thus, not only is his rebuke talked of as a judgment,[7] but he is assigned a series of legal tasks – indictment, pronouncement of judgment, and its execution. The forensic aspects of his activity, already present in the dream symbolism, are further intensified in the interpretation. After this, he will deliver the rest of the

people in the land of Israel and rejoice with them until the time of the
end and the day of judgment (12:34).

It has been suggested that certain editorial adjustments have been made
within this vision, in the verses touching on the Messiah.[8] These are the
addition of the phrase "whom the Most High hath kept unto the end of
days" (12:32) and the whole of 12:34. The basis for these suggestions are
alleged "contradictions" in the book's ideas about the Messiah. Preexistence supposedly contradicts Davidic descent, whereas 12:34, referring to
the deliverance of the survivors and their joy in the Messianic kingdom
until the day of judgment, is an addition – it is "out of harmony" with
the "purely political" expectations of the vision.

These supposed anomalies are, in fact, far less serious than they seem.
They arise because modern critics apply to the book rigid categories of
logic and consistency that are inappropriate.[9] To take one example, it is
illuminating to compare this Messianic figure, with its supposedly incompatible heavenly origin and Davidic descent, to Melchizedek as presented
by 2 Enoch. There, Melchizedek is born before the flood and assumed to
heaven in order to appear later at the appointed time. This is no less
strange, indeed perhaps more so, than a Messiah of Davidic descent who
is preexistent (see 2 Enoch Chap. 71).

Nonetheless there is one major difference between what is said about
the Messiah in 4 Ezra Chapters 11–12 and in 7:28f. There the Messiah
appears after the inception of the Messianic kingdom and his central task
in the *Eagle Vision* (Chapters 11–12), viz. the indictment and destruction
of the Roman empire, is not hinted at. In the *Eagle Vision,* moreover, the
Messiah's action is described in legal terms, reminiscent of the language
of God's judicial activity (see, e.g., 7:37). Yet, as distinct from the judgment in Daniel 7 or in The Similitudes of Enoch, which is unmistakably
cosmic in scope, the elements of universality and resurrection, usually
associated by 4 Ezra with final judgment, do not appear, nor do those that
serve to typify judgment as cosmic in the other sources mentioned. So,
although the Messiah judges in Chapters 11–12, his judgment is prior to
the day of judgment (see n. 23 below).

Where does the form of the Messiah's judicial function found in this
vision originate? Is it to be seen as a modification of the concept of the
Redeemer as cosmic judge, which is to be found, for example, in The
Similitudes of Enoch, or may it be seen as a legalization of the eschatological battle as is already to be observed in Daniel 7?

In this connection it is useful to consider 2 Apocalypse of Baruch 39–
40. In spite of the intimate connections between 2 Apocalypse of Baruch
and 4 Ezra, these chapters do not seem to have a literary relationship with
4 Ezra 11–12. 2 Apocalypse of Baruch 39–40 is a four empires vision (as

is 4 Ezra 11–12). Like the indictment in 4 Ezra 11:38–43, this passage refers to the last wicked empire in "antichrist" terminology similar to that used in the little horn in Daniel 7. The legal nature of the judgment of the leader of the last empire (40:1), as well as the idea of a temporary Messianic kingdom (40:3), are also features shared with 4 Ezra. Yet in neither vision is there any mention whatsoever of the cosmic, universal aspects of the redeemer's judgment that are found in other contexts such as The Similitudes of Enoch and 11Q Melchizedek. Various events along the eschatological timetable involve a separation of the good from the wicked without constituting the final judgment.[10] The Messiah's destruction of the Roman Empire is one of them.

The chief activity that the Messiah performs in both this and the next vision is the destruction of the Roman Empire. This is a reflection of the idea of the eschatological battle between good and evil, which is particularly prominent in the dream in Chapter 13. Yet even though in both 4 Ezra and 2 Apocalypse of Baruch the Messiah's activity is described in legal terms, in both works final judgment is clearly the realm of God alone. So we are led to conclude that behind the situation in 4 Ezra and 2 Apocalypse of Baruch lie the separation of the eschatological battle from final judgment and the subsequent legalization of the eschatological battle.

Consequently it should be stressed once more that the role attributed to the Messiah in the *Eagle Vision* differs greatly from that in 7:28f. precisely on this point. There, the Messiah is said to do nothing but "rejoice" the survivors for 400 years. Here he destroys the wicked kingdom.

The Messiah also plays a large role in the second dream *(Son of Man)* vision (Chapter 13). In the dream itself, Ezra sees a man who arose from the sea. He flew with the clouds of heaven and his glance and voice melted all who encountered them (13:1–4). He was attacked by a multitude, carved out a great mountain for himself, and flew upon it (13:5–7). Weaponless, he fought the multitude, and fire from his mouth burnt them up (13:8–11). Then a multitude gathered to him, some joyful and some sad (13:12–13). In the interpretation, the man from the sea is identified as the one whom God reserved for many ages to deliver the survivors (13:26). His stand against the multitude means that at the end all peoples will unite to fight the Man (13:32–34) who will stand on mount Zion and reprove them and destroy them by the law – symbolized by fire – (13:35–38). The peaceable multitude are the ten tribes who will return (13:39–47). Moreover, the survivors in the borders of the holy land will be saved and he will defend them and show them wonders (13:48–50). An additional note stresses the hiddenness of the son (or: servant) (13:52).

The point of view of Box and others who maintain that the whole of the *Son of Man Vision* is drawn from another source and adapted by the redactor has been found wanting.[11] Yet when the dream is compared with its interpretation and when the interpretation itself is examined, a series of severe literary problems arise. An analysis of these leads to the conclusion that the author wrote his own interpretation to a previously existent allegory.[12] This explains the contrast between the closely structured allegory and confused interpretation as well as the overall contrast between this confused interpretation and the carefully structured interpretation of the *Eagle Vision*.

The Messiah is called "man" in both the dream and the interpretation, but the title "servant" is to be found only in the interpretation,[13] which treats the title "man" as a symbol of which the meaning is "my servant" (see 13:25, 32, 51), just like the lion in Chapter 12. Consequently, "the man" is never the subject of action in the interpretative sections.[14]

Box characterized the figure described in the vision as the transcendent Son of Man. The actual expression "Son of Man" is not found in Chapter 13, and although this title probably originally meant simply "human being,"[15] the consistent use of "Son of Man" in The Similitudes of Enoch and the New Testament shows that it early became formulaic. It is important to observe that even if the man in the dream was the traditional "Son of Man," the author had to interpret that figure to his readers. Moreover, the author has shorn the Son of Man of all his particular characteristics in the interpretation and treated him as a symbol. This would be inconceivable if the Son of Man concept was readily recognizable to him and his readers.

In the dream the figure is presented predominantly as a warrior, which contrasts with the presentation of the Messiah in the *Eagle Vision,* where judicial traits predominate and the figure of the eschatological warrior can be discerned, at most, in the background. The "Man" is not entitled "Messiah," nor is the symbolism pregnant with hints in that direction (contrast the lion in the previous vision). On the other hand, he is described with symbolic language drawn largely from biblical descriptions of epiphanies of God, particularly as warrior. God is regularly preceded by winds,[16] and the clouds come before him or are his chariot.[17] Fire is also typical of theophanies and is one of God's chief weapons against his enemies.[18] The melting of enemies is also appropriate to the Divine Warrior.[19]

All of these elements had been freed from the concept of God as Warrior before the time of 4 Ezra, and they are attributes of the man in the symbolic dream. Consequently, it is of great significance that none of them is taken up in the interpretation except the fiery elements that are explicitly interpreted in legal terms.[20]

The cosmic features of the Divine Warrior are attracted to the man in the dream but are all excluded or changed in the interpretation. The forensic aspect is less prominent here than in the *Eagle Vision,* but is treated in the same way. There is rebuke, perhaps sentencing,[21] and destruction by the Messiah's righteous pronouncement.[22] Moreover, the interpretation adds features not present in the dream, including the showing of wonders (13:50), the companions (13:52), and the Messiah's role in the destruction of the hostile host (13:26, 49–50).

The very elements that are found in the interpretation and not in the dream show the greatest connection with the rest of the book. Moreover, the unique traits of the figure in the vision, its cosmic features and unadorned military characteristics, are found nowhere else in 4 Ezra. This situation is congruent with the conclusion, drawn on literary grounds, that the vision is an originally independent piece, and the interpretation has been added by the author.

As in Chapters 11–12 and in opposition to 7:28f., the activity of the Messiah commences before the beginning of his kingdom, and he is active in the overthrow of the nations.

In 14:9, there is the only incidental reference to the Messiah in the book, in connection with the promise of assumption made to Ezra. He is said to be preserved with the assumed righteous until the end of time. He is called "servant," but no other details are given.

In general, the following may be observed:

1. All four texts seem to say that the Messiah is preexistent, although the extent and nature of this preexistence are not made explicit.
2. Where information is provided, he is expected to take care of the righteous survivors (except in 14:9 and the dream of Chapter 13).
3. His kingdom is not stated to be eternal and, in two sources, is stated to come to an end (7:29 and 12:34). This matter is not discussed in Chapters 13 or 14.
4. The term "survivors" is common to all relevant sources except the dream in Chapter 13.
5. He is called Messiah in 7:26 and 12:32 and "servant" in 7:29, 13:32, 13:37, 13:52, and 14:9.

Thus in these categories, the common features of the Messianic figure are prominent. Only the dream in Chapter 13 is distinguished from the other sources. Moreover, in spite of the title "Messiah," the Davidic descent, and the lion symbol by which he is represented, the Messiah is nowhere talked of in the language of kingship. He makes the survivors rejoice (7:28, 12:34), delivers them (12:34, cf. 13:26), defends (13:49) or orders them (13:26); he never rules over them. In 7:22ff., the author's attention is devoted to the ensuing events, the resurrection, and the day of judgment, and the Messiah and his kingdom are mentioned summarily, merely as stages on the way to those events. The direction of this presentation is reinforced by the fact that even Visions 5 and 6, for which the advent of the Messianic kingdom is the climax, say nothing about it except in the most general terms.[23]

The Messiah in the Overall Thought of the Book

In terms of the overall thought of the book, it must be observed that the Messianic figure occurs predominantly in those parts of the book that have best claim to be drawing on prior traditions, the two dream visions. In the long first three visions, with their extensive discussion of eschatological matters, he plays only a more or less incidental role in the systematic exposition of 7:26–44. Moreover, even his chief role as destroyer of Rome, which could have been most appropriately mentioned in the first three visions, never occurs. This could, of course, be attributed to the different sort of material in these chapters, but other explanations might also be sought, such as the fact that the dream visions represent the beliefs of the seer after his conversion, when he has taken up, once more, the traditional explanations and they comfort him.[24]

Moreover, the Messiah and his kingdom are consistently held to be temporary. Thus, they cannot be the final resolution of the writer's problems. Clearly he is most preoccupied with the Messiah and his role in ensuring the passing of Rome and the rule of "the saints of the Most High." In these broad terms the way that the Messiah is presented responds to the major concern of the first part of the book. There will be a vindication of Israel and a redress of the balance.

One or two further comments seem in order at this point. Whatever the circles in which 4 Ezra originated, it is clear that the establishment of the Messiah as king did not play a major role in their expectations. Furthermore, the fact that his activities vis-à-vis Rome are predominantly formulated in legal terms rather than military ones provides another possible insight into their hierarchy of values.

The Type of Community and Interests That Can Be
Inferred from These Views

These questions lie at the heart of the concerns to which this paper is addressed, yet they are very difficult to answer. The issue of the sociological matrix of the apocalypses has remained basically intractable. There is no source external to 4 Ezra that provides any information about its authors, and almost nothing can be learned within the book itself. The only more or less secure facts are the following (all inferred from internal data within the book):

1.   The book is written in response to the destruction of the Second Temple. It clearly expresses yearning for the end of the Roman empire and the vindication of Israel.
2.   It seems to have been written in the land of Israel and in the Hebrew language.
3.   It seems to have been written about the year 100 C.E. or shortly before that date.[25]

The framework of the book is pseudepigraphical; it contains no information about the way of life or habits of its author and no external information for this exists either. Moreover, we do not know how the book functioned, or toward whom it was directed. Perhaps two minor pieces of information fill this lacuna somewhat: (1) it has been argued that the apocalypses reflect, either directly or indirectly, some genuine religious experience;[26] (2) the esotericism of the apocalypses does not seem to be the reflection of a conventicle with secret teachings.[27]

W. Harnisch attempted to use a sort of "opposition criticism," i.e., taking the viewpoints urged by the angelic authority in 4 Ezra as refutations of specific views that are cultivated by some groups in Jewish society and are set in the seer's mouth.[28] This assessment, as Breech rightly notes, runs against the obvious sense of the book. Yet the questioning of Harnisch's evaluation of the roles of the seer and the angel does not invalidate the methodology he employed. The paradigm for it is, perhaps, to be found in studies of the Pauline Epistles, where the study of what Paul is attacking is assumed to illuminate the views of his opponents. Yet with the case of 4 Ezra, we do not even know that what is being attacked is a distinct polemical opponent. Gunkel suggested that it is the author's internal conflict that is here being reflected.[29] This is, given our ignorance of the apocalypses in general and of 4 Ezra in particular, as plausible as the point of view suggested by Harnisch.

Conclusions

In light of all the above considerations, then, we find it to be exceedingly difficult to answer the broader questions of what may be learned from 4 Ezra's views of Messiah and redemption about the dynamics of the group or individual that produced the book. The generalities are clear: They were deeply distressed by the destruction of Israel. They eagerly awaited divine vindication of the righteousness of Israel. The Messiah played a role in that vindication, and an important role in the progress of the eschatological events. He was conceived of primarily as acting in legal terms rather than in military ones; his coming as king was not expected.

Inasmuch as the destruction and the consequent issue of theodicy are mainsprings of the book, it is natural that the issue of redemption is also pivotal. In this overall context, it seems to be notable that, although central in the latter visions, which are most dependent on preexisting traditions and sources, the Messiah plays no role in the first four visions, except for his brief appearance in 7:28ff. So, although part of the author's repertoire of eschatology, he is not so essential as to have to be mentioned every time it might have been possible to do so.

As we have explained, reasons inherent in the very *materia* of the apocalypses make questions about their social functioning particularly difficult to answer, including the very significant questions set as the agenda of this volume. We could simply throw up our hands and pronounce the issues intractable; and perhaps they are at the present stage of knowledge. But it is also possible that the accumulation of new perceptions and knowledge about various aspects of the apocalypses over recent years may gradually lead us to a measure of insight into their context of composition.

Some advances are methodological. Only in recent decades have form-critical methods been applied to the apocalypses. Such methods involve not merely a particular approach to analysis of the literary phenomena of the pericopae under discussion, but seek to relate those literary phenomena to various sorts of social *Sitze im Leben*. Form-critical enquiries have sharpened concern about the definition of "apocalypse" and the relationship between literary phenomena and conceptual constructs. Such concerns are often presented as the need to distinguish the pattern of ideas commonly called "apocalypticism" from the literary form "apocalypse."[30] In a recent paper, E. P. Sanders pointed out that to draw a distinction between apocalypse and apocalypticism, which many scholars have felt to be essential, runs against a basic assumption of form criticism, that every form must have a *Sitz im Leben* and consequently the description of forms should include features other than purely literary ones.[31]

Yet, following Sanders himself, we may question whether form-critical criteria and methods that have been developed to deal with smaller literary units *(Gattungen)* can really be applied appropriately to whole works. Moreover, on another level, the criticism that may have leveled at the assumption that "apocalypticism" is the ideology of the apocalypses need not conflict with the idea that the apocalypses have an ideology that may be discussed. It should only affect the particular issue of whether what many scholars call "apocalyptic(ism)" is really the ideology of the apocalypses.[32] This discussion heightens our sensitivity to the questions of context and function. These are proper questions that must be posed to the apocalypses. It is doubtful, however, that a single *Sitz im Leben* can be found, or should even be sought, to explain the genre apocalypse.

"Opponent criticism" as practised by W. Harnisch raises another methodological option. Can something be learned of the social setting of the apocalypses by studying points of view they are opposing? Perhaps so, in some cases, but not all the apocalypses are polemical in nature (cf. e.g., 3 Apoc. Bar.). Even in a work that may very well reflect the struggle of ideas, such as 4 Ezra, we have noted above how difficult it is to determine whether what we perceive is a sociological or psychological struggle (or perhaps both). Seeking in the apocalypses hints at their purpose, function, and social setting, has produced some fruit. Thus, a good deal may be inferred from the "pseudo-esotericism" of the apocalypses. It has been argued that whereas these works present themselves as esoterically transmitted information (cf. 4 Ezra 3:14 and 14:5–6, 45–8) they were in fact not esoteric, that is they were not the actual secret teaching of hidden conventicles.[33] This does not mean that some of the apocalypses may not have originated in discrete social contexts. A case has recently been made that certain groups of apocalypses, such as some Enoch writings, do come from very self-conscious sectarian contexts[34] and these have even been identified with historically known groups. The argument is made first on the basis of the actual texts of the works themselves. Ideas and terminology of self-designation were isolated that reflect sectarian self-consciousness. Historical connections were then sought, in this case with some success.[35]

This sort of conclusion about the Enochic literature was made possible by various pieces of information within the books, both details that can be interpreted historically and also elements of terminology.[36] Yet 4 Ezra is not so kind to the scholar, and in his parallel treatment of this work, John Collins, whose conclusions about the Enoch books are so far-reaching, finds himself nonplussed and can say nothing definite at all about its circles of origin or social function.[37]

It has been suggested that 4 Ezra has particular connections with Rabbinic circles.[38] It is certainly more like the rabbinic literature than some other apocalypses, but then so is its sister-work, 2 Apocalypse of Baruch, and (to a lesser extent) Apocalypse of Abraham.

Indeed, the relationship between 4 Ezra and 2 Apocalypse of Baruch is significant. The two books also show affinities with the Apocalypse of Abraham, and to an even lesser extent with the *Biblical Antiquities* falsely attributed to Philo. The three first works are apocalypses, all dating from the period after the destruction of the Temple and all reflecting a deep concern for the questions of theodicy raised thereby.[39] If 2 Apocalypse of Baruch is in some way responding to 4 Ezra or to concerns very similar to those raised by 4 Ezra (or, indifferently from the point of view of our argument, if the reverse is true), this provides some hint about the creation and transmission of the works. Not only are they consciously in a tradition of apocalyptic teaching,[40] but they are related to one another. This must imply that those who composed them were socially coherent enough to cultivate a common tradition, and one that was clearly at home in the Judaism of the period following the destruction.

In light of this, then, the pseudo-esotericism of 4 Ezra, and the claim for divine authority made by the last vision (Chapter 14, note particularly vv. 44–8) seem to imply a deliberate social function and role. Since 4 Ezra is first and foremost a response to the destruction of the Temple and the issues raised thereby, and since its message is in the final analysis an assertion of the traditional hope of redemption, it may be seen as representative of one group or trend's response to that destruction.[41]

But when all this is said, it still leaves open the questions raised in the first paragraph of this paper. How is the Messianic view of 4 Ezra a reflection of the social and political situation of its author and his group? From the analysis of his actual teaching on the matter of the Messiah a number of particular emphases emerged. He very much underplayed the Messiah's role as king and to a somewhat lesser extent as warrior. In the book, the Messianic kingdom is expected to be but a stage on the way to final judgment. At its end the Messiah will die (7:29). Consequently it seems clear that the restoration of the ideal situation of the Davidic monarchy did not play a major role in the author's expectations for his ideal future polity. The destruction of the Roman empire was very important and it is the point of the two dream visions, the *Eagle Vision* and the *Son of Man Vision*. However, the destruction of Rome was expected to take place through the Messiah's exercise of judgmental rather than military functions. This again seems to reinforce his nonmonarchical view of the future state. It is impossible, at least at present, to determine what may be inferred about the actual situation of the author from this. The vindication of divine justice through the final day of judgment stands at the peak of the author's expectations (7:30–44) and the restoration of David's empire was not central for him. These views hint, so it may be maintained, at the sorts of ideals the author fostered.

NOTES

1   The actual analysis of the material was first published in my "The Concept of the Messiah in IV Ezra," *Religions in Antiquity*, ed. J. Neusner (Leiden: Brill, 1968) 295–312. This analysis has recently been reviewed in the composition of *The Messiah in 4 Ezra*, an excursus in the commentary on 4 Ezra presently under preparation by the author for the series *Hermeneia*.

2   Moreover, the very notion of "traditional concepts" is deceptive, for in fact the best comparative material is offered by other representatives of the Apocrypha and Pseudepigrapha, which are as unknown as 4 Ezra as far as context of composition is concerned.

3   Here we have sustained the term "community" introduced into the discussion by J. Neusner. This implies certain assumptions about the nature of the author(s) of the apocalypses and of 4 Ezra in particular. In fact, one of the great conundrums is precisely this question of who produced the apocalypses and for what purposes: See Stone, "Apocalyptic Literature," *Jewish Writings of the Second Temple Period* (Compendia Rerum Iudaicarum ad Novum Testamentum, 2.2; Assen Philadelphia: Van Gorcum & Fortress, 1984) 433–5.

4   It has also been suggested that the son in Vision 4 is the Messiah but this seems unlikely. See E. Sjöberg, *Der Menschensohn im aethiopischen Henochbuch* (Lund: 1946) 134–9 for bibliography and critique. On the problematic of the terminology and for a survey of the term *mashiaḥ* and equivalents in the Pseudepigrapha see J. H. Charlesworth, "The Concept of the Messiah, in the Pseudepigrapha" *Aufstieg und Niedergang der Römischen Welt*, Vol. 19, Part 2, ed. W. Haase (Berlin: de Gruyter, 1979) 188–218.

5   Knibb gives a conspectus of the history of this title. See R. J. Coggins and M. A. Knibb, *The First and Second Books of Esdras* (Cambridge Bible Commentary; Cambridge: Cambridge University Press, 1979), 168–9. The literature on it is vast; in general on redeemer figures in Judaism see G. W. E. Nickelsburg and M. E. Stone, *Faith and Piety in Early Judaism* (Philadelphia: Fortress, 1983) 161–201 and additional references there.

6   This perhaps resembles the idea of the snatching away of the Messiah remarked upon by W. Zimmerli and J. Jeremias, *The Servant of God* (London: SCM, 1957). One of their references, 1 Enoch 70:1 refers to Enoch himself, but he is identified as the Son of Man in the next chapter (71:14–16). Still, 4 Ezra's reference to the Messiah's death remains unparalleled.

7   W. Baldensperger pointed out that in Daniel 7 the eschatological battle is given a forensic formulation and that this is relevant to the description in 4

Ezra here; see *Das Selbstsbewusstein Jesu im Licht der messianischen Hoffnungen seiner Zeit* (3rd ed. rev.; Strassburg: Heitz und Mundle, 1903) 98–9, cf. 161.

8   See Stone, "Messiah in 4 Ezra" 296–300, where literary critical issues are addressed in detail.

9   Ibid., 297–300.

10   Such is most evident in ideas about the post-mortem state of the souls (7:78–99) and the messianic woes (6:25, 7:27, 12:34). See also note 23 below.

11   Stone, "Messiah" 304–5. The interpolation theory developed by Box leaves the interpretation with the same literary and structural problems vis-à-vis the vision (Box puts his views in *The Ezra–Apocalypse* [London: Pitman, 1912], pp. 285–6). Other hypotheses are even more complex and are not demanded.

12   Stone, "Messiah," 305–6, provides detailed argumentation.

13   The title "Son of Man" for a redeemer is clearly used in The Similitudes of Enoch and in the NT. It has been the subject of intensive study: See, e.g., the extensive bibliography quoted in *Theological Dictionary of the New Testament* 8.400–77. Naturally, it is derived from Dan. 7, where this figure appears with God and exercises cosmic functions: see ibid., 420–3. It should be noted that in the interpretation of Dan. 7, as here, the human figure is treated as a symbol to be interpreted. Box, Volz, and others have suggested, on the basis of the title, that this man is to be identified with the *Urmensch.* In his treatment of the much more clearly defined Son of Man in 1 Enoch, Sjoberg concluded that, while the figure was influenced by the *Urmensch,* it is not identified with him. The Son of Man is identified neither with Adam nor with the *Urmensch.* See *Menschensohn* 190–8; cf. P. Volz, *Die Eschatoloqie der juedischen Gemeinde im NT Zeitalter* (Tuebingen: Mohr, 1934) 214–17. On the Son of Man as *Urmensch* in 4 Ezra see his arguments on pp. 189–90.

14   In 13:32 he is identified as "my servant," and "my servant" continues to be the subject of action in 13:37; the argument for "servant" rather than "son" is set forth in M. E. Stone, *Features of the Eschatology of IV Ezra* (unpublished Ph.D. dissertation; Harvard University, 1965), 71–5.

15   See Vermes's ongoing polemic on this; G. Vermes, "The Present State of the Son of Man Debate," *Journal of Jewish Studies* 29 (1978), 123–34.

16   See 1 Kings 19:11–12, Zech. 9:14, Job 40:6, etc. These elements are also featured in Daniel 7, which is clearly at play here in 4 Ezra.

17   Preceding theophanies: Exod. 13:21, 19:9, 16, Num. 12:5, 14:14, 1 Kings 8:10f., Ezek. 1:4; as his chariot Exod. 19:9, Isa. 14:14, 19:1, Nah. 1:3, Pss. 68:5, 104:3; note *rkb 'rpt* as title of deity in Ugarit.

18   Ps. 97:2–3, cf. 2 Sam. 22:9f. See also Ps. 18:9f., 1 Kings 19:12, Ezek. 10:2, etc.

19   Mic. 1:4, Ps. 97:5; see Jth. 16:15, 1 Enoch 1:6.

20   Box points out that the mountain might also be related to cosmic war, but it is unambiguously interpreted as Mount Zion. This figure clearly derives from Dan. 2:45, as is explicit from 4 Ezra 13:7.

21   The verse (13:38) is problematic, however, and might refer to future judgment.

22   See Isa. 11:4, Wisd. of Sol. 12:9, 18:15f., 1 Enoch 62:2, 2 Thess. 2:8; cf. Isa. 49:2. Rebuke is also destruction in Chapters 11–12.

23   As noted, the differences between the vision in Chapter 13 and all of the other passages dealing with the Messiah accorded with our hypothesis that that vision comes from another context. Moreover, the difference between 7:28f., in which the Messiah plays no role in the destruction of the wicked kingdom, and the Visions 5 and 6 where his role is central, are significant. We might be tempted to harmonize this, saying that in 7:28ff. the author is not really interested in the Messiah and his doings, while these form the very point of Vision 6 and play a very major role in Vision 5. However, there are enough similar unresolved contradictions elsewhere in the book to make this sort of explanation a little suspect, although it is rather neat.

24   See M. E. Stone, "Reactions to Destructions of the Second Temple," *Journal for the Study of Judaism* 12 (1982) 202–4.

25   This is the present consensus opinion: see most recently B. M. Metzger, "The Fourth Book of Ezra" in J. H. Charlesworth, ed., *The Old Testament Pseudepigrapha* (Garden City: Doubleday, 1983), 1:519–21. For the detailed arguments, see the bibliography set forth by Metzger on p. 524.

26   See D. S. Russell, *The Method and Message of Jewish Apocalyptic* (Philadelphia: Westminister, 1964), 158–77; Stone, *Jewish Writings,* 429–31.

27   Stone, ibid., 431–2. On the "conventicle" theory of apocalyptic origins, see J. J. Collins, *The Apocalyptic Imagination* (New York: Crossroad, 1984), p. 29.

28   W. Harnisch, *Verhaengnis und Verheissung der Geschichte* (Goettingen: Vandenhoeck & Ruprecht, 1969). See the comments on this by E. Breech, "These Fragments I have Shored Against my Ruins: The Form and Function of 4 Ezra," *Journal of Biblical Literature* 92 (1973), 269.

29   H. Gunkel, "Das vierte Buch Esra," in E. Kautzsch, ed., *Die Apokryphen und Pseudepigraphen des Alten Testaments* (Tuebingen: Mohr, 1900), 2.339–42.

30   The bibliography is extensive. By way of illustration, see K. Koch, *The Rediscovery of Apocalyptic* (Abingdon: Naperville, 1972) 28–33; M. E. Stone, "Lists of Revealed Things in Apocalyptic Literature," *Magnalia Dei*, ed. F. M. Cross et al. (Garden City: Doubleday, 1976), 440–2; H. D. Betz, "On the Problem of the Religio-Historical Understanding of Apocalypticism," *JTC* 6 (1969), 134–5; P. D. Hanson, *Interpreters Dictionary of the Bible, Supplement Volume,* 27–34.

31   E. P. Sanders, "The Genre of Palestinian Jewish Apocalypses," *Apocalypticism in the Mediterranean World and in the Near East,* ed. D. Hellholm (Tuebingen: Mohr, 1983), pp. 447–59.

32   See sources cited in note 30. The results of the Society for Biblical Literature genre project are summarized by J. J. Collins in a very perspicacious definition of the literary genre:

> Apocalypse is a genre of revelatory literature with a narrative framework, in which a revelation is mediated by an otherworldly being to a human recipient, disclosing a transcendent reality which is both temporal, inso-

far as it envisages eschatological salvation, and spatial insofar as it involves another, supernatural world.

[J. J. Collins, ed., *Apocalypse: The Morphology of a Genre* (*Semeia* 14; Missoula: Scholars Press, 1979), 9]. Collins went on to present the apocalypses as an attempt to bring order and structure into a disordered reality (ibid., 27), or even as the "transposition of the frame of reference from the historical" and its setting in the perspective of transcendent reality "which is both spatial and temporal" [Collins, "The Apocalyptic Technique: Setting and Function in the Book of the Watchers," *Catholic Biblical Quarterly* 39 (1977), 111]. These observations might well be subjected to the criticism that they remain too exclusively in the realm of literary considerations and historical development of ideas. But in a recent work, Collins has broadened his canvas to include a much greater range of features of the apocalypses with an attempt to stress the question of social matrix; see *Imagination,* particularly pp. 1–32.

33 See Stone, *Jewish Writings,* pp. 431–2. On the "conventicle" theory of apocalyptic origins, see Collins, *Imagination,* 29.

34 The commonality of certain of the Enoch writings, as well as differences between various of them, are well known facts; see recently J. C. Greenfield and M. E. Stone, "The Enochic Pentateuch and the Similitudes of Enoch," *Harvard Theological Review* 70 (1977), especially 55–6.

35 See Collins, *Imagination,* pp. 58–63, basically operating with all of 1 Enoch except the Similitudes and identifying the works as originating in Hasidean circles.

36 See Collins, ibid.

37 Collins, ibid., pp. 168–71.

38 An extreme case was made by Rosenthal and it has not held up. He would connect 4 Ezra with the teaching of R. Eliezer ben Hyrkanos [*Vier apokryphische Buecher aus der Zeit und Schule R. Akibas* (Leipzig: Schulze, 1885)]. Many concepts in the work, however, do find close analogies in Rabbinic writing as is evident from the commentaries. Yet differences are also quite clear. The idea of a parallel set of revealed books (as distinct from a tradition) is not to be found among the Rabbis. The sharpness of the contrast between the two ages is also atypical for the Rabbis (see Schaefer, discussed by Collins, *Imagination,* n. 41, p. 245).

39 See Collins, *Imagination,* pp. 178–80, who discusses the relationship between these works and gives further bibliography in his notes there. Although the arguments are not decisive, it seems likely that 4 Ezra has priority. G. W. E. Nickelsburg, *Jewish Literature between the Bible and the Mishnah* (Philadelphia: Fortress, 1981), p. 287, is more skeptical about the relationship of the two works.

40 4 Ezra 12:11 refers to Daniel explicitly and, moreover, the *Eagle Vision* as a whole is dependent on the beasts in Daniel 7. That chapter has also influenced 4 Ezra 13.

41 This formulation, it seems to us, does not foreclose the question of whether 4 Ezra contains the record of the inner struggle of the author. It does mean

that in his own overall view and understanding, the author was not an isolated individual. It is, of course, quite impossible at the present state of our knowledge to gain any insight into the question of what role the author and those who held and cultivated views like his held in society.

11

From Jewish Messianology to Christian Christology
Some Caveats and Perspectives

J. H. CHARLESWORTH

Jews often assume a Christian is one who claims that Jesus was the Messiah. They rightly see the problems involved in such a belief, but they fail to note that from the beginning until the present those who follow Jesus have expressed their beliefs by employing a wide range of terms or titles that are often interpreted with considerable freedom, a fact which frequently seems astounding to an outsider.

Christians often claim that Jesus' followers knew he was the Messiah, a well known concept in Judaism, and that Christianity obtained its eponymous cognomen from the conviction and proclamation that Jesus was the Christ. They rightly discern that very early in the first century, indeed by the time of Paul's epistles, Jesus of Nazareth was known as Jesus Christ, but they fail to perceive the abundant misunderstandings in the way their claim is articulated. They will be surprised to learn that none of the creeds, especially those recited in unison Sunday morning, contains the confession that Jesus is the long-expected Messiah.

The present chapter in this important book, which should help turn the tide of understanding regarding messianism, seeks to illustrate how difficult it is to move from a first-century Jewish belief in the Messiah to a Christian confession in Jesus' messiahship. The phrase "the Jewish belief" is itself, as we shall see, problematic, yet it is facilely defined by excellent scholars as the contention that at the end of time, or near it, God will send his Messiah, or Anointed One, to restore the harmony of Eden. The Christian confession is customarily put simply: Jesus was the Messiah expected. To obtain this equation between messianology[1] and christology three factors are essential: (1) Palestinian Jews held a recognizable and definable, if not common, messianic belief, (2) this belief was both widespread and to some extent normative, and (3) the Jews who followed Jesus grasped who he was by applying this developed title to him.

225

This chapter proceeds, therefore, by asking three questions: What did first-century Palestinian Jews mean by the title "the Messiah"? Is it not true that almost all Jews expected in the near future a Messiah? Did not Jesus' earliest followers recognize and categorize him as the Messiah and call him Jesus the Christ, or simply Jesus Christ? Before addressing each of these questions, we must dismiss a misconception, perceive what is meant by "Judaism," define our major terms, and clarify the proper methodology.

A Common Misunderstanding by Authorities

Pierre Grelot in his important article titled "Messiah" in the authoritative *Sacramentum Mundi: An Encyclopedia of Theology* rightly warns against the misuse of this term:

> In theology and apologetics, Messianism if often made to include all that concerns the promise and expectation of salvation, since it all prepared for the coming of Jesus Christ.[2]

Wilhelm Vischer, Professor of Old Testament at the University of Montpelier, France, called attention to Luther's argument that *universa scriptura de solo Christo est ubique,* "everywhere the scripture is about Christ alone." Vischer wisely affirms that in neither testament "does God meet men at a point beyond their historical existence,"[3] and that "the revelation in Jesus Christ" cannot be known "apart from the Old Testament."[4] His argument is directed against Rudolf Bultmann, and he astutely contends that Christian theology must not be abstracted from its base in history. Vischer, however, is vunerable to this same critique, for he argues that "the New Testament asserts *(sic),* that God's *deed in Jesus Christ is not merely one but rather THE decisive event for the history of Israel"* (italics his).[5] Such statements in apologetics were very close to polemics because they are not informed by what contemporary specialists in first-century history and theology are perceiving.

During this century we have learned how counterproductive is research bound to terms expanded beyond their usefulness. It was once thought that the Prayer of Manasseh was a Christian work because it sounded "Christian"; and the 23rd Psalm is often still labeled a Christian composition. Systematic theologians may claim that the fourth-century process of canonizing the so-called Old Testament and the subsequent habit of binding both testaments into one volume implies that the Church has christianized the pre-Christian works incorporated. Others, especially first-century historians, will stress that the canon was then still open – some documents in the Bible were not yet written – and that the pre-

Christian writings in Israel and Judaism cannot be ordered under the rubic "the Messiah" without remolding them by discarding what is deemed unfit. Here one must simply make a choice, either to read ancient writings so that they confirm one's own beliefs, or to struggle with the demanding task of attempting to discern what an author was intending to say to whom and who was influenced by him. Here, obviously, I shall try to throw some light upon a major contemporary misperception by focusing on first-century Palestinian Jewish phenomena, since Christianity was born and developed in that time, place, and culture.

"Judaism" as a Problem

C. Geertz has articulated a thought that is exceedingly important for the commencement of our task. He argues,

> The mere use of such terms as 'Islam,' 'Buddhism' . . . and so on, tends to make us think of a religion as a kind of block, an eternal object that is always the same – somehow outside of the historical process.[6]

The contention that "Judaism" might surreptitiously suggest a fixed entity with neat contours and not a swirling dynamo full of life and contradictions is the reason I tended to avoid the term, as well as the equally malign concept "religion," in *The Old Testament Pseudepigrapha and the New Testament: Prolegomena for the Study of Christian Origins.*[7] A similar sensitivity, with added perspicacity, leads Jack Neusner to admit, "I study not a religion but a library"; and to warn against the supposition that we are working with a religion, when in fact we are struggling to grasp "religions." We must not treat the extant early Jewish texts as if they are, using Neusner's words, "testimonies to a single system and structure, that is, to Judaism."[8] Since we are dealing not with one normative structure, but with many structures and substructures, each conceived as normative in its own way and to its own religious group, we must resist the old methodological approach that assumed a coherent messianology in Early Judaism. The old approach tended to systematize, and only subsequently analyze, the messianic passages in early Jewish literature. Lost in the process was understanding. Judaism was posited; messianism was assumed.

No one seemed to perceive, and thence understand, that most of the Dead Sea Scrolls and the Pseudepigrapha, and all of the Apocrypha, contained not one reference to "the Messiah." The view was obscured because numerous nouns were interpreted to denote messianic figures. At least to a certain extent this work, conducted by Christians, was informed by the presuppositions of christology and the assumption that developed messianology flowed smoothly into nascent christology. In order to perceive the erroneous elements in this constructed system and in order to be trusted by others with whom we wish to share some precious insights, we must clarify our definitions and methodologies.

Definitions and Methodologies

The present study differs from most previous examinations of first-century messianisms because of what it excludes and includes. I shall not be looking for the appearance of messianic figures in early Jewish literature; and so excluded will be all references to the Son of Man, the Man, the Shepherd, the Son, and David's Son, which is usually a surrogate for "Messiah." The explanation for this omission is that I am convinced the entire enterprise has been undermined by scholars who mix clear references to the Messiah with vaguely possible, and at times unlikely, messianic passages. Certainly not included at this stage are the portions of ancient writings in which a figure is probably messianic but not called "the Messiah." It will be easy to supplement the present study with such insights when we are convinced that we have developed precise methodologies for assuring that these passages are definitely messianic.

Since our first question pertains to the use of the title "Messiah" in first-century Palestinian Judaism, we are justified in focusing solely on Palestinian texts that contain the Hebrew term "Messiah," the Greek translation of that term, "Christ," and the meaning of each of these, namely "the Anointed One." We may now proceed to attempt to comprehend and then answer our first question.

What Did First-Century Palestinian Jews Mean by the Title "the Messiah"?

Long before the first century C.E., Jews and earlier Israelites used the Hebrew term *Māshîᵃh* to denote a person who was anointed by God. He was almost always either a king or a high priest, although he was on occasion a prophet. Outside of Qumran and other priestly dominated communities, Jewish messianic hopes often tended to idealize the monarchy, and the initial success of the Hasmoneans heightened this dream; hence, as W. Harrelson states, David "became the prototype of the Lord's Anointed, God's Messiah."[9]

During the conflict between David and Saul, according to the account in 1 Samuel, David cut off the skirt of Saul's robe while he was in a cave in order to relieve himself. David subsequently laments his action in these words:

The Lord forbid that I should do this thing to my lord, to the Lord's anointed *(lim'shî'ḥ y'hwāh)*, to stretch out my hand against him, for he is the Lord's anointed *(kî-m'shî'ḥ y'hwāh)*. (1 Sam. 24:7 [Heb.] 6 [Eng.])

Without any doubt the Hebrew noun *Māshî'ḥ* should be translated here not as "Messiah," but as "anointed." David is referring to God's selection of Saul, which was publicly confirmed when Samuel anointed Saul's head with a vial of oil (cf. 1 Sam. 10).

Almost a millenium before the destruction of Jerusalem in 70 C.E., the Hebrew noun *Māshî'ḥ* denoted a king selected and anointed by God. R. de Vaux correctly pointed out that "it is certain that all the kings of Judah were anointed, and it is probably true of all the kings of Israel." He continues, "The king, a consecrated person, thus shares in the holiness of God; he is inviolable."[10]

According to Leviticus 4, ordinances are written for the high priest who sins unwittingly and breaks one of the Lord's commands. The high priest is specified as *hakkôhēn ham-māshî'ḥ*, "the anointed priest" (Lev. 4:3,5). It is obvious, therefore, that anointing was not a technical term reserved only for the king. But more, much more must be perceived.

Many passages in the Old Testament or Tanach refer to the anointing of the high priest or of the priest, but there is a consensus that these passages are edited or composed by the priests after the sixth-century exile. R. de Vaux offers the opinion that during the monarchy only the king was anointed, then "after the disappearance of the monarchy, the royal anointing was transferred to the high priest as head of the people, and later extended to all the priests" (p. 105). Significantly for our present purposes, there is no evidence in the hellenistic period that priests were anointed, and we are justified in concluding that this custom had ceased long before the first century C.E. and that the investiture of the high priest at that time was celebrated by the putting on of the special, cherished, traditional vestments.[11]

This insight is of great paradigmatic significance and is often lost in discussions of the meaning of "the Messiah" in the first century. It must be emphasized that the cessation of the ceremonial act of anointing of the priest, or high priest, and the collapse of the kingship meant that *there was no anointed one among God's people.*

When we come upon the term *MShH* or any of its cognates or upon a transliteration or any translations of it we must be extremely careful. On the one hand, many of our documents are unusually conservative and may refer back to archaic traditions, like the anointing of God's agent, especially a king or priest; on the other hand, something new and unprecedented will be in the air, namely the yearning for God to send another anointed one, "the Messiah." The unique characteristics of this figure will be the terminus technicus "Messiah," or "Christ," the futuristic dimension of the thought, and the titular aspect of the term, which will reflect either a king, a priest, both, or two persons, one a king and the other a priest. As S. Mowinckel stated long ago, "The word 'Messiah' by itself, as a title and a name, originated in later Judaism as the designation of an eschatological figure; and it is therefore only to such a figure that it may be applied."[12]

The question now before us concerns how Palestinian Jews in the first century used the term "Messiah," its cognates and translations. In order to answer this question we may turn to only two collections of early Jewish documents: the Dead Sea Scrolls and the Old Testament Pseudepigrapha. Some of the Targumin (*viz.* Pseudo-Jonathan, Gen. 49:1, Num. 24:17–24) do contain impressive passages regarding the Messiah, but all of these are far too late in their present form to aid us in attempting to define the content of first-century Palestinian Jewish belief in the Messiah.[13]

The Dead Sea Scrolls

In "Qumran Messianology: An Assessment of Critical Research,"[14] I discuss the concept of "the Messiah" or "the Messiahs" in the Dead Sea Scrolls. The following brief comments may suffice to summarize that discussion.

This procedure is appropriate; there is simply insufficient space to attempt here an assessment of the present debate on the references to "the Messiah" or "the Messiahs" in these texts; we must keep in focus the question before us. The major passages must be reviewed in light of our overall concern.

What is novel and important in Qumran messianism is not the denial of a kingly Messiah, but the addition of a priestly Messiah who shall not only accompany the messianic king but also dominate him. The tendency to elevate the preisthood and place all others, especially the ruling king, in subordination to it is to be expected among priests in exile and in tension with the ruling body; this tendency has now been clarified impressively in the Temple Scroll.

In "the rule for all the Congregation of Israel at the end of days (*l'khôl 'dhath Yisrā'ēl b' ah'rîth hayyāmim:*, 1QSa 1.1) are some obtuse references to "the Messiah." Again we confront the idea that God will raise up the Messiah from among the men of the Yahad (the community); here we learn that God will beget the Messiah, perhaps implying that the Messiah will be God's son. "When God begets the Messiah *(hammāshîᵃḥ)* among them" (1QSa 2.11–12), the following meal will take place. The priest shall enter first, and only later shall "[the Mess]iah of Israel" *([Mᵉsh]îᵃḥ Yisrā'ēl)* enter and be seated. The priest shall bless the meal, and only afterwards shall "the Messiah of Israel" *(Mᵉshîᵃḥ Yisrā'ēl)* extend his hands over the bread (1QSa 2.20–21). Some scholars have interpreted this passage to imply (or denote) that the priest is also anointed, a priestly Messiah. If not, the princely Messiah is still subordinated to the priest. This passage is important for us because it placards the lack of clarity in the concept of the Messiah in the Dead Sea Scrolls.

The two most important documents for understanding the concept of the Messiah or the Messiahs in the Qumran Scrolls are the Rule of the Community and the Damascus Document. In the Rule of the Community is the following significant section:

> And they shall be judged by the first judgments (or ordinances) in which the men of the Yahad (or community) began their instruction, until the coming of a prophet and the Messiahs (or the Anointed Ones, *Mᵉshîḥei*) of Aaron and Israel. (1QS 9.10–11)

According to these lines the Qumran community (at least in one stage in its evolution) expected the appearance of three eschatological figures: a prophet, the Messiah of Aaron, and the Messiah of Israel. Without any doubt this column contains the Qumran expectation of two Messiahs. In fact 1QS 9.10–11 is the *locus classicus* for that belief. It is also implied in other writings that have strong affinities with the Dead Sea Scrolls. In the Testaments of the Twelve Patriarchs, portions of which are represented in an early form among the Qumran fragments, we read about the coming of two eschatological figures, who seem to be the priestly Messiah and the princely Messiah: "For the Lord will raise up from Levi someone as high priest and from Judah someone as king" (Testament of Simeon 7:2; *Old Testament Pseudepigrapha*, vol. 1, p. 787).

We are rightly frustrated by this terse line in 1QS. All that we learn about the Messiahs is that they are expected in the future. But, we naturally ask, when – in the near future or after some decades; what are the functions of these Messiahs; what will be the result of their coming; and how shall they be recognized? These and many other questions simply disclose how little we may know about Qumran messianic beliefs. In 1QS 9.11 the belief in the appearance of the Messiahs is used to exhort the members of the community "not to depart from any maxim of the Torah" but to be "governed (or judged) by the first ordinances (or judgments) with which the men of the Yahad" began (1QS 9.9–10). We are not presented with a treatise on the Messiahs.

1QS, however, despite the unexamined assumption of many scholars, is not the only copy of the Rule. Although it is dated paleographically to 100–75 B.C.E., it is not the oldest copy of the Rule. An older copy is announced by J. T. Milik, who merely published

> une liste choisie des leçons variantes (et des additions pour les lacunes de 1QS) que fournissent les mss fragmentaires de la Regle de la Communauté provenant de la Grotte 4 de Qumrân; et ensuite la liste complète des passages identifiés de 4QS (a selected list of variant readings [and additions for lacunae in 1QS] which are furnished by the fragmentary manuscripts of the Rule of the Community deriving from Qumran Cave 4; and following that, a complete list of passages identified in 4QS).[15]

One frustratingly brief sentence pertains to 1QS 9.10–11: "In 4QS^c, on the corresponding line, *byd mšh* (in 8.15) is immediately followed by 9.12ff." (p. 413). This laconic statement means that 4QS^c omits the words found in 1QS from *byd mwšh* in 8.15 to the beginning of 9:12. What is *not* contained in 4QS is the *locus classicus* for two Messiahs. In my judgment, the reference to two Messiahs is a later redactional addition.

This information increases the difficulties for anyone who desires to organize into a system all the references to the Messiah in the Qumran Scrolls. It is possible that Qumran messianism appears only after the death of the founder of the Yahad; but both redacted and earlier copies of the Rule were still available to the members of the community in the first century C.E.; they were hidden in 68 in the caves. It is conceivable that first-century Qumran Essenes were divided in their belief about the coming of the Messiah (or Messiahs).

The second most important document for understanding the Qumran belief in the Messiah or the Messiahs is the Damascus Document, which reached only its final form at Qumran, but apparently contains traditions that predate the founding of the community.[16] It may also represent communities contemporaneous with the Qumran covenanters; perhaps those of the Essenes who lived somewhere else in Palestine than at Qumran. Here are the noteworthy passages:

> And this is the rule of those who dwell (in) camps: They shall walk continuously in these (ordinances) in the time of evilness until shall arise the Messiah (*M^{e}shû^{a}h,* an error for *M^{e}shî^{a}h*) of Aaron (13) and Israel. . . . (12.23–13.1)

> And this (is) the clarification of the ordinances (or judgments) [in] which [they shall walk continuously in the time of evilness until shall arise the Messi]ah ([*M^{e}shî*]^{a}h) of Aaron and Israel. (14.19)

And they who obey him, they are the poor of the flock; these are they who shall be allowed to escape in the time of the visitation. But the remainder shall be delivered to the sword when he comes (sing. part.), namely the Messiah *(Mᵉshîᵃh)* of (11) Aaron and Israel, as it occurred in the time of the first visitation. (19.9–11)

[. . .] the teacher of the Yahad *(hayyāḥîdh,* an error for *hayya-ḥadh)* until shall arise the Messiah *(Māshîᵃh)* from Aaron and from Israel. (20.1)

We are obviously confronted with a formulaic way of referring to the coming of "the Messiah." It is conceivable that the Damascus Document reflects a late, or post-, Hasmonean belief that one person would be the Messiah, and that he will inherit not only the princely but also the priestly lineage (as was attributed to Jesus in some early Christian writings, like Luke). This possibility leads some scholars to suggest that the Damascus Document contains the absorption of the traditional Davidic messianic beliefs by the concept of a priestly Messiah (cf. Schürer's *History,* ed. Vermes et al., 1979, vol 2, p. 552).

The temptation to systematize all the messianic passages in the Dead Sea Scrolls must be resisted. I am impressed by imprecise contexts and content. When it seems clear that the usual expectation is for the appearance of the Messiahs of Aaron and Israel it also becomes obscure why no functions are attributed to them. Moreover, some of the major scrolls, namely the Hodayoth and the Temple Scroll, do not contain the technical term "the Messiah."

The Qumran community existed during three centuries; the original group of monks that wandered there, following the Righteous Teacher, are different from the much larger body of Jews who resided at Qumran about the time of Alexander Jannaeus; and each of these are not to be confused with the small band of Jews who lived at Qumran in the first century C.E., which is, of course, our major interest at this time.[17] Qumran theology was not monolithic.

We must conclude this review of Qumran messianology with the acknowledgment that there is no clear development or consistent content. The Qumran Scrolls do not present a unified view regarding messianism. In some periods in their history the belief in the coming of the Messiah was probably not a major doctrine for them. It also seems certain that no clear development of doctrine is discernible.[18] We must not suggest that the Essenes had developed a messianology that could be easily converted into christology. We simply do not know which of the earlier traditions were most dear to the Essenes living at Qumran in the first century C.E.[19]

The Old Testament Pseudepigrapha

To some readers a brief examination of the Qumran Scrolls has concluded with a dissappointment; no system is discernible; it is impossible to move easily from a Qumran messianology to an early Christian christology. Turning to the Old Testament Pseudepigrapha they are justified in expecting to find in these sixty-five documents much more data for an assessment of the move from messianology to christology. Certainly, they may contend, we will find in these writings a discussion of the relationship between such titles as the Messiah, the Son of Man and the Suffering Servant;[20] titles which many of the earliest Christians claimed adequately defined the status of Jesus of Nazareth, and which were probably accepted by Jesus.

Such readers will discover that their expectations are neither fully frustrated nor fulfilled. The Pseudepigrapha is a mass of documents, and we must proceed with the knowledge that some Jewish works are too late for a study of first-century messianism, and some references to "the Messiah," or "the Christ," were appended to other Jewish writings by Christians living in the second or third centuries, or even later. The latter phenomenon is particularly evident when working with some Sibylline Oracles, The Fourth Book of Ezra, the Martyrdom and Ascension of Isaiah, the Testaments of the Twelve Patriarchs,[21] 2 Enoch, the Apocalypse of Abraham, and the Testament of Adam.

To avoid the confusion that is found in some publications we shall begin by examining the original sources, and by approaching them with the self-same question addressed to the Dead Sea Scrolls, namely, how is the term "the Messiah" and its cognates and translations used in the documents? Our focus will be limited to those Pseudepigrapha that are Jewish and prior to 100 C.E. Four documents, consequently, come before us for study: the Psalms of Solomon, 1 Enoch 37–71, 4 Ezra (not the Fourth Book of Ezra, but the Jewish chapters 3–14), and 2 Baruch.[22] Each of these contains the major references to the Messiah in the Jewish Pseudepigrapha; and each was composed in Palestine. That discovery is significant in itself; and it augurs well for some profitable discussion of the relation between messianology and christology in first-century Palestine.

Psalms of Solomon. This document was composed in the first century B.C.E., in Jerusalem, and reflects the piety of a group of Jews who were not Pharisees necessarily but shared much with that group.[23] The document is written against the horrifying actions of the Romans, especially their occupation of Palestine in 63 (cf. 17:6–14), and it celebrates the just death of Pompey in Egypt (cf. 2:31). The author and his group yearn for the defeat of the Romans at the hands of the long-awaited Messiah. This hope is concentrated in Psalms 17 and 18.

The *terminus technicus* appears in both the Greek and Syriac, the two significant recensions of the Psalms of Solomon.[24] In 17:32[36] we confront the following important phrase:

kai basileus autōn christos kurios (Greek)

wmlkhwn mshyḥ' mry' (Syriac)

"and their king (shall be) the messiah of the Lord" (ET)

In this psalm *christos* and *mshyḥ'* should be translated "the Messiah" and neither "the Anointed One" nor "an anointed one." The pertinent verses of Psalm 17 are as follows:

> See, Lord, and raise up for them their king,
>> the son of David, to rule over your servant Israel
>> in the time known to you, O God.
> Undergird him with the strength
>> to destroy the unrighteous rulers,
>> to purge Jerusalem from gentiles
>>> who trample her to destruction;
>> in wisdom and in righteousness to drive out
>>> the sinners from the inheritance;
>> to smash the arrogance of sinners like a potter's jar;
>> to shatter all their substance with an iron rod;
>> to destroy the unlawful nation with the word of his
>>> mouth;
> At his warning the nations will flee from his presence;
>> and he will condemn sinners
>>> by the thoughts of their hearts.
> He will gather a holy people
>> whom he will lead in righteousness;
>> and he will judge the tribes of the people
>>> that have been made holy by the Lord their God. . . .
> There will be no unrighteousness among them in his days,
>> for all shall be holy,
>> and their king shall be the Lord Messiah.
> (For) he will not rely on horse and rider and bow,
>> nor will he collect gold and silver for war.
> Nor will be build up hope in a multitude for a day of war.
>> (Psalm of Solomon 17:21–33)[25]

The messianic figure depicted in this psalm is clearly "the Messiah"; and his functions are clarified by the active verbs: "to destroy the unrighteous rulers," "to purge Jerusalem from gentiles," "to drive out the sinners," "to smash the arrogance of sinners," "to shatter all their substance," "to destroy the unlawful nation," to "condemn sinners," to "gather a holy people," and to "judge the tribes." Nowhere else in early Jewish literature are the functions of the Messiah so well delineated. The Messiah, however, is totally subservient to God. He appears only "in the time known" to God, and acts only according to God's will. In 17:45–46 it is clear that God himself will accomplish the tasks of the Messiah:

> May God dispatch his mercy to Israel;
>   may he deliver us from the pollution of profane enemies;
> The Lord himself is our king forever more.

Either this verse is a non sequitur with the preceding verses, or – more probably – the author affirms the belief in the coming Messiah and stresses that he is performing God's acts in history. It is clearly stated that the Lord God himself is both King and the Lord of the Messiah (*kurios autos basileus autou*, 17:34).

The Romans are mirrored in the frequent descriptions of the enemies; note the following surrogates for the Romans taken from verses 21–33: "the unrighteous rulers," "gentiles who trample her (Jerusalem) to destruction," "the sinners," and "the unlawful nation." The hatred of the Romans is thorough; but the Messiah is not portrayed as a vengeful bloody warrior, as in the Targum of Pseudo-Jonathan:

> How noble is the king, Messiah, who is going to rise from the house of Judah. He has girded his loins and come down, setting in order the order of battle with his enemies and killing kings with their rulers . . . reddening the mountains with the blood of their slain. With his garments dipped in blood, he is like one who treads grapes in the press. (Targum to Genesis 49:11)[26]

He is a Messiah who does not rely on the horse or the bow; he shall "destroy the unlawful nation (the Romans) with the word of his mouth" (*olethreusai ethnē paranoma en logō stomatos autou*, 17:24). The Messiah is able to win the war against the Romans because he is undergirded by God and is righteous. He shall usher in the messianic age, gathering "a holy people whom he will lead in righteousness." His reign will be paradisiacal; there will be "no unrighteousness among" his people "in his day." In contrast to the Romans, and the later Hasmoneans, he will not seek gold or silver and shall not amass armaments for war. In summation, the Messiah will be the prefect king, who shall guide a people who will embody the truth that "the Lord himself is our king forever more" (*kurios autos basileus ēmōn eis ton aiōna kai eti,* 17:46).

1 Enoch 37–71. After decades of debate in which the date assigned to the Similitudes of Enoch ranged from the first century B.C.E. to the third century C.E., labeling it either as a Jewish or a Christian writing in toto, scholars have now come to an impressive consensus.[27] Virtually all specialists agree that these chapters were written by a Jew.[28] One scholar is still convinced that they may postdate the destruction of Jerusalem in C.E. 70; others, namely G. Nickelsburg, M. Black, E. Isaac, M. E. Stone, D. W. Suter, J. C. Greenfield, and J. VanderKam, rightly date these chapters before seventy, and perhaps in the first century B.C.E.[29] The provenance of 1 Enoch 37–71 is surely Palestinian.

This Book of Enoch contains numerous terms for messianic figures, namely "the Son of Man," "the Righteous One," "the Elect One," and notably a transliteration of *Māshîaḥ,* which can be translated "the Messiah," "the Anointed One," or "the Christ." The term appears only in two passages.

The first passage, 1 Enoch 48:10, has been translated as follows:

> For they (the kings of the earth) have denied the Lord of Spirits and His Anointed.[30]

> . . . for they denied the Lord of Spirits and his Messiah.[31]

> For they have denied the Lord of the Spirits and his Messiah.[32]

There is no function attributed to the Messiah and we learn virtually nothing about him; the brief verse seems to imply that the kings of the earth and the mighty landowners (verse 8) will "burn before the face of the holy ones and sink before their sight" because they have denied the Lord of the Spirits and His Messiah. Chapter 48 is not about the Messiah; it is about the Son of Man who was given a name, in the presence of the Lord of the Spirits, "before the creation of the stars."

The second passage, 1 Enoch 52:4, has been translated in the following fashion:

> And he said unto me: "All these things which thou hast seen shall serve the dominion of His Anointed that he may be potent and mighty on the earth." (Charles)

> And he said to me: "All these (things) which you have seen serve the authority of his Messiah, that he may be strong and powerful on the earth." (Knibb)

> And he said to me, "All these things which you have seen happen
> by the authority of his Messiah so that he may give orders and be
> praised upon the earth." (Isaac)

In this verse the translation by Knibb is appreciably different from the one
by Isaac. According to the latter scholar the Messiah is more active; this
translation may represent the superior reading. Manuscripts B (Princeton
Ethiopic 3 of the 18th or 19th century) and C (EMML 2080 of the 15th,
perhaps 14th, century) have "to the Messiah" (supplying the translation
presented by Knibb and Charles); but manuscript A (Kebra 9/II of the
fifteenth century) contains "by the Messiah." If Isaac has caught the original intention of the author of this Book of Enoch, then the Messiah has
been quite active. By the authority of the Messiah all Enoch has seen has
happened, namely, according to 52:1, "all the secret things of heaven and
the future things." Because of his authority and activity the Messiah is
empowered to give orders and shall "be praised upon the earth." The
sweeping generality of "all" leaves quite unclear what are the specific
functions of the Messiah. Perhaps the author believed that the Messiah
will, in the eschaton (the passage is clearly eschatological), perform all the
functions necessary in order to achieve the desired harmony in creation.
The details are shrouded in secret.

According to Knibb's translation all that Enoch has seen will serve the
Messiah when he appears on the earth. The Messiah will be exceedingly,
indeed invincibly, "strong and powerful on the earth." According to all
translations, the Messiah will come to the earth in the future; but the time
is not indicated.

The discussion of the Messiah in 1 Enoch 37–71 is incomplete until
some attention is given to the relationship of this title to the other messianic figures in this book, namely "the Righteous One," "the Elect One,"
"the Chosen One," and "the (or that) Son of Man." Any attempt to distinguish between these figures fails because of the indefiniteness of the
resumptive pronoun "he" in Semitics and the phenomenological similarity of the place of these creatures, specifically before the Lord of Spirits,
the identical functions performed by them, the glory given to each of
them, and their exaltation on the throne of glory. I have come to the
conclusion that as many titles are given to the Angel of Truth in the Rule
of the Community, so these different titles or terms[33] in 1 Enoch 37–71
are united not only in setting and functions but in one and the same
person.

Not only are these creatures similar in characteristics and perform identical functions, but it is impossible to discern any chronological relation
between them. One does not follow after another. There is no sequence

or chronology. These different names are essentially distinguishable attributes of one eschatological figure. Hence, since the Son of Man shall be a staff for the righteous ones (48), and since "This is the Son of Man to whom belongs righteousness, and with whom righteousness dwells" (46:3), it is only to be expected that the Son of Man is none other than "the Righteous One." No distinction should be stressed between these two and the Elect One, because in his days righteousness shall prevail (39:6).

The equation between these only apparently different figures seems to be presented in cryptic language, typical of the apocalypses and the Pseudepigrapha, in chapters 48 through 53. In 48:6 the author boldly reveals that the Son of Man became the Chosen One. Note the development of thought in 48:2–6, which is clarified by excerpting it and highlighting it as follows:

> At that hour, that Son of Man was given a name in the presence of the Lord of the Spirits, the Before–Time, even before the creation of the sun and the moon, before the creation of the stars, he was given a name in the presence of the Lord of the Spirits. He will become a staff for the righteous ones in order that they may lean on him and not fall. He is the light of the gentiles and he will become the hope of those who are sick in their hearts. All those who dwell upon the earth shall fall and worship before him; they shall glorify, bless, and sing the name of the Lord of the Spirits. For this purpose he became the Chosen One; he was concealed in the presence of [the Lord of the Spirits] prior to the creation of the world, and for eternity.

The Son of Man is clearly the Chosen One; he is given a name before the creation of the world. Our attempt to obtain some insight into the identity of the figures by looking at the titles is paralleled by the penchant of the author to refer to, but never to disclose, the name given to the Son of Man.

In 48:10 the Son of Man and the Chosen One seem equated with the Messiah, and that association will prove to be significant in our present search for the meaning of the Messiah in first-century Judaism. Both the Son of Man and the Messiah are shown in the same setting, and are moving in identical ways in the drama. They both are similarly related to the Lord of the Spirits: Both serve before him. The drama in chapter 48 would be needlessly twisted if one were to posit a distinction between the Son of Man and the Messiah. Note the flow of thought:

> At that hour, that Son of Man was given a name, in the presence of the Lord of the Spirits. . . . All those who dwell on the earth shall fall and worship before him . . . he became the Chosen One

> ... the righteous ... will be saved in his name. ... In those days the kings of the earth and the mighty landowners shall be humiliated ... for they have denied the Lord of the Spirits and his Messiah.

The righteous are oppressed by the kings and landowners; the former shall be saved but the latter consumed because one worshipped whereas the other denied the Lord of the Spirits and that Son of Man, the Messiah.

Similarly, the Elect One seems paralleled with the Son of Man, in 49:2. And in 49:4 the Elect One seems identical to the Chosen One, who is the Son of Man. In 53:6 the author identifies the Righteous One and the Elect One; observe the thrust of that verse: "After this, the Righteous and Elect One will reveal the house of his congregation. From that time, they shall not be hindered in the name of the Lord of the Spirits." This pellucid equation tends to confirm the suggestion developed above, that is that the Elect One, the Righteous One, the Messiah, and the Son of Man are different titles for the same messianic and eschatological figure.

This conclusion does not warrant the appealing corollary, that the functions and descriptions given to these other titles can readily be transferred to the Messiah. There is far too much work, research, and thinking to be done, to say little of the debates the preceding comments will evoke, before we are justified in moving in that direction. For the present it is sufficient to emphasize once again how complex is the terrain covered by early Jewish messianism. We are observing no set concept of the Messiah; rather we are impressed by the brilliant and fertile minds of the early Jews.

This research resulted in a conclusion that seemed speculative and in sharp contrast to the tendency of almost all modern scholars, who emphasize that "Son of Man" and "Messiah" are quite different terms, or titles, and must not be associated. I was surprised to find that my thoughts were corroborated by two of the finest specialists on 1 Enoch.

R. H. Charles, the leading scholar on 1 Enoch in the first half of this century, contended that the "Messiah is variously named: 'the Righteous and Elect One,' 53:6; 'the Elect One of righteousness and of faith,' 39:6; 'the Elect One,' 40:5, 45:3, 49:2, 4, 51:3, 5, 52:6, 9, 53:6, 55:4, 61:5, 8, 10, 62:1; 'The Messiah,' 48:10, 52:4."[34] He continued by stating that the "Messiah is conceived in the Parables as (1) the Judge of the world, (2) the Revealer of all things, (3) the Messianic Champion and Ruler of the righteous."[35]

Nickelsburg, certainly one of the leading experts today on the Books of Enoch, astutely argues that the "Elect One combines the titles, attributes, and functions of the one like a son of man in Daniel 7, the Servant of the Lord in Second Isaiah, and the Davidic Messiah." He continues by affirming that "the Elect One" is indeed another title for "the Righteous One." Extremely important for our present concern to find reliable ways to understand the movement from Jewish messianology to Christian christology is his perception of one aspect of first-century messianism:

> It is noteworthy that both this document and the early church conflated the originally separate figures of the Servant, the one like a son of man, and the Messiah.[36]

My own research has led me to precisely this same conclusion.

Before C.E. 70, two groups in Early Judaism held messianic beliefs in which the Messiah was identified with the Servant and one like a Son of Man. One group portrayed the Elect One with terms, functions, and attributes derived from the traditions associated with the Isaianic Suffering Servant, the Davidic Messiah, and the Danielic Son of Man figure; the other group depicted Jesus of Nazareth in the same manner. Moreover, the author of the Similitudes states that the Messiah, or more specifically, the Son of Man, is hidden, "At that hour, that Son of Man was given a name, in the presence of the Lord of the Spirits . . . he became the Chosen One; he was concealed in the presence of (the Lord of the Spirits) prior to the creation of the world, and for eternity" (48:2–6). The hidden Messiah, the Son of Man, or the messianic secret, is also a major feature in the earliest gospel, Mark. Similarly, the author of the Similitudes contends that the righteous "will be saved in his name" (48:7); the pronoun "his" may refer back to a preceding "the Lord of the Spirits" or to "that Son of Man." Klausner of the Hebrew University, Jerusalem, wisely contended, "In this there is much of the views found in the Gospels, which of course were popular Jewish views of an earlier time."[37]

It is conceivable that these Jewish and Christian traditions emanated from Galilee. With these insights we come close to peering into the historical period when there was a paradigm shift and a flow from messianology to christology. For at least 40 years, from 30 to 70, the Palestinian Jewish Movement was a group within Early Judaism; it is often misleading to use terms such as "Jewish" versus "Christian" during this early phase of Christian Origins.

4 Ezra. Shortly after the destruction of Jerusalem and the defeat of Israel in seventy, a devout and distraught Jew wrote one of the great masterpieces in the history of literature – 4 Ezra. He was torn by two irreconcilable opposites: God has promised in his Torah that he will be faithful to his promises to Adam, Noah, Abraham, and David, essentially that he will be a father to his son, Israel, and guard and protect him in a promised land, Palestine. Now, the smoke rises from the charred remains of the house of Yahweh in the "holy city" of a land devastated because a pagan and idolatrous nation, Rome (i.e., Babylon), has defeated Israel, slaughtering thousands of Jews, including women and children, and carrying off many into slavery. The piercing question is focused:

> And now, O Lord, behold, these nations, which are reputed as nothing, domineer over us and devour us. But we your people, whom you have called your first-born, only begotten, zealous for you, and most dear, have been given into their hands. If the world has indeed been created for us, why do we not possess our world as an inheritance? (6:57–59)[38]

The questions in this document are so penetrating, and present such real crises, that the answers supplied are pale in comparison. It is out of this social, political, economonic, and above all religious crisis that the hope in the coming of a Messiah is articulated.

The author of 4 Ezra inherits the tradition that time is bifurcated into "this world" and "the world to come" (7:50, 8:1 – *Hoc saeculum fecit Altissimus propter multos, futurum autem propter paucos*). Surprisingly the Messiah does not belong to the future world, which is often portrayed in other documents as the eschatological day or messianic age; he belongs to the present age.

The future of this world is trifurcated into periods. The first "will come" and "the city which now is not seen shall appear, and the land which now is hidden shall be disclosed" (7:26). The author struggles for an answer as to how he can comprehend the desecration of God's holy and promised land and his holy city. At this time the Messiah shall appear:

> For my son the Messiah shall be revealed with those who are with him, and those who remain shall rejoice four hundred years. And after these years my son the Messiah shall die, and all who draw human breath. *(Et erit post annos hos. et morietur filius meus Christus et omnes qui spiramentum habent hominis. Syriac: wnhw' mn btr hlyn shny' nmwt bry mshyḥ' wklhwn 'ylyn d'yt bhwn nshmt' dbrnsh'.)* (7:28–29)[39]

This is the only passage in the literature of Early Judaism in which it is stated that the Messiah shall die.

How do we explain this passage? The Messiah dies, but he has performed no functions. Let us examine each of these factors in order to understand the messianism in 4 Ezra.

Is not the reference to the death of the Messiah an alteration of the text by a Christian? There is no doubt that the text of 4 Ezra has been altered by Christian scribes. For example, in 7:28 of the original Jewish version – represented perhaps by the Armenian "God's anointed,"[40] the Syriac "my son the Messiah," or the Latin "my son the Messiah" (or "Christ": *filius meus Christus*) – was changed by Christians, in the Latin version, to *filius meus Jesus,* "my son Jesus" (cf. Latin MSS. Phi, CMV).

Alterations, either accidental or intentional (as in 7:28), by copying scribes must not be confused with Christian redactions or interpolations.[41] The question is focused: Is the reference to the Messiah in 4 Ezra 7:26–44 an interpolation or redaction by a Christian?

First, we should ask if the Messiah performs any functions. The answer is no, except in the Armenian version: "Then God's anointed will appear manifestly to men and he will make those happy who persisted in faith and in patience" (7:28). But the actions and results in the subsequent verses in the Armenian tradition are because of "the voice of God" and "the Most High." One must raise some doubts whether a Christian would add a passage about the Messiah and attribute to him no functions, which is an impressive aspect of the Latin and Syriac versions, as well as most of the Armenian version.

Are there salvific effects of the death of the Messiah? Is his death linked with some explanation of the suffering endured by Jesus on the cross, and is there some allusion to or explanation of the effects of his death for the atonement of sinners? All of these dimensions of the death of Jesus are conspicuously absent in 4 Ezra 7. The author states simply, "my son the Messiah shall die" (7:29). The passage cannot be Christian, since postseventy Christianity stressed the efficaciousness of Jesus' crucifixion (or – among the Ebionites and other docetic Christians – denied that Jesus had died).

What is the meaning of this Jewish belief? It must be related to the holocaust of seventy, that disaster in which the Roman brutality to the Jews was exceeded only by the internecine horrors perpetrated by Jews against Jews, the armed youth against the defenseless elderly, and even starving mother against infant son.[42] It does not reflect an anti-Christian polemic, "a biblical counterblast to the Christian faith in the Jesus (who has died) as the Messiah."[43] Stone may well be correct; while the role of the Messiah in 4 Ezra "is difficult to assess," and while "the place of the Messiah in the author's eschatological scheme cannot be doubted," the paucity of references to the Messiah outside chapters 11 through 13 and 7:28–44 may be because "the Messiah was not the answer to the questions that Ezra was asking."[44] As stated earlier, the questions in this document are so penetratingly unbridled that no adequate answers are possible; Messianic ideas are on the side of the answers, hence they are not sufficient to counterbalance the force of the devastating questions.

It becomes obvious now how difficult it is to use the references to the Messiah in 4 Ezra to comprehend the movement from Jewish messianology to Christian christology before seventy. This caution does not belie the fact that 4 Ezra incorporates many pre-seventy Jewish traditions; but its author, because of his social setting, was forced to recast these traditions for a new and different period in Jewish history.

Returning to 4 Ezra 7, it is clear that the Messiah dies within "this age." He inaugurates no messianic age. After his death "the world shall be turned back to primeval silence for seven days . . . And after seven days the world" shall be transformed, and the final judgment shall occur. The resurrected dead shall be sent either, because of "unrighteous deeds," to "the pit of torment" or, because of "righteous deeds," to "the Paradise of delight." The judge is not the Son of Man or the Messiah; he is "the Most High" (*Altissimus;* 7:33,37).

The future is different from the eschaton. The future, as indicated above, is divided into three periods: the time of the Messiah, the seven days of silence, and the period of judgment. After this future period, this world and this age will come to an end. Observe the import of 7:43[113]–44[114]:

> But the day of judgment will be the end of this age and the beginning of the immortal age to come, in which corruption has passed away, sinful indulgence has come to an end, unbelief has been cut off, and righteousness has increased and truth has appeared.

Two other significant references to the Messiah in 4 Ezra are not so novel as the ideas found in chapter seven; and they are reminiscent of the messianic ideas encountered already in pre-seventy Jewish documents. In chapters 11 and 12 we read about "a creature like a lion" (11:37) who is identified as the Messiah. Ezra is told:

> And as for the lion that you saw . . . speaking to the eagle (i.e., the Roman empire, with its eagle insignias) and reproving him for his unrighteousness . . . this is the Messiah whom the Most High has kept until the end of days, who will arise from the posterity of David, and will come and speak to them; he will denounce them for their ungodliness and for their wickedness, and will cast up before them their contemptuous dealings. (12:31–32)

The Messiah (*unctus;* Syriac: *mshyḥ'*) will sit in judgment, destroying "them" (an imprecise reference to the Romans) and delivering "the remnant of my people," to "make them joyful until the end comes." Here we encounter the well known concept of the Messiah who is a warrior (although there is no mention of his using weapons of war, a similarity with the Psalms of Solomon) and a judge.

The messianic passage, 13:1–14:9, does not contain the technical term "the Messiah," but it is relatively certain that the author of this document (which is not composite) has in mind the Messiah, whom he has already identified as God's son (recall "And after these years my son the Messiah shall die. . . ."). In this section "my son" appears as a man from the sea *(virum ascendentem de corde maris)*. This man is "he whom the Most High has been keeping for many ages, who will himself deliver his creation; and he will direct those who are left" (13:26). Reminiscent of the author's comments in chapters 7, 11, and 12, and also a remnant of ancient messianic tradition, is the explanation of the advent of the Messiah: "Just as no one can explore or know what is in the depths of the sea, so no one on earth can see my Son or those who are with him, except in the time of his day" (13:52). Impressively reminiscent of the Psalms of Solomon is the description of how he shall defeat a warring multitude:

> After this I looked, and behold, all who had gathered together against him, to wage war with him, were much afraid, yet dared to fight. And behold . . . he neither lifted his hand nor held a spear or any weapon of war; but I saw only how he sent forth from his mouth as it were a stream of fire, and from his lips a flaming breath, and from his tongue he shot forth a storm of sparks. . . . All these . . . fell on the onrushing multitude . . . and burned them all up. . . . (13:8–11)

Surely the Messiah shall partake of supernatural dimensions, as would be befitting the son of God. The author probably does not attribute to the Messiah the use of military means for destroying the Romans, because the debacle of 66–74 was a grim reminder that militant messianism had led to the defeat of Israel.[45] The social setting of the apocalypse helps provide the proper exegesis: The Messiah does not become entangled with the heinous enemy; from a distance he destroys them with fire.

No attempt should be made to systematize the author's messianic ideas, or to attribute the contrasting chapters to different authors or documents.[46] He was writing under exasperating circumstances that would preclude consistent reflection; he was one of the apocalyptists, and they were circuitous in the development of thought and self contradictory. Even more so, it is unwise to organize and categorize what had been left unrelated in Early Judaism. At the end of this section we shall seek to discern to what extent that advice is appropriate regarding messianism in Early Judaism.

2 Baruch. Klausner stated long ago "that there is no Pseudepigraphical book in which are found so many detailed Messianic expectations as in the

Syriac Book of Baruch; and there is no other Pseudepigraphical book the Messianic expectations of which are so like *those in the earliest parts of the Talmud and Midrash*."[47] 2 Baruch was composed around 100 C.E., probably shortly after 4 Ezra (conceivably as a correction to his pessimism), and probably also somewhere in Palestine. Like 4 Ezra, 2 Baruch is a literary unity. "The Messiah" *(mshyḥ')* is mentioned in 29:3, 30:1, 39:7, 40:1, and 72:2; and the references appear in three self-contained discussions.

Chapters 29 and 30 comprise the first section. With the coming of the Messiah (or the Anointed One), "when all that which should come to pass in these parts has been accomplished" (29:3), then Behemoth and Leviathan will appear and "will be nourishment for all who are left" (29:4). A passive Messiah, who has no functions to perform, simply appears; he does not even judge the wicked or protect the righteous. His appearance coincides with the resurrection of the righteous; the wicked "will the more waste away," probably in their graves.

The following passage has been problematic:

> And it will happen after these things when the time of the appearance of the Messiah (or Anointed One) has been fulfilled and he returns with glory, that then all who sleep in hope of him will rise. (30:1)

The problem centers on the clause *wnhpwk btshbwḥt'*.[48] R. H. Charles translated it as follows: "that he shall return in glory." He understood this clause "to mean that after His reign the Messiah will return in glory to heaven."[49] P. Bogaert followed Charles's interpretation, stating that the Messiah's reign is limited and he will return to glory.[50]

This interpretation is problematic in itself. As W. O. E. Oesterley stated, "It does not say definitely where (the Messiah) will come from, but it is apparently implied that he will come from Heaven, since immediately upon his appearance the Resurrection is to take place. . . . "[51] Oesterley is obviously influenced by Charles. The author of 2 Baruch does not say where the Messiah is from or to where he returns. Only context and the perception of other early traditions regarding the Messiah can supply a reliable exegesis.

An equally significant problem caused by Charles's interpretation is that the Messiah seems to appear and then vanish. After he has disappeared the resurrection occurs.

I am convinced that the Syriac clause should be pointed as follows: *wᵉnehpôch bᵉteshbûḥtā'*, "and he returns (or shall return) with (not *in* or *to*) glory." The Messiah returns to the land ('R'' 29:2), the earth, with glory. He is perhaps preexistent (cf. 1 En. 46:1–2; 48:3; 62:7; 4 Ezra 12:32, 13:26), and had been in Paradise, or Eden, with Adam. He was taken away from the earth (Paradise was conceived either on an unreachable place on the earth or in one of the heavens, usually the third) and now *returns*. These traditions were circulating in the Adam cycle before the time of 2 Baruch, and it is conceivable the author was assuming the reader knew them.[52]

Chapters 39 through 42 comprise the second messianic section in 2 Baruch. In these chapters the Messiah is a militant figure. He shall capture, convict and kill the last leader *(NQṬLYWHY)*. But he will "protect the rest of my people." There is a long messianic kingdom: "And his dominion *(RShYTH)* will last forever until the world of corruption has ended and until the times which have been mentioned before have been fulfilled."

Chapters 72 through 74 contain the longest and final messianic section. As in the second, but in contrast to the first section, the Messiah in 72–74 is active. He shall summon all the nations (72), sparing those who have not oppressed or known (an interesting aside) Israel, and slaying those who have conquered and ruled her.

Of particular importance is the description of the Messiah's kingdom *(DMLKWTH)*: "The joy will be revealed and rest will appear" (73:1). That place and time is paradise redivivus; there will be no illness, fear, or tribulation, no one will die untimely; all unpleasant things will be no more. But there is more: "And the wild beasts will come from the wood and serve men, and the asps and dragons will come out of their holes to subject themselves to a child." Woman will no longer suffer the pains of giving birth, and workmen will no longer struggle to provide food, "because the products of themselves will shoot out speedily, during the time that they work on them in full tranquility" (74:1). These verses inherit many traditions, notably those we know from Isaiah 11 (especially verse 6), the Papias quotation in Irenaeus (*Adv. Haer.* 5.33.3–4) and the History of the Rechabites.

The Messiah is here portrayed quite clearly as a militant warrior. He slays all the gentiles who have ruled over Israel (*KWL 'LYN DYN D'ShṬLTW 'LYKWN:* 72:6). In contrast to the Psalms of Solomon and 4 Ezra 13 the Messiah shall kill with the sword (*LḤRB'; 72:6*).

The First Question: No Easy Answer

We are finally in a position to answer our first question, "What did first-century Palestinian Jews mean by the title 'the Messiah'?" Our examination of the Dead Sea Scrolls left us with numerous possibilities for reflection but no clear insight into what the Qumran Essenes were thinking about the Messiah in the first century C.E. Some may have held no messianic beliefs, others – probably most of them – yearned for the coming of one or two messiahs. The latter group has left us no clue by which to recognize the Messiah or Messiahs; we are given no blueprint or script for him or them. There is no content for messianism left by the Essenes. Significantly, the War Scroll, which probably dates from the Roman period, is singularly silent on the role of the Messiah in the great eschatological war.

From the Pseudepigrapha we learn that only a very few documents contain a clear reference to "the Messiah." And these passages are either frustratingly ambiguous or contradictory. We are presented with various beliefs, not one belief about the Messiah. The functions of the Messiah are not clear; there is again no script. When it is stated that he defeats the enemy, some texts (especially the Psalms of Solomon and 4 Ezra 13:8–10) claim that he will not rely on military weapons, others (namely 2 Baruch 72) assert that he will use the sword. In some texts (cf. 2 Baruch 72–74) he inaugurates or participates in the messianic age, in others (notably 4 Ezra 7) he dies before the eschaton and inaugurates no messianic age. In some documents (4 Ezra 7:28–29 [contrast the Armenian]; 2 Baruch 29–30) he is passive, performing no functions, in others he is militantly active (2 Baruch 39–42). In a few documents (viz. 4 Ezra 13:8–13) he apparently acts on his own initiative, in others he is totally subservient to God (viz. Psalms of Solomon 17 and 18). Frequently he is portrayed as a judge (4 Ezra 12:31–32), in other passages the Messiah is removed so that God himself sits in judgment (viz. 4 Ezra 7:26–44).

These are the major discrepancies; they must not be ignored in an attempt to construct a content for Jewish messianism. Definitions of messianism must be rewritten to absorb the aforementioned complexities. Now unrepresentative is the following classic definition:

> Messianismus is "im wesentlichen der religiöse Glaube an das Kommen eines Erlösers, der auf universaler oder partikularer Ebene der gegenwärtigen Ordnung ein Ende setzen und eine neue Ordnung der Gerechtigkeit und des Glücks begründen wird" (Messianism is "essentially the religious belief in the coming of a Redeemer, who on a universal or particular level, brings an end to the present order, and establishes a new order of righteousness and prosperity.").[53]

This definition errs in particularly assuming that the Messiah is always active. First-century Palestinian Jews held many different, often mutually exclusive, ideas and beliefs regarding the Messiah. There was no developed and set messianology ready to be used in christological didache and kerygma. The implications of this discovery will be assessed when we confront our third question; we turn now to the second question raised at the outset.

The Second Question

Most of the publications now on the shelves of our libraries, including even some books by scholars, tend to assume that most first-century Palestinian Jews expected the coming of a Messiah. One reason for this assumption, still lingering on, is based on the conviction that the belief in the coming of the Messiah is part of the Eighteen Benedictions. For example, W. Koester and J. Schmid conclude an article with the following: "After 135 C.E. the concept of the Messiah lost its power to influence history; it lived on in the 15th of the Eighteen Benedictions."[54] This terse statement is essentially accurate, but it is potentially misleading. Many readers will think that the present benediciton, the Amidah or the Shemoneh Esreh, popularly called outside of the synagogue "the Eighteen Benedictions," contains a blessing on David as the Messiah and a plea for the reestablishment of his throne in Jerusalem. In fact these prayers are found in the synagogue services today. Note the following benediction:

> Return in mercy to thy city Jersualem and dwell in it, as thou hast promised; rebuild it soon, in our days, as an everlasting structure, and speedily establish in it the throne of David *(u*Kissê Dhāwidh)*. Blessed art thou, O Lord, Builder of Jerusalem.[55]

On the basis of this benediction, and on the widespread knowledge that the Eighteen Benedictions predate C.E. 70, many will assume that the belief in the coming of the Messiah was the basis for a common prayer in the synagogue, and was, therefore, part of the essence of Early Judaism before the destruction.

It must be emphasized that while the Eighteen Benedictions are early – pre-seventy – only their number, order, and occasion for recitation were set; their precise wording was not yet finalized.[56] The above passage is appreciably different in the old Palestinian form; note the older wording:

> Have compassion, O Lord our God, in thine abundant mercy,
> On Israel thy people,
> And on Jerusalem thy city,
> And on Zion, the abode of thy glory,
> And upon the royal seed of David, thy justly anointed.
> Blessed art thou, O Lord, God of David, Rebuilder of
> Jerusalem.[57]

The Hebrew of the pertinent section above, *W'L MLKWT BYT DWYD MShYH,*[58] is impressive and could be translated, "and upon the kingdom of the house of David, the Messiah." The import of this version, however, is significantly different. In place of the modern appeal for God to return and dwell in Jerusalem, and to rebuild it and to "establish in it the throne of David," is the exhortation for God to have "compassion" on Jerusalem and on David. There is no messianic belief contained in the old form.

It is pertinent now to ask, as a logical sequence to our first question, "Is is not true that almost all (first-century Palestinian) Jews expected in the near future a Messiah?" The answer is clearly "no."

The term "the Messiah," along with its cognates and translations, does not appear in the Apocrypha, Philo,[59] and Josephus (except for allusions), and the framers of the Mishnah avoided "the Messiah-myth."[60] Philo probably avoided the term because of his own philosophical interests and allegorical methodology. Josephus and the compilers of the Mishnah may have ignored it, because of the holocaust produced by revolutionary messianic Jews.[61]

As we have stated, the terminus technicus *MShYH* – "the Messiah," "the Anointed One," or "anointed one" – is found in early Jewish literature only in the Dead Sea Scrolls and the Old Testament Pseudepigrapha. But even in these two collections it is not abundant. Of ninety-six significant documents produced by the Qumran Essenes, the Damascus Document, only 11Q Melchizedek, 4Q Patriarchal Blessings, 1QSa, and 1QS contain this technical term. The latter document – the Rule of the Community – furthermore, is preserved partially in a fragment from Cave IV; and it does not contain the famous reference to two Messiahs. Of 65 documents in the Pseudepigrapha many are too late for inclusion in our present quest; yet only a small minority of the remaining early Jewish writings contain explicit references to the Messiah. We have presented and discussed each of these, namely the Psalms of Solomon, the Similitudes of Enoch (which are entwined with intricate thoughts about the Messiah and his other titles), 4 Ezra, and 2 Baruch (the authors of the latter two have inherited but not really digested a wide range of traditions regarding the Messiah). In many of the Pseudepigrapha, namely Jubilees, the Testament of Moses, Pseudo-Philo, and the Life of Adam and Eve, the term "the Messiah" is surprisingly and conspicuously absent.

Some early Jews did not look for the coming of a Messiah. They contended that God himself would act; he would punish the gentiles. Listen, for example, to the words of the author of the Testament of Moses:

> For God Most High will surge forth,
> the Eternal One alone.

In full view will he come to work vengeance on the nations.
Yea, all their idols will he destroy.
Then will you be happy, O Israel!
And you will mount up above the necks
and the wings of an eagle.
Yea, all things will be fulfilled.
(10:7–8)

The statement, "the Eternal One alone," is conceivably an antimessianic pronouncement and a caution against overt revolutionary action. Since this document was either composed or redacted in the first century C.E., such seemingly pacifistic statements are highly significant in our present search.

During the time of Jesus of Nazareth some religious Jews were apparently arguing that trust and hope should be placed in God alone and not in the advent of a Messiah, and that one must not revolt against the heathen Romans because God himself is to defeat them. So articulated, the thoughts of the Testament of Moses are reminiscent of the War Scroll. They also recall the words attributed to Jesus and assembled into the great Sermon on the Mount, notably the blessing on the peacemakers (Matt. 5:9), the injunction to turn the other cheek (Matt. 5:38–42), and the exhortation to love one's enemies (Matt. 5:43–48).

The Third Question

Our third question is the following: "Did not Jesus' earliest followers recognize and categorize him as the Messiah and call him Jesus the Christ, or simply Jesus Christ?" The answer may seem simple, but it is complex. There are four stages to be covered in attempting to answer it.
Stage I. By the time of Jesus, or the beginning of the first century C.E., Palestinian Jews had developed deep and variegated beliefs regarding the coming of the Messiah. They may not have been as widespread as many publications tend to indicate, yet they are part of the first-century Palestinian Jewish Zeitgeist.[62] As E. Rivkin states, the messianic idea (or ideas) had emerged "as a viable concept in the time of Jesus."[63] If we are impressed with the absence of any reference to the Messiah in some Dead Sea Scrolls and Pseudepigrapha it is because we have found it impressively articulated in others.
Stage II. The conclusion that Jesus' earliest followers recognized and categorized him as the Messiah is impossible. The gospels are unanimous in recording that the disciples were confused men; according to Mark, the disciples are unable to comprehend who Jesus is or what he intends to

accomplish. They are portrayed following him as somewhat stupefied men.

Apparently Peter told Jesus, "You are the Christ" (*su ei ho christos;* Mark 8:29). But this brief verse is the famous exception to the rule; and we have no clues as to what Peter may have meant by this word, which is certainly a title.[64]

Most Christians assume Jesus accepted Peter's confession. In the Marcan narrative, our earliest source, the next word Jesus says to Peter is, "Get behind me Satan." Did Jesus accept the confession of Peter?

The conservative scholar G. E. Ladd recognizes the difficulties inherent in the usual unexamined assumption. He concludes, therefore, that "by Messiah, Peter means the one who is to fulfill the Old Testament messianic hope, *even though it is not in terms of a conquering king.*"[65] This solution is informed and does struggle with the problems, but there is absolutely no indication that this meaning is the one intended by Peter; moreover, Peter is said to have used the terminus technicus "the Messiah" (Greek translation: "the Christ").

Many scholars have concluded, perhaps reluctantly, that Jesus did not accept Peter's confession, and that Matthew totally rewrites the entire tradition of this pericope. Many specialists are persuaded that Mark or earlier Christians have added the prediction of future suffering by Jesus (Mark 8:31–32a) and that originally the tradition read as follows:

> And [Jesus] asked them, "But, who do you say that I am?" Peter, answering, said to him, "You are the Christ." But turning and seeing his disciples, he rebuked Peter, and said, "Get behind me, Satan! You are not on the side of God, but of men."

R. H. Fuller is thereby persuaded to conclude that "Jesus rejects Messiahship as a merely human and even diabolical temptation."[66]

If this tradition can finally be traced back to Jesus himself, as many scholars, myself included, are persuaded, then Jesus rejects the title "the Messiah." Why would he do this?

There are numerous answers. Since there were many definitions of the title, even contradictory ones (as we have seen), then chaos could have resulted by accepting an ill-defined title, especially one that would have aroused strong emotions.[67] The most persuasive reason – according to my own research – is that if Jesus thought he was the Messiah he would have falsified the very possibility of being the Messiah by any messianic claim, since only God himself may announce the Messiah's identity, according to some early Jewish texts. The questions regarding Jesus' own self-understanding, however, are not those we are now trying to comprehend and answer.[68]

We are presently focusing on the claim that the earliest followers used the term "the Messiah" or "the Christ" to articulate the particular significance of Jesus. The early pre-Pauline confession in Romans 1:3–4, probably the earliest confession we possess,[69] is highly significant in our examination of this claim. According to it, Jesus is hailed as "Christ." The good news Paul received is,

> concerning his (God's) son
> who came
> from the seed of David
> according to the flesh,
> who was designated Son of God
> in power
> according to the spirit of holiness
> by the resurrection from the dead,
> Jesus Christ *(Christou)* our Lord.

The confession, however, is really about the celebration of the identity of "God's Son." That is the central title in this confession. Its presence here should warn us not to focus on the title "Christ" and so become blind to the many other titles attributed to Jesus. K. Wengst, H. von Campenhausen, and more recently J. C. Beker have clarified the multiple kerygmata in the early Christian communities.[70] There was no set creed, no normative confession, no pontificated title that was binding. Many early Christians may well have denied that Jesus had been the Messiah; some may have expected him to return as the Messiah (cf. Acts 3:20); others may have believed that "Lord," "Servant," "Prophet," "Son of Man," "the Righteous One," "the Lamb," or "Wisdom" were more representative titles.

The kerygma attributed by Luke (the author of Acts) to the earliest followers of Jesus in Jerusalem is most accurately reflected in Acts 3, according to many critical scholars.[71] Note the numerous titles employed by Luke (according to Acts):

> The God of Abraham and of Isaac and of Jacob, the God of our fathers, glorified his *servant* Jesus, whom you delivered up and denied in the presence of Pilate, when he had decided to release him. But you denied *the Holy and Righteous One,* and asked for a murderer to be granted to you, and killed the *Author of life,* whom God raised from the dead. (Acts 3:13–15; Revised Standard Version; italics mine)

According to this kerygma the citizens of Jerusalem are not forced to believe that Jesus had been, or is, the Messiah or the Christ.

Stage III. By about 50 C.E. in many, but not all, circles the dominant title was "the Christ." By about that time it had been so closely identified with Jesus of Nazareth that he was called Jesus Christ. Paul customarily uses "Christ" as a proper name and refers to Jesus as Jesus Christ, Christ Jesus, or simply Christ.

Stage IV. The early Christians inherited four main sources for comprehending and explaining the term "Christ." They obviously inherited the many tributaries of Early Judaism, not only those concerning the Messiah and other messianic figures, but also the independent one concerning the belief in the resurrection of the dead. The title attributed to Jesus was shaped profoundly by the claim that Jesus had been raised from the dead by God. Also, the messianic consciousness of the early Christians was shaped by the crucifixion of Jesus. Finally, Jesus' own life and teachings helped remint traditional concepts and titles.

A brilliant and erudite Jewish scholar, Rivkin, very perceptively framed the essential insight:

> Yet we know, Jews no less than Christians, that the cross was the beginning, not the end. It was the birth of a viable and vital messianic idea, an idea proclaimed by Jews, for Jews, and out of the stuff of regnant Judaism. What gave life to the crucified Messiah was the Pharisaic belief in the resurrection of the dead. . . . It dawned on them [the disciples and other early Christians] that the proof of Jesus's claim to be Christ was his resurrection. . . . For them, to deny that they had seen him resurrected was as inconceivable as to deny that he had been crucified.[72]

It certainly can be doubted that Jesus claimed to be Christ, that there was a regnant Judaism, and that the belief in the resurrection of the dead should be labeled Pharisaic. The central thrust is axiomatic: The study of christology begins within the history of Early Judaism, and it is also indissolubly linked with the particularity of Jesus' own life, teachings, death, and resurrection (as described by the members of the Palestinian Jesus Movement).[73] Perhaps we must now also include the possibility that christology has some relation to Jesus' own self-understanding and intentionality.

Conclusion

The above discussion reveals that we must attend carefully to the extant documents and assess each passage in terms of its own peculiar context, and each word and phrase in light of its own particular function. It would be a non sequitur to the preceding methodology to summarize our position. Suffice it to be stated now that Jewish messianology does not flow majestically into Christian christology. From the thirties of the first century until today those who have followed Jesus have found the essence of the faith not centralized in one title or even a series of titles. They have often found, as did many of the devout in early Judaism, that the ineffable embodies the essential.

> Jesus said to his disciples, "Make a comparison to me and tell me whom I am like." . . . Thomas said to him, "Master *(sah)*, my mouth is incapable of saying whom you are like."
> (Gospel of Thomas Log. 13)

NOTES

1 This is a neologism I have created in order to clarify and simplify a comparison of Jewish beliefs in a Messiah and Christian contentions that Jesus is the long-awaited Messiah; or succinctly to juxtapose and compare messianology and christology. For the thoughts that led to this neologism see my 1985 inaugural lecture published in *The Princeton Seminary Bulletin* 6 (1985) 98–115.

2 P. Grelot, "Messiah," in *Sacramentum Mundi: An Encyclopedia of Theology* (New York: Herder, 1969) vol. 4, p.14.

3 W. Vischer, "Everywhere the Scripture is about Christ Alone," in *The Old Testament and Christian Faith: A Theological Discussion,* ed. B. W. Anderson (New York, London: Harper, 1963), p. 100.

4 Ibid., p. 101.

5 Ibid., p. 97.

6 C. Geertz, "The Discussion," in *Religion and Progress in Modern Asia,* ed. R. N. Bellah (New York: Free Press, 1965), p. 155.

7 J. H. Charlesworth, *The Old Testament Pseudepigrapha and the New Testament: Prolegomena for the Study of Christian Origins (Studiorum Novi Testamenti Societas* Monograph Series 54: Cambridge: Cambridge University Press, 1985).

8 J. Neusner, *Revisioning the Written Records of a Nascent Religion* (Formative Judaism: Religious, Historical, and Literary Studies, 5th Series; Brown Judaic Studies 91; Chico, Calif.: Scholars, 1985); see pp. 2–5.

9 W. Harrelson, "The Messianic Hope," in *Judaism, 200 B.C.–A.D. 200,* ed. J. H. Charlesworth (Evanston, Ill.: Religion and Ethics Institute, 1983), J3, p.1.

10 R. de Vaux, *Ancient Israel: Its Life and Institutions,* trans. J. McHugh (London: Darton, Longman & Todd, 1965 [2d. ed.]), pp. 103–4.

11 For good discussions of the priests and high priests in the first century C.E. see J. Jeremias, "The Clergy," in *Jerusalem in the Time of Jesus: An Investigation into Economic and Social Conditions During the New Testament Period,* with author's revisions, trans. F. H. and C. H. Cave (London, Philadelphia: Fortress, 1969) pp. 148–221; H. D. Mantel, "The High Priesthood and the Sanhedrin in the Time of the Second Temple," in *The Herodian Period,* ed. M. Avi-Yonah, assistant editor Z. Baras (The World History of the Jewish People, First

Series, Volume 7; Jerusalem, New Brunswick, N.J.: Rutgers Univ. Press, 1975), pp. 264–81; M. Stern, "Aspects of Jewish Society: The Priesthood and Other Clases," in *The Jewish People in the First Century: Historical Geography, Political History, Social, Cultural and Religious Life and Institutions* (Compendia Rerum Iudaicarum ad Novum Testamentum; Section 1, volume 2; Assen/ Amsterdam: Van Gorcum, 1976), pp. 561–630.

12 S. Mowinckel, *He That Cometh,* trans. G. W. Anderson (New York: Abingdon, 1956), p. 3. Of course, not only a king and a priest were designated God's anointed one, but these two figures are the dominant ones. Any one who was deemed to be "anointed" by God and commissioned to perform a significant function in the history of salvation could be called "the anointed one" with or without capitals, since such distinctions are impossible in Hebrew, Aramaic, and Greek. Even a foreigner, like the Persian Cyrus (cf. Isa. 45), could be called "the Anointed" of the Lord. For a brief study see Charlesworth, "Messiah," in *Illustrated Dictionary and Concordance of the Bible* (Jerusalem: Jerusalem Publishing House, in press).

13 I use the singular "belief" at this time intentionally; of course, it will become clear that we are confronted with beliefs. For a recent study of the concept of the Messiah in the Targumim, see S. H. Levey, *The Messiah: An Aramaic Interpretation: The Messianic Exegesis of the Targum* (Monographs of the Hebrew Union College 2; New York: Hebrew Union College Press, 1974).

14 The study will be published in the near future. See the contributions in this volume by S. Talmon.

15 J. T. Milik, in his review of P. Wernberg-Møller's *The Manual of Discipline Translated and Annotated, with an Introduction,* in *Revue biblique* 67 (1960): 411. On the absence of the *locus classicus* in 4QS see the judicious comments by Caquot in *Qumrân: Sa piété, sa théologie et son milieu,* ed. M. Delcor (Bibliotheca Ephemeridum Theologicarum Lovaniensium 46; Paris: Duculot, 1978), p. 237: "À l'époque même de Jean Hyrcan, si l'on se fie à la datation maintenant proposée pour le plus ancien rouleau de la *Règle* (4Q Se), le messianisme essénien est encore dans les limbes puisque la phrase du rouleau de la grotte I (IQS 9, 11) ' . . . jusqu'à le venue du prophète et des messies d'Aaron et d'Israël' n'y figure pas." Also see E. M. Laperrousaz in *L'attente du Messie en Palestine à la veille et au début de l'ère chrétienne* (Collection empreinte dirigée par Henri Hierche; Paris: A. and J. Picard, 1982), pp. 81–92. Laperrousaz rightly contends that "le premier témoignage d'une attente messianique, dans les textes de Qoumrân, serait, justement, ce passage de la *Règle* (IX, 11)" (p. 87).

16 See J. Murphy-O'Connor, "An Essene Missionary Document? CD (Damascus Document) II, 14–VI, 1," *Revue biblique* 77 (1970): 201–29; "A Literary Analysis of Damascus Document VI, 2–VIII, 3." *Revue biblique* 78 (1971): 210–32; "The Original Test of CD 7:9–8:2 = 19:5–14." *Harvard Theological Review* 64 (1971): 379–86; "The Critique of the Princes of Judah (CD VIII, 3–19)," *Revue biblique* 79 (1972): 200–16; "The Translation of Damascus Document VI, 11–14," *Revue de Qumran* 7 (1971): 553–6; "A Literary Analysis of Damascus Document XIX, 33–XX, 34," *Revue biblique* 79 (1972):

544–64. Murphy-O'Connor tends to agree with H. Stegemann's reconstruction of the history of the Essenes just prior to the exodus to Qumran; the Wicked Priest is Jonathan, and most importantly, the Righteous Teacher was the Zadokite high priest who was deposed by Jonathan. In his *Die Entstehung der Qumrangemeinde* (Bonn, 1971) Stegemann critically examined CD. More recently P. R. Davies, in *The Damascus Covenant: An Interpretation of the "Damascus Document"* (Journal for the Study of the Old Testament, Supplement Series 25; Sheffield: Journal for the Study of the Old Testament Press, 1983), concludes that CD "*as a whole is basically older than the Qumran community,* and that our available manuscripts (from Cairo and presumably also from the Qumran caves) represent a Qumranic recension" (p. 2; italics his).

17 For an assessment of the evolutionary history of the Qumran Essenes, see Charlesworth, "The Origin and Subsequent History of the Authors of the Dead Sea Scrolls: Four Transitional Phases Among the Qumran Essenes," *Revue de Qumran* 10 (1980): 213–33.

18 The editors of the new Schürer mislead their readers when they conclude a study of "The Qumran Messiahs and Messianism" with the following advice:

> If the messianism of Qumran originated in a political movement to restore a rightful High Priest to the pontifical throne, it developed in time into a full-blown messianic doctrine *(sic)* within the context of an apocalyptic eschatology having a transcendental as well as a historical dimension. (Vol. 2, p. 554)

We have shown why this conclusion is improper; unfortunately Vermes and his co-workers are not informed of the redactional nature of 1QS and the important fragments of the Rule found in Cave IV.

19 I have tried to demonstrate why in the study of the Dead Sea Scrolls *all* methodologies are requisite. We must be fully informed of all aspects of Qumran research, including those which are archeological, paleographical, orthographical, philological, theological, historical, and redactional. These are the seven methodologies of Qumran research. To avoid the errors of the past we must be informed by, and indeed utilize, each of them; moreover, we must consult all copies or fragments of a document, avoid the tendency to posit developments, acknowledge the evolutionary theology reflected by the history of the Qumran Essenes, be open to the possibility that more than a group of so-called Essenes were living at Qumran in the early portions of the first century B.C.E., and acknowledge the partial knowledge with which we historians must struggle (how many of the Qumran Scrolls have been lost, intentionally or inadvertently destroyed in this century, or decayed over the last millennium?).

20 On the concept of the Suffering Servant, see the following books by L. Ruppert: *Jesus als der leidende Gerechte? Der Weg Jesu im Lichte eines alt- und zwischentestamentlichen Motivs* (Stuttgarter Bibelstudien 59; Stuttgart: KWB Verlag, 1972); *Der leidende Gerechte: Eine motivgeschichtliche Untersuchung zum*

Alten Testament und zwischentestamentlichen Judentum (Forschung zur Bibel 5; Würzburg: Echter Verlag, 1972); *Der leidende Gerechte und seine Feinde: Eine Wortfelduntersuchung* (Würzburg: Echter Verlag, 1973).

21 The Testaments of the Twelve Partriarchs is a Jewish composition that has been heavily redacted by Christians. See Charlesworth, *The Old Testament Pseudepigrapha and the New Testament,* pp. 36, 38–40. For discussions of the messianism in the T12P see the following: P. Volz, *Die Eschatologie der jüdischen Gemeinde im neutestamentlichen Zeitalter* (Tübingen: Mohr, 1934) pp. 180–1. J. Klausner, *The Messianic Idea in Israel from its Beginning to the Completion of the Mishnah,* trans. W. F. Stinespring (London: George Allen and Unwin, 1956), pp. 310–16; V. Tsakonas, "The Teaching Concerning the Messiah in the Testaments of the Twelve Patriarchs," *Timetikos Tomos V. M. Vellas* (Athens, 1969 [in modern Greek]), pp. 687–93; B.-A. Shemer, *The Messianic Idea of the Testaments of the Twelve Patriarchs* (Tel Aviv, 1970 [in modern Hebrew]). M. de Jonge, *Studies on the Testaments of the Twelve Patriarchs: Text and Interpretation* (Studia in Veteris Testamenti Pseudepigrapha 3; Leiden: Brill, 1975) pp. 183–246. P. G. R. de Villiers, "The Messiah and Messiahs in Jewish Apocalyptic," *Neotestamentica* (1979): 1–29; Laperrousaz, *L'Attente du Messie,* pp. 138–48; Charlesworth, "The SNTS Pseudepigrapha Seminars from 1976 to 1983; 1976 (Durham, N.C.; Duke University): The Testaments of the Twelve Patriarchs," in *The Old Testament Pseudepigrapha and the New Testament,* pp. 94–102.

22 See my methodological discussion in "The Concept of the Messiah in the Pseudepigrapha," in *Aufstieg und Niedergang der Römischen Welt,* Vol.2.19.1 (Berlin, N.Y.: Walter de Gruyter, 1979) pp. 188–218, see especially pp. 195–6. Other publications on the concept of the Messiah in the Pseudepigrapha are the following selected works: Volz, *Die Eschatologie der jüdischen Gemeinde;* Klausner, *The Messianic Idea in Israel;* U. B. Müller, *Messias und Menschensohn in jüdischen Apokalypsen und in der Offenbarung des Johannes* (Studien zum Neuen Testament 6; Gütersloh: Mohn, 1972); P. G. R. de Villiers in *Neotestamentica* (1979): 1–29. Charlesworth, "Messianism and Christology: A Major Problematic Term," in *The Old Testament Pseudepigrapha and the New Testament,* pp. 87–90. For a bibliographical list see Charlesworth, "Messianism," in *The Pseudepigrapha and Modern Research, with a Supplement* (Society of Biblical Literature, Septuagint and Cognate Studies Series 7S; Chico, Calif.: Scholars Press, 1981), pp. 57–61, 265–6. Also, see many of the publications listed in the preceding footnotes.

23 In *Die Psalmen Salomos: Ein Zeugnis Jerusalemer Theologie und Frömmigkeit in der Mitte des vorchristlichen Jahrhunderts* (Arbeiten zur Literatur und Geschichte des Hellenistischen Judentums 7; Leiden: Brill, 1977) J. Schüpphaus concludes that the Psalms of Solomon is the "klassische Quelle für den Pharisäismus" (p. 158). This conclusion is not probable; see the reasons given in my review of this book in the *Journal of the American Academy of Religion* 50.2 (1982): 292–3. Unfortunately many scholars still incorrectly assume that the Psalms of Solomon is Pharisaic. S. Holm-Nielsen offered the opinion that "die PsSal

der pharisäischen Geistesrichtung entsprechen, kann nicht bezweifelt werden" (p. 59). See his *Die Psalmen Salomos* (Jüdische Schriften aus hellenistischrömischer Zeit 4.2; Gütersloh: Mohn, 1977). M. de Goeij claimed, "Tot voor enige decennia werd algemeen aangenomen dat de pss afkomstig waren uit farizeese kringen" (p. 16). Consult his "Psalmen van Salomo," in *De Pseudepigrafen* (Kampen: Kok, 1980).

Long ago R. Kittel contended,

> So werden die Gegner, d.h. die Sadduzäer und ihr Anhang, als Ganzes verurteilt, und sie sind darum schon an sich die Gottlosen und Sünder, wogegen des Dichters Freunde, die Pharisäer, schon an sich die Frommen, Gerechten und Heiligen sind." (p. 129)

These comments were published in the classic German edition of the Pseudepigrapha; cf. Kittel's "Die Psalmen Salomos," in *Die Apokryphen und Pseudepigraphen des Alten Testaments,* 2 vols., ed. E. Kautzsch (Darmstadt: Wissenschaftliche Buchgesellschaft, 1975 [reprint: Tübingen, 1900, 1921]. The author(s) of the Psalms of Solomon may have had the Sadduccees as opponents and the Pharisees as friends; but such speculations do not make the document Pharisaic. We must be far more critical in our historical reconstructions. First-century B.C.E. Jerusalem was characterized by many Jewish groups; and the Pharisees were themselves subdivided into numerous subgroups. J. Neusner rightly stresses that "the three sources of Pharisaism – Josephus, the Gospels, and the Talmudic traditions about pre-70 'rabbis,' all of them shaped after 70 A.D. – cannot be moulded into a single continuous narrative" (Jacob Neusner, *From Politics to Piety: The Emergence of Pharisaic Judaism* [New York, Englewood Cliffs, N.J.: Prentice-Hall, 1979; 2nd ed.] p. xx).

24 J. Trafton has been able to show that the Syriac recension is important. His study is the first thorough comparison of the Greek and Syriac, and he concludes that the Syriac is sometimes dependent upon the Greek and probably sometimes upon the lost Hebrew original. See his forthcoming monograph on the Psalms of Solomon.

25 The division of lines brings out the functions of the Messiah and is by me; the translation is by R. B. Wright and is published in *The Old Testament Pseudepigrapha*, ed. J. H. Charlesworth (Garden City, N.Y.: Doubleday, 1985) Vol. 2, in press. All translations of the Pseudepigrapha, unless otherwise noted, are according to this edition (Vol. 1 is dated 1983).

The brilliant philologist and historian, A. Piñero Sáenz aptly states:

> En medio del lamento pro la triste situación moral del pueblo elegido brilla la esperanze del Mesías. Dios suscitará su Ungido (17,21), como cumplimiento de su alianza y promesa (7,10;17,4), que vendrá a poner orden en un caos pecaminoso. El Mesías es un ser maravilloso, recipiendiario de los dones del Espíritu divino (17,37), lugarteniente de Yahvé sobre la tierra, ejecutor de su teocracia.

See his "Salmos de Salomon," in *Apocrifos del Antiguo Testamento,* ed. A. Diez Macho et al. (Madrid: Ediciones Cristiandad, 1982) Vol. 3, p. 19.

26 J. Bowker, *The Targums and the Rabbinic Literature* (Cambridge: Cambridge University Press, 1969), p. 278. For another translation see S. H. Levey, *The Messiah: An Aramaic Interpretation. The Messianic Exegesis of the Targum* (Monographs of the Hebrew Union College 2; New York: Hebrew Union College Press, 1974) p. 9.

27 See the report on the two SNTS seminars, one in Tubingen and the other in Paris, on the date and character of the Similitudes of Enoch; it is published in Charlesworth, *The Old Testament Pseudepigrapha and the New Testament,* pp. 102–10. Also, see the judicious comments on 1 Enoch in the present volume by G. W. E. Nickelsburg.

28 The conclusion to the Similitudes is the revelation that Enoch is himself the Son of Man (cf. 1 En. 71:14) and this attribution is unthinkable for a Christian in the first century, according to my understanding of that period. This argument is developed by B. Lindars in "Re-enter the Apocalyptic Son of Man," *New Testament Studies* 22 (1975/1976): 52–72.

L. Fusella wisely states,

> Gli argomenti del Milik non sono convincenti. . . . Scrivere un'opera sul messianismo cristiano senza che ci sia nessun accenno alla vita di Gesù, e in particolare alla sua sofferenza, è impossibile.

See his "Libro di Enoc," in *Apocrifi dell'Antico Testamento,* ed. P. Sacchi (Classici delle religioni, La religione ebraica; Turin: Unione Tipografico–Editrice Torinese, 1981), pp. 436–37.

29 The odd man out is M. A. Knibb, who thinks that the Similitudes of Enoch were composed around "the end of the first century A.D." (p. 359). See his "The Date of the Parables of Enoch: A Critical Review," *New Testament Studies* 25 (1979): 324–59. In a recent study, G. Bampfylde concludes his examination of the date of the Similitudes with these words: "The original parables or psalms in Sim. En. were composed by 50 BC at the latest" (p. 31). See his "The Similitudes of Enoch: Historical Allusions," *Journal for the Study of Judaism* 15 (1984): 9–31. Also see the brilliant article by J. C. Greenfield and M. E. Stone titled "The Enochic Pentateuch and the Date of the Similitudes," *Harvard Theological Review* 70 (1977): 51–65. A full monograph is devoted to the date of the Similitudes: D. W. Suter, *Tradition and Composition in the Parables of Enoch* (Society of Biblical Literature Dissertation Series 47; Missoula, Mont.: Scholars Press, 1979). For other publications see Charlesworth, *The Pseudepigrapha and Modern Research, with a Supplement.* After the present chapter was completed I received for review M. Black's erudite commentary on 1 Enoch; regarding the date of 37–71 he has much to say and concludes as follows: "In brief, Halévy and Charles were right in proposing a Hebrew *Urschrift* for the Book of the Parables, which I would date to the early Roman period, probably pre-70 A.D." (p. 188). See Black's *The Book of Enoch or I*

Enoch: A New English Edition (Studia in Veteris Testamenti Pseudepigrapha 7; Leiden: Brill, 1985).

30   The translation of R. H. Charles, published in *The Apocrypha and Pseudepigrapha of the Old Testament in English* (Oxford: Clarendon, 1913), Vol. 2, p. 127.

31   The translation of M. A. Knibb, published in his *The Ethiopic Book of Enoch: A New Edition in the Light of the Aramaic Fragments,* 2 vols. (Oxford: Clarendon, 1978), Vol. 2, p. 134.

32   Isaac in *OTP,* Vol. 1, p. 36.

33   G. W. E. Nickelsburg rightly points out that "Son of Man" in the Similitudes of Enoch is almost always qualified; He is called "that Son of Man," (e.g., 48:2, 69:29, 70:1, 71:17), or "the Son of Man," (46:3), or some other qualifying phrase is appended. Nickelsburg, however, goes too far when he states that "'Son of Man' is not a title" in the *Similitudes;* it is not a title in the same way "the Messiah" or "the Lord of the Spirits" is a title. Nickelsburg correctly states that "it cannot be excluded that the author (of the Similitudes) has in mind a human being glorified in heaven, with a face 'like one of the holy angels' (46:1)." See his *Jewish Literature Between the Bible and the Mishnah: A Historical and Literary Introduction* (Philadelphia: Fortress, 1981), p. 215.

34   R. H. Charles, *The Book of Enoch or 1 Enoch* (Oxford: Clarendon, 1912), p. 70, notes.

35   Ibid, p. 87. My research has led me to agree with Charles, and to disagree with many good scholars, namely D. H. Wallace, who concluded, "The Book of Enoch is best known for its doctrine of the Son of Man which has many messianic overtones. Yet he is not the Messiah, but a person much like Daniel's Son of Man." See his "Messiah," in *Baker's Dictionary of Theology,* p. 350.

36   Nickelsburg, *Jewish Literature,* p. 223. Similar conclusions have been announced by other excellent scholars. See J. Theisohn, *Der auserwählte Richter: Untersuchungen zum traditionsgeschichtlichen Ort der Menschensohngestalt der Bilderreder des Äthiopischen Henoch* (Studien zur Umwelt des Neuen Testaments 12; Göttingen: Vandenhoeck & Ruprecht, 1975); and F. Corriente and A. Piñero, "Libro 1 de Henoc *(et y gr),*" in *Apocrifos del Antiguo Testamento,* ed. A. Diez Macho et al. (Madrid, 1984), Vol. 4, p. 23.

37   Klausner, *The Messianic Idea in Israel,* p. 294.

38   B. M. Metzger in *OTP,* Vol. 1, p. 536. M. A. Knibb correctly states that 4 Ezra "takes as its starting-point the question whether the fate of Israel, with Jerusalem destroyed and her inhabitants taken into captivity, can be reconciled with the promises which God had made to her" (p. 100). See his "The Second Book of Esdras," in *The First and Second Books of Esdras,* by R. J. Coggins and M. A. Knibb (The Cambridge Bible Commentary; Cambridge & New York: Cambridge University Press, 1979). See the discussion on 4 Ezra in the present volume by M. E. Stone.

39   The Latin is taken from the new definitive edition: A. F. Klijn, *Der Lateinische Text der Apokalypse des Esra,* with an index grammaticus by G. Mussies (Texte und Untersuchungen zur Geschichte der altchristlichen Literatur 131; Berlin:

Akademie-Verlag, 1983). The Syriac is from the excellent edition by R. J. Bidawid: "4 Esdras," in *The Old Testament in Syriac According to the Peshitta Version,* Part IV, fascicle 3. Leiden: Brill, 1973.

40   See M. E. Stone, ed. and trans. *The Armenian Version of IV Ezra* (University of Pennsylvania Armenian Texts and Studies 1; Missoula, Mont.: Scholars Press, 1979), pp. 108–9.

41   See the discussion of the differences between redactions and interpolations in Charlesworth, *The Old Testament Pseudepigrapha and the New Testament,* pp. 99–102.

42   "Among the residents of the region beyond Jordan was a woman named Mary . . . eminent by reason of her family and fortune, who had fled with the rest of the people to Jerusalem and there become involved in the siege . . . while famine coursed through her intestines and marrow and the fire of rage (against the brutality of fellow Jews in Jerusalem) was more consuming even than the famine. . . . Seizing her child, an infant at the breast, . . . she slew her son, and then, having roasted the body and devoured half of it, she covered up and stored the remainder" (Josephus, *War* 6.201–8). For the Greek and English translation (presented above) see H. St. J. Thackeray, *Josephus* (The Loeb Classical Library; Cambridge, Mass.: Harvard, 1928, 1968), Vol. 3, pp. 434–7.

43   These are the words of Mowinckel in the English translation by Anderson of *He That Cometh,* p. 330; they were directed against the Targumic development of the concept of the Messiah. Medieval Jewish traditions must not be confused with pre-seventy Jewish beliefs.

44   Michael Stone, "The Concept of the Mesiah in IV Ezra," in *Religions in Antiquity: Essays in Memory of Erwin Ramsdell Goodenough,* ed. J. Neusner (Studies in the History of Religions 14 [Supplements to *Numen*]; Leiden: Brill, 1970), pp. 295–312. The quotation is from p. 312. See Stone's comments in the present work.

45   P. G. R. de Villiers correctly suggests that the avoidance of military means is because of the social setting: "Pseudo-Ezra was put wise by his experience of history: his Messiah is one accusing, denouncing and destroying the Romans – and then particularly in a judicial sense." *Neotestamentica* (1979): 21.

46   A good review of such attempts was published by A. L. Thompson, *Responsibility for Evil in the Theodicy of IV Ezra: A Study Illustrating the Significance of Form and Structure for the Meaning of the Book* (Society of Biblical Literature Dissertation Series 29; Missoula, Mont.: Scholars Press, 1977).

47   Klausner, *The Messianic Idea in Israel,* p. 331 (italics his).

48   The Syriac is taken from the excellent edition by S. Dedering: "Apocalypse of Baruch," *The Old Testament in Syriac,* Part IV, fascicle 3 (1973).

49   Charles in *Apocrypha and Pseudepigrapha of the Old Testament,* Vol. 2, p. 488.

50   P. Bogaert, *Apocalypse de Baruch,* 2 vols. (Sources chrétiennes 144, 145; Paris: Les Editions du Cerf, 1969), Vol. 1, p. 416.

51   R. H. Charles, *The Apocalypse of Baruch,* with an introduction by W. O. E.

Oesterley (Translations of Early Documents; London: Adam & Charles Black, 1918), p. xxxi.

52   See the review of the Adamic traditions by S. E. Robinson in his *The Testament of Adam: An Examination of the Syriac and Greek Traditions* (Society of Biblical Literature Dissertation Series 52; Chico, Calif.: Scholars Press, 1982), pp. 3–18.

53   H. Desroche, "Messianismus," *Die Religion in Geschichte und Gegenwart,* 3rd ed., Vol. 4, col. 895.

54   W. Koester and J. Schmid, "Messias," in *Lexikon für Theologie und Kirche,* 2nd ed., Vol. 7, col. 339.

55   For the Hebrew and English see P. Birnbaum (translator and editor), *Daily Prayer Book: Ha-Siddur Ha-Shalem* (New York: Hebrew Publishing Co., 1977), pp. 205–6.

56   See the definitive work by J. Heinemann, *Prayer in the Talmud: Forms and Patterns,* trans. R. S. Sarason (Studia Judaica: Forschungen zur Wissenschaft des Judentums 9; Berlin, N.Y.: W. de Gruyter, 1977); see especially p. 26.

57   Ibid., pp. 28–9.

58   The Hebrew is taken from S. Schechter, "Genizah Specimens," *The Jewish Quarterly Review* O.S., 10 (1898): 654–9.

59   R. D. Hecht in the present volume discusses the implications of the fact that Philo does not mention the term *christos.*

60   In addition to his chapter in the present volume, see the following major studies by J. Neusner: *Messiah in Context: Israel's History and Destiny in Formative Judaism* (Philadelphia: Fortress, 1984); "Messianic Themes and the Differentiation of Documents in the Rabbinic Canon of Late Antiquity," in the Delcor Festschrift, in press. For a considerably different perspective see B. Z. Wacholder, *Messianism and Mishnah: Time and Place in the Early Halakhah* (The Louis Caplan Lecture on Jewish Law; Cincinnati: Hebrew Union College Press, 1978). Also, see the brilliant reflections by E. E. Urbach in *The Sages: Their Concepts and Beliefs,* trans. I. Abrahams (Jerusalem: Magnes, 1979), Vol. 1, 308–14, 682–9, and vol. 2, notes.

61   Consult Josephus' account of the first Jewish war against Rome in the handy Loeb Classical Library edition, and the documents pertaining to the second Jewish war assembled by P. Schäfer, entitled *Der Bar Kokhba-Aufstand* (Texte und Studien zum Antiken Judentum 1: Tübingen: Mohr, 1981). An authoritative and brief review of the first war is found in P. Schäfer's *Geschichte der Juden in der Antike* (Stuttgart: Katholisches Bibelwerk, 1983), 135–57. Also see the erudite study by Martin Hengel, entitled "Messianische Hoffnung und politischer 'Radikalismus' in der 'jüdisch-hellenistischen Diaspora': Zur Frage der Voraussetzungen des jüdischen Aufstandes unter Trajan 115–117 n. Chr.," in *Apocalypticism in the Mediterranean World and the Near East,* ed. D. Hellholm (Tübingen: Mohr, 1983), pp. 655–86.

62   See the comments by A. Diez Macho in "Reino mesiánico en este mundo y reino de Dios en el mundo futuro," in *Introducción general a los apocrifos del*

Antiguo Testamento, ed. Diez Macho, et al. (Madrid: Ediciones Cristiandad, 1984), Vol. 1, pp. 376–88.

63   E. Rivkin, "The Meaning of Messiah in Jewish Thought," *Union Seminary Quarterly Review* 26 (1970/71): 383–406; the quotation is from p. 384.

64   See the insightful comments in the present volume by H. C. Kee and G. MacRae.

65   G. E. Ladd, *A Theology of the New Testament* (Grand Rapids, Mich.: Eerdmans, 1974), p. 142 (italics his).

66   R. H. Fuller, *The Foundations of New Testament Christology* (New York: Scribner, 1965), p. 109.

67   M. Smith has emphasized in numerous publications the "mutually contradictory programs" for the Messiah, the lack of uniformity within one group, and the absence of even one text that is a literary unity. He has also pointed out that the "most likely way to become a messiah was to begin as a robber." See his pertinent publications: "What is Implied by the Variety of Messianic Figures?" *Journal of Biblical Literature* 78 (1959): 66–72; "Messiahs: Robbers, Jurists, Prophets, and Magicians," *Proceedings of the American Academy for Jewish Research* 44 (1977): 185–95; the quotations above are from pp. 185 and 189 respectively.

68   See my reflections in the inaugural lecture published in the *Princeton Seminary Bulletin* 6 (1985): 98–115, and in *Jesus Within Judaism* (The Gunning Victoria Jubilee Lectures at the University of Edinburgh), in press.

69   The most recent study of this confession is by R. Jewett: "The Redaction and Use of an Early Christian Confession in Romans 1:3–4," in *The Living Text: Essays in Honor of Ernest W. Saunders,* ed. D. E. Groh and R. Jewett (Lanham, Md., New York, & London: University Press of America, 1985), pp. 99–122.

70   K. Wengst, *Christologische Formeln und Lieder des Urchristentums* (Studien zum Neuen Testament 7; Gütersloh: Mohn, 1972); H. von Campenhausen, "Das Bekenntnis in Urchristentum," *Zeitschrift für die neutestamentliche Wissenschaft* 63 (1972): 210–53; J. C. Beker, *Paul the Apostle: The Triumph of God in Life and Thought* (Philadelphia: Fortress, 1980), see especially 127–9.

71   See especially R. F. Zehnle, *Peter's Pentecost Discourse* (Society of Biblical Literature Monograph Series 15; New York: Abingdon, 1971), p. 136.

72   Rivkin in *Union Seminary Quarterly Review* 26 (1970/1971): 398.

73   See the following major contributions to the study of the earliest christologies (in chronological order): W. Marxsen, *The Beginnings of Christology,* trans. P. J. Achtemeier and L. Nieting, with an introduction by J. Reumann (Philadelphia: Fortress, 1969, 1979); M. Hengel, *The Son of God: The Origin of Christology and the History of Jewish–Hellenistic Religion,* trans. J. Bowden (Philadelphia: Fortress, 1976); C. F. D. Moule, *The Origin of Christology* (Cambridge & New York: Cambridge University Press, 1977, 1980); M. Hengel, *The Atonement: The Origins of the Doctrine in the New Testament,* trans. J. Bowden (Philadelphia: Fortress, 1981); M. Hengel, *Between Jesus and Paul: Studies in the Earliest History of Christianity,* trans. J. Bowden (Philadelphia: Fortress, 1983).

12

Mishnah and Messiah

JACOB NEUSNER

The Mishnah in the Context of Earlier Uses of the Messiah Theme

When the Temple of Jerusalem fell to the Babylonians in 586 B.C.E., Israelite thinkers turned to the writing of history to explain what had happened. From that time onward, with the composition of the Pentateuch and the historical books, Joshua, Judges, Samuel, and Kings, to teach the lessons of history, and of prophetic and apocalyptic books to interpret and project those lessons into the future, Israel explained the purpose of its being by focusing upon the meaning of events. The critical issue then was salvation: From what? For what? By whom? In that context, the belief in a supernatural man, an anointed savior or Messiah, formed a natural complement to a system in which teleology took the form of eschatology. Israelites do their duty because of what is happening and of where events will lead. All things point to a foreordained end, presenting the task of interpreting the signs of the times. No wonder, then, that when the Temple of Jerusalem fell to the Romans in C.E. 70, established patterns of thinking guided writers of Judaic apocalypse to pay attention to the meaning of history. In that setting, Jesus, whom Paul had earlier grasped in an essentially ahistoric framework, now turned out, in the hands of the writers of the Gospels, to be Israel's Messiah. He was *the* Messiah at the end of time, savior and redeemer of Israel from its historical calamity, thus a historical-political figure: king of the Jews.

The character of the Israelite Scriptures, with the emphasis upon historical narrative as a mode of theological explanation, leads us to expect Judaism to evolve as a deeply Messianic religion. With all prescribed actions pointed toward the coming of the Messiah at the end of time, and all interest focused upon answering the historical-salvific question – "how long?" – Judaism from late antiquity to the present day presents no surprises. Its liturgy evokes historical events to prefigure salvation; prayers of petition repeatedly turn to the speedy coming of the Messiah; and the experience of worship invariably leaves the devotee expectant and hopeful. Just as Rabbinic (now-normative) Judaism is a deeply Messianic religion, secular extensions of Judaism for their part have commonly proposed secularized versions of the established pattern of focus upon history and interest in the purpose and denouement of events. Teleology once more takes the form of eschatology embodied in messianic symbols.

Yet, for a brief moment, a vast and influential document presented a kind of Judaism in which history did not define the main framework, in which the issue of teleology took a form other than the familiar, eschatological one, and, in consequence, in which historical events were absorbed, through their trivialization in taxonomic structures, into a non-historical system. In the kind of Judaism at hand in this document, messiahs did figure. But these "anointed men" played no historical role. They undertook a task quite different from that assigned to Jesus by the framers of the Gospels. *Messiahs were merely a species of priest, falling into one classification rather than another.*

That document is the Mishnah, ca. C.E. 200, a strange corpus of normative statements we may, though with some difficulty, classify as a law code or a school book for philosophical jurists. The difficulty of classification derives from the contents of the document, which deal with the topics to the bulk of which we should be reluctant to assign the title "law." Composed in an age in which, on the Roman side as well, people were making law codes, the Mishnah presents a systematic account of the life of Israel, the Jewish people in the Land of Israel. The Mishnah comprises sixty-three tractates covering six categories of activity. These begin with rules for the conduct of the economy, that is, agriculture, with special attention to the farmers' provision of priestly rations. Second come rules for various special holy days and seasons, with special attention to the conduct of the sacrificial service and life of the Temple cult on such occasions, and corresponding conduct in the home. Third are rules governing the status of women, with particular interest in the transfer of a woman from the domain of one man to that of another. Fourth is a code of civil laws, covering all aspects of commercial, civil, and criminal law, and offering a blueprint for an Israelite government based on the Temple in Jerusalem and headed by a king and a high priest. Fifth, we find rules for the Temple's sacrificial service and for the upkeep of the Temple buildings and establishment, with emphasis upon the life of the cult on ordinary days. Finally, the Mishnah details taboos affecting the cultic life in the form of unclean things and rules on how to remove their effects.

This brief account of the document points toward its principal point of interest: sanctification. At issue is the life of Israel under the aspect of holiness, lived out in relationship to the Temple and under the governance of the priesthood. What has been said indicates also what the document neglects to treat: salvation, that is, the historical life of the Jewish nation, and where it is heading and how to get there. The Mishnah omits all reference to its own point of origin, thus lacking a historical account or a mythic base. The framers of the code likewise barely refer to Scripture, rarely produce proof texts for their own propositions, never imitate the modes of speech of ancient Hebrew, as do the writers of the Dead Sea Scrolls at Qumran. They hardly propose to explain the relationship between their book and the established holy Scriptures of Israel. As we shall see, the absence of sustained attention to events and a doctrine of history serves also to explain why the Messiah as an eschatological figure makes no appearance in the system of the Mishnah.

Accordingly, the later decades of the second century C.E., after the defeat of Bar Kokhba, witnessed the composition of the Mishnah, a vast book, later received as authoritative and turned into the foundations of the two Talmuds, one composed in Babylonia, the other in the Land of Israel, which define Judaism as we know it. If, then, we ask about the context in which this foundation-document of the rabbinic canon came into being, we find ourselves in an age that had witnessed yet another messianic war, fought by Israel against Rome, this one under Bar Kokhba, from 132 to 135. That war, coming three generations after the destruction of the Temple, aimed to regain Jerusalem and rebuild the Temple. It seems probable that Bar Kokhba in his own day was perceived as a messianic general, and the war as coming at the expected end of time, the eschatological climax to the drama begun in 70. If so, the character of the Mishnah, the work of the survivors of the war, proves truly astonishing. Here, as I said, we have an immense, systematic, and encompassing picture of the life of Israel, in which events scarcely play a role. History never intervenes. The goal and purpose find full and ample expression with scarcely a word about either the end of time or the coming of Messiah. In a word, the Mishnah presents us with a kind of Judaism possessed of an eschatology without Messiah, a teleology beyond time. When the point of insistence is sanctification, not salvation, in the Mishnah, we see the outcome.

The Messiah in the Mishnah

We now ask the Mishnah to answer the questions at hand. What of the Messiah? When will he come? To whom, in Israel, will he come? And what must, or can, we do, while we wait, to hasten his coming? If we now reframe these questions divested of their mythic cloak, we ask about the Mishnah's theory of the history and destiny of Israel and the purpose of the Mishnah's own system in relationship to Israel's present and end: the implicit teleology of the philosophical law at hand.

Answering these questions out of the resources of the Mishnah is not possible. The Mishnah presents no large view of history. It contains no reflection whatever on the nature and meaning of the destruction of the Temple in C.E. 70, an event that surfaces only in connection with some changes in the law explained as resulting from the end of the cult. The Mishnah pays no attention to the matter of the end-time. The word "salvation" is rare, "sanctification," in numerous forms, is commonplace. More strikingly, virtually silent on the teleology of its own system, the framers of the Mishnah never tell us why we should do what the Mishnah tells us, let alone explain what will happen if we do. Incidents in the Mishnah are preserved either as narrative settings for the statement of the law, or, occasionally, as precedents. Historical events are classified and turned into entries on lists. But incidents in any case come few and far between. True, events do make an impact. But it always is for the Mishnah's own purpose and within its own taxonomic system and list-making, rule-seeking mode of thought. To be sure, the framers of the Mishnah may also have had a theory of the Messiah and of the meaning of Israel's history and destiny. But they kept it hidden, and their document manages to provide an immense account of Israel's life without explicitly telling us about such matters. To what may be implicit I confess myself blind and deaf: I see and hear only thin echoes of a timeless eternity governed by orderly rules.

Let me digress to provide an important qualification to the argument that is to come. Since the Mishnah constitutes the foundation-document of its kind of Judaism, our interest is in that document as such, and not in other ideas that may or may not also have been held by its framers. Of these the Mishnah tells us nothing. What is assigned or attributed to them in later documents testifies only to what the framers of those documents thought their predecessors had stated long ago. Whether or not the Mishnah's authorities had actually made such statements we do not know. In the Mishnah we have ample evidence concerning the statements they did make in the document for which, along with Scripture, they secured recognition as Israel's constitution. Accordingly, the Mishnah, and the Mishnah alone, defines the original boundaries of the canon of Judaism as the rabbinic system. Whatever else second century thinkers may have believed surfaced only later on. It was not until the third, fourth, or fifth centuries that these other opinions, allegedly held in the second century, proved important and made their impact upon the public and collective statement in literature coming forth from rabbinical institutions and defining Rabbinic Judaism. So in the Mishnah we deal with what was official and definitive at the beginnings.

Now, to return to the argument, when we walk the frontiers laid out by the Mishnah, we turn inward to gaze upon a portrait of the world at rest, in which, as I said, events take place, but history does not. It is a world of things in the right place, each with its proper name, all in the appropriate classification. In the Mishnah's world, all things aim at stasis both in nature and in society, with emphasis upon proper order and correct form. As we saw, the world of the Mishnah in large part encompasses the cult, the priesthood, and protection of the cult from sources of danger and uncleanness. So the Mishnah presents a priestly conception of the world, creating a system aimed at the sanctification of Israel under the rule of the priests, as a holy people. The world subject to discussion encompasses a Temple, whose rules are carefully studied; a high priest, whose actions are meticulously chronicled; a realm of the clean and the holy, whose taboos are spelled out in exquisite detail.

But, since none of these things existed when the framers of the Mishnah wrote about them, the Mishnah turns out to be something other than what it appears. It purports to describe how things are. But it tells us about a fantasy much more than about the real, palpable world, the world concretely known to the people who wrote about it. So the Mishnah is a work of imagination – made up in the minds of the framers of the Mishnah. The Mishnah does not undertake a description of a real building out there, maintained by real flesh-and-blood people, burning up kidneys of real lambs whose smoke you can smell and see. It is all a realm of made-up memories, artificial dreams, hopes, yearnings. When we turn from the inner perspective to the sheltering world beyond, we see how totally fantastic was the fantasy. For the Mishnah provides prescriptions for preserving a world of stable order. But, living in the aftermath of Bar Kokhba's defeat, the framers of the Mishnah in fact carried on through chaos and crisis, paying the psychic, as much as the political, costs of catastrophic defeat.

Lacking a Temple or credible hope for one, for the first time in Israelite history in the millennium from the rule of David onward, the sages confronted an Israel without blood-rites to atone for sin and win God's favor. Under the circumstances, their minds might well have turned back to the time of David, therefore forward to the age in which David's heir and successor would come to restore the Temple and to rule Israel as God's anointed. Perhaps they did. Maybe in writing the Mishnah, they meant to describe how David's son would do things just as David had done things long ago. But if that was their purpose, they did not say so. And the one thing any student of the Mishnah knows is that its framers are pitiless in giving detail, in saying everything they wish, and in holding back – so far as we can tell – nothing we might need to know to plumb their meaning.

Yet we do not have to argue from their silence to find out what was in their minds. True, they speak little of the Messiah and rarely refer to events perceived as history. But they do record the events of the day when it serves their purposes. They do hint at the Messiah's coming. So, rather than harping on the absence of evidence, let us rapidly survey some facts. If, for example, they give us no doctrine of the Messiah, no stories about him, no account of where he will come from, how we shall know him, and what he will do, still, they do use the word "messiah." How do they use it?

In a legal context, the Mishnah's framers know the anointing of a leader in connection with two officials: the high priest consecrated with oil, in contrast to the one consecrated merely by receiving the additional garments that indicate the office of high priest (M. Mak. 2:6, M. Meg. 1:9, M. Hor. 3:4), and the (high) priest anointed for the purpose of leading the army in war (M. Sot. 7:2, 8:1, M. Mak. 2:6). When the Mishnah uses the word "messiah," in legal contexts the assumed meaning is always the anointed priest (M. Hor. 2:2, 3, 7, 3:4, 5).

Yet the Mishnah's framers know a quite separate referent for the same term. When they wish to distinguish between this age and the world to come, they speak (M. Ber. 1:5) of "this world and the days of the Messiah." That Messiah can only be the anointed savior of Israel. The reference is casual, the language routine, the purpose merely factual. Likewise, at M. Sotah 9:9–15 there is a reference to "the footsteps of the Messiah," again in the setting of the end of time and the age to come. That passage, a systematic eschatology, is critical for us in assessing whatever the Misnah offers as a theory of Israel's history, so we shall review it in its entirety. (Biblical verses are cited in italics.)

M. Sotah 9:9–15
9:9

> I. A.   When murderers became many, the rite of breaking the heifer's neck was cancelled.
>
> B.   [This was] when Eleazar b. Dinai came along, and he was also called Tehinah b. Perishah. Then they went and called him, "Son of a murderer."
>
> II. C.   When adulterers became many, the ordeal of the bitter water was cancelled.
>
> D.   And Rabban Yohanan b. Zakkai cancelled it, since it is said, *I will not punish your daughters when they commit whoredom, nor your*

daughters-in-law when they commit adultery, for they themselves go apart with whores (Hos. 4:14).

III. E. When Yose b. Yoezer of Seredah and Yose b. Yohanan of Jerusalem died, the grape-clusters were cancelled,

F. since it is said, *There is no cluster to eat, my soul desires the first ripe fig* (Mic. 7:1).

9:10

A. Yohanan, high priest, did away with the confession concerning tithe.

B. Also: He cancelled the rite of the Awakeners and the Stunners.

C. Until his time a hammer did strike in Jerusalem.

D. And in his time no man had to ask concerning doubtfully tithed produce.

9:11

IV. A. When the Sanhedrin was cancelled, singing at wedding feasts was cancelled, since it is said, *They shall not drink wine with a song* (Isa. 24:9).

9:12

V. A. When the former prophets died out, the Urim and Tummim were cancelled.

VI. B. When the sanctuary was destroyed, the Shamir-worm ceased and [so did] the honey of *supim.*

C. And faithful men came to an end,

D. since it is written, *Help, O Lord, for the godly man ceases* (Ps. 12:2).

E. Rabban Simeon b. Gamaliel says in the name of R. Joshua, "From the day on which the Temple was destroyed, there is no day on which there is no curse, and dew has not come down as a blessing. The good taste of produce is gone."

F. R. Yose says, "Also: the fatness of produce is gone."

9:13

A. R. Simeon b. Eleazar says, "[When] purity [ceased], it took away the taste and scent; [when] tithes [ceased], they took away the fatness of corn."

B. And sages say, "Fornication and witchcraft made an end to everything."

9:14

I. A. In the war against Vespasian they decreed against the wearing of wreaths by bridegrooms and against the wedding-drum.

II. B.   In the war against Titus they decreed against the wearing of wreaths by brides.

C.   And [they decreed] that a man should not teach Greek to his son.

III. D.   In the last war [Bar Kokhba's] they decreed that a bride should not go out in a palanquin inside the town.

E.   But our rabbis [thereafter] permitted the bride to go out in a palanquin inside the town.

9:15

A.   When R. Meir died, makers of parables came to an end.

B.   When Ben Azzai died, diligent students came to an end.

C.   When Ben Zoma died, exegetes came to an end.

D.   When R. Joshua died, goodness went away from the world.

E.   When Rabban Simeon b. Gamaliel died, the locust came, and troubles multiplied.

F.   When R. Eleazar b. Azariah died, wealth went away from the sages.

G.   When R. Aqiba died, the glory of the Torah came to an end.

H.   When R. Hanina b. Dosa died, wonder-workers came to an end.

I.   When R. Yose Qatnuta died, pietists went away.

J.   (And why was he called *Qatnuta*? Because he was the least of the pietists.)

K.   When Rabban Yohanan b. Zakkai died, the splendor of wisdom came to an end.

L.   When Rabban Gamaliel the Elder died, the glory of the Torah came to an end, and cleanness and separateness perished.

M.   When R. Ishmael b. Phiabi died, the splendor of the priesthood came to an end.

N.   When Rabbi died, modesty and fear of sin came to an end.

O.   R. Pinhas b. Yair says, "When the Temple was destroyed, associates became ashamed and so did free men, and they covered their heads.

P.   "And wonder-workers became feeble. And violent men and big talkers grew strong.

Q.   "And none expounds and none seeks [learning] and none asks.

I. R.   "Upon whom shall we depend? Upon our Father in heaven."

S.   R. Eliezer the Great says, "From the day on which the Temple was destroyed, sages began to be like scribes, and scribes like ministers, and ministers like ordinary folk.

T.   "And the ordinary folk have become feeble.

U.   "And none seeks.

II. V. "Upon whom shall we depend? Upon our Father in heaven."

W. With the footprints of the Messiah presumption increases, and dearth increases.

X. The vine gives its fruit and wine at great cost.

Y. And the government turns to heresy.

Z. And there is no reproof.

AA. The gathering place will be for prostitution.

BB. And Galilee will be laid waste.

CC. And the Gablan will be made desolate.

DD. And the men of the frontier will go about from town to town, and none will take pity on them.

EE. And the wisdom of scribes will putrefy.

FF. And those who fear sin will be rejected.

GG. And the truth will be locked away.

HH. Children will shame elders, and elders will stand up before children.

II. *For the son dishonors the father and the daughter rises up against her mother, the daughter-in-law against her mother-in-law; a man's enemies are the men of his own house* (Mic. 7:6).

JJ. The face of the generation is the face of a dog.

KK. A son is not ashamed before his father.

III. LL. Upon whom shall we depend? Upon our Father in heaven.

MM. Pinhas b. Yair says, "Heedfulness leads to [hygienic] cleanliness, [hygienic] cleanliness leads to [cultic] cleanness, [cultic] cleanness leads to abstinence, abstinence leads to holiness, holiness leads to modesty, modesty leads to the fear of sin, the fear of sin leads to piety, piety leads to the Holy Spirit, the Holy Spirit leads to the resurrection of the dead, and the resurrection of the dead comes through Elijah, blessed be his memory, Amen."

This is a long and rather complex construction. Concluding the tractate at hand, it is located after a legal passage on the topic of murder. I see the following large, free-standing units: (1) M. Sotah 9:9–12, on the gradual cessation of various rites, with an insertion at M. Sotah 9:10 and an addition at M. Sotah 9:13; (2) M. Sotah 9:14, a triplet appropriately inserted. The melancholy list (3) about how the deaths of various great sages form a counterpart to the decline in the supernatural life of Israel, M. Sotah 9:15 A–N, presents a rabbinic counterpart to the cultic construction at the outset. (4) M. Sotah 9:15 O–MM is diverse. But the main beam – the phrase, "Upon whom shall we depend? Upon our Father in heaven" – does show. It appears to me that M. Sotah 9:15 O–R form the bridge, since the theme of the foregoing, the decline of the age marked by the decay of the virtue associated with sages, is carried forward, while the key-phrase in what is to follow is introduced. W–LL then go over the matter yet again.

The Messiah, we notice, occurs rather incidentally and tangentially at M. Sotah 9:15W. The important statement is at M. Sotah 9:15M.M., Pinhas b. Yair's account of the steps toward the end of time. The important fact is that the Messiah does *not* mark off a rung. Instead Pinhas lays emphasis upon personal virtues, the very virtues any one may master if he keeps the law of the Mishnah, with its interest in particular in cultic cleanness, on the one side, and holiness, on the other. The virtue of each person governs the passage to the resurrection of the dead; everyone is supposed to be modest, fear sin, attain piety. All then are candidates, as potential sages, to receive the Holy Spirit. So far as the Mishnah's pages contain a view of history and a statement of the teleology of the law, it is in this brief statement of Pinhas, *and here alone.*

The insertion of Elijah as herald of the resurrection of the dead, of course, draws upon the well-known biblical allusion at Malachi 4:5, "Behold, I will send you Elijah the prophet before the great and terrible day of the Lord comes." The Mishnah's authors refer to Elijah as the forerunner of the end at M. Sheqalim 2:5, M. Baba Mesia 1:8, 2:8, 3:4–5. His task is defined as settling various disputed questions, in particular involving genealogy (M. Eduyyot 8:7). Allusion to Elijah here follows what again is a routine convention, established in Scripture, and in no way proposes a revision of it. For the philosophers of the Mishnah the figure of the Messiah presents no rich resource of myth or symbol. The Messiah forms part of the inherited, but essentially undifferentiated, background of factual materials. The figure is neither to be neglected nor to be exploited.

We therefore may hardly find astonishing the failure of the Mishnah's lawyers to pay attention to the possibility of a false Messiah, nor do we even know what sort of Messiah would fall into that classification. The main concern expressed in the law on people who might mislead Israel focuses upon false prophets (M. San. 11:1B, 11:5), and blasphemers (M. San. 7:2S). The principal concern is that people of this sort pose the danger of incitement to idolatry.

Accordingly, the figure of a Messiah at the end of time, coming to save Israel from whatever it is that Israel needs to be saved, plays a negligible role in the Mishnah's discourse. It follows that fear of the wrong sort of Messiah likewise scarcely comes to the surface. Whether, at M. Sanhedrin 7:2ff, idolatry or blasphemy in general served to encompass people who might falsely claim to inaugurate the end of time or to do the work of eschatological forgiveness of sins and the ultimate salvation of Israel, no one can say. It seems unlikely.

In all, the Messiah in the Mishnah does not stand at the forefront of the framers' consciousness. The issues encapsulated in the myth and person of the Messiah are scarcely addressed. The framers of the Mishnah do not resort to speculation about the Messiah as a historical-supernatural figure. So far as that kind of speculation provides the vehicle for reflection on salvific issues, in mythic terms – we cannot say that the mishnah's philosophers take up those encompassing categories of being: Where are we heading? What can we do about it? That does not mean questions found urgent in the aftermath of the destruction of the Temple and the disaster of Bar Kokhba failed to attract the attention of the Mishnah's sages. But they treated history in a different way, offering their own answers to its questions.

Eschatology without Messiah, Teleology beyond Time

At issue is the direction of eschatology in the foundation-document and its continuations. It is not merely whether, or how frequently, the figures of the Messiah and Elijah make an appearance, how often "the days of the Messiah" come under discussion, or how many references we find to "the end of days" or events we regard as historical. We focus upon how the system laid out in the Mishnah takes up and disposes of those critical issues of teleology worked out through messianic eschatology in other, earlier versions of Judaism. These earlier systems resorted to the myth of the Messiah as savior and redeemer of Israel, a supernatural figure engaged in political-historical tasks as king of the Jews, even a God-man facing the crucial historical questions of Israel's life and resolving them: the Christ as king of the world, of the ages, of death itself. Even though the figure of a Messiah does appear, when the framers of the Mishnah speak of "the Messiah," they mean a high priest designated and consecrated to office in a certain way, and not in some other way. The reference to "days of the Messiah" constitutes a given, a conventional division of history at the end-time but before the ultimate end. But that category of time differentiated plays no consequential role in the teleological framework established within the Mishnah. Accordingly, the Mishnah's framers constructed a system of Judaism in which the entire teleological dimension reached full exposure with scarcely a hint of a need to invoke the person or functions of a Messianic figure of any kind. Perhaps, in the aftermath of Bar Kokhba's debacle, silence on the subject served to express a clarion judgment. I am inclined to think so. But, for the purpose of our inquiry, the main thing is a simple fact, now fully expounded and illustrated.

The issue of eschatology, framed in mythic terms, draws in its wake the issue of how, in the foundation-document of Judaism, history comes to full conceptual expression. History as an account of a meaningful pattern of events, making sense of the past and giving guidance about the future, begins with the necessary conviction that singular events matter, one after another. The Mishnah's framers present us with no elaborate theory of events, a fact fully consonant with their systematic points of insistence and encompassing concern. Events do not matter, one by one. The philosopher-lawyers exhibited no theory of history either. Their conception of Israel's destiny in no way called upon historical categories of either narrative or didactic explanation to describe and account for the future. The small importance attributed to the figure of the Messiah as a historical-eschatological figure, therefore, fully accords with the larger traits of the system as a whole. Let me speak with emphasis: *If what is important in Israel's existence is sanctification, an ongoing process, and not salvation, understood as a one-time event at the end, then no one will find reason to narrate history.* Few then will form the obsession about the Messiah so characteristic of Judaism in its later, rabbinic mode. But the Messiah then will wear rabbinical cloak and draw Israel to accept the Talmuds' ironic conception of the holy life. Salvation comes through sanctification – just as M. Sotah 9:15 indicates. Then the salvific figure becomes an instrument of consecration and so fits into a system quite different from one built to begin with around the Messiah in particular.

When, in analyzing the foundations of Judaism, we move from species and eschatology upward to genus and teleology, we find ourselves addressing head-on the motives and goals of the mishnaic system. The system is so constructed as *not* to point toward a destination at the end of time. But still it does speak of last things. Accordingly, we ask, where, if not in the eschaton, do things end up? The answer provided by Mishnah-Tractate Abot, the Mishnah's first apologetic, is clear: "Where do we head? Where do we go? Below, below, below." Death is the destination. In life we prepare for the voyage. We keep the law in order to make the move required of us all. What is supposed in Abot to make the system work, explaining why we should do the things the Mishnah says, is that other end, the end to which history and national destiny prove remote, or, rather, irrelevant. So, as is clear, Abot constructs a teleology beyond time, providing a purposeful goal for every individual. Life is the antechamber, death, the destination; what we do is weighed and measured. When we die, we stand on one side of the balance, our life and deeds on the other.

The Mishnah's teleology supplied by Abot presents a curious contrast to the focus of the Mishnah itself. Abot addresses the life of the individual, but only incidentally the construct of the nation. But the system of the Mishnah, for its part, designs a whole society, one component after another. Mishnaic discourse speaks of the individual in the context of the national life of collective sanctification. Self-evidently, tensions between individual and community reach ready resolution; that is hardly the point. The main thing is that the Mishnah addresses not the stages or phases of individual life, but the constituents of the life of village and Temple – the former shaped, where possible, into the counterpart and mirror image of the latter. To the system of sanctification imagined in the Mishnah, the individual is not a principal building block. The householder and his ménage form the smallest whole unit of social construction. So, as I said, the teleology contributed by Abot to the mishnaic system turns out to be no more just a fit than the one that might, but did not, come out of messianic eschatology. Yet the world beyond historical time to which Abot makes reference provides precisely the right metaphysical setting for the system of order and stasis, or proper and correct classification, that underlay, as foundation and goal, the Mishnah's authorities' own detailed statements.

But Judaism at the end did indeed provide an ample account and explanation of Israel's history and destiny. These emerged as the generative problematic of Judaism, just as they framed the social reality confronted by Jews wherever they lived. So, to seek the map that shows the road from the Mishnah, at the beginning, to the fully articulated Judaism at the end of the formative age in late antiquity, we have to look elsewhere. For as to the path from the Mishnah to tractate Abot – this is not the way.

It could never have been the way because, in my view, the Mishnah with its documents of continuation and succession proposed to ignore the actualities of the social condition of Israel. The critical issues confronting the Jewish nation emerged from its sorry political condition. In the most commonplace sense of the word, these were *historical* issues. Any sort of Judaism that pretended the history of Israel could be reduced to lists of events sharing the same taxonomic traits, and that the destiny of Israel might be absorbed into an essentially imaginary framework of sanctification attained through the human heart and mind, demanded what the Jewish nation could not give. For people could not pretend to be other than who they were and what they were. Israel constituted a defeated people, driven from its holy place, yet reminded, every time they opened their ancient Scriptures, of God's special love for them and of their distinctive destiny among nations. Israel lived out an insufferable paradox between God's word and world, between promise and postponed fulfillment. So the critical issue confronting any sort of Judaism to emerge in late antiquity reached definition and attained urgency in the social reality, the everyday experience, of Israel: When? By whom? To the Jewish nation history proved very real indeed. The political question of Israel's destiny settled by the myth of the promise of the Messiah's coming salvation – a concrete, national, and historical salvation – could not be wished away. It demanded response: How long, O Lord? So, as is clear, the Mishnah's system would have to undergo revision and reformation. The labor of renewal would demand fresh and original thinkers: exegetes of a remarkably subtle capacity.

The Next Stage

The Mishnah, the first document in the canon of formative Judaism, ca. C.E. 200, presented a system of Judaism aimed at the sanctification of Israel. That system invoked a teleology lacking an eschatological dimension. What happened next? The several successive documents of exegesis – the Talmud of the Land of Israel, the exegetical compositions organized around scriptural books, and the Talmud of Babylonia – from 400 to 600 then supplied the larger system of formative Judaism, resting upon the constitution of the Mishnah, with that well-established, eschatologically oriented teleology of Messiah and his salvation that the Mishnah's framers had rejected. The Judaism that emerged was, and now remains, profoundly devoted to questions of history and its meaning, promising salvation attained through holy deeds of eschatological and salvific value. So the Mishnah, a system aimed at sanctification and built upon the mainbeams of nature and supernature, was drawn nearer to the orbit of the ongoing everyday life of Israel. The document of a Judaism of sanctification ended up as the foundation of a Judaism of historical salvation. How so? The Talmuds and (in lesser measure) collections of scriptural exegeses presented a system of Judaism focused upon salvation and promising to carry Israel to the age of the coming of the Messiah and the end of history as it was then suffered. Yet, the Messiah in the Talmudic sector of the formative canon emerged as a figure meant to encourage and foster precisely those emphases upon life above time and beyond history, life lived in full acceptance of God's rule in eternity and rejection of man's rule in history, that the Mishnah had originally made the foundation of its system. Accordingly, when the canon of Judaism had reached the end of its formative period, it presented a version of the Messiah-myth entirely congruent to the character of the foundation-document, the Mishnah. Judaism emerging from late antiquity then would deliver to Israel an enduring message of timeless sanctification, garbed in the cloak of historical, and hence eschatological salvation.

So we here adumbrate the first stage – the Mishnah's part – of two reciprocal processes, first the "remessianization" of the canon of formative Judaism, second, the reformation of a Messiah-myth itself to fit into the larger system expressed in that canon. In the end we shall be helped to grasp what is happening if we compare the Messiah in the canon of formative Judaism to the unfolding of the Messiah-myth in the Christian understandings of Jesus as the Christ. Early on, Christ, the Messiah, marked the end of history, the expectation of the imminent resurrection of the dead. Later on, the eschatological Messiah would become Jesus: rabbi, teacher, preacher, wonder-worker, God-man, perfect priest, and oblation – many other things, human and heavenly alike. So the ongoing life of the Church turned Christ, the Messiah-Savior at the eschaton, into whatever Christians needed the Christ, Jesus, to be through the eternity of time. The Messiah-myth, originally defined in terms of antecedent, Israelite conventions, entered the grid of Christian being, to be reframed and reformed within that ongoing experience of the enduring "life in Christ." So too, in the formation of Judaism, the eschatological Messiah (so critical to Paul's Christ) was initially rejected as a category useful to the Mishnah's stratum of the canon. The Messiah-myth would then regain pride of place within the Talmuds' sector of the canon. But this only in terms wholly natural to the points of insistence of the system inaugurated and defined by the Mishnah. So the established conventions, whatever they were, would give way. The Messiah would serve Israel precisely as Israel's rabbis wanted him to – just as the Messiah would serve the Christian Church as Christians wished.

We now recognize that the figure of the Messiah serves diverse purposes, defined by the framers of the larger systems in which the Messiah-myth will find a place. We know that the authors of the Mishnah assigned an insubstantial role to the Messiah. But did the framers of the ultimate rabbinical system, in particular the great encyclopedists of the Talmud of Babylonia, simply open the gate to admit "the Messiah" at large? I think not. What we find in the talmudic sector of the formative canon of Judaism is not merely an established, general conception of the Messiah, now invited to serve (as it supposedly had so well elsewhere) as the principal teleological justification of the rabbinical system. True, the Messiah enters. But he does so only on the rabbis' terms. So he is incorporated into the rabbinical realm through a process of assimilation and (from the viewpoint I think dominant among the Mishnah's philosophers) also neutralization.

Under the circumstances, it is difficult to see that the rabbis had much choice. The vivid expectation of the imminent advent of the Messiah could hardly continue indefinitely. For instance, decades after Paul's dec-

larations on that matter, people were still dying, the assembled people of
God still suffering, as the Gospels' authors realized. So the Messiah had to
find secondary, long-term embodiment in some form: rabbi, priest, master
and divine model on earth – God-with-us, the word made flesh, Son of
Man in the image of God – and in heaven, yet other tasks. So the ahistorical Christ of Paul, lacking all biography, becomes the Jesus of Q, Matthew, Mark, and Luke, ends up as the Jesus Christ of John and of everyone
beyond: no longer merely the celebrant of the end of time, but now the
center and pivot of all time, all being, all history. Shall we then conclude
that the established, inherited conception of *the* Messiah, as termination
of life and time, defined for the heirs and continuators of Christ in the
church what they would see in him and say about him? Quite to the contrary. They inherited, but also reshaped the inheritance. Whatever happened in the beginning, Christ as Messiah continued to serve, long after
the moment that should have marked the end of time. Now as the ever-
stable focus and pivot of Christian existence, the Messiah became something other and far more useful. So far as the apocalyptic expectations
were not realized, indeed, could not have been realized, the Messiah had
to become something else than what people originally expected. True, he
will still be called Christ. But he will be whatever the Church needs him
to be: anything but terminus of a world history that – up to now – refuses
to come to an end.

So too was the case of the Messiah in the formative canon of Judaism.
That is, if we take for granted that people to begin with imagined the
Messiah in accordance with the promises of old, we must assume that at
the outset they saw the Messiah as an apocalyptic figure, coming at the
end of time. As dominant and definitive pattern, that version of the Messiah-myth then passed from the center of the stage of the Messiah. Other
patterns – attempts to explain the same unclassifiable figure – came into
use. As to the Mishnah's part of the canon, at the beginning the authors
wished so far as possible to avoid all reliance upon the Messiah as an apocalyptic figure. Even the language was given a meaning not primary in the
prior writings, "messiah" as (mere) high priest, "messiah" as something
other than eschatological savior, whether priest or general, whether from
David's line or the house of Joseph. But then, in the Talmuds' sector of
the canon, the figure of the Messiah, and the concerns addressed through
discourse about that figure, came to the fore in powerful expression. So,
to state my thesis briefly and with emphasis:

> *(1) Established conventions of the Messiah-myth served the Church
> merely to classify Jesus at the outset, but later on, other taxa came into
> play. (2) The Messiah-myth found no consequential place in the rabbin-*

ical canon at the outset, that is, in the Mishnah, but later on that same myth became the moving force, the principal mode of teleological thought in the talmudic sector.

If I had to guess why the Talmuds gave prominence to a concept ignored in the Mishnah, I should have to appeal to the evidence of what the nation, Israel at large, had long had in mind. It seems to me self-evident that a Judaism lacking an eschatological dimension must have contradicted two established facts. First, the people read Scripture, which told them about the end of days. Second, the condition of the people, deteriorating as it was, called into question the credibility of the ahistorical construction of the Mishnah. So, I should imagine, for the Mishnah to be of any practical use, it required not only application to diverse circumstances, which the rabbis gave it. Its system also required expansion, not only by augmenting what was there, but also by exploring dimensions not contained therein at all. By reshaping the teleology of the mishnaic system into an eschatological idiom – indeed, by restating the eschatology in the established Messianic myth – the rabbis of the Talmud made the Mishnah's system over.

But if the Mishnah was thus forced into that very grid of history and eschatology that it had been formulated to reject, the Mishnah's mode in turn drastically modified the Messiah-myth. For the latter was recast into the philosophical mode of thought and stated as teleology of an eternally present sanctification attained by obedience to patterns of holiness laid out in the Torah. This grid is precisely the one that the framers of the Mishnah had defined. So by no means may we conclude that what changed, in the end, was the Mishnah's system. Its modes of thought intact, its fundamental points of insistence about Israel's social policy reaffirmed, the Mishnah's system ended up wholly definitive for Judaism as it emerged in the canon at the end of its formative centuries, the "one whole Torah of Moses, our rabbi."

How so? The version of the Messiah-myth incorporated into the rabbinic system through the Talmuds simply restates the obvious: Israel's sanctification is what governs. So if Israel will keep a single Sabbath (or two in succession), the Messiah will come. If Israel stops violating the Torah, the Messiah will come. If Israel acts with arrogance in rejecting its divinely assigned condition, the Messiah will not come. Everything depends, then, upon the here-and-now of everyday life. The operative category is not salvation through what Israel *does,* but sanctification of what Israel *is.* The fundamental convictions of the Mishnah's framers, flowing from the reaction against the apocalyptic and messianic wars of the late first and early second centuries, here absorbed and redirected precisely those explosive energies that, to begin with, had made Israel's salvation through history the critical concern. So, whereas the Talmuds introduced a formerly neglected myth, in fact in their version the Messiah became precisely what the sages of the Mishnah and their continuators in the Talmud most needed: a rabbi-Messiah, who will save an Israel sanctified through Torah. Salvation then depends upon sanctification, so is subordinated to it.

The Mishnah proposed to build an Israelite world view and way of life that ignored the immediate apocalyptic and historical terrors of the age. The Mishnah's heirs and continuators, who produced the other sector of the formative canon, did two things. They preserved that original policy for Israelite society, but they also accommodated an ongoing social and psychological reality: the presence of terror, the foreboding of doom, and Israel's iron-clad faith in the God who saves. Israel remained the old Israel of history, suffering, and hope. The Mishnah's fantasy of an Israel beyond time, an Israel living in nature and supernature, faded away. It was implausible. The facts of history contradicted it.

Yet Israel's condition, moral and social, must govern Israel's destiny – in accordance with the Torah's rules, but also precisely as biblical prophecy and mishnaic doctrine had claimed. What then could Israel do about its own condition? How could Israel confront the unending apocalypse of its own history? Israel could do absolutely nothing. But Israel could be – become – holy. That is why history was relegated to insignificance. Humble acceptance of the harsh rule of gentiles would render Israel worthy of God's sudden intervention, the institution of God's rule through King–Messiah.

What the rabbinic canon set forth at the end, in its rich eschatological-messianic myth and symbolism, states precisely what the Mishnah at the outset had defined as its teleology, but in the idiom of life and death, nature and supernature. The rabbinical canon in its ultimate form delivered the message of sanctification, garbed in the language of salvation – but not garbled by that expression. So diverse systems of Judaism make use of messianic materials to make their own statements. In the case of the Messiah-theme in the Mishnah's successor-documents, if the hands are the hands of the inherited eschatological faith of prophecy and apocalypse, the voice remains the true voice of Jacob, that is, speaking through the Mishnah.

General Index

Index to Biblical and Hermeneutical Texts